LIVING IN THE FUTURE

.

VICTORIA W. WOLCOTT

Living in the Future

Utopianism and the Long
Civil Rights Movement

THE UNIVERSITY OF CHICAGO PRESS
Chicago and London

The University of Chicago Press, Chicago 60637
The University of Chicago Press, Ltd., London
© 2022 by The University of Chicago
Published 2022
Paperback edition 2024
Printed in the United States of America

33 32 31 30 29 28 27 26 25 24   1 2 3 4 5

ISBN-13: 978-0-226-81725-5 (cloth)
ISBN-13: 978-0-226-83680-5 (paper)
ISBN-13: 978-0-226-81727-9 (e-book)
DOI: https://doi.org/10.7208/chicago/9780226817279.001.0001

Publication of this book has been aided by a grant from the
Meijer Foundation Fund.

Library of Congress Cataloging-in-Publication Data

Names: Wolcott, Victoria W., author.
Title: Living in the future : utopianism and the long Civil Rights
Movement / Victoria W. Wolcott.
Other titles: Utopianism and the long Civil Rights Movement
Description: Chicago : The University of Chicago Press, 2022. |
Includes bibliographical references and index.
Identifiers: LCCN 2021035849 | ISBN 9780226817255 (cloth) |
ISBN 9780226817279 (ebook)
Subjects: LCSH: Civil rights movements—United States. |
Pacifism—United States. | Utopias.
Classification: LCC E185.61 .W8 2022 | DDC 323.0973—dc23
LC record available at https://lccn.loc.gov/2021035849

♾ This paper meets the requirements of ANSI/NISO Z39.48-1992
(Permanence of Paper).

To my daughters:
Nora and Maya

Contents

Illustrations, Table, and Map

Introduction

We want freedom now. . . . We do not want freedom fed to us in
teaspoons over another 150 years.

MARTIN LUTHER KING JR.[1]

In the spring of 1952, a young African American woman, Coretta Scott,
gave a book to a seminary student she had befriended. The book was Edward Bellamy's 1888 utopian novel, *Looking Backward: 2000–1887*, which
predicted a socialist America. A graduate of the progressive Antioch College,
Scott was active in the pacifist movement and closely followed the nonviolent
direct-action work of Bayard Rustin. She inscribed her gift, "Dear Martin, I
should be interested to know your reaction to Bellamy's predictions about our
society." Martin Luther King Jr. responded in a long letter two months later:
"I welcomed the book because much of its content is in line with my basic
ideas. I imagine you already know that I am much more socialistic in my economic theory than capitalistic. . . . Today capitalism has outlived its useful-
ness. It has brought about a system that takes necessities from the masses to
give luxuries to the classes." He finished his letter, "Let us continue to hope,
work, and pray that in the future we will live to see a warless world, a better

distribution of wealth, and a brotherhood that transcends race or color. This is the gospel that I will preach to the world."[2] Bellamy's imagined socialist and egalitarian future helped shape the twentieth century's most powerful social movement. And while utopian thought and writing influenced Coretta Scott and Martin Luther King Jr., some of their contemporaries went even further and lived their utopian dreams, creating small communities that modeled Bellamy's vision.

Two years before reading *Looking Backward*, King was introduced to Mahatma Gandhi's teachings at the Fellowship House in Philadelphia. The Fellowship House was part of a matrix of interracial communities that provided a safe haven for activists and trained them through a radical pedagogy. Although each had its own unique history, they were "utopian" in their rejection of gradualism and their demands for immediate change. And they lived according to these values in the present, rather than waiting for complete societal transformation. The activists who inhabited these communities were neither racial liberals employing moral suasion, nor were they part of the communist Left. Rather they were socialist in orientation and deeply influenced a generation of activists in the interconnected labor, civil rights, and peace movements. From the 1920s through the 1960s, they built labor colleges, folk schools, ashrams, interracial churches, and urban and rural cooperatives. This book traces the connections between those institutions: workers' education schools such as Brookwood Labor College and Highlander Folk School, a Mississippi cooperative, the Father Divine movement, Fellowship Houses and churches, and a myriad of pacifist and civil rights organizations and enclaves.

Three central tenets united the activists who demanded immediate change in the face of racial and economic inequality. They believed in building cooperatives as an alternative to capitalism. They practiced interracialism in their religious worship, social activism, and communal housing. And they developed a form of Gandhian nonviolent direct action that was more aggressive than the passive resistance promoted by the traditional pacifist peace churches, such as the Quakers and Mennonites. By living cooperatively and communally, they created a new reality that served as a model for civil rights activists. More pragmatically, the members of these communities trained activists in radical nonviolence and created real change in the economic and political fortunes of African Americans. This history also suggests lessons for contemporary social movements. The small-scale communities that are emblematic of American utopianism acted as a leavening agent for large-scale social justice movements. In isolation, these communities could be marginalized, but by training activists, publicizing their work, and envisioning a new world, transformational change was possible. Living in experimental communities also acted as a buffer against reactionary politics, which views radical breaks as inherently dangerous and destabilizing. King's reading of Bellamy, for example, helped him to envision an egalitarian future and develop tactics to hasten its arrival.

Because utopian ideas and practices proved so generative in the long civil rights movement, we should not overlook their centrality. But deploying the concept of utopia comes with its own dilemmas, inherent in its coining by Sir Thomas More in 1516. More combined the Greek word for "place" (*topos*) with the "u" from the word for "no" (*ou*) to construct "utopia" (no place).[3] Thus, from the term's inception, people considered utopias to be fantastical and out of reach, a world best left to fiction rather than lived reality.[4] But the social imagination necessary to envision utopia could also power dramatic social change by insisting on "freedom now," in King's words. The activists who circulated among folk schools, communes, and Fellowship Houses also insisted on freedom now. Their work was linked with a long history of utopian communalism and intentional communities within the United States.[5] In the eighteenth and nineteenth centuries, both religious and secular utopian communities proliferated, including cooperative towns founded by British utopianist Robert Owen and millenarian religious groups such as the Shakers. By the early twentieth century, utopian communities ranged from anarchist and single-tax enclaves to student cooperatives and Christian socialist communities.

But what made them utopian? The political scientist Lyman Tower Sargent defines utopianism as a form of "social dreaming" that "allows communities to envision a radically different society than the one in which the dreamers live."[6] Similarly, Robin D. G. Kelley writes about the "freedom dreams" of the Black community: "I have come to realize that once we strip radical social movements down to their bare essence and understand the collective desires of people in motion, freedom and love lay at the very heart of the matter."[7] These freedom dreams could not wait for an imagined future. For those, like King, who hoped for a "warless world" and a "socialistic future," utopian dreaming required transformative experimentation in the present. The militant optimism of utopianists was not complacent or passive. They put their bodies on the line. Civil rights and peace activists, like Bayard Rustin, languished in prisons and embarked on hunger strikes. Labor organizers manning picket lines suffered the blows of police and were attacked by white mobs. And intentional communities like the Delta Cooperative Farm and Highlander Folk School were under constant threat by white supremacists and state authorities. The social dreams of utopia sometimes elicited a waking nightmare of reactionary violence.

For progressive thinkers, utopianism has long been an arena of conflict.

Edward Bellamy was part of a group of utopian socialists in the late nineteenth century that "scientific socialists," or followers of Friedrich Engels and Karl Marx, widely criticized.[8] Utopian socialists did not believe in revolution, or at least not in violent revolution. For this reason, scientific socialists were disdainful of Bellamy, whose novel *Looking Backward* suggested that a peaceful but swift evolution of society would lead to a socialist utopia.[9] Marx decried Bellamy and his followers' lack of class analysis and their claims of universal emancipation, cooperation, and brotherhood. Because Bellamy posited a "velvet revolution," his ideas became popular among pacifists who feared the chaos of class conflict but still desired revolutionary change.[10] This idea of peaceful revolution was central to utopian socialists and radical pacifists well into the twentieth century. In 1940, for example, the famed white pacifist A. J. Muste called for "pacifism as a revolutionary strategy."[11] The desire to prevent violence meant that some utopianists had an ambivalent relationship to strikes and other working-class political action. And they openly criticized the sectarian politics of the communist Left. But their goals paralleled those of other radical thinkers, a new society. They wanted a revolution, a nonviolent revolution.

Utopian socialists' framework for social change involved giving the ends and means of social struggle the same weight. The white British author Aldous Huxley, highly influential in pacifist and radical circles, was one popularizer of this model. Best known for his dystopian novel *Brave New World*, Huxley was an active promoter of utopian thought and practice. While living in California during the 1930s, utopian socialists introduced Huxley to Vedanta mysticism, a philosophical branch of Hinduism, and he later wrote a utopian novel, *Island*.[12] His 1937 essay collection, *Ends and Means: An Inquiry into the Nature of Ideals*, was widely read by political radicals. In this work he promotes nonviolent solutions to revolutionary change. On cooperatives, a key institution for utopian socialists, Huxley writes, "Co-operatives and mixed concerns already exist and work extremely well. To increase their numbers and to extend their scope would not seem a revolutionary act. . . . In its effects, however, the act would *be* revolutionary; for it would result in a profound modification of the existing system."[13] Cooperatives provided a revolutionary end through peaceful means, ameliorating the worst excesses of capitalism and promoting egalitarianism.

The relationship between means and ends is also captured in the term "prefigurative," coined by the political scientist Carl Boggs in 1977: "By 'prefigurative,' I mean the embodiment, within the ongoing political practice of a movement, of those forms of social relations, decision-making, culture, and human experience that are the ultimate goal."[14] Like Huxley, Boggs identified movements where the means and ends converged. And he characterized the New Left of the 1960s and early 1970s as the recipient and popularizer of this tradition. Sociologist Wini Breines, in her 1982 work *The Great Refusal*, expands on the prefigurative nature of New Left politics. This politics encompasses "the effort to build community, to create and prefigure in lived action and behavior the desired society, the emphasis on means and not ends, the spontaneous and utopian experiments that developed in the midst of action while working toward the ultimate goal of a free and democratic society."[15] Central to this concept was the creation of "counter-institutions," like the cooperatives, ashrams, and interracial churches activists founded in the mid-twentieth century.[16] But while we associate New Left politics with such counter-institutions, in fact a generation of "Old Left" activists pioneered these practices.

This amnesia about earlier experimentation reflects the fact that the New Left's prefigurative politics emerged from what appeared to be a relatively conformist and contained post–World War II nation that rejected utopianism. In the late 1940s, the twin horrors of fascism and Stalinism suggested to many liberals that utopian thinking was dangerous. Arthur Schlesinger Jr.'s *The Vital Center*, Daniel Bell's *The End of Ideology*, and Judith Shklar's *After Utopia*, as well as texts by political philosophers Hannah Arendt and Theodor Adorno, argue that utopian thinking had led to totalitarianism.[17] These works emphasize the horrendous costs of "blueprint" utopias that were inflexible and dictatorial.[18] "The urge to construct grand designs for the political future of mankind," notes Shklar, "is gone. The last vestiges of utopian faith required for such an enterprise have vanished."[19] The anti-utopian thinking of the mid-twentieth century inaccurately tied totalitarian states to American utopian communities. But cooperation, not domination, was a central tenet of communal utopianism. Indeed, most radical pacifists, who generally defined themselves as socialists or anarchists, were deeply critical of the Soviet Union and were among the first to speak out about the dangers of fascism.

Anti-utopian arguments corresponded with the rise of the cold war in the late 1940s and the decline of the labor movement. These powerful trends masked the ongoing organizing work of radical pacifists and their increased affiliation with the Black freedom struggle. Some formed small intentional communities. But these communities did not mark a retreat from politics, as activists trained others in nonviolent direct action and published political and intellectual works calling for mass resistance. Their social dreaming and hopeful utopian planning proved more effective in building a mass movement than most observers could imagine. In *The Vital Center* (1949), liberal pragmatist Schlesinger lambasts such dreaming: "On the one hand

are the politicians, the administrators, the doers; on the other, the senti-
mentalists, the utopians, the wailers." Writing about civil rights in the wake
of President Truman's 1947 report on civil rights, "To Secure These Rights,"
Schlesinger believed that the politicians and administrators could address
this vital problem. "The South on the whole accepts the objectives of the
civil rights program as legitimate," argues Schlesinger, "even though it may
have serious and intelligible reservations about timing and method."[20] In fact,
the South "on the whole" fought against the civil rights movement with violent terror and racist laws. It was Schlesinger's "utopians" and "wailers" who
challenged their power directly and, with time, won many battles. Thus, the
mistakes of midcentury intellectuals, who dismissed radical pacifism, should
not blind us to the vital role of utopianism.

Of the three central tenets—cooperatives, interracialism, and nonviolence—that bound utopian socialist communities together, interracialism most directly challenged the laws and mores of Jim Crow America. But
the ideological and practical forms of interracialism varied. Some activists,
like those who ran Fellowship Houses or YWCA and YMCA programs, promoted a liberal interracialism that viewed education and moral suasion as
the primary way to foster racial understanding. This work was valuable as
liberal interracialists created spaces for dialogue and fought against white
supremacy. But their efforts were often limited to elites, and they generally
argued for a gradual approach rather than immediacy. Krishnalal Shridharani, one of the leading interpreters of Gandhi for American pacifists, wrote
in 1941: "Many an isolated reformer has organized inter-racial house parties
and dances, and this Y.M.C.A. method does bring a few Negro girls and boys
in contact with a few whites. But it is a process of individual reform and not
a broad social solution."[21] A broader social solution required a more direct
challenge to segregation than education and conversation would allow.

In contrast, labor interracialists, such as those who ran Brookwood Labor
College and founded Highlander Folk School, fostered a class-based movement to create strategic alliances across racial lines. First generated by progressive unions such as the International Ladies' Garment Workers' Union
and propagated through workers' education, labor interracialism elevated
racial cooperation among the working classes to foster a more egalitarian
future. In the 1920s, Black socialists such as A. Philip Randolph also took
up the mantle of labor interracialism, and the Communist Party soon joined
these efforts, promoting interracial alliances to build a broad pro-labor coalition. During the Great Depression, leftist activists built a popular front of
like-minded radicals to address racial violence and economic disenfranchisement.[22] These labor interracialists envisioned a future of full racial equality

and lived that future in the present by integrating their unions and social movement organizations.

Finally, utopian interracialism went beyond these more strategic approaches. Utopian communities, such as Father Divine's Peace Mission and the Harlem Ashram, called for immediate and radical change and prefigured that change by sharing labor, property, and politics. These groups took up nonviolent direct action as the most effective means to challenge racial segregation and inequality through wide-scale training and implementation. Utopian interracialism often subverted racial hierarchies. White followers of Father Divine, for example, accepted the diminutive African American man as an embodiment of God himself. Black Nationalists such as Floyd McKissick, who created the utopian town Soul City, also inverted racial hierarchies when reaching out to white allies. "Soul City will be an attempt to move into the future," explains McKissick, "a future where black people welcome white people as equals."[23] In these cases, Black leaders and activists invited white people to join them, a model in sharp contrast to both liberal and labor interracialism, which often originated with white leaders and activists. Radical pacifists in the Congress of Racial Equality (CORE) also practiced utopian interracialism in their communal homes and training centers. This culture and politics later became central to the Student Nonviolent Coordinating Committee (SNCC) when they launched major civil rights campaigns in 1960. Thus, far from being a uniform and moderate call for integration, interracialism contained revolutionary potential driven by utopian freedom dreams.

A second tenet that profoundly shaped the work of utopian socialists and radical pacifists was a commitment to cooperatives as an economic alternative to capitalism and as a broader metaphor for unity across class, race, and gender lines. Since the nineteenth century, cooperatives have been a central component of European and American utopian communities. America's mid-twentieth-century cooperatives were generally modeled after the Rochdale cooperative system in England, founded in 1844 by a group of weavers who formed the Rochdale Society of Equitable Pioneers. The Pioneers drew up a set of Principles, which allowed their cooperative to be replicated internationally. Rochdale cooperatives refused to discriminate in their membership and offered everyone an equal vote. Workers founded the first American cooperatives based on Rochdale's rules in 1863, and they proliferated throughout the late nineteenth century.[24] Because of the egalitarian nature of the Rochdale system, these cooperatives often promoted interracialism. As a character in Upton Sinclair's 1936 novel *Co-op: A Novel of Living Together* states, "A true co-operative has to be based on human brotherhood; we ought to state at the outset that we are open to all men without distinction of race or color or creed or party."[25] African Americans found cooperatives particularly appealing, as they allowed them to maximize scarce resources in the decades following emancipation. In addition to providing some economic independence, Black cooperatives were an expression of political power and self-help. In the first decades of the twentieth century, African American leaders, such as W. E. B. Du Bois, George Schuyler, Ella Baker, and A. Philip Randolph worked to promote both consumers' and producers' cooperatives as viable economic solutions to Black economic problems. By the 1970s, Black cooperatives, particularly in the agricultural South, became a major project of Black Nationalist organizers. And today, cooperatives play a central role in both urban and rural experiments in social activism, from Detroit to rural Mississippi.

White utopian socialists in the early twentieth century who promoted labor interracialism also embraced cooperatives. Progressive workers' education and folk schools trained their Black and white students in how to run cooperatives, most notably at Brookwood Labor College and Highlander Folk School. Indeed, these schools were run as cooperatives similar to nineteenth-century utopian communities, such as Robert Owen's New Harmony colony in Indiana. But it was during the Great Depression that the cooperative movement was at its strongest. Two examples exemplify this trend. The Delta and Providence cooperative farms in rural Mississippi were highly influential model communities that drew hundreds of outside activists and influenced New Deal programs. Founded by a white Protestant missionary, Sherwood Eddy, the farms provided housing and a cooperative livelihood for Black and white sharecroppers who had been kicked off their land and terrorized during the height of the Great Depression. The farms largely disbanded after white supremacists' attacks in the mid-1950s, but their legacy was felt when a decade later Mississippi was at the front lines of the civil rights movement. Freedom Summer in 1964 brought young volunteers to rural Mississippi, much as the farms had decades earlier. And through the 1960s and 1970s, there were numerous experiments in cooperative farming in Mississippi that offset rural Black poverty and built on the cooperative farms' legacy.

But the most successful interracial cooperative was the Father Divine Peace Mission, a utopian community that erased racial categories altogether and blurred gender lines. The labor interracialism of workers' education schools and the Delta and Providence cooperative farms challenged a segregated society. But Father Divine promoted a utopian interracialism that actively challenged segregation using nonviolent direct action and provided housing, recreation, and sustenance to thousands devastated by the Great Depression. Father Divine borrowed from earlier utopian communities, including the Shakers, by promoting celibacy, owning property in common, and instituting a matrix of cooperatives. His followers were "angels" who lived their heaven on earth by creating the society they envisioned. Divinites, however, were also deeply political. They purchased property in white communities to challenge the color line, and by the early 1940s they used nonviolent direct action to challenge segregated public accommodations. Thousands of Divinites also took to the streets of Harlem in support of the Scottsboro Boys, Black teenagers accused of rape and facing execution, and anti-lynching legislation. And the Peace Mission's low-cost hotels, restaurants, and resorts were open to all, providing much-needed leisure to African Americans who had to negotiate a segregated landscape. Although often dismissed by his contemporaries as a charlatan, Father Divine demonstrated that cooperation combined with religious teachings and a utopian perspective could prove highly attractive to both Black and white people.

The third belief system that united the utopian experiments was nonviolence, and by the late 1930s it was the application of Gandhian nonviolent direct action to the American context. Those most engaged in labor interracialism, particularly at the Highlander Folk School, did not always fully embrace nonviolence. Myles Horton, Highlander's white founder, had seen horrific brutality unleashed against southern workers attempting to organize and would not fully commit to pacifism.[26] But the primary figures of workers' education institutions, Fellowship Houses and churches, and early civil rights organizations identified as pacifist, and most were active members of the Fellowship of Reconciliation (FOR). For example, Howard Thurman, a Black theologian who was the first African American to meet Gandhi, helped establish San Francisco's Church for the Fellowship of All Peoples, an ecumenical and interracial religious center. And Marjorie Penney, a white Quaker woman from Pennsylvania, led the interracial Fellowship House for several decades starting in the early 1930s.

While they initially stopped short of the utopian interracialism of the Divine movement or CORE, Fellowship Houses and churches communicated Gandhian ideas and trained a new generation of radical pacifists. Thurman's religious teachings, particularly his 1949 book *Jesus and the Disinherited*, profoundly influenced Martin Luther King Jr. and the major organizers of CORE. Penney's connections spanned from the founders of the Delta and Providence farms to major civil rights leaders, who used Fellowship Houses as their organizing base. By the 1950s, fellowshippers began to engage more actively with radical nonviolence, and in the early 1960s, they became important participants in the mass civil rights movement. Training for the Freedom Rides in the early 1960s, for example, took place at Fellowship Houses where seasoned pacifists worked with young student volunteers.

By the 1940s and 1950s, a matrix of intentional communities and an expansion of nonviolent direct-action training by FOR and CORE situated utopian interracialism and radical nonviolence at the center of the civil rights movement. Young activists who embraced radical pacifism founded utopian communities such as Ahimsa Farm in Ohio and the Harlem and Newark Ashrams. They carried out desegregation campaigns and developed workshops to train other activists. CORE and FOR members circulated through these communities and expanded their training efforts across the country, teaching hundreds of workshops and race relations institutes. These activists convinced A. Philip Randolph's March on Washington Movement (MOWM) to embrace nonviolent direct action and wore down mainstream civil rights organizations' resistance to nonviolence, which they had viewed as lawbreaking and too dangerous. By the early 1950s, more radical civil rights groups, such as the Peacemakers, called for communal living, nonpayment of taxes, and total nonresistance when engaging in protests. Pacifist farms, such as Koinonia and Macedonia in Georgia, echoed the cooperative and communal Brookwood, Highlander, and Delta and Providence farms. These served as crucial havens for exhausted activists recovering from violent civil rights campaigns as the southern struggle escalated. By the time of the 1955 Montgomery Bus Boycott, a cadre of well-trained activists could be deployed to the emerging civil rights hotspots. Most had experienced the utopian interracialism of an ashram, a Fellowship House, or an interracial church.

Many radical pacifists also had in common an ecumenical and prophetic Christian faith that propelled their utopian experimentation.[27] They were part of what broadly can be termed the Christian Left. Following theologian Reinhold Niebuhr, and departing from the optimistic liberalism of the Progressive Era's Social Gospel movement, they expressed little faith in American institutions and the prospect for gradual societal change.[28] Instead, leaders such as Muste modeled themselves after the Hebrew prophets and viewed the world as inherently sinful.[29] Muste wrote in 1940, "Our concern has been with the problems and crisis of modern civilization as a whole; with the achievement of a dynamic, beautiful, and noble social order, the realization of the ancient prophetic dream of the Kingdom of God on earth."[30] This prophetic tradition resonated strongly with African Americans, who had long practiced what historian Gary Dorrien terms the "black social gospel," which "combined an emphasis on black dignity and personhood with protest activism for racial justice, a comprehensive social justice agenda, an insistence that authentic Christian faith is incompatible with racial prejudice."[31] These traditions met in the cotton fields of Mississippi, at labor colleges, and in radical pacifist circles.

In order to create Muste's kingdom on earth, Christians needed to engage with the world politically, both at home and abroad. Theologians of the prophetic tradition internationalized their teachings by creating the World Council of Churches in 1937 and promoting missionary work worldwide. Christian Left activists traveled extensively, visiting experimental folk schools in Denmark, Soviet industrial cities, and South Asian ashrams. Christian pacifists, such as the white British activist Muriel Lester, circulated globally, visiting utopian communities and pacifist communes from India to North America.[32] Leaders of the Christian Left, particularly Howard Thurman, also incorporated mysticism in their religious teachings and practices. While traveling in South Asia, where he met with Gandhi, Thurman experienced a mystical vision that inspired him to build the Church for the Fellowship of All Peoples in San Francisco.

Less often recognized as part of this tradition, the Father Divine Peace Mission movement also drew from mystical beliefs as Father Divine and his followers sought a union with God. This unity with the sacred undergirded Divine's teaching that racial divisions were illusory and all humans were equal. Divine also drew from the nineteenth-century Protestant New Thought tradition that argued that the power of the mind could heal a sick body and create a prosperous life. The Peace Mission's cooperative empire and well-fed followers provided evidence for these teachings' efficacy, which proved attractive to Black and white seekers. Like Thurman, Father Divine immersed himself in the teachings of Gandhi and Eastern religion. This mystical element of the Christian Left was more prevalent in the utopian communities of pacifists and socialists than mainstream civil rights groups. And it allowed activists to pursue their freedom dreams through meditation, imagination, and reverie.

Although Protestant activists make up the majority of the groups in this study, the Catholic Worker Movement also served as a model for small pacifist communes and the possibilities of labor interracialism. Dorothy Day and Peter Maurin started the Catholic Worker Movement in May 1933, calling for houses of hospitality and farming communes for the unemployed and suffering. These offered non-state solutions for poverty-stricken women and men in the depths of the Great Depression. Before founding the movement, Day spent her young adulthood as a journalist and writer working in New York City among the Greenwich Village avant-garde, sometimes known as the "lyrical left." These years, which also saw the rise of workers' education and social unionism, were suffused with a utopian excitement. Day remembers, "Each of the radical groups had its own vision, and each was terrified that immediate gains would make the masses content and not willing to go further toward the new earth they were envisioning."[33] During this period, she wrote for progressive publications including the *Call* and the *Masses*, spending long evenings with playwright Eugene O'Neill and an eclectic group of socialists, anarchists, and communists.

After her conversion to Catholicism in 1927, Day embraced a voluntary poverty and with the help of the French thinker Peter Maurin launched her movement in 1933.[34] The movement's publication, the *Catholic Worker*, became the primary means of spreading Day and Maurin's message of peace and equality. And it reflected some of the same utopian spirit of Day's radical youth. One of Maurin's "Easy Essays," short and catchy poems he used to communicate their teachings, was titled "The Case for Utopia." "The world would be better off," begins the poem, "if people tried to become better. And people would become better if they stopped trying to become better off."[35] This work appeared in the inaugural issue, which also documented the struggles of Black sharecroppers in the rural South. The most visible sign of the movement's commitment to interracialism was on the *Catholic Worker*'s masthead: a Black worker and a white worker shaking hands. This image was the suggestion of Arthur Falls, an African American doctor in Chicago who wrote to Day after reading the first issue. Falls headed up the Catholic Worker house in Chicago and made interracialism a centerpiece of Catholic activism in that city. Berenice Fisher, one of the founding members of CORE, consulted with Falls when launching the civil rights group in 1940. But even in Chicago, the Catholic Worker Movement was predominantly white and focused primarily on supporting the labor movement.[36] While they called for racial tolerance and always allowed African Americans full access to their houses of hospitality, racial politics and civil rights were not at the forefront of the movement.

The Catholic Workers' closest relationships with civil rights activists centered around their shared commitment to pacifism. Muste and Day, who were friends and admired each other deeply, helped shepherd in a pacifist culture in the 1930s and 1940s that would profoundly impact emerging civil rights organizations such as CORE, as well as pacifist organizations like the Peacemakers.[37] The houses of hospitalities were also model small pacifist communes, leading the white pacifist David Dellinger to reach out to his Catholic Worker friends when he established the Newark Ashram in the early 1940s.[38] Dellinger was also attracted to the Catholic Workers' anarchist tendencies. They were anti-statist, decentralized, and made up of a loose network of small communities. An ideal world, for Day and many of her followers, would consist of intentional communities without a controlling and alienating state apparatus.[39] Many of the Protestant pacifists in this study had a similar vision. White FOR member Douglas Steere, for example, called for small groups to form "peace cells" that would be "the vigilant guardian of the rights of the under-privileged in its community and should know at first hand the problems and their treatment."[40] And the workers' education schools, Fellowship Houses, and cooperatives were all independent of government funding and support. Some pacifists, such as those in the Peacemakers, refused to pay taxes to support increased militarism, a view shared by Day. And Father Divine's Peace Mission and Dorothy Day's Catholic Worker Movement both refused to accept any government welfare.

Anarchism was also a major ideological source for the more secular branch of the pacifist movement, particularly the War Resisters League (WRL). Secular groups such as the WRL worked in coalition with the Christian Left communities but did not form peace cells, ashrams, or other utopian experiments to the same extent. American communists were also secular in orientation, and although they had many of the same goals as the Protestant pacifists and worked in alliance with Father Divine, among others, they did not share a commitment to nonviolence. By the early 1940s, communists had also alienated some Black activists such as A. Philip Randolph, who viewed them as divisive and potentially dangerous. His antipathy to communists led Randolph, in his March on Washington Movement, to exclude white activists who might be communist infiltrators. Randolph's strategy of restricting the MOWM to African American followers can also be seen in Black Nationalist organizations such as Marcus Garvey's Universal Negro Improvement Association (UNIA) and the Nation of Islam, among others. Black Nationalism clearly had utopian leanings; indeed, Robin D. G. Kelley's invocation of "freedom dreams" largely describes these groups.[41] Garvey, like Father Divine, was a proponent of cooperatives, and the pacifist conscientious objectors of World War II shared prison cells with members of the Nation of Islam. Black Nationalists in the late 1960s inherited and expanded on some of the utopian strategies I investigate here, particularly the use of cooperatives and communal farms, a fact explored in the afterword of this book. But their rejection of interracialism, in all its forms, sets them apart from the utopian socialists and radical pacifists.

The religious, activist, and communitarian traditions examined in *Living in the Future* have been siloed into several disparate fields. Recent religious histories have explored the legacy of the Christian Left for the long civil rights movement. But these works exclude the Father Divine movement and do not delve into the secular labor movement that was so crucial to the early decades of civil rights struggles. In the field of peace studies, scholars have examined the radical pacifists and some of the intentional communities in which they lived. And there are substantial biographies of many of the major figures explored in this book, including A. J. Muste and Howard Thurman.[42]

Finally, most recent civil rights histories that focus on the 1930s through the early 1950s have downplayed both the role of pacifism and religion.[43] Many of these scholars have focused on the communist Left, praising their class politics and their radicalism. Indeed, some historians view CORE's attacks on segregated public accommodations as a retreat from the labor orientation of the 1930s.[44] In this narrative, the cold war gutted the class politics of the early civil rights movement, making way for a narrower rights discourse that failed to call for full economic equality. For these historians, the emergence of CORE is a sign of the breakup between labor and civil rights, not the fruition of a new and revolutionary form of activism.

In reality, although utopian socialists sought a peaceful revolution, they were always invested in class struggle. Many intentional communities actively supported organized labor and created cooperatives to offer an alternatives to competitive capitalism. Organizers built workers' education institutions, such as Brookwood and Highlander, to convey the values of social unionism, which offered a vision of a new society built on racial and gender equality. And radical pacifists on the noncommunist Left directly addressed economic rights and employed tactics honed in the labor movement, particularly the sit-down strike. These movements offered broad and inclusive visions of solidarity that went beyond trade unionism. A CORE publication in 1944 remarked, "More cooperation between people of different races exists in the labor unions than among 'educated' people. A different kind of education, that of living and working with people, has shown them that all people are human and have fundamentally the same need which should be satisfied, to give and take on equal terms in our **brave new world** for which we are fighting."[45] Thus, far from abandoning the class politics of the Great Depression, a vision of a "brave new world" of class and racial equality lived on in CORE and its radical pacifist allies.

During the war, the Communist Party largely set aside its civil rights activism to focus wholly on its support for the Soviet Union. Mainstream and liberal civil rights organizations, most notably the NAACP, supported the war effort as part of the Double V campaign, which called for both a military victory against fascism and the defeat of American racism. But activists on the noncommunist Left rejected these positions and focused on gaining Black economic, social, and political rights. Radical pacifists were committed to nonviolent revolution, and their interracialism reflected their utopian sensibilities, rather than moderation. White radical pacifist John Swomley notes, "From the outset I rejected liberalism, with its efforts at modest reforms, for a more radical analysis of history and contemporary events and for more radical action."[46] Utopian socialist and radical pacifists like Swomley called for an immediate break with the segregated and racist society in which they lived by prefiguring a future they envisioned. This utopian experimental strain in the Black freedom struggle had an ambivalent relationship with communism and racial liberalism. And its commitment to interracialism set it apart from Black Nationalism. But slighting its significance in the long civil rights movement gives us an incomplete picture of midcentury activism and does little to explain the success of radical nonviolence both in the North and in its most celebrated manifestation in the South.

By mapping interconnected ideas and institutions that were deeply influenced by utopian thought and practice, *Living in the Future* weaves together a variety of historical threads. Take, for example, the early career of African American activist Pauli Murray, who went on to be a leading figure in the feminist and civil rights movements. As a young woman, she studied at Brookwood Labor College, an experience she found transformative. Building on this training during the late 1930s, Murray worked with the Works Progress Administration to set up workers' education projects in Harlem. Divinites attended those programs in large numbers, encouraged by Father Divine to further their education. Murray no doubt encountered them in classrooms and made use of their low-cost cooperative restaurants and hotels while living in the city. After leaving Harlem, Murray attended Howard University, where she became close with Howard Thurman, who advised her throughout her career. Murray also helped establish the Washington, DC, Fellowship House, modeled after Marjorie Penney's Philadelphia Fellowship House. Finally, while traveling to help train activists in nonviolent direct action, Murray routinely stayed at the Harlem Ashram. In isolation, each of these encounters may not appear significant, but multiply Murray's experience by the larger civil rights community, and the connections take on greater import.

The prefigurative politics of utopian thinkers in the first half of the twentieth century played a crucial, if overlooked, role in the long civil rights movement. The backlash against utopian thinking after World War II lessened their visibility. It would take a new generation of dreamers in the early 1960s to fly the utopian flag again. Like earlier activists, they sought to avoid some of the traps of the sectarian Left by invoking a universal fellowship. As Daniel Bell wrote in 1960, "One can begin anew the discussion of utopia only by being aware of the trap of ideology."[47] By the mid-1960s, the New Left had revived many of the ideas and practices of utopian socialists and radical pacifists. Although they did not always live up to these ideals, the multiple movements that flourished in the 1960s and 1970s made utopia relevant again.

We are currently living in a moment when there is newfound interest in cooperatives, communal living, and racial equality. Critical theorists who seek to influence contemporary politics—such as Fredric Jameson, Erik Olin Wright, and David Graeber—have all explored how utopian thought can shape an imagined future.[48] Contemporary popular culture is also suffused with utopia, from the blockbuster film *Black Panther* to the science fiction television anthology *Black Mirror*. And social movements—such as the cooperative experiments in Jackson, Mississippi, the alter-globalization movement, Black Lives Matter, and the World Social Forum, to name a few—continue the legacy of the civil rights struggle by borrowing heavily from utopian thought.[49] The crises of climate change, economic inequality, racial disparities, and the coronavirus pandemic have also sparked experimentation in social and political practice. Policies such as the ambitious Green New Deal and Universal Basic Income, for example, have found new traction. Such ambition would have been familiar to the utopianists of an earlier generation. Ella Baker, A. J. Muste, Father Divine, Pauli Murray, and so many others refused to live in a world with profound injustice and violence. So they created new societies, on a small scale, to model what a more just society that equally valued ends and means would look like. They lived their freedom dreams, impatiently, and with profound consequences.

1

The Workers

I have to *experience* ideas, rather than *think* them. I have to learn what they mean in practice, have to act them out. Also, as I have indicated before, life . . . means to me being involved in the struggle against injustice and tyranny. It means acting "politically," trying to help build a new world, or new social forms.

A. J. MUSTE[1]

If you want love and brotherhood, you've got to incorporate them as you go along, because you can't just expect them to occur in the future without experiencing them before you get there.

MYLES HORTON[2]

In roomy farmhouses in upstate New York and rural Tennessee, Black and white laborers, activists, and intellectuals met on equal footing to plot out a utopian future. They envisioned a new world and impatiently created institutions to enact that world in the here and now. Renowned civil rights activists like Ella Baker and Rosa Parks sat around outdoor campfires singing labor songs and plotting movement strategies. They shared food, housing, and recreation alongside white labor organizers and intellectuals. Far from factory floors and city streets, these women and men declared that the working classes could only rise on the basis of full racial equality. Their work ushered in the largest mass movement in twentieth-century America.

In the 1920s, a remarkable movement for workers' education grew rapidly in the United States. It grew despite the conservative political climate of that decade and the lack of a thriving labor movement. The more radical branches of workers' education, the Brookwood Labor School and Highlander Folk

School, had a direct and lasting impact on the long civil rights movement. Workers' education went beyond trade unionism to advocate for a new and more just world that would embrace racial and gender equality. Students and instructors at labor schools enacted that world in the present by promoting labor interracialism, a cooperative economy, and a nonviolent future. Workers' education had its roots in the Social Gospel movement of the late nineteenth and early twentieth centuries, which proclaimed that Christians had an obligation to change unjust social structures, rather than simply working toward individual salvation.[3] Similar experiments in northern Europe, where a more robust and successful labor movement flourished, also influenced American workers' education. Finally, socialist utopian communities, such as the Ruskin Cooperative Association in Tennessee and Llano del Rio in California and Arkansas, shaped labor schools.[4] Like those colonies, Brookwood and Highlander offered safety and sanctuary to socialists who sought to create a new social order in the present, rather than waiting for the future.

Historian Lewis Mumford cautioned in 1922 that workers' education "is to be no mere antidote against a 'capitalist' educational system and a 'capitalist' press; for counteracting a poison is not the same as establishing a regimen of health."[5] By taking their students out of the factories and mines and placing them in an idyllic landscape free to explore a variety of strategies for full social and economic justice, Brookwood and Highlander were prescribing "a regimen of health." Both schools were nonsectarian, although primarily socialist in orientation, and both welcomed all-comers. They also embraced some of the leading Black intellectuals and activists of the day, such as W. E. B. Du Bois and A. Philip Randolph. These men, and others, believed that the class struggle and organized labor would entail cooperation across racial lines. In addition to exposing students to Black intellectuals, the schools nurtured a new generation of Black activists, many of them women. Ella Baker, Pauli Murray, and Rosa Parks were just a few of the leading lights who found their way to the freedom struggle through workers' education.

A Workers' Utopia

During the Progressive Era, workers' education in America was a feminist project. Its early proponents were working and middle-class women who sought both pragmatic organizing skills and a political perspective that reflected their own experiences in the workplace. Although Brookwood is often called the first residential workers' education institution, that claim belongs to the Women's Trade Union League's (WTUL) Training School for Women

Organizers, which opened in Chicago in 1914. The school was explicitly interracial, reaching out to Black female workers in Chicago's stockyards and
elsewhere.[6] In their announcement of the school, the WTUL argued, "Self-
government is essential to the making of a free people, and self-government
in the day[']s work can be had only by the united action of the workers."[7] The
female students learned how to negotiate contracts, speak in public, and organize workers.[8] The WTUL would later support the Bryn Mawr Summer
School and was the first union to hold a summer institute at Brookwood.
Closely allied with the WTUL was the International Ladies' Garment Workers' Union (ILGWU). They launched a workers' education program the same
year the Chicago school opened, advocating "social unionism," which promoted "workers' need for recreation, education, health care, and housing."
Social unionism tied the growth of the labor movement to a larger movement
of social change that would create a more egalitarian world.[9] To create this
new world, the ILGWU opened "unity houses" in major cities and offered a
"unity center" in the Catskills to provide respite and education for female
workers.[10] These havens invited recent Jewish immigrants, southern Black
migrants, and laboring native-born whites to share their experiences and
their vision for a more just future.

Fannia Cohn, a founding member of Brookwood and head of the ILGWU's
workers' education program, argued, "It has always been our conviction that
the Labor Movement stands, consciously or unconsciously, for the reconstruction of society. It dreams of a world where economic and social justice
will prevail, where the welfare of mankind will be the aim of all activity, where
society will be organized as a cooperative commonwealth."[11] This utopian vision of a labor movement's potential was institutionalized in labor colleges.
By 1932 there were three hundred workers' schools in the United States.[12]
Workers' education, and the labor movement more generally, was the primary path to a new future of cooperative brotherhood, racial equality, and
women's rights. Len De Caux, a communist who spent time at Brookwood,
noted, "Out of the workers' struggles—and the capacities they developed—
the power should come to transform society, to make it serve the needs of the
many rather than the profits of the few."[13] Female workers, Black workers, and
ethnic industrial workers would make up a revolutionary force that would
transform America. And workers' education would be the primary means
to train and prepare them for that transformation.

The year 1921 proved to be a bellwether for workers' education. Advocates
like Cohn and the white pacifist, minister, and labor organizer A. J. Muste
founded the Workers' Education Bureau (WEB) as a clearinghouse for the
burgeoning new institutions. That same year, Bryn Mawr College opened

its summer school for women workers, which recruited African American women as well as immigrants and native-born white women.[14] And in idyllic Katonah, New York, Muste opened Brookwood Labor College. Writing in the proceedings of the first national conference on workers' education, educator H. B. Brougham reported on the establishment of Brookwood Labor College: "It will be based frankly on the hypothesis that a new social order is coming and that it is not necessary or desirable to aid in bolstering up the present social order which is passing."[15] Muste noted that Brookwood was the "spiritual child" of the Comradeship, a radical faction of the pacifist organization the Fellowship of Reconciliation (FOR). Those in the Comradeship wished to "order our lives today as if the Kingdom were already here." Creating a cooperative intentional community was their goal, and Brookwood embodied their social dreams. "The community," wrote Muste, "was a model of how society should, and eventually might, be organized."[16] Brookwood founders' dreams were centered around anti-capitalism and labor interracialism. But they encompassed broader goals, including racial and gender equality, peace, and creating a cooperative commonwealth.

Located in picturesque Katonah, New York, an hour's train ride from the city, Brookwood even looked like a utopian community. Historian Charles F. Howlett notes, "Brookwood's rambling fifty-two acres possessed many of the same qualities and characteristics of Robert Owen's nineteenth century utopian venture at New Harmony, Indiana."[17] Students and teachers lived communally and collaborated on curriculum. They referred to themselves as "cooperators" who would carry out "the principle of democratic control by those living and working in the college."[18] Much like the members of the Student Nonviolent Coordinating Committee (SNCC) in the 1960s, the cooperators donned a working-class uniform of overalls and flannel shirts. They performed all the labor needed to run the school, from cooking to carpentry.[19] And through their training of industrial workers, they sought to create a new social order. For Brookwooders, the labor movement was "a great social force in the modern world, charged with the responsibility of building a planned economy under the control of the workers, in which the good life should be possible for all men." That "good life" would be open to all, including women, the foreign born, and African Americans. This inclusion reflected "that spirit of brotherhood and comradeship which we trust will be universal in a nobler social order when economic classes have been wiped out."[20]

Although overtly socialist in orientation, Brookwood practiced ideological inclusion with no litmus test for political beliefs. Students and faculty alike generally opposed the "pure and simple trade unionism" of the American Federation of Labor (AFL), which promoted conservative craft unions. As a result, in 1928 the AFL denounced Brookwood and told their affiliated unions to withdraw support from the school. Although some students, such as Len De Caux, were Communist Party members, most were part of the noncommunist Left that would dominate the pacifist civil rights community for decades to come. The students, 40 percent of which were female, were generally in their early twenties and had some experience in the industrial workforce.[21] Many attended the school on scholarships supplied by unions, or in the case of Black students, the National Association for the Advancement of Colored People (NAACP). They lived and worked communally and sought to spread Brookwood's tactics and ideas from the shop floors of automobile factories to the homes of sharecroppers in the Deep South.

Training for the Future

Brookwood's curriculum reflected the progressive ideas of John Dewey, the American philosopher and educational reformer who actively supported the school. Following Dewey, Brookwood's instructors promoted a democratic classroom and pragmatic, hands-on teaching. As historian Joyce L. Kornbluh explains, "Dewey's assertion that the *process* of a democratic education would lead to a democratic society became the maxim of adult educators in general, and workers' education leaders in particular."[22] Brookwood instructors frequently brought students to picket lines and protests as they emphasized the importance of doing as well as learning. The first year of the two-year program included general classes such as English and economics, while the second year incorporated courses in labor journalism, labor history, and public speaking.[23] Central to their economic instruction was creating producers' and consumers' cooperatives that could serve as alternatives to capitalist enterprises. Muste wrote in 1926, "Cooperation, like workers' education, is one of the tools with which the working class hacks its way out of the wilderness into the promised land of the new social order." The school itself ran as a cooperative, which was designed to "bring about a fundamental economic change, a better kind of civilization." And in the summer of 1929, Brookwood held a "Consumers Cooperative Institute."[24] Brookwood's students would carry out the vision of a "cooperative commonwealth" into the broader society for years to come.

One of those standard-bearers for cooperatives was Ella Baker, perhaps the long civil rights movement's most effective organizer. Baker's first organizing job was as director for the Young Negroes' Co-operative League (YNCL). It was founded by the editor of the *Pittsburgh Courier*, George Schuyler, in 1930 as the Great Depression began to devastate Black communities. Schuyler traveled to Brookwood in the summer of 1931 to speak about cooperatives. "The increasing pauperism of the American Negro," said Schuyler, "due partially to the collapse of the capitalist system and mostly to the swiftly developing industrial Jim Crowism, is gradually forcing him to adopt co-operative methods."[25] Baker took this message from city to city, educating young African Americans about cooperatives' power in the early 1930s. In 1931 she deepened her education when the Cooperative League USA awarded her a scholarship to attend Brookwood for a semester. Her experience with workers' education at Brookwood was transformative as she relished the democratic atmosphere and progressive politics. Over the next few years, Baker helped establish more than twenty affiliated councils in cities nationwide that built new cooperatives to help African American communities survive the ravages of the Depression.[26]

Under Baker's leadership, the YNCL echoed many of the principles and teachings of Brookwood. It was egalitarian and democratic, encouraging widespread participation by young Black women and eschewing the hierarchical structures that marked the dominant racial reform organizations of the time, like the NAACP and the National Urban League. According to Baker's biographer Barbara Ransby, the young participants viewed the cooperative movement as "a microcosm of a new social order and embodied the idealistic vision held by many of its proponents."[27] The YNCL ended its work in 1933 due to financial difficulties, but Baker continued to deploy Brookwood's lessons as a consumer education teacher for the Workers' Education Project run by the Works Progress Administration (WPA) in 1936, where she served as supervisor for consumer education in New York City.[28] Four years later she became the NAACP's most successful field secretary and went on to work with Martin Luther King Jr.'s Southern Christian Leadership Conference and to advise SNCC, an organization that resembled the inclusive and experimental activism at Brookwood.

Baker was not the only well-known civil rights activist to train at Brookwood. The feminist and civil rights lawyer Pauli Murray worked with Ella Baker at the Workers' Education Project in Harlem. While there she choose to take a brief leave of absence to attend Brookwood in 1937, the last year of the school's existence.[29] Murray described an "almost religious fervor" at Brookwood, "which would be seen two decades later in the civil rights movement and in the women's movement of the early seventies." Workers' education, both with the WPA and at Brookwood, also expanded Murray's horizons during the 1930s. "As I became more immersed in workers' education, my conceptions of racial identity and of injustice began to undergo a significant change," writes Murray in her autobiography. "The study of economic oppression led me to realize that Negroes were not alone but were part of an unending struggle for human dignity the world over."[30] This insight was central to the promise of labor interracialism, linking movements for racial, gender, and economic equality.

A few years later, while a law student at Howard University, Murray would spearhead a pioneering sit-in movement to desegregate public accommodations in Washington, DC, and go on to become a leader in both the feminist and civil rights movements. Baker and Murray were no doubt attracted by Brookwood's avowed commitment to gender equality and organizing women workers. Indeed, Brookwood's commitment to racial equality, and their experience with women such as Baker and Murray, encouraged the active recruitment of Black women. Assisting them in this endeavor was the Bryn Mawr Summer School for Women Workers in Industry, founded in the same year as Brookwood by its feminist president, M. Carey Thomas.[31] Although Thomas was well known for her support of suffrage and her advocacy of women's higher education, she was also notoriously anti-Semitic and racist. Her biographer, Helen Lefkowitz Horowitz, notes, "When she thought about women she imagined those like herself, privileged and educated Anglo-Saxon Protestants."[32] But the summer school for workers opened when Thomas was abroad and it was under the direction of white liberal Hilda Worthington Smith, who in 1926 invited Black students to the campus for the first time.[33] "Bryn Mawr gathers together women workers in industry from all sections of the country," reported a Brookwood publication, "from all types of industrial activity, with every kind of racial background; and in two months of the summer serves as a diminutive melting pot to the labor movement."[34] With help from the school, a subset of these women moved on to Brookwood's two-year program.

Typical of a Black Bryn Mawr student who went out to study at Brookwood was Beatrice Eve. After eight weeks at Bryn Mawr, she was recommended to A. J. Muste as an ideal student. Gertrude Wilson, New York City's industrial secretary, wrote of her, "She has the background of knowing people of various races and nationalities and a very keen sense of the contribution which colored workers have to make to industry and their need of organization."[35] Eve had immigrated from Haiti and was a textile worker living in Harlem who had a reputation for being "radical, rebellious and energetic."[36] This description was provided by a classmate, Floria Pinkney, another African American union worker and activist who attended both Bryn Mawr and Brookwood. Pinkney, like other Black students, obtained a scholarship from the NAACP to attend the school. Because most AFL unions excluded Black workers, they generally only provided scholarships for white students. African Americans, then, needed to rely on civil rights organizations or progressive groups like the Bryn Mawr

Summer School for funding. Fannia Cohn, familiar with Pinkney through the ILGWU, nominated her for the scholarship, and the author and NAACP leader James Weldon Johnson also supported her application.[37] Although the language of labor was the unifying theme of workers' education, notably African Americans did not have the close ties to organized labor shared by their white and immigrant comrades.

When Pinkney arrived in Katonah, New York, in 1925, she was twenty-two years old and a dressmaker from Brooklyn, New York. Pinkney had led an industrial girls' club at a Brooklyn YWCA and was president of the Industrial League of Brooklyn, an organization of employed young women of all races.[38] She had also gained organizing experience with the WTUL working with the Laundry Workers Union. Pinkney was one of the two first Black students at Brookwood, recruited by Muste to "bring about an even better understanding between the white and colored workers in this country." One white male southern student apparently resisted the arrival of Pinkney and fellow African American student Thomas Dabney, telling Muste that Brookwood had taught him "that all people are equal," but noting, "I know it now although I don't feel it yet." Muste reported that after a year, this student "associated in study, work and play with the colored students just as naturally and unaffectedly as with any of the others."[39] For Muste, racial understanding was a process that took place in the context of communal living, transforming the mindset of working-class whites who harbored anti-Black sentiments. This was the hope of social unionism and workers' education, that by living and working together, solidarity could be forged. Pinkney had a difficult time that first year, losing weeks to an appendicitis attack and concerned about her finances. However, upon returning to the city that summer, the ILGWU, which employed many of Brookwood's female students, hired her as an organizer.[40] At the end of her second year, her fellow students unanimously chose Pinkney to be their commencement speaker. Upon graduation she moved back to the city and organized laundry workers with the WTUL and led an organizing drive for the ILGWU.[41]

In 1930, now a seasoned organizer, Floria Pinkney traveled to Denmark on a scholarship provided by the National Urban League and the New York School of Social Work to attend the renowned folk school the International People's College (IPC).[42] Opened, like Brookwood, in 1921 after the carnage of the Great War, the IPC had also hosted Myles Horton, who would attempt to duplicate its teachings at Highlander Folk School. It promoted an international version of social unionism, which emphasized social and economic equality across racial and political borders. The following summer, the YWCA's Industrial Assembly chose Pinkney as their representative for the world YWCA

FIGURE 1.1 Floria Pinkney, fourth from the right, posing with fellow organizers from the International Ladies' Garment Workers' Union at Brookwood Labor College in 1927. Credit: Walter P. Reuther Library, Archives of Labor and Urban Affairs, Wayne State University.

in Geneva, Switzerland.[43] Geneva housed "an international women's community" as the headquarters of both the Women's International League for Peace and Freedom and the YWCA.[44] While the YWCA remained segregated until 1946, the more progressive Industrial Assemblies were often interracial, particularly outside of the South. Organizing women workers into industrial unions necessitated working across racial divisions and challenging the limits of liberal interracialism. The YWCA channeled students into workers' education programs like Bryn Mawr and Brookwood, encouraging those schools' integration, and actively promoted organized labor. Indeed, of the forty-three industrial workers who attended the 1932 YWCA convention, eighteen had attended summer schools for women workers.[45] For Black women, these urban spaces offered training, shelter, and employment.

Pinkney's growing reputation led to an invitation to attend a major 1933 conference in Washington, DC, of activists demanding unemployment relief, which led to an incident involving the white leader of the American Socialist Party, Norman Thomas. Thomas was popular among Black activists, including Pinkney, Baker, and Murray, as well as many Brookwooders. The conference's New York delegation, which included both Pinkney and Thomas, was housed at the Cairo hotel, but when Pinkney appeared in the lobby they barred her from registration. With Thomas in the lead, hundreds withdrew their reservations and marched in her support. This act led Martin Luther King Jr. to later call Thomas the "bravest man I ever met." King lauded Thomas for standing "firmly for the integrity of ends and means."[46] Like King in later years, Thomas demanded that the struggle's interracial tactics must match its goal of full racial equality. By the 1930s Thomas, as well as the Socialist Party, became more outspoken about racial equality. When the party created the Workers Defense League (WDL) in 1936, for example, they recruited Pauli Murray to be one of their organizers. Future Congress of Racial Equality (CORE) founders James Peck and James Farmer also worked with the WDL.[47] When Pinkney returned to New York, the Workers' Education Project hired her to teach courses in labor economics and related topics alongside both Murray and Ella Baker.[48] The education Pinkney received at Bryn Mawr and Brookwood gave her experience and visibility within the linked labor and civil rights movements.

Pinkney was not the only African American student whose time at Brookwood created opportunities for extensive travel in a period in which segregation limited Black mobility. Her fellow student in 1925, Thomas Dabney, also won a NAACP scholarship to attend Brookwood. Because he had a stronger academic background than Pinkney, Dabney stayed at Brookwood for only one year, focusing on honing his skills as a labor journalist. After that year, in the summer of 1926, he was appointed as a member of the American Student Delegation to the Soviet Union.[49] Dabney traveled extensively in Russia and spent several weeks in London meeting "several labor leaders, mostly editors and writers." He reported to Muste that "Brookwood has opened up new vistas of future hope and work for me. The Russia trip enabled me to get some sort of idea of the value of labor education."[50] When Dabney returned, he moved to Philadelphia to work with the communist American Negro Labor Congress (ANLC). Dabney hoped to organize "mass meetings on current questions affecting the Negro such as the Haitian occupation, lynching, peonage, segregation of Negro children in Northern schools, discrimination of labor unions against Negro workers."[51] Although he did not achieve his aims, he did organize interracial conferences and worked with the Philadelphia Committee for Interracial Cooperation. Eventually lack of funds led him to return to the South and become the principal of a "colored high school" in Virginia. However, Dabney continued to find time to investigate and write about racial discrimination in industry. In 1928, for example, the National Urban League sent him on a southern tour to investigate racial discrimination.[52]

Dabney's interracial work in the South led white supremacists to label him a communist, a common refrain among white supremacists. In his case the accusation was somewhat justified because for a brief period after his trip to the Soviet Union, Dabney did work for the party. By the early 1930s, however, Dabney had moved away from the Communist Party, writing Muste that there

FIGURE 1.2 Thomas Dabney at Brookwood Labor College, 1926. Credit: Walter P. Reuther Library, Archives of Labor and Urban Affairs, Wayne State University.

was a "need for an organization to give leadership to the workers which will be revolutionary and at the same time free from the terrific mistakes made by the Communists."[53] Despite his renunciation of the party, when he called for equal pay for Black teachers in Virginia, state leaders hounded him and he was ostracized by some in the Black community.[54] Dabney's confrontations with state officials over equal pay for teachers, his ongoing labor journalism, and his engagement with the growing interracial movement in the South were rooted in his education at Brookwood. For Dabney, as for other Brookwood students, labor interracialism remained at the center of his activism.

Dabney and Pinkney, Brookwood's pioneering Black students, were followed by dozens more, including Ella Baker and Pauli Murray. A number of them went on to play significant roles in the labor and civil rights movements. Historian Thomas Sugrue calls 1931 graduate Henry Lee Moon, for example, "one of the most influential Black political strategists of his time."[55] Moon came from a prominent Black family in Cleveland, Ohio, with deep ties to the NAACP. A graduate of Howard University with a master's degree from Ohio State, Moon honed his journalistic skills at Brookwood, and after graduation became a reporter for the *Amsterdam News*. Like Dabney, in 1932 Moon also traveled to the Soviet Union with artists and activists, including writer Langston Hughes, to make a film documenting African American life. He went on to work with New Deal agencies and the Congress of Industrial Organization (CIO) as a field organizer in the South. Moon was best known for his 1948 book, *Balance of Power*, which argues that African Americans could provide a crucial swing vote in national elections that would force both political parties to support civil rights legislation. Working with the NAACP, Moon promoted voter registration campaigns to make this prediction a reality in the 1940s and beyond. Moon ended his illustrious career as the fourth editor of *The Crisis*, the NAACP's journal.[56]

A protégé of A. Philip Randolph and a sleeping car porter, Ben McLaurin followed Moon to Brookwood, graduating in 1935. McLaurin went on to work with the Brotherhood of Sleeping Car Porters (BSCP) and was Randolph's trusted adviser. Like Randolph, McLaurin believed the causes of labor and civil rights were deeply intertwined. Traveling the country setting up locals for the BSCP, McLaurin reported to Randolph that some porters "are unable to see the larger aspect of the Brotherhood's mission." But he was determined to apply his Brookwood training in workers' education to the BSCP. "We need these men," wrote McLaurin, "and hence we will have to cultivate and educate them into the larger philosophy."[57] He went on to apply this philosophy in the early 1940s while working on Randolph's March on Washington Movement (MOWM) as its national secretary. The MOWM embraced nonviolent direct action and pressured Franklin Roosevelt to end job discrimination in the war industries. McLaurin was active in the labor movement in the postwar years, ending his career as the chairman of New York City mayor John V. Lindsay's Committee on Exploitation of Workers.[58] Randolph long admired A. J. Muste and Brookwood Labor College, sending organizers like McLaurin to the college when he had enough funds to do so. Randolph's crucial linking of issues of labor, race, and nonviolence in the MOWM echoed Brookwood's teaching and would shape the burgeoning civil rights movement for decades to come.

Although only 40 percent of Brookwood students were female, Black women made up about 60 percent of the African American student body.[59] There are a number of likely reasons for this. Brookwood recruited students from AFL unions, most of which excluded African Americans. Thus the male industrial workers who attended the school were largely white, with a few exceptions. A few Black students were coal miners who worked in integrated unions in the upper South and others worked with the all-Black BSCP. In contrast, Black women who attended Brookwood often had affiliations with the progressive ILGWU, and many attended the Bryn Mawr Summer School. Thomas Dabney wrote to Muste about one Black textile worker, Florence Marie Baker, whom he tried to recruit for Brookwood. He remarked, "I think the ILGWU is exhibiting fine spirit in helping and encouraging its intelligent and alert Negro members. That is more than can be said of most of the International Unions. It appears that the women trade unionists are more liberal and alert than the men not only towards Negro workers but towards organizing work."[60] It would take a mass movement to create the industrial unions that would welcome Black male workers into the fold.

Training for the Future

One of the most effective tools in the long civil rights movement was the training institute. Often held in the summer months to attract students, institutes lasted a few days or several weeks. Activists around the country gathered to learn nonviolent direct action, boycotting, picketing, and other tactics they could deploy in their own communities. Brookwood helped to hone this practice through early institutes and small conferences that created networks of like-minded activists and intellectuals and generated ideas for constructing a new social order. Brookwood provided a place where the heavy hitters of early twentieth-century racial reform could meet and talk, often long into the night. A cooperative and egalitarian society was the common goal, but the path there ranged from liberal NAACP president Walter White's legislative reform to A. Philip Randolph's socialist state. At Brookwood the path to a new social order was the path of labor interracialism. Given their commitment to an interracial labor movement, the rampant discrimination practiced by the AFL unions posed a major barrier to racial and economic equality. But for most Brookwooders, the Far Left was also problematic. Writing in 1928, Muste said that communism, although sympathetic to African Americans, was too divisive. In contrast, "the hope of the negro worker is in a militant, progressive trade unionism, which is in earnest about organizing the great masses in the basic industries, which to that end wishes to break down all barriers of color, race and creed between workers, which seeks to develop a political expression for the interests and aspirations of labor, and to which the labor movement is not merely a machine for getting higher wages and shorter hours, immediate material gains, but a great social force, aiming to bring in the good life for all men."[61] Black workers couldn't wait for the unions to come to them; they needed to train and organize to create the "good life" for "all men."

In May 1927, Brookwood held the first of two institutes that focused on

African Americans. "Negro in Industry and the Labor Movement" brought together a diverse group of labor and civil rights leaders. They included the BSCP leader A. Philip Randolph, the sociologists and authors E. Franklin Frazier and Charles S. Johnson, Socialist Party leader Norman Thomas, and the economist Abram Lincoln Harris Jr., among others. Of all the participants, Randolph had the most experience organizing Black workers, and his attendance at the institute was key to its success. He told those gathered that Black workers could not wait for the AFL to organize them, but as the porters had done, they needed to organize themselves. "A movement of this kind," hoped Randolph, "will demonstrate to the white worker that there are some white workers superior to other whites; some Black people superior to other Black people; some white people superior to Black people and some Black people superior to white people."[62] The institute participants agreed that the AFL was the primary barrier to organizing Black workers. Rienzi Lemus of the Brotherhood of Dining Car Employees argued, "Until and unless the movement in entirety soon gets too fundamentally sound, too basically democratic, too cardinally humanitarian, too intrinsically American to foster and nourish race and color prejudices the check will fail to balance and the movement itself will be chief victim of its folly."[63] In addition to organizing Black unions such as the BSCP, the future of the labor movement depended on the ability of white unions to invite African Americans, industrial workers, and women into their ranks.

Major African American and progressive periodicals published articles reporting on the Brookwood institute including *The Survey*, the leading social work journal; *The Messenger*, co-edited by socialists Randolph and Chandler Owen; the National Urban League's *Opportunity*; the NAACP's *Crisis*; *The Nation*; and the then-liberal *New Republic*.[64] This wide publicity, which directly attacked the AFL craft unions, may account for the timing of the AFL's denunciation of Brookwood in 1928 as a dangerously radical institution. The AFL publicly condemned Brookwood for promoting "the cause of Communism extolled through example, teaching and writings" and urged all its affiliated unions to no longer support the college.[65] The following year the AFL wrenched control of the Workers' Education Bureau from its more progressive and visionary founders. The chair of the WEB, James Maurer, whom the AFL ousted, lamented that the AFL "had denied that the basic purpose of such education was an 'intelligent guide to a new social order' and had limited such education 'to study of trade union routine only.'"[66] As Thomas Dabney found in Virginia, calls for racial equality made individuals and institutions vulnerable to accusations of communism. Despite these denunciations, the Brookwood staff held a second conference on "Workers Education for Negroes" in December 1930.

This second conference had equally illustrious participants, including W. E. B. Du Bois. Du Bois had long been interested in cooperatives and workers' education. As early as 1907, while at Atlanta University, Du Bois was promoting cooperatives for African Americans. "The lack of co-operation," argued Du Bois, "is a handicap which the race must overcome if it would hold its own or win a larger place in the industrial world."[67] In 1918 Du Bois founded the Negro Cooperative Guild to promote cooperatives within the Black community, and he spent the next decades fostering cooperatives as an alternative to capitalism that would promote self-reliance.[68] Because a central teaching in workers' education was the planning and execution of cooperatives, DuBois was invested in Brookwood's program. Although he was primarily interested in creating cooperatives controlled by the Black community, he was open to interracial cooperatives. Indeed, "cooperation" had a wider meaning in the context of utopian thought and practice. As Muste stated in a promotional letter for the conference, "How can the workers, regardless of creed, race, or color, be educated to cooperate for the building of a militant, progressive labor movement in the United States?"[69] Cooperation was economic but also social, and labor interracialism was central to its success.

Joining Du Bois were several men who had attended the first conference, including the Howard University economist Abram L. Harris and the sociologists Ira de Reid and E. Franklin Frazier. The Harlem Renaissance writer Langston Hughes was also on hand. Attending as well were several of Brookwood's African American students including Floria Pinkney and Henry Lee Moon.[70] Also present was the executive committee of a new organization, the Conference for Progressive Labor Action (CPLA), that Muste created in the wake of Brookwood's break with the AFL. The CPLA, Muste hoped, would offer an alternative to the AFL by promoting the organization of industrial workers, including African Americans, and advocating for a planned economy. Activists on the noncommunist Left who joined Muste worked both for industrial unionism and broader societal transformations, which explicitly included racial and gender equality as well as the formation of a socialist state.[71]

The discussions at the conference similarly went beyond the need for labor organization. "While recognizing that the Negro problem is pre-eminently economic and similar to the problem of workers organizing the low paid unskilled workers of other groups," read a press release, "speakers gave numerous illustrations of the extent of discrimination of Negroes as Negroes and the resultant intensification of Negro race consciousness."[72] Blacks did not suffer discrimination solely because of their economic status, and thus solutions to poverty and inequality must be enacted on multiple fronts. Like other "New Negroes" of the Harlem Renaissance, the conference participants rejected older bourgeois strategies of racial uplift. In a joint statement, they agreed, "Even more so than other American workers, they [Black workers] have been led to believe that education, loyalty, thrift, business enterprise and political activity (save in the South) will lift them from the ranks of workers and place them on a plane of equality with middle class America."[73] Workers' education could remedy these false beliefs, whether in formal schools or at training institutes.

Practicing Performance

Brookwood provided a space separate and apart from the turmoil of picket lines and city streets for activists to meet, strategize, and talk. This was a key function for communal utopias that offered weary women and men respite from daily political struggles. But at times Brookwood became mobile and brought its message of a new social order to dozens of working-class communities. Brookwooders did this through theater, which by the 1930s had become a means to communicate subversive ideas to the masses. Soviet Russia's agitprop theater, which used mobile theater groups to "agitate" audiences to support the communist cause, was one model for Brookwood's theatrical work. By the early 1930s, a number of agitprop groups in the United States organized a League of Workers' Theaters. These small theaters were a crucial part of what historian Michael Denning terms the "cultural front" of the 1930s. "The heart of this cultural front," explains Denning, "was a new generation of plebeian artists and intellectuals who had grown up in the immigrant and Black working-class neighborhoods of the modernist metropolis."[74] This vibrant interracial movement helped to "labor" American culture, placing working-class intellectuals at the center of the cultural Left. At Brookwood, these plays tended to be optimistic, offering a vision for a more just society. Onstage, Brookwooders played out a vision of the future where the workers were triumphant and a fully egalitarian society was realized.

Brookwooders did not wait for the tumultuous 1930s to begin their theater program. At the height of the conservative turn against labor in the mid-1920s, students and teachers began to write and perform plays. Like workers' education generally, workers' theater was deeply influenced by the feminist movement. In 1925 Hazel MacKaye became Brookwood's first drama teacher. MacKaye was well known as a radical suffragist from a prominent theatrical family who staged huge pageants promoting the suffrage cause.[75] MacKaye brought these skills to Katonah, proclaiming: "Every cemetery has a number of Shakespeares buried in it for want of opportunity to develop their talent."[76] Although MacKaye only stayed at Brookwood for a year, other dramatic instructors followed her methods, and Brookwood became a model for dra-

FIGURE 1.3 The Brookwood Labor Players' bus. Credit: Walter P. Reuther Library, Archives of Labor and Urban Affairs, Wayne State University.

matics in workers' education programs, including the Bryn Mawr Summer School and Highlander Folk School.[77] MacKaye sought to create a student-led program, with many of the plays authored and produced by students, drawing from their experiences in industrial workplaces. Drama at Brookwood was a collective endeavor. By 1926 students were taking weekly courses in "Labor Drama" and had formed the traveling Brookwood Labor Players. The Labor Players visited major cities and in 1932 performed "fifty-three shows, traveled nearly 2,300 miles, and saw a total audience attendance of over 13,000."[78] Students also performed on a radio show, *The Brookwood Hour*, on WEVD in New York City, singing labor songs and making speeches for an urban audience.[79] By 1936 there were three full companies of Brookwood Players on tour, reaching one hundred cities in twenty-three states.

The theater program gained momentum when the Great Depression hit. In 1932, for example, the students built a theater on school grounds to stage plays. Brookwood's Barn Theater was the setting for one of their most successful plays, *Mill Shadows*, which the Brookwood Players took on the road in 1932. This play, like most of Brookwood's repertoire, portrayed collective action as the solution to labor conflict.[80] They also allowed audiences to observe interracial and inter-ethnic actors working cooperatively. Helen G.

Norton, a Brookwood instructor, wrote of the play *The People* performed at the Labor Temple in New York City, "There were seven nationalities represented among the twelve players—English, Hebrew, Italian, Negro, Finnish, Slav, and American."[81] Even during the worst years of the Great Depression, the plays' tone remained optimistic.[82] The WPA's Federal Theater Project embraced that sense of possibility during the New Deal. Union locals also performed workers' theater after Brookwood and other schools closed.[83] But it was the Brookwood Players who helped pioneer the cultural front and performed the language of labor interracialism.

Workers' theater had a direct application to the civil rights movement. Nonviolent direct action was inherently performative, as a Woolworth counter or a picket line became a theatrical space. Activists needed training to anticipate how the drama would play out. During workshops to train civil rights protesters, activists staged skits so Black and white participants could learn how to operate in the theater of the freedom struggle. Understanding the role of performative protests, Brookwood teachers introduced nonviolent direct action and the teachings of Gandhi into Brookwood's curriculum by the early 1930s. And the Brookwood Players not only performed labor plays but also antiwar plays that discussed Gandhian nonviolence.[84] One of the key texts that introduced nonviolence to labor activists was Richard B. Gregg's *The Power of Nonviolence*. Widely circulated at Brookwood in the last two years of the school's existence, Gregg emphasizes the performative nature of radical nonviolence, offering a choreography of protest. The resister "accepts blow after blow, showing no signs of fear or shrinking or resentment, keeping steadily good-humoured and kindly in look of eye, tone of voice, and posture of body and arms," writes Gregg. "To violence he opposes non-violent resistance."[85] Brookwood's popular labor dramas would evolve into the sociodramas of CORE and SNCC, used to train a generation of nonviolent civil rights activists.

Deploying the Sit-Down

Perhaps the most influential play performed by the Brookwood Players was *Sit-Down*, a dramatization of the 1936 Flint sit-down strike that helped build the United Auto Workers (UAW).[86] The connection between Brookwood and the historic 1936 strike was direct. Three leaders of the strike, Merlin Bishop and two of the infamous labor-organizing Reuther brothers, Roy and Walter, had attended and taught at Brookwood. In 1935 Brookwood's staff invited Roy Reuther to help train a generation of labor organizers who would usher in industrial unionism and create an alternative to the AFL, the Congress of Industrial Organizations (CIO).[87] The labor leader John L. Lewis broke from the AFL that same year to create the CIO, which Brookwood students would play a crucial role strengthening. "From 1933 to 1937," argues historian Charles Howlett, "Brookwooders, either through local unionizing efforts or in holding leadership positions within the new national federation[,] were able to help push the CIO to the forefront of the American Labor Movement."[88] In December 1935, all three Reuther brothers convened at Brookwood to discuss the growing movement and plan for the future. Victor Reuther agreed to become an extension worker for Brookwood, traveling the country speaking to industrial workers. And his two brothers threw themselves into the work of organizing new industrial unions.

The 1936 sit-down strike proved to be the turning point in the struggle to organize industrial unions. The sit-down was a nonviolent, but militant, tactic that attracted activists across the Progressive Left. It was a labor strategy dating back to the late nineteenth century in the United States and had been practiced by the Industrial Workers of the World (IWW) and other progressive unions.[89] But the Reuthers and Bishop built on this tactic through their study of Gregg's book and their understanding of Gandhi's nonviolent direct-action movement in India. Roy Reuther was particularly active in antiwar activities, serving as a student representative to the Anti-War Congress in 1934. Roy Reuther and Bishop had discussed the sit-down tactic at Brookwood, information that Bishop brought into the UAW as its educational director. Bishop stressed the importance of labor plays and songs and encouraged the sit-downers in Flint to sing during their occupation of the plant, sending in lyric sheets of labor songs. The Reuthers also sent the workers' theater group, the Contemporary Theater of Detroit, into the plants to perform a two-act play, *Virtue Rewarded*. Labor activists adapted this play for the sit-downers from a Brookwood Labor College play.[90] Thus, Brookwood's teachings on the importance of industrial unionism that was inclusive and democratic lay at the heart of the CIO.

In contrast to the AFL, the CIO encouraged interracial organizing and supported civil rights legislation throughout the freedom struggle. Although weakened by the cold war, this link continued well into the twentieth century. In 1963, for example, Walter Reuther joined Martin Luther King Jr. for Detroit's Walk to Freedom March. By then Walter Reuther's staunch support for the movement had earned him the title of the "white Martin Luther King, Jr." Although he was initially skeptical about a larger march in Washington, DC, the success of the sizable and peaceful Detroit protest convinced him of its utility.[91] Therefore, later that same summer, Reuther joined King again at the March for Jobs and Freedom in Washington, DC. There Reuther, along with other speakers like A. Philip Randolph, directly linked fair employment to civil rights. "We will not solve education or housing or public accommodations," proclaimed Reuther, "as long as millions of American Negroes are treated as second class economic citizens and denied jobs."[92] This link between economic and racial equality had been made decades earlier in Katonah, New York.

Decline of Workers' Education

The success of the sit-down strikes and creation of the CIO reflected the inclusive and democratic impulses of workers' education and the growing popularity of labor interracialism. However, in many ways, workers' education became a victim of its success. The final years of Brookwood were tumultuous. Muste believed that given the crisis of the Great Depression, workers' education should take a back seat to "labor action."[93] Therefore, in 1933 he left Brookwood to devote further time to the CPLA and work with a Trotskyist group, the Workers Party. In 1937 he re-embraced pacifism and Christian socialism and dedicated his life to FOR. As the Depression deepened, Brookwood's financial status was in constant jeopardy, but until 1937 they managed to continue functioning. By 1936, 420 workers had graduated from Brookwood.[94] In the school's final years, the faculty emphasized their pacifist message and the utility of Gandhian nonviolent tactics. In the summer of 1936, for example, they sponsored a Workers Anti-War Summer School and connected peace education to labor interracialism.[95] But after 1937, it was the unions themselves, particularly the new CIO unions, that would take up the cause of workers' education. And between 1933 and 1942, the federal government created its own workers' education program, the Workers' Education Project, under the auspices of the New Deal.[96] The need for a private institution like Brookwood, always difficult to fund, seemed to have passed.

When activists like Muste and Fannia Cohn organized the Workers' Education Bureau in 1921, they had broad goals for workers' education, including the creation of a "new social order." But in the late 1930s, unions and the federal government downplayed this utopian message. Even though the CIO was more progressive and inclusive than the sometimes-reactionary 1920s-era AFL, institutionalized workers' education lacked the broad vision of creating a cooperative society and did not promote labor interracialism as vociferously. Historian Susan Stone Wong notes that by the late 1930s, "Workers' education had become labor education, and the link between education and social action was broken. Whereas workers' education had aimed to teach workers to build a new and better world, labor education endeavored to instruct them to manage the world in which they lived."[97] The utopian strain in workers' education dissipated, only to be replaced by a more pragmatic and narrow agenda.

Labor interracialism was not an inevitable outcome in socialist utopian communities or workers' education schools. A number of Brookwood's contemporary institutions excluded African Americans entirely. Commonwealth College in Mena, Arkansas, for example, grew out of a utopian community but did not directly challenge the racial mores of the South. The origins of Commonwealth were in the socialist utopian community of Llano del Rio. Founded in 1914 outside of Los Angeles, the community members sought to create a cooperative commonwealth. Llano del Rio attracted hundreds of adherents, but could not support the growing community as a result of a water shortage. In 1917 members founded a second utopian community in Vernon Parish, Louisiana, which they called New Llano. Even in the original California colony, the leaders refused to admit any African Americans. According to their publication, *The Western Comrade*, "The rejection of these applications are [*sic*] not due to race prejudice but because it is not deemed expedient to mix the races in these communities."[98] The families who left California for Louisiana continued this practice of racial exclusion. In 1923 they decided to launch a labor college that, like Brookwood, would be "nonfactional, wedded to no specific ideology, group, or school of thought."[99] In 1924 the new institution, now called Commonwealth College, moved to an all-white community in Polk County, Arkansas.

Commoners, as they labeled themselves, believed that "nothing would have destroyed the College's relations with its neighbors more quickly, venomously, and permanently than the presence of African Americans on campus."[100] They also pointed to the fact that Arkansas law deemed integrated schools illegal. In contrast to Brookwood, which imported some food, Commonwealth College was a completely self-sufficient cooperative where students and faculty engaged in extensive manual labor to produce all their food and other needs. During the height of the Great Depression, Commoners did begin to work with the Southern Tenant Farmers' Union (STFU), organizing Black and white sharecroppers. This marked a shift to extension work and pragmatic union organizing that other workers' colleges experienced. As historian William H. Cobb argues, "The Left, particularly the non-communist Left, was forced to concentrate its efforts on the organizational struggles of the workers and their unions rather than the utopian vision of creating a new social order."[101] After 1937 members of the Communist Party dominated Commonwealth, alienating it from socialists doing similar work. In 1940 state officials shut down the school, charging it with "anarchy."[102]

It is notable that the segregationist governor of Arkansas, Orval Faubus, attended Commonwealth College. Notorious for his defiance of school integration in Little Rock in 1957, Faubus came from a liberal family. His father, Sam Faubus, was a socialist who enlisted many of his neighbors in rural Arkansas in the cause. Influenced by these ideas, Orval attended Commonwealth in 1935, where he was elected president of the student body. Although he renounced socialism, during Roosevelt's presidency he supported the New Deal and continued to view himself as a liberal throughout his political career.[103] But he was also a staunch segregationist, a viewpoint that Commonwealth did not directly challenge. The example of Commonwealth demonstrates that not all factions of the Left viewed interracialism as a primary goal. At Commonwealth the idea of racial equality was for the future, not the present.

The utopian goals of Brookwood Labor College—seeking a cooperative, nonviolent, interracial world—did not disappear with the bureaucratization of workers' education. They may have failed to bring a fully new social order, but Brookwood spawned other experiments in labor interracialism and created a new generation of labor leaders for whom racial equality was a central measure of success. Of these interracial experiments, the most significant was the Highlander Folk School.

A Danish Folk School in the Rural South

Brookwooders had a comparable community in Tennessee. Highlanders, like their northern counterparts, shared a utopian spirit that sought a new social order. Highlanders were, in the dialogue of the 1937 documentary *People of the Cumberland*, "the people of tomorrow." They were living in the future, or at least the future they envisioned. Highlanders lived communally and much of their days were filled with building and providing for their folk school. Like Brookwooders, they ran cooperatives and had an expansive vision of the role that organized labor could play in a new society. They had no political affiliation, although most Highlanders identified with Norman Thomas's Socialist Party. But unlike Brookwood, Highlander survived the Great Depression, and when the labor movement became more conservative after World War II, they did not close their doors. Instead, they turned their attention toward the struggle for racial equality, particularly desegregation and voting rights. In doing so, they became what historian Aldon Morris terms "a classic movement halfway house."[104] Highlander offered respite, training, and music to the leading figures of the civil rights movement, including Martin Luther King Jr., Rosa Parks, and the young students of SNCC.

Although the early years of Highlander, founded in 1932, resembled Brookwood, there were crucial differences between the two institutions. Katonah, New York, was not Monteagle, Tennessee, and the problems of rural south-erners differed from the urban industrial workers who traveled to Brook-wood. Brookwood's founder, A. J. Muste, also differed from the guiding light of Highlander, the white reformer Myles Horton. Unlike the sophisticated Muste, Horton came of age in rural Tennessee and graduated from Tennes-see's Cumberland College in 1928. After graduation he worked as a student secretary for the YMCA, but ran afoul of the Y's leadership for holding a series of interracial meetings. The Y's liberal interracialism did not go far enough for the young radical. Horton soon left the South to attend the highly influential Union Theological Seminary, where he studied with Reinhold Niebuhr and joined Niebuhr's Fellowship of Socialist Christians. Niebuhr, a radical theologian who also influenced Martin Luther King Jr., would remain a staunch supporter of Highlander throughout his life. While in New York, Horton visited Brookwood in 1929 but found it too "academically oriented" and urban focused.[105] Horton also made a point of visiting utopian communi-ties, including the Rugby and Ruskin colonies in the Cumberland Mountains, and Oneida in New York. Although these communities had largely disbanded by the time of Horton's visits, he met with the few surviving members. They appealed to him "because of their spiritual, religious and economic back-ground," but he was concerned that they were too "escapist," separate from the world.[106] He found the model of the school he would eventually establish much farther away, in Denmark.

Before exploring the Danish folk schools, Horton spent time at the Uni-versity of Chicago studying sociology with Robert Park and meeting with famed settlement house founder, Jane Addams, who encouraged him to open an experimental southern settlement.[107] In 1931, with Niebuhr's encourage-ment, he earned enough money to travel to Denmark, where he visited the renowned folk schools. Danish reformers first established these schools in the 1840s as an attempt to preserve the cultural traditions and language of the Danish peasantry. By the early twentieth century, they were running suc-cessful cooperatives and trade unions.[108] And they institutionalized a philos-ophy about teaching and learning that became central to Horton's worldview: "Adults had to learn how to live a new social and economic order before they could teach it."[109] Like Brookwooder Floria Pinkney, Horton also attended the International People's College at Elsinore. He returned home in 1932 de-termined to open a "southern mountain school" that would go beyond more traditional workers' education by allowing the people themselves to set the agenda, rather than following a set curriculum. Horton, along with fellow activist Don West, was able to secure land from Lillian Johnson, a former suffragist and strong proponent of cooperatives, in the "highlands" of Tennessee. There they created a "new society" that was envisioned "as a democratically conceived, cooperatively administered center for the community."[110] It was also an interracial community from the outset, a direct violation of the state's segregation statutes and a stark contrast to Commonwealth College and other southern workers' education institutions.

A New Democracy

Highlander opened in one of the poorest districts in the South in the midst of the Great Depression. Horton and his fellow teachers believed that by establishing a new democratic model based on cooperatives and organized labor, southerners could be lifted from poverty. "Labor unions and cooperatives," argued Horton, "by practicing democracy within themselves, by assuring equality of economic and political democracy for all Southern citizens regardless of creed or color, could liberate basic and latent Southern initiative and dynamism from the feudal landowners and baronial industrialists' choking grip."[111] For the next two decades, Highlanders labored tirelessly to create this new democratic order and promote labor interracialism, and to some extent they succeeded. Like Brookwood, Highlander played a key role in the emergence of the CIO and the promotion of interracial unions. But challenging segregation and exploitation came at a significant cost as white supremacists repeatedly attacked the school through legal and extralegal means. Mob violence, backed by the state, would accelerate when Highlander increasingly turned to training civil rights activists in the late 1940s.[112]

Horton's educational philosophy was more flexible than Muste's, but the two agreed that students learned best by doing. Indeed, one of Highlander's original teachers, Zilla Hawes Daniel, attended Brookwood in 1932 and moved to Highlander the following year to teach labor history.[113] But Horton explained that teachers were "not teaching reading, or some work skill, or how to get along with society as it was."[114] Instead, the staff listened to those who came to Highlander and shaped their programs around the needs of the participants. For the desperately poor local residents, this meant assisting them in forming cooperatives and providing day care for working mothers. Highlanders also joined striking workers throughout the South, providing training, teaching them union songs, and often putting their own lives at risk. During the 1934–35 general textile strike, for example, staff and students visited "strike scenes, armed with mimeographed song sheets, some unorthodox ideas of workers' education and a high sense of a movement in the making."[115] The textile strikes failed but set the stage for the more successful CIO organization, the Textile Workers Organizing Committee, in 1937. Horton was hopeful that this new union, which became the Textile Workers Union of America in 1939, would become a "democratic, radical, social movement."[116] Highlanders spread out across the South to assist in the organizing efforts and held numerous workshops to train union leaders in a safe, supportive space. The textile workers campaign solidified Highlander's relationship with the newly emerging CIO, which viewed the community as organized labor's primary southern training ground.

The CIO's commitment to labor interracialism appealed to Highlanders committed to full racial equality. When in the field, they encouraged Black workers to pledge their loyalty to the unions and tried to persuade whites that racial unity would only strengthen their cause. In the early years, few Black students attended Highlander, but the staff did bring in African American speakers to discuss the plight of Black workers. In 1934, for example, a Black sociology professor from Knoxville College, J. H. Daves, spoke on the "relation of Negro workers to the labor movement in the South," violating the state law that prohibited Blacks and whites from eating or sleeping together under the same roof. Hearing of the visit, local whites threatened to dynamite the school, and guards had to be posted while Daves was there.[117] Zilphia Horton, Myles Horton's first wife, noted: "We have thought it a more practical way to attack the problem of racial relations in the southern unions by having students meet and talk with Negro guests who visit the school and [by] making it a point to have as lecturers during the term distinguished Negroes."[118] In this limited way, soon to be dramatically expanded, Highlander encouraged interracial organizing on school grounds. Black visitors ate, danced, and worked alongside the white participants, modeling the possibility of an interracial society.

Highlanders faced constant threats of violence from white vigilantes. For this reason, they never fully embraced nonviolence. Highlanders stockpiled weapons to defend participants against white supremacists. And Horton argued that conflict was necessary in labor struggles, based on his experiences on the picket line. He believed that social struggles were "a matter of determining what was the lesser violence, not choosing between violence and nonviolence."[119] Highlanders, however, did recognize that nonviolence could work as an effective tactic. They offered teachings on Gandhi and closely followed the early labor sit-ins.[120] Highlander applied these tactics in 1939 when working with a WPA union. The workers were disgruntled with the state administrator who closed many works projects in retaliation for unionization, leaving over seven hundred with no relief. Union members staged a "stay-in" of the Grundy County WPA office. Nearly five hundred families occupied the building for ten days. Highlander helped them organize committees and publish a newspaper, and led them in singing "We Shall Not Be Moved." The stay-in received national publicity, and donations of food and clothing poured into the community. An investigation by the federal WPA office led to praise for the union and a return of relief payments for many.[121] Nonviolent direct action and the movement music developed by Highlander would soon become central to the broader civil rights movement.

Highlanders' activism and training helped to foster a growing coalition of liberals and radicals who sought to improve race relations in the South by the end of the 1930s. In 1938 this coalition formed the Southern Conference for Human Welfare (SCHW). Their first meeting in Birmingham brought socialists like Horton, union organizers, and First Lady Eleanor Roosevelt, who was a strong supporter of Highlander. Until the SCHW's demise in 1948, Highlander played a central role in the organization, pushing southern liberals to directly address segregation and African Americans' low economic status. The SCHW's open membership, which ranged from communists to moderate Democrats, reflected Highlander's own nonsectarian position. By 1948 the participation of communists would be a major factor in SCHW's demise, a threat that hounded Highlander as well.[122] The SCHW, argues historian John Egerton, "would long be remembered, not for what it achieved, but for what it aspired to and what it attempted."[123] This inclusive vision of a new society marked what was most progressive in New Deal politics and helped fulfill the promise of labor interracialism.

Civil Rights Unionism

The 1939 WPA stay-in was the beginning of the most fruitful period in Highlander's interracial labor organizing. By 1949 Highlander had trained 7,200 workers, Black and white, industrial and agricultural. Their extension work reached twice that number. In 1940 Highlander announced that the school would not hold training sessions for any union that discriminated against African Americans. Consistent with their growing commitment to civil rights, they also integrated their previously all-white board of directors and actively recruited Black students, farmers, and workers to come to the school. With the rise of the defense industry during World War II, the number of southern unionized workers rose and Highlander was in an ideal position to work with the CIO on training workers. These efforts peaked in 1944 when the UAW held a fully integrated training session at Highlander, the largest session it had ever run and the first southern interracial union school. Highlander's location in the mountains allowed union members to relax and strategize away from the pressures of the union hall or shop floor. Although Horton had criticized utopian communities' isolation from the outside world, the isolation of his mountain folk school created the possibility of full racial equality.[124]

Throughout the 1940s, Highlander sponsored an interracial summer school for CIO members that proved transformative for some. One white textile worker from Georgia reported, "Highlander gave me strength where I had a little weakness—the Negro question. I know now there are no superior races—we are all human beings."[125] Highlander had a particular powerful role in its home state of Tennessee. Most Tennessee CIO leaders had spent time in Highlander, absorbing the lessons of labor interracialism. Highlander also did not ignore rural workers during this period. Between 1944 and 1950, they created a Farmers Union designed to bring Black and white sharecroppers and small farmers together.[126] A pamphlet highlighting this work shows photographs of African Americans and whites "living, playing, working together." It boasts, "Highlander students learn that artificial barriers are erected between the Negro and white workers and farmer in the South. They learn that cooperative effort creates an environment in which not only civil liberties, but also higher standards of living can thrive." One white Alabama farmer, J. D. Mott, reported, "I'll bet I've shaken hands with five hundred colored farmers—and organized them into the Farmers Union. We're all getting together as farmers to solve our mutual problems." Extension work also promoted interracial understanding. An extension program in Alabama encouraged Black workers to "describe barriers which keep them from voting." After much discussion, white and Black students reportedly made "plans for the next election."[127] Labor interracialism prepared Highlanders for their central role in the emerging southern civil rights movement.

Hoping to further strengthen unionization in the South in 1946, the CIO launched "Operation Dixie" in a coordinated attempt to organize Black and white workers. But the progressive politics of the New Deal era had given way to a more conservative climate and a fervent anti-communism. This political shift marginalized Highlander, as well as the progressive SCHW, in the labor movement. Operation Dixie, as a result, was less inclusive and more limited than the 1930s campaigns, fading after a year of failed strikes and frustrations. Only the most progressive CIO organizers were willing to actively recruit Black workers into the new unions, and some CIO organizers harbored racist views and feared the taint of communism. Operation Dixie was the harbinger of a new era of anti-communism and anti-labor sentiment. By 1947 less than 10 percent of CIO members lived in the South.[128] That year Congress passed the Taft-Hartley Act, which limited the kinds of strikes that labor unions could embark on and allowed state legislatures to pass anti-labor legislation at will. In the years that followed, southern state legislatures passed hundreds of anti-labor laws, and the rift between Highlander and the CIO grew dramatically. As had happened with Brookwood, unions began to embark on their own workers' education program rather than sending students to the embattled institution. "Today many unions are in a position to do much of their own training," read Highlander's 1953 annual report.[129] More significantly, in the growing cold war climate, unions were reluctant to associate with a school run by an avowed socialist who openly violated the state's segregation laws. Thus, Highlander did not leave the labor movement voluntarily—the labor movement abandoned Highlander.

In 1949 the CIO demanded that Highlander change its statement of purpose by "declaring that the Highlander Folk School is opposed to all kinds of totalitarianism including communism, fascism and Nazism." The board refused and told the CIO that it would continue to work with expelled unions suspected of communist infiltration. This had implications for the civil rights movement as progressive unions were much more likely to be integrated. In response the CIO instructed its locals that they should no longer associate with the folk school.[130] Just as the AFL had rejected Brookwood's inclusive goals, the postwar CIO rejected Highlander and largely gave up the project of interracial organizing in the South. Highlander's board did issue a new statement of purpose in 1949, but one that reflected a broad and deep commitment to radical democracy. "We reaffirm our faith in democracy as a goal that will bring dignity and freedom to all; in democracy as an expanding concept encompassing human relations from the smallest community organization to international structures; and permeating all economic, social and political activities."[131] "Dignity and freedom to all" included African Americans. This commitment drew the ire of local whites, and in 1950 the Federal Bureau of Investigation (FBI) began harassing the school as Highlander ramped up its civil rights activity.[132] Highlanders recognized that the cold war had undermined organized labor, particularly in the South, and so they turned their attention to the broader search for racial equality.

A Civil Rights Revolution

White workers and labor leaders' resistance to labor interracialism was a central reason that organized labor was unable to effectively organize in the South. By 1953 Highlander's staff understood that they could no longer productively work with organized labor and met to discuss what lay ahead. In the 1940s they had already broadened their interracial activism, bringing Black and white students and community leaders to the school to discuss issues ranging from segregation, the United Nations, and poverty. In the early 1950s, Black students who would be in the vanguard of SNCC—including Marion Barry, James Bevel, Diane Nash, and John Lewis—attended Highlander workshops.[133] Like the white union members who learned to work with African Americans at Brookwood, these young Black activists experienced a fully interracial community. Sharing food, songs, and labor, Highlander activists developed a set of strategies and a culture that would shape the civil rights movement at the height of its powers. As they lived together and trained activists to enact immediate change, Highlander's culture shifted from labor interracialism to utopian interracialism.

Highlander began its civil rights campaigns in earnest in 1953, holding two workshops on school desegregation in preparation for the *Brown v. Board of Education* decision. These workshops, which were broadened to include other forms of segregation, continued until 1957. The first workshop, "The Supreme Court Decisions and the Public Schools," brought together Black and white ministers, farmers, teachers, students, and community leaders. Crucially the workshop drafted a handbook that organizers could bring back to their home communities outlining steps toward school desegregation and best practices. They encouraged participants to set up independent committees that could inform the public and pressure school boards. Highlanders also produced a filmstrip on the "High Cost of Segregation" that could be shown at community meetings. Segregation, they argued, hurt all children, and the ultimate goal was "better educational opportunities for all children of the South."[134] Horton deemed the workshops a success. "Instead of trying to get official endorsements and resolutions from top leaders and organizations," he argued, "this program would be reaching out into the homes of the workers from the mills and factories, the farmers on their land, and the church and school people in their communities."[135] The tools that Highlander had used in the labor movement, empowering ordinary people to act, were now harnessed to address racial inequality.

The experience of fully integrated living at the Highlander workshops could be transformative for southern African Americans. That was the case for one of its most famous participants, Rosa Parks. Parks often reflected back on the experience of waking up to "the smell of bacon frying and coffee brewing and know[ing] that white folks were doing the preparing instead of me.'"[136] E. D. Nixon, a Black labor activist who had worked with Highlander in the 1930s to organize an Alabama union, and Virginia Durr, a liberal white woman who served on Highlander's board, both urged Parks, then youth secretary for the Montgomery NAACP, to attend the 1955 summer workshop.[137] Although she was nervous at first, Parks found the two-week workshop invigorating and returned to Montgomery inspired. During the workshop she took copious handwritten notes, giving us a sense of Highlander's teaching. One note simply reads: "Never make compromises—Seek truth—Practice brotherhood." Throughout her notes the need and efficacy of immediate change, rather than gradualism, is evident. "Desegregation proves itself," wrote Parks, "by being put in action not changing attitudes."[138] Workshoppers were also attentive to the potential drawbacks of school integration, including the potential for Black teachers to lose their positions, and strategized possible solutions. This reflected a pragmatic sensitivity to the plight of the Black middle class that Parks appreciated.

Parks arrived at Highlander exhausted and pessimistic about the possibility of real change. She left with a new vision after finding "for the first time in my adult life that this could be a unified society, that there was such a thing as people of all races and backgrounds meeting and having workshops and living together in peace and harmony." She was struck by living, if only temporarily, in a community of equality and brotherhood. "I had heard there was such a place, but I hadn't been there."[139] Montgomery was certainly not such a place, and even after the workshop Parks was pessimistic about the possibility of real change in the city. Five months later, her decision not to relinquish a seat on a Montgomery bus and the boycott that followed would prove her wrong. Parks experienced utopian interracialism briefly at Highlander, and that vision helped launch the mass civil rights movement.

The Montgomery Bus Boycott also brought another civil rights leader, Martin Luther King Jr., to the attention of Highlander. Horton invited King to be the keynote speaker at Highlander's 1957 twenty-fifth anniversary, an event also attended by Parks and civil rights activist Ralph Abernathy. King's stirring address includes this passage:

> But there are some things in our social system to which I am proud to be maladjusted and to which I suggest that you, too, ought to be maladjusted. I never intend to adjust myself to the viciousness of mob rule. I never intend to adjust myself to the evils of segregation and the crippling effects of discrimination. I never intend to adjust myself to the tragic inequalities of an economic system which takes necessities from the masses to give luxuries to the classes. I never intend to become adjusted to the madness of militarism and the self-defeating method of physical violence. I call upon you to be maladjusted.[140]

His comprehensive linking of violence, segregation, and economic inequality echoed the teachings at Highlander during the previous quarter century. Although Horton disagreed with King on nonviolence, and preferred a more

FIGURE 1.4 Septima Clark and Rosa Parks at Highlander, 1955. Credit: Library of Congress, Prints and Photographs Division, Visual Materials from the Rosa Parks Papers, LC-DIG-ppmsca-47364.

grassroots and dispersed leadership style in the movement, the two remained close throughout the remainder of King's life.[141] But King's relationship with Horton and Highlander had significant consequences. At that 1957 meeting, the Georgia Commission on Education, a right-wing group set up by the segregationist governor, sent an agent to photograph the participants. Unbeknownst to those at Highlander, a columnist for the communist newspaper the *Daily Worker* also attended the event. Using those photographs, the Georgia Commission produced fifty thousand pamphlets, *Martin Luther King at a Communist Training School*. Right-wing groups also produced postcards and billboards, plastering the South with the accusation of treason.[142] Segregationists and the FBI used this material to portray King as a communist until his death. Parks also appeared in the photographs and suffered subsequent attempts to smear her and other civil rights activists.[143]

The anti-Highlander billboards remained well into the 1960s. For example, Horton told this story about the 1965 Selma march:

> On the way to the capital, I dropped back beside an elderly Montgomery Negro who was having trouble keeping pace. After several silent miles he told me that he joined the march to finish the freedom walk he started ten years ago during the bus boycott. He had only confided in me, however, after we passed a large billboard outside the

FIGURE 1.5 Billboard accusing Martin Luther King Jr. of being a communist for attending a Highlander event, 1965. Credit: Library of Congress, Prints and Photographs Division, NYWT&S Collection, LC-USZ62-120215.

> *White Citizen's Council headquarters purported to show Rev. Martin Luther King, Jr. at a "communist school." My marching companion recognized my picture and that of Mrs. Rosa Parks, whom he had known before she came to Highlander, in the picture with Rev. King. Later, Mrs. Parks was introduced as the "Mother of the Movement." In her quiet impressive way, she spoke of being a student at Highlander, where, ten years ago, she learned "not to hate white people."*[144]

Clearly white supremacist propaganda did not have the intended impact on those committed to the freedom movement. But the constant harassment from state authorities and white supremacists alike took its toll on Highlander and the activists associated with it. The same year that the Georgia Commission on Education smeared Highlander, the school lost its tax-exempt status, with the approval of the notoriously racist anti-communist Senator James Eastland of Mississippi. Supporters of the school scrambled to raise funds for the tax bill, and Highlander had its tax-exempt status reinstated a year later.[145] The final years of Highlander's existence in Monteagle, Tennessee, saw constant crises and harassment. That fact makes the accomplishments of the school even more remarkable.

The credit for perhaps the most significant program Highlander ever launched goes to Septima Clark, who, unlike King and Parks, never became a household name. But her work with Highlander exemplified the democratic leadership they embraced. Clark, an African American teacher, first came to Highlander in 1954, after being fired from her teaching job in Charlestown, South Carolina, for her membership in the NAACP. Impressed by Highlander's civil rights work, the next summer she transported three groups of African Americans to the school and mentored Rosa Parks when she attended the pivotal 1955 workshop. Recognizing her talent at reaching students, the following year Horton appointed Clark director of workshops for Highlander. Clark convinced Horton that in order to enfranchise Blacks, they needed first to be taught to read and write. Working with Esau Jenkins, an African American activist who lived on Johns Island, Clark developed a program of "citizenship schools." She soon was bringing dozens of African Americans to Highlander and training them to transport the literacy program to their home communities. Adult students met in beauty parlors, kitchens, and churches to share their struggles and learn the skills necessary to pass literacy tests. Responding to their immediate needs, the teachers also helped them open bank accounts, find employment, and improve their living conditions. "By the spring of 1961," according to Clark, "eighty-two teachers who had received training at Highlander were holding classes in Alabama, Georgia, South Carolina, and Tennessee."[146] Under constant attack by local police and the FBI, Horton decided to have the Southern Christian Leadership Conference (SCLC) take over the program under Clark's direction in 1961. Other civil rights organizations joined the effort, and in 1962 they created the Voter Education Project, which went on to train close to 10,000 teachers for citizenship schools. When the 1965 Voting Rights Act passed, many thousands of Black voters were ready to register thanks to the efforts of Clark and her army of citizen teachers.

Although Clark worked with King in SCLC, like Horton she was critical of his leadership, particularly his need to be always visible. "I thought that you develop leaders as you go along," said Clark, "and as you develop these people let them show forth their development by leading."[147] This echoed Ella Baker's famous quote "Strong people don't need strong leaders." Embracing this philosophy, the white staff at Highlander recognized that the citizenship schools needed to be controlled by African American teachers and students, without white interference. Horton noted, "Even whites with the best of intentions could not long work with blacks without telling them how to do what was supposedly good for them."[148] Listening and deferring thus also meant whites giving up control. Black leadership was a key component of utopian interracialism, in contrast with the liberal and labor interracialism that too often placed whites at the center. Clark's educational ethic was a centerpiece of workers' education and the Dutch Folk School movement, empowering ordinary people to take control of their lives. Both Clark and Baker believed deeply that listening to the people and allowing them to set the agenda was central to building a social movement. And they were always looking to the future. "The only thing that's really worthwhile is change," remarked Clark near the end of her life. "It's coming."[149] When Highlander started listening to African American college students, the change came rapidly.

Starting in 1954, Highlander invited African American students from historically Black colleges to discuss segregation, atomic war, and global issues and to strategize on possible solutions. As always, the students set the agenda and found at Highlander a peaceful yet powerful setting to have their voices heard.[150] When the sit-in movement began in Greensboro and Nashville in February 1960, Highlander invited the young activists to attend a workshop and strategize about their next steps. On April 1, 1960, seventy-five students, two-thirds of whom were Black, converged on Highlander from fourteen southern universities. There they debated whether to focus on direct action to challenge segregation or voter registration. Crucially they came to a consensus to pursue both strategies and set an agenda for a follow-up meeting in Raleigh, North Carolina. At that meeting, the students declared their independence from existing organizations and created the Student Nonviolent Coordinating Committee (SNCC). Throughout the freedom movement of the early 1960s, Highlander would continue to provide training for young SNCC workers. Before heading to volatile Mississippi, for example, SNCC volunteers trained at Highlander from 1961 through the "Freedom Summer" of 1964.[151] In the 1930s and 1940s, Highlanders had faced the racial terror of white supremacy and violence against organized labor. They had been shot at, put in jail, and hounded by the FBI. Thus, they could provide the kind of training and support needed by this new generation of activists facing white racial terror.

Highlander's central role in the student movement came at a considerable cost. During the 1960 student workshop, white supremacists terrified participants, riding by Highlander at night with their shotguns. Terror also came from the state. Tennessee officials had long sought a way to shut down Highlander, and in 1961 the Tennessee legislature finally succeeded in closing the school, charging it with selling alcohol and practicing racial integration in violation of state law. After losing a series of appeals, the state took possession of Highlander in Monteagle. Highlander staffers moved to Knoxville, Tennessee, where they opened the Highlander Research and Education Center. It was there that SNCC students held their training workshops and strategized.[152] But the Knoxville location was not the idyllic retreat that Monteagle had been and did not have the space the former school provided. Highlander remained active throughout the 1960s, including helping to organize Martin Luther King Jr.'s 1968 Poor People's Campaign; indeed, it still exists today and continues its social justice work. By listening to the people, rather than dictating to them, Highlander helped transform the freedom movement. As Horton said, "What ought to be, rather than what is—that is Highlander's mission."[153]

Despite the importance of Highlander's prefigurative politics to the labor and civil rights movements, what is most often remembered about its contributions is the music that was created there and taught to activists. The person most responsible for developing a powerful repertoire of freedom songs was Zilphia Mae Horton, who was a talented musician. During the 1930s and 1940s, she traveled to picket lines and taught striking workers to sing old folk songs and spirituals with updated militant lyrics. Labor leader John L. Lewis called the "southern union movement" a "singing army."[154] Zilphia had a rich store of music to work from, particularly from Black culture. "Because of those deep-rooted traditions of singing in churches and homes," remembered Highlander Ralph Tefferteller, "it was very natural that singing should develop in the Southeastern part of the country as a natural adjunct to the struggle to overcome inhuman situations and to deal with them in song."[155] Zilphia and the folk singer Pete Seeger were responsible for modifying a traditional African American spiritual to create the anthem for the civil rights movement, "We Shall Overcome." Famed song leader and active participant at Highlander, Bernice Johnson Reagon, argues that Highlander served as a "custodian" of the song. "They had kept it alive by singing it as a song of struggle but were proud to be able to see it reclaimed by Black people. And reclaimed it was."[156] During the first SNCC workshop in 1960, Guy Carawan, who carried on the song tradition for Highlander after Zilphia's untimely death, taught the students "We Shall Not Be Moved," "Keep Your Eyes on the Prize," "This Little Light of Mine," and "We Shall Overcome."[157] After activists reclaimed these songs, and many others, they were further shaped and changed for the movement as verses were added and singing styles evolved.

Labor and civil rights activists found Highlander workshops filled with music, and they took those songs with them as they traveled back to the front lines of struggle. Communal singing had long been an important component of utopian communities, with the Shakers being perhaps the best example. It promoted unity among diverse groups of activists and was an outlet for powerful emotions. The importance of singing is epitomized by the reaction of activists when Highlander was raided by police in 1959. Huddled in the dark while the police searched the premises, they began to sing "We Shall Overcome." A young Black woman from Montgomery spontaneously added the verse "We are not afraid" to the song.[158] That same night police placed Septima Clark in a filthy jail cell and denied her a phone call. Unsure of what to do, she decided to sing. "We had had a workshop," Clark later remembered, "and Harry Belafonte had been there, teaching us 'Michael Row.' So I just sat up there and sang that, until they came to get me out of that room."[159] Thousands of activists in jail, at mass meetings, and marching in picket lines pulled songs from Highlanders' repertoire during the height of the movement. These songs are much better known today than Highlander itself. But they reflect the basic goal of the folk school and the radical workers' education movement of the 1920s and 1930s: brotherhood, cooperation, and nonviolence. During his speech at Highlander's twenty-fifth anniversary, King said, "Men hate each other because they don't know each other; they don't know each other because they can't communicate with each other; they can't communicate with each other because they are separated from each other."[160] Labor plays and protest music were a powerful way to connect women and men together across racial and class lines.

Conclusion

Much like "We Shall Overcome" moved from a union to a civil rights song, activists deployed sit-down strikes in the cause of labor activism before applying them to civil rights. But that labor activism was broad and inclusive. Social unionism and civil rights unionism went well beyond simply organizing trade unions—they advocated labor interracialism and the building of a new society. At Brookwood and Highlander, men like Muste and Horton imagined a new world of cooperation and brotherhood. They borrowed heavily from an earlier feminist labor vision and reached out to African Americans. In the short term, they helped create a powerful industrial union movement that, despite its flaws, left behind the narrow focus of AFL craft unions. In the long term, they trained a generation of activists who would take their expansive vision nationwide and beyond. Muste, and especially Horton, emphasized cooperation over hierarchy and sought to foster a truly democratic form of education where students set the agenda and wrote the curriculum. But in reality these two white men dominated their respective institutions and surely drowned out voices that had less power. However, the labor interracialism promoted by Brookwood and Highlander allowed Ella Baker, Pauli Murray, Rosa Parks, and many others to obtain valuable training and glimpse a vision of the future. Their work shifted labor interracialism toward a utopian interracialism that was not centered on white leadership.

Until the mid-1950s at Highlander, the number of African Americans who attended workers' education schools was relatively small. But particularly in the South, those small numbers posed a broad challenge to the existing racial system. And living interracially had a profound impact on both whites and Blacks. "Highlander was like a little oasis down South," remembered Pete Seeger. "There weren't that many places in the South where you could go and find Black and white sitting down eating together and drinking together and kidding each other and teasing each other, and dancing together."[161] Labor interracialism was not the liberal integrationism of racial moderates, who called for gradual change through moral suasion. Rather it marked a radical and immediate break from the current system. Workers' education was not merely about studying, but doing. It was also not prescriptive, but called for careful attentiveness to ordinary people's needs. This flexible and democratic approach would serve the civil rights movement well. The activists who attended these schools or were part of the labor movement they promoted, brought these lessons into the freedom struggle. An experiment in economic cooperation and labor interracialism in Mississippi exemplified this broad vision of a utopian future in the here and now.

2

The Cooperators

To the disinherited belongs the future.

HOWARD KESTER[1]

The great object of the Cooperative Farms is to build a new type of
manhood and a new social order amid the decay of the old system.

SHERWOOD EDDY[2]

In the blistering hot Mississippi Delta during the depths of the Great Depression, displaced Black and white sharecroppers toiled shoulder to shoulder in the fields of a cooperative farm. Their children played together on a nearby swing set and ran across the open fields. White college students from the North did small jobs on the farm and joined in nightly discussions at the community center. A health clinic, a rarity in rural Mississippi, treated the surrounding Black community suffering from chronic illness. And visiting dignitaries wrote long letters home extolling the virtues of cooperative living and labor interracialism. This was the Delta Cooperative Farm. An experiment in utopian socialism in the depths of the Great Depression, it became a model for successful organizing in the Deep South.

In 1936 racial and economic turmoil upended the southern social order. The exploitative sharecropping system crumbled under the weight of New Deal agricultural policy and decimated crop prices. Landowners threw

Black and white sharecroppers off their land and refused to share government payments with them. The sharecroppers fought back, creating the socialist Southern Tenant Farmers' Union (STFU) in Arkansas and the communist Alabama Sharecroppers Union. In response, southern sheriffs, with
the support of the Ku Klux Klan (KKK) and other white supremacist groups,
arrested union members, beat them mercilessly, and terrorized their families. In 1936 the white Protestant missionary Sherwood Eddy traveled to
Arkansas to investigate racial violence against displaced Black and white
STFU members. The local sheriff promptly arrested him. In a local jail cell,
Eddy heard the sharecroppers' stories of brutality and the abject poverty suffered by the dozens of families evicted from their farms. With the backing
of Reinhold Neihbur and other prominent intellectuals and activists, Eddy
purchased land in rural Mississippi and transported twenty-four families to
a new interracial community. The Delta Cooperative, which later expanded
to a second farm, became a model producers' and consumers' cooperative.
"We emphatically believe that cooperation by itself is 'not enough' to establish
a new social order," argued Eddy. "But it may be one important non-violent
method by which we may pass from an old, outworn order to something new
and better."[3] Cooperation, across racial lines and against a corrupt agricultural system, fueled a successful utopian experiment in labor interracialism
that lasted two decades before virulent white backlash brought it down.

Workers' education programs had been actively promoting cooperatives
since the 1910s, including at Brookwood and Highlander. And African American leaders, such as W. E. B. Du Bois, Ella Baker, George Schuyler, and A. Philip
Randolph worked to promote both consumers' and producers' cooperatives as
viable economic solutions to Black economic problems. Cooperatives among
African Americans had a particularly long history in Mississippi. In the years
following emancipation, freedpeople formed "Union Leagues," which Jessica
Gordon Nembhard calls "hatcheries of radical economic experiments."[4] In
Mound Bayou, Mississippi—an all-Black town modeled on the utopian ideas
of Robert Owen—cooperatives thrived and the community served as a refuge
for activists during the civil rights era, including NAACP secretary Medgar
Evers.[5] But it was during the Great Depression that the cooperative movement
was at its strongest. At the end of the 1930s, African American journalist Alethea H. Washington wrote, "The cooperative movement is based on the deep
and abiding religious principles of honesty, justice, equality, brotherhood,
and love. The cooperative movement is inter-faith, inter-class, and inter-race.
Therefore it gives us that common meeting ground which produces the best
setting for working together."[6] During the 1930s, Black activist and entrepre-
neur Jacob L. Reddix ran a thriving set of cooperative stores in Gary, Indiana.[7]

And Father Divine led a cooperative empire, both in urban Harlem and in rural New York. By the 1930s, then, African Americans from the rural South to the urban North were familiar with cooperatives, and many were eager to use this tool to offset the devastation of the Great Depression. A group of white Christian socialists, who viewed cooperatives as the pathway to a new social order, joined them in this effort.

Cooperatives were a partial remedy to a capitalist system that was brutalizing southern workers, particularly during the Great Depression. Organized labor was another, and southern interracial activism in the 1930s and 1940s, such as Highlander's many campaigns, focused on mobilizing Black and white workers. This was a period of civil rights unionism, when activists looked to mass unionization as offering the best hope to address racial inequality and class oppression. Like the social unionism that defined Progressive Era workers' education programs, civil rights unionism sought to create a new social order, rather than settle for incremental reforms. Civil rights unionism also promoted labor interracialism and the active participation of whole families in the movement, including women and children. Cooperatives and interracial unions sought alternatives to capitalism that went beyond the picket line. And at the Delta Cooperative Farm, people lived that alternative reality in their daily lives.

The Sharecroppers' Rebellion

Myles Horton was not the only southern radical pushing for interracial cooperation, socialism, and equality. He was part of a generation of Black and white activists determined to use labor interracialism to attack white supremacy. Southern African Americans, in alliance with white radicals, organized the STFU and challenged the racial status quo during the Great Depression.[8] They blended socialist politics with religious practices, developing what historian Anthony P. Dunbar terms the "radical gospel," a revolutionary take on the Social Gospel movement of the early twentieth century. Those who preached the radical gospel "conceived that the world might be redeemed not through man's good works but through the rising up of the poor."[9] In the South, sharecroppers made up the poorest of the poor, and organizing them to "rise up" meant committing fully to an interracial vision of the future. The dramatic conflicts that resulted from this movement brought the plight of the sharecroppers to a national, and even international, audience. This visibility led directly to the founding of an interracial cooperative in the Mississippi Delta.

The central figure in the STFU, and a strong ally of the Delta Cooperative Farm, was Howard Kester, who exemplified the white southern radical tradition. Like Myles Horton, Kester started his career working for the YMCA and encouraging interracial meetings in the 1920s. He went on to work as a youth secretary for the Fellowship of Reconciliation (FOR) and eventually became their southern secretary. During this period, Kester made a point of violating segregation laws by riding in the Jim Crow section of trains and buses. He was impatient with the southern white liberals' moderation. For example, reformers promoting liberal interracialism founded the Commission on Interracial Cooperation (CIC) in 1919 in response to a wave of southern racial violence at the end of WWI. The CIC investigated lynchings and spoke out against white supremacists groups such as the KKK, but they did not directly challenge segregation. Criticizing the CIC, Kester argued in a 1933 report to FOR, "To attempt to emancipate the mass of white and Negro workers in the South . . . only through the methods of goodwill, moral suasion and education is to invite the continued exploitation misery and suffering of generations yet unborn."[10] Seeking a more aggressive model for challenging economic exploitation and racial discrimination, Kester worked with Reinhold Niebuhr in two organizations, the Committee on Economic and Racial Justice and the Fellowship of Socialist Christians. Kester also investigated twenty-five southern lynchings for the NAACP during the 1930s.[11] When two white socialist organizers, H. L. Mitchell and Henry Clay East, founded the STFU in 1934, Kester was ready and eager to join the struggle.[12]

Like Kester, white labor organizer Claude Williams used religion to mobilize southern progressive forces. He was a minister who was deeply committed to organizing Blacks and whites who had not been part of the traditional labor movement. To further this cause, Williams opened the New Era School of Social Action and Prophetic Religion in 1936, which offered training to sharecroppers away from the violence of the cotton fields. After a short stint directing Commonwealth College in the late 1930s, Williams reorganized his New Era School into the People's Institute of Applied Religion in 1940, holding interracial institutes to organize Black and white workers and preach his radical gospel. In 1942 Williams took his organizing skills to Detroit to work with southern migrants in the United Auto Workers (UAW). When he returned south three years later, he reestablished his People's Institute in Birmingham, Alabama. Williams was a dynamic and effective organizer, but he was also a divisive figure. Unlike Kester, who was an avowed socialist and follower of Norman Thomas, Williams was a communist. A schism between the two men reflected the ways that sectarian politics weakened radical social movements like the STFU.[13]

Williams and Kester, among others, shaped civil rights unionism, working not only for organized labor but for the revitalization of a region and a people. They would not have had the success they did if African American sharecroppers were not already open to joining forces to fight against their oppression. From Union Leagues during the Reconstruction era to the proliferation of cooperatives in the early twentieth century, southern African Americans had a rich tradition of political engagement and economic experimentation. In the 1880s, for example, in the midst of the populist era, landless Blacks and a small group of whites formed biracial lodges of the Cooperative Workers of America (CWA) in South Carolina and built cooperative stores and schools.[14] Southern Blacks also had distinct memories of the brutal retaliation against earlier organizing efforts. In particular, the 1919 Elaine massacre cast a long shadow over Arkansas's sharecroppers. In the communities around Elaine, Arkansas, Black sharecroppers organized a chapter of the Progressive Farmers and Household Union of America in 1918. They hoped to sell their crops directly to the market by setting up cooperatives. When local whites attempted to disrupt an organizing meeting, two were shot in the ensuing mêlée. This led to wholesale retaliation by white vigilante groups assisted by federal troops. They murdered and arrested hundreds of African Americans in the days that followed.[15] At least some of the survivors later joined the STFU and again faced the dangers of challenging white supremacy.[16]

Conditions among sharecroppers in the Delta region had long been dire. But the early years of the Great Depression and the policies of Franklin Roosevelt's New Deal made them significantly worse. Reinhold Niebuhr called the sharecroppers "the most exploited group of workers in any part of the western world."[17] In the late 1920s, before the rest of the country experienced the economic crisis, the Delta was already beset by natural disasters, including the 1927 Mississippi flood and periodic droughts. Overproduction also led to plummeting cotton prices. When Roosevelt came to office in 1933, he sought to aid farmers by passing the Agricultural Adjustment Act (AAA), which paid landowners for voluntarily reducing their crops. The federal government instructed landowners to share these payments with their tenants, but they often refused or evicted tenants altogether. They did so with the knowledge that the southern white power structure fully supported them.[18] Evicted tenants were destitute, often in poor health and with meager belongings. "The AAA policies of the federal government," noted Kester, "intensified the already deepening misery of the southern sharecropper and acted as a climax to the long and bitter struggle which he had been waging against poverty, disease, ignorance and semi-slavery."[19] In the midst of this despair, the STFU's civil rights unionism and labor interracialism found fertile ground.

Our images of evicted sharecroppers and tenant farmers come to us from the haunting photographs of New Deal photographers.[20] Dorothea Lange, for example, extensively photographed sharecroppers, including those who found a home at the Delta Cooperative Farm. But an image of an evicted sharecropper gaunt with hunger, wearing torn clothing, with no shoes and no possessions, conveys a helplessness and passivity that is inaccurate. The women, men, and children were not waiting for northern white saviors to rescue them from their plight. Rather, their network of fraternal lodges and churches, and their previous experiences with cooperatives and unionization, were responsible for the STFU's limited success. African Americans shaped the distinct culture of the STFU. They usually met in secret to protect themselves from vigilante justice. Black sharecroppers often incorporated rituals, such as pledges of loyalty, which reflected the fraternal organizations and secret societies that pervaded southern small towns. Many belonged to the Masons or other lodges and borrowed from their iconography and ceremonies. And they used the Bible to mobilize and train sharecroppers within the union. Indeed, many of the Black organizers were themselves ministers, skilled in oration and able to translate the sharecroppers' possible future to the biblical language of redemption.[21]

Two white southern socialists, H. L. Mitchell and Henry Clay East, tapped into this Black organizing tradition when they founded the STFU in 1934. That year the wholesale eviction of sharecroppers had reached a crisis point. The organizers were familiar with a parallel effort in Alabama where the Communist Party had established a sharecroppers' union.[22] Within two years, the STFU had thirty-one thousand members and over two hundred local unions. They sought to pressure landowners to share AAA payments with their tenants, as mandated by law. As Kester noted, "For every tenant who has received his share of the government money without endless delay one hundred have never received anything."[23] And they demanded higher wages for cotton pickers as well as the establishment of cooperatives. Their first strike, in 1935, was also their most successful, raising the rate of pay for cotton pickers. But it also brought down upon the union the full wrath of white planters and their political allies. Sherwood Eddy reported, "Whenever an old economic or social order is disintegrating and the owners or beneficiaries of that order are threatened with loss and have their backs to the wall, they always look with fear upon the rise of a new order and become ruthless in its suppression." The fact that this "new order" was an interracial one deeply threatened some southern whites. An African American who survived the Elaine massacre and was present at the first meeting of the STFU is credited with pushing for an interracial union, pointing out that "they could not hope to succeed until the two races stood together in economic cooperation."[24] For the next decade, this union would fight the white power structure and suffer ongoing violence and repression.

In addition to their labor interracialism, the STFU shared much in common with Brookwood and Highlander. Like those institutions and earlier southern agrarian movements, the STFU incorporated women fully into their organizing efforts. Women were more likely to be literate, and thus often served as secretaries for the union. And they were fully equal members, rather than serving in an auxiliary.[25] Even in the face of horrific violence, STFU members also embraced nonviolence, deploying picket lines and sit-ins as tactics. Like the organizers at Highlander, union members sang songs from the rich repertoire of African American traditional music.[26] The egalitarian ethos of the STFU, its foundation in religious teaching, and its socialism all made it part of the utopian strain in the long civil rights movement. By founding a cooperative farm, Sherwood Eddy and his allies hoped to foster this culture and politics more fully.

Creating a Christian Cooperative

In January 1936, plantation owner C. H. Dibble evicted nearly one hundred sharecroppers from his farm in Arkansas. Hearing the news, a white southerner, Sam H. Franklin, who had served as a missionary in Japan with Sherwood Eddy, contacted his old friend and invited him to come to Arkansas to see how dire the sharecroppers' plight had become. This kind of trip was becoming increasingly common among socially conscious intellectuals. Norman Thomas, for example, traveled to the Delta in 1934 and published *The Plight of the Sharecropper* to publicize and fundraise for the fledging STFU.[27] Franklin and Eddy met in Memphis, and although activists warned them that they would likely be arrested, they traveled to northeastern Arkansas. There they quickly came across the evicted families from the Dibble plantation and other farms. Nineteen Black families were staying in makeshift tents by the side of the road. When the local sheriff heard Eddy and Franklin were interviewing sharecroppers, he arrested the two men and locked them in a cotton store. Planters confronted them there and threatened to carry out another Elaine massacre unless they left immediately. Eddy remembered, "During the threatening and bullying that accompanied the arrest, when we saw the danger in which the tenants lived, the purpose began to form in our minds: 'Let us stop talking, get out of here as soon as we can, and look for a farm where we can assist these people to save themselves.'"[28]

Franklin and Eddy found that farm in Mississippi, safely distant from the worst violence afflicting Arkansas. After securing a loan, they purchased over two thousand acres of land in Bolivar County near Hillhouse, Mississippi. They hoped that this would be "the first of a chain of similar projects among the eight million sharecroppers of the South."[29] And they were able to act quickly because early New Deal programs had already developed plans for cooperative colonies, making such an endeavor more appealing. In particular, the Tennessee Valley Authority (TVA) provided a plan for a model town, which Franklin and Eddy followed. The town promised "a fuller, more completely balanced life" for its unemployed residents.[30] The crucial difference, however, is that the TVA's model town excluded African Americans.[31] Eddy tapped five trustees to hold the property and organize the farm, including Reinhold Niebuhr, and Franklin became its resident director. Calling the farm "the most significant experiment in social Christianity now being conducted in America," Niebuhr spent a significant amount of time overseeing its operations.[32]

Within days, twenty-four displaced families settled on the farm and began the backbreaking work of building new homes and tilling the fields. The residents named the farm after the region and in consultation with the trustees laid out four foundational principals. The first was "efficiency in production and economy in finance through the cooperative principle." Delta Cooperative Farm would run both a consumers' and producers' cooperative. The land would be owned and farmed cooperatively with goods sold at the cooperative store or directly to the market. Second, residents would participate in "the building of a socialized economy of abundance." Cooperators supported labor unions, particularly the STFU of which they remained members, and worked to build a socialist future. Third, they committed to "the principle of interracial justice." Although Franklin argued they were not violating Mississippi's law against "social equality," he considered Blacks and whites at the farm equals, and all lived side by side.

The final principle was the seeding of "realistic religion as a social dynamic." Like the Black ministers and organizers in the STFU, those at the Delta farm sought to return Christianity to its "prophetic mission of identification with the dispossessed."[33] These teachings reflected the theology of Christian realism, which rejected the optimism of liberal Progressives. Instead, religious realists argued that it was necessary for Christians to engage in politics to prevent totalitarianism and fascism.[34] Niebuhr was the most prominent theologian of this group, and his teachings and writings deeply impacted both Eddy and Franklin. But unlike Niebuhr, they held out hope that the Kingdom of God could be found on earth, and their prefigurative politics sought to create that vision at the Delta farm.[35] This prophetic tradition among Protestants, which advocated concrete solutions for social ills, also tied itinerant ministers like Claude Williams to an international matrix of missionaries and intellectuals. And a prophetic Christianity that combined Niebuhr's realism with utopian aspirations drove the religious base of the mass civil rights movement.

The Christian realists at the Delta farm were wedded to the cooperative principle. They modeled their system after the Rochdale cooperative in England, founded in 1844 by a group of weavers who formed the Rochdale Society of Equitable Pioneers. The group drew up a set of principles, which allowed their cooperative to be replicated internationally. Rochdale cooperatives were voluntary groups who refused to discriminate in their membership. They had democratic principles with members investing equally and receiving dividends based on their purchases. Workers founded the first American cooperatives based on Rochdale's rules in 1863, and they proliferated throughout the late nineteenth century.[36] By 1940 African American educator John Hope II reported that "the Rochdale cooperative movement is beginning to take root in the thinking Negroes over a wide area, both rural and urban."[37] Similarly, in 1942 Black economist Samuel Lloyd Myers lauded the proliferation of cooperatives and hoped for a future when "individuals will be born in cooperative health centers, will live in cooperative houses, will meet their needs from cooperative stores, will be protected by cooperative law, and, in the end, will be buried by cooperative burial associations." Myers was careful to separate these endeavors from the private enterprises promoted by the National Negro Business League and other moderate civil rights groups. Cooperatives, in contrast, were not "only an economic plan" but were "educational, social, and in a sense religious as well." And he pointed to the Delta Cooperative Farm as a model for this vision, proving that "Negroes and whites, by substituting cooperation for competition, may work harmoniously together."[38] In recognition of the important heritage of Rochdale cooperatives, the Delta cooperators christened their new post office, store, community center, and school as "Rochdale."[39]

The fact that Delta worked as both a producers' and consumers' cooperative proved particularly challenging. Since the late nineteenth century, Black sharecroppers had attempted to undercut the exploitative plantation stores by forming consumer cooperatives.[40] But adding a producers' cooperative, where products such as livestock and lumber were collectively produced, was relatively novel. Delta's founders knew that such a cooperative could not rely on cotton production alone. From the outset, they diversified their crops to include alfalfa and purchased a steam sawmill to process lumber from the farm's extensive forest. Soon they added poultry, hogs, and dairy cattle. Despite a late start planting in 1936, the farm managed to provide dividends for

FIGURE 2.1 Blacks and whites working together at the Delta Cooperative Farm, 1936. Photograph by Dorothea Lange. Credit: Library of Congress, Prints and Photographs Division, FSA/OWI Collection, LC-USF34-009553-C.

all the cooperative families in the first year. Upon seeing these results, one visiting government administrator from the TVA wrote in the farm's visitors' book, "A miracle has happened."[41] But it was a miracle that required backbreaking labor in extreme heat and the motivation to negotiate daily life with other families. This reliance on individual motivation for the cooperative's greater good was the most contested aspect of the farm, as is the case in many intentional communities. "In the producers cooperative," noted the members' manual, "everyone works where he can best serve the farm and receives a share of whatever the farm earns."[42] A council of five elected members, no more than three of one race, ran the producers' cooperative, although they were beholden to the wishes of the entire cooperative. Similar to the gender egalitarianism of the STFU, the cooperative gave full voting power to women, allowed them to serve on the council, and receive equal pay for equal work.[43]

Given the immediate needs of the displaced sharecroppers, Eddy and Franklin also set up a credit cooperative. Sharecroppers had been crippled for generations by excessively high credit rates for basic goods. The first year of the Delta Cooperative Farm, for example, an African American sharecropper from a neighboring plantation approached them for help. Her son had been killed in a cotton gin years previous, but the plantation owner refused to pay any damages and charged her excessive prices for seed and her food staples.[44] In contrast to the planters' monopoly, at Delta all members of the producers' cooperative belonged to the credit cooperative. They could apply for small loans to meet their needs at a very low interest rate, ordinarily 2 percent per year. If at the end of the year there were earnings above those needed for basic expenses, cooperative members received dividends based on the amount of interest they paid on their loans.[45] Thus, cooperators had the security in knowing that a sudden death, illness, or other mishap would not displace or bankrupt them.

Delta's second year was not as propitious as its first. Cotton prices fell in 1937 and heavy rainfall damaged crops. The cooperators had to be evacuated from the rain and mud-soaked farm for a time to ensure their safety.[46] As a result of these natural and economic setbacks, trustees, wishing to further diversify rather than relying heavily on cotton, purchased a second farm in Holmes County, Mississippi. Cooperators set up a creamery and general store on the 3,000-acre farm, named Providence. Unlike Delta, though, it was populated at first solely by white families.[47] However, African Americans, who made up the majority of the county's population, had access to Providence's resources, including the store, church, and community center. These Black community members' use of Providence would create racial tensions in the years that followed. And at Providence farm, the dream of a producers' cooperative would fade after World War II. In its wake a wider social mission that focused on educating and providing health services for the surrounding African American community would take precedence and ultimately would challenge Mississippi's white supremacist power structure.

While the first members of Delta farm were primarily refugees from the Dibble plantation gathered together by Sam Franklin, in later years the Cooperative Council chose new members. After two years' probation, cooperators invited these new families to become full members.[48] During the depths of the Depression, and as the farms gained more publicity, letters requesting membership poured in. Dot McPhail wrote Sherwood Eddy in 1936, "We are the working class of white and have no home or work to do." Her family, like so many others, was living with her in-laws and trying to survive on one WPA salary for two families.[49] Another letter from an African American man, S. M. Magsby, pleaded for the safety and security of Delta. "In short now Dr. we are tired of the white collar bossing us for a little meat and bread so we want you to set us out in life and see the while will turn. Now Mr. Eddy we are all neggers [*sic*] tenants farmers hear [*sic*] is a list of each family who want to be with you 1937." Unfortunately for Magsby and the families he represented, who had been "drifting from place to place and from land to land," there was limited space at the Delta farm.[50]

The families the council did select engaged in a process of democratic community building to ensure a cohesive community. Religion was always central to that community. The "realistic religion" of the Delta and Providence farms centered around its cooperative economy. The members' manual stated that "if we are trying to live a Christian life, the cooperative may help us to live it better."[51] Cooperation was based on the idea of helping one another rather than being in competition and putting profits ahead of the common welfare. And this cooperation happened across racial lines, including in the church. Franklin claimed that the Rochdale Community Church at the Delta farm was the first integrated church in Mississippi.[52] Not all white families, however, were comfortable with interracial worship. "Race prejudices die very hard," reported Franklin in 1939, "and still keep some of our people from church."[53] The farms held regular religious meetings, often led by visiting Christian socialists such as Howard Kester. Their worship reflected a utopian perspective. "What we do desire," wrote Franklin, "is that Christianity should challenge the old order, not with mere condemnation, but with the immediate and attainable goals of a better way."[54] Visitors to the farm often noted that cooperators lived as "true" Christians. For example, after a trip to see Delta, A. J. Muste wrote, "I came away feeling that here was the nearest thing I had ever seen to an early Christian community, attempting in the name of brotherhood with incredible courage to build a totally new pattern of communal life."[55] At Delta and Providence, prophetic religion was enacted in daily life.

Health services were central at both Delta and Providence farms. From the very beginning of the experiment, the ill health of the cooperators was a major challenge, and the solution benefited not only those living at Delta and Providence, but impoverished sharecroppers in the surrounding communities. One African American family from the Dibble plantation included a five-year-old boy, whom a visiting representative from the Church League for Industrial Democracy described in *The Witness* magazine: "His general health was poor, due to malnutrition, and he had a serious heart and kidney complication." When Franklin found the boy's family in Arkansas, they had not eaten anything except beans for four days. As a result, the boy's mother was "thin and emaciated."[56] Many of the farmers suffered from syphilis as well as malnourishment. In response to the myriad health problems, Franklin recruited a nurse, Lindsey Hail, to join the farm. Hail was the daughter of Christian missionaries in Japan who met the Franklins when they served overseas.[57] Soon Dr. David Minter joined her and, with the help of the cooperators, they built a two-story clinic. During the first year of its operation in 1938, the clinic served over six hundred individuals, both at the Delta farm and in the surrounding community. Because of the dangers of venereal disease and the relatively large average family size, the trustees were particularly interested in providing safe birth control to farm residents. They enlisted Margaret Sanger, the well-known birth control proponent, to visit the farm and educate its inhabitants. Franklin supplied Minter's clinic with "contraceptive jelly" and pamphlets on birth control.[58] Minter also held luetic (syphilis) clinics and well-baby clinics for the region. And unlike other southern medical facilities, the clinic was open to both Black and white patients.[59]

Providence Cooperative Farm, located in a county with no medical facilities for African Americans, made health care central to its mission. Holmes County was 70 percent Black but had no Black doctors or dentists. To address this situation, during the 1940s the Black sorority Alpha Kappa Alpha sent social workers and medical personnel to run a series of clinics for the surrounding impoverished community. Dentists, nutritionists, teachers, and doctors served hundreds of Black sharecroppers during their weeks at the farm.[60] This missionary work proved vital to a generation of poor Black families in Holmes whose lives were significantly improved through access to basic health care. And it predated similar efforts during the Great Society, when Black Mississippians spearheaded an effort to bring the health and education benefits of the War on Poverty programs, particularly Head Start, to their state.[61]

In addition to ill health, one of the barriers experienced by sharecroppers, particularly African Americans, was limited schooling. On southern tenant farms, children began to work in the cotton fields starting at age six. In contrast, both Delta and Providence farms did not allow anyone under the age of twelve to perform fieldwork of any kind.[62] Off the farms, schools were often dilapidated one-room buildings with little heating, and generally no transportation was provided. Howard Kester described the plight of sharecropping children: "Thinly clad, often without shoes, trudging to school with no books, paper or pencil, to be there all day without anything to eat is not a very pleasant thing for a normal youngster."[63] Even that small possibility was cut off for six to eight months per year to allow children to work in the fields. In the region of the Delta farm, twenty-four thousand African American children had no consolidated school whatsoever. Franklin and Eddy were able to convince the state to open a second Black school near the farm to provide for sharecroppers' education. They also opened an interracial nursery school and kindergarten at the farm itself. And all of these facilities were available for adults in the evening to gain literacy skills.[64]

As a result of increased schooling and delayed fieldwork, Black and white children on the farms had significantly increased leisure time, captured by Dorothea Lange's gripping photographs. At Delta their playtime also allowed for interracial mixing, in contrast to the segregated schoolhouses. In 1937 some of these children's voices were captured in a farm publication, "The Children's Book." First they described what they had experienced in the past:

Our houses were old and bad. They leaked. We had pasteboard instead of glass windows. The doors were split from top to bottom. We ate turnips and cabbage and bread. If we had no jobs, we ate hominy and nothing else. We could not go to school much in winter. We had no shoes. We put rags on our feet. Some of us had one month of school. Some of us had three months of school. When we were six or eight we picked cotton. We picked a hundred or more pounds of cotton. When our fathers complained because they were not paid, the boss put all the families off the plantation and we lived in a tent. Some of our fathers were put in jail.[65]

They went on to describe their families joining the STFU and being thrown off their farms. Arriving at the Delta farm, they learned about the cooperatives and their benefits. "The store pays extra money to our mothers and fathers," wrote the children, "because it is a cooperative store."[66] The children devised games and songs that fit their new life. "The Children's Cooperative Song," for example, was sung to the tune of the "Battle Hymn of the Republic."

We are growing up together in a new and different world;
The flag of help-each-other is the banner we've unfurled
We work not for ourselves alone but for our neighbors too
To make a dream come true.

Let us work and play together;
Let us work and play together
Let us work and play together
As all true neighbors do

We can show that we are growing by the happiness we find
In co-operation always and in work and being kind
In remembering the rules we make and helping others to—
We can make our dream come true[67]

Reflecting the STFU's civil rights unionism, children also sang a version of "We Shall Not Be Moved" that they titled "The Children's Union Song." "We work, we play, we're friendly," they sang. "We shall not be moved."[68] They

FIGURE 2.2 Children at the Delta Cooperative Farm, 1936. Photograph by Dorothea Lange. Credit: Library of Congress, Prints and Photographs Division, FSA/OWI Collection, LC-USF34-017356-C.

meant that they would not be moved from the farms' safety and relative prosperity.

The farms' many visitors often remarked upon the interracial play and songs of children. Utopian communities from the Shakers and Oneida in the nineteenth century to the socialist New Llano colony in the twentieth had welcomed visitors and tourists as they served as living examples of model communities and sought to attract new members. Delta and Providence farms continued this tradition. For example, the Travel Bureau of Cooperative Distributors organized a "Social Survey Tour" of US cooperatives. "Many Americans have rushed to Europe to see Cooperation in action there," noted the organization, "while completely overlooking the great things that are happening at home."[69] The travelers visited the Delta farm as well as the New Llano Cooperative Colony and the Tennessee Valley Authority. One of the prime attractions of their visit was the Rust cotton picker. An image from their brochure shows dozens of visitors crowding around the new mechanized picker. This machine was on the farm thanks to its inventors, John and Mac Rust. The Rust brothers were socialists who lived for a time at the New Llano utopian community. Together they invented the mechanical cotton picker and donated one of the first machines to the farm. Kester accurately predicted that the cotton picker "will produce a major social revolution." It had the capability of picking enough cotton in one hour to match the labor of four cotton pickers working a full day. Rather than reject mechanization, however, the founders of the Delta farm sought to harness its power for the good of the greater community. In fact, the Rust brothers hoped to invest 90 percent of the profits from their cotton picker in a series of cooperative farms and stores, as well as interracial education projects. Because of competition from International Harvester, their dream was never fully realized, but their invention proved a major draw for visitors.[70]

The number of visitors to Delta and Providence reflected one of the key characteristics of Christian socialists' lives; their constant travel. Indeed, the constellation of radicals that created and sustained the Delta and Providence farms can only be understood in an international context. There had long been a tradition of political tourism among activists, leading, for example, to the adaptation of Danish folk schools at Highlander, a school sparked by Myles Horton's contemplative time spent in Europe. And the tactics of Gandhian nonviolence found their way to the United States because of individuals like Howard Thurman, who traveled to India and met with Gandhi. Sam Franklin was also part of this tradition. He was from the South but had continued his education at the influential Union Theological Seminary in New York. He went on to get a doctorate in philosophy in Edinburgh. Following that experience, he headed east to Japan, where he worked with Toyohiko Kagawa. Kagawa was a Christian pacifist who advocated for the poor and championed the establishment of consumer cooperatives. Franklin's commitment to cooperatives came directly from Kagawa. "There has been a wide-spread conviction among Christians in recent years that the cooperative movement offers the best opportunity for achieving by methods in harmony with Christian principles an economic order which shall more nearly approximate the Christian ideal than does the present." Wrote Franklin to one trustee, "This conviction has often been urged by Dr. Toyohiko Kagawa whom I came to know intimately during my five years as a missionary in Japan."[71]

Franklin first met Sherwood Eddy in Japan, where they became close friends. Also a graduate of the Union Theological Seminary, the independently wealthy Eddy carried out missionary work in Asia and Europe for the YMCA. Starting in 1921, Eddy created the "American Seminar," an annual summer study trip that began in Great Britain and ended in the Soviet Union. These tours introduced theologians and social activists to their international counterparts and demonstrated the ravages of World War I and the advances of socialism.[72] Similarly, a steady stream of international visitors toured the farms as model cooperatives and communities. In 1939, for example, a Chinese doctor and the secretary for rural work in China stayed at the Delta farm for several days.[73] The white Quaker reformer Marjorie Penney, who founded Philadelphia's Fellowship House, spent a summer at the Delta farm. She returned to her city shaken by the experience and newly committed to building her Fellowship movement. A. J. Muste was also a frequent guest at the farm and a strong supporter of its practice of labor interracialism.[74]

Also attracting visitors were a series of institutes and conferences held at both Delta and Providence and reminiscent of the work at Highlander and Brookwood. Relatively large community centers were among the first buildings to be erected to house these events. The farms held community institutes at least twice a year since their founding. These institutes explored the benefit of cooperatives, changes in agriculture, and social issues including the possibility of southern racial equality. In the early years of the Delta farm, Black and white members of the STFU met to train and discuss strategy in a series of two-week summer institutes taught by Kester and H. L. Mitchell. In 1938 Delta held a Negro Ministers' Institute that brought together Black clergy from throughout the South to discuss practical religion. The following year, the Southern Socialist Conference also held a fully integrated meeting at Delta.[75] Throughout the 1940s, Providence farm held large institutes that offered a variety of services to the surrounding Black community. Eddy bragged in 1943 that the institutes "mobilized many of our neighbors within several miles of the farm to make a constructive attack upon the evil condition under which they have been living." That condition included "abject poverty and denial of elementary civil rights."[76] Participating in the farms' cooperatives would loosen the grip of landowners' power over these families. Full civil rights would be longer in the making.

The visibility of the farm in the national and international press offered some safety to the farms' inhabitants, who were under constant threats by surrounding white planters and the white power establishment. As Muste noted, visitors were important, "not only for the educational results on themselves, but because they constitute a way of saying to the community round about Delta Farm that this Farm has many friends all over the nation. With the danger of violent interference very real, this protection is not to be overlooked."[77] The racial terror experienced by STFU members in Arkansas would not go unnoticed in this Mississippi experiment. The wish to support and popularize the farm motivated some reformers, who traveled from one utopian community to another during the 1930s. F. E. Danner, for example, visited Amana, Louisiana; Benton Harbor, Michigan; Oneida, New York; Koreshan

Unity, Florida; and New Harmony, Indiana, before visiting the Delta farm. These were all either current or historic utopian communities. He spent eight months living in New Llano as well and visited the Fairhope Single Tax Colony in Alabama. Danner may have been planning to start his own cooperative community, but his form of utopian tourism was hardly unique. Believing that "cooperation is the only hope of the human race," William Ressell wrote of his intentions to visit the farm after having also spent time at New Llano. Over just a three-year period, according to the farm's members' manual, one thousand visitors had signed the farm's guest book.[78]

Many of those visitors were young. Despite the blistering heat, summers were the most active time for young visitors at Delta and Providence farms. Drawing from progressive universities, YWCAs and YMCAs, Christian groups, and the American Friends Service Committee (AFSC), college students and young people flocked to the farms in the summer to work and learn about this new experiment. Even the very first summer in 1936, students "from many colleges were working along with the farmers and the lumbermen— many even paying for the opportunity."[79] Theologian Howard Thurman recommended students from Howard University, where he was Dean of Rankin Chapel, to spend time at Delta.[80] Professors sometimes took their students for shorter visits to the farm, such as one delegation from Nashville's Scarritt College for Christian Workers in 1937. A similar group traveled much farther, from California, representing the Student Christian Association of the College of the Pacific, Stockton. Starting in 1937 the AFSC established a summer work camp at Delta, recruiting students from throughout America and the Caribbean.[81] These students lived and worked at the farm and were exposed to the same racial threats as the residents. This broader tradition of summer social welfare work gives more context for the well-known Freedom Summer program in 1964. White and Black students gathering in rural Mississippi to educate and aid impoverished sharecroppers was a tradition that dated back to the 1930s.

Race and Troubled Waters

The Delta Cooperative Farm was founded on the principle of racial equality. African Americans and whites received the same returns on the cooperatives and were ensured an equal vote on farm councils. However, Sherwood Eddy and Sam Franklin believed they could not openly violate Mississippi's segregation laws. Therefore, the farms practiced a limited form of segregation that stopped short of calling for "social equality," which might suggest interracial sexual relations. Delta farm's council declared that they believed in "voluntary separation but not segregation."[82] Organizers segregated some social events, such as dances, but any aspect of the farm that involved labor and running of the cooperatives was fully integrated. As Eddy explained, "We endeavor to develop a sense of solidarity and to bring the workers of both races to a realization of the necessity of facing their mutual economic problems together."[83] As in the case of workers' education and civil rights unionism, the farms' founders and participants saw racial equality as a means to achieve a socialist future. Social mixing, then, seemed a lesser priority than labor interracialism and an invitation for attack. Rose Terlin, a white Christian economist, wrote, "It would be sheer foolhardiness to run into legal difficulties over something (segregation) which is not really the central issue: economic justice."[84] The cooperators understood that racial and economic justice were linked, but they prioritized the needs of the cooperative over full interracialism.

At the Delta farm, two rows of small homes, one inhabited by whites and the other by Blacks, faced each other with vegetable gardens grown in between. They had screened windows and multiple rooms, a far cry from the shacks the displaced sharecroppers had come from. Black sharecroppers, in particular, arrived at the farm in dire straits. Perhaps no family was more desperate than the "widow" of Frank Weems and her eight children. Eddy and Franklin believed that Arkansas planters killed Weems for marching in a STFU parade. In fact, he barely escaped with his life and had made his way to Chicago. The children had no shoes and only the clothes on their backs. The family became a cause célèbre for the farm, which raised money to house and clothe them.[85] Other African Americans came from similar violent and impoverished backgrounds. A Black man, Mr. "A," was the son of slaves who had become active in the STFU while farming in Arkansas. After he was arrested on trumped-up charges, the union helped get him released. His landlord then confronted him with a pistol in his face, warning him to leave the union. The STFU sent him to Delta farm to live in safety for at least a year with his family. Mrs. "D" was an African American sharecropper who, along with her husband, joined the STFU in Arkansas. Their landlord threw them off the property, and they lived for a time in a tent city with other displaced workers. Then their landlord left a stick of dynamite at their tent with a note threatening, "Nigger, you'd better be gone in twenty-four hours." Franklin and Eddy were able to take her and her family to the farm soon thereafter.[86] Some of these families stayed for a few months and others for years.

Some northerners who wished to visit Delta during the summer to aid the cooperative effort were displeased with any degree of racial separation. Franklin found himself constantly defending the practice and initially he

FIGURE 2.3 Cabins at the Delta Cooperative Farm, 1937. Photograph by Dorothea Lange. Credit: Library of Congress, Prints and Photographs Division, FSA/OWI Collection, LC-DIG-fsa-8b38670.

only invited southerners to visit. In 1936 he noted, "A large number of college young people have offered to come to the farm to work this summer but we have felt in general that it was best to receive only southerners due to the race problem." The following year, in correspondence about the possibility of Leo Tolstoy's daughter coming to the farm, Franklin warned, "Any one not fully conversant with the whole situation and sympathetic with our policies might invite disastrous consequences by departing from the accustomed procedure of the farm."[87] Eddy was particularly concerned about Black students volunteering at the farm "unless they come knowing that they are going to work exclusively for and with the Negro group and not to have their social life with the white students." He deliberately discouraged two "brilliant" Black students from coming "because they would never understand the method of separation and would be too sensitive." Those African American students who were invited lived separately from their white counterparts. Eddy wrote to Howard University student Lucius Miles Tobin that he was welcome to join a group of white students "in all their discussions and lectures but living with some of your own people while on the Farm." "I think you know enough of conditions in the deep South," wrote Eddy, "to know that it is the bitter necessity of the situation there that requires such limitations."[88] Franklin had another motivation to discourage young Black men from volunteering at the farms. Unused to local mores, they could endanger themselves and others in the community. But his policy also highlights the limits of labor interracialism, which fell short of full equality.

In public the trustees and Sam Franklin described the early years of the farm, and particularly its race relations, as uniformly successful. However, behind the scenes there were problems almost immediately. Although Eddy and Franklin set up an interracial council on the farm, the board of trustees was entirely white. Celestine Smith, an African American woman active in the YWCA, wrote the white economist and Christian leader Rose Terlin that "Negroes should be represented on this Advisory or Trustee Committee group as well as in the workers' council itself." Charles S. Johnson, the renowned African American sociologist, finally integrated the board in 1938.[89] The producers' cooperatives on the farm also rarely turned a profit, despite all of the positive publicity in the progressive press. Within just a few years, the white trustees began complaining that the cooperators did not work long enough hours. Apparently the ten hours per day they did work was not enough to fully sustain the producers' cooperative.[90] Accusations of laziness or lack of commitment to the endeavor continued in the years that followed, accusations that often reinforced racial stereotypes.

In 1936 Delta housed eighteen Black families and twelve white families, but within a year that ratio would shift. A number of the African American women refused to work in the cotton fields, and their husbands defended them to the council and Franklin. Deploying a savvy economic strategy, at least some of these women hired themselves out to adjacent planters to bring in extra cash.[91] Although likely not known by the white members of Delta, this refusal was reminiscent of freedwomen's refusal to work in the fields following emancipation. Freedom from slavery and freedom from sharecropping ideally should entail greater control over one's own labor, these women believed. And not having women engaging in fieldwork also marked their respectability. As a result of these tensions, four Black families left the farm after the first year. In addition to their objection to women's field labor, the families were disappointed with the dividends they received at the end of the year, suspecting they had been shortchanged. The farm secretary reported that "they seemed unable to conceive of such a being as a white man smart enough to cheat them but honest enough not to do it."[92] Franklin had hired a white manager for the farm, which the families disliked. And local plantation owners also tried to lure them away with offers of higher pay. Franklin saw their departure not as the fault of the farm management but rather the "natural restlessness of the Negro."[93] This attitude demonstrated his inability to fully comprehend the Black families' choices. Franklin's goal was to keep the two races equal in number, but as that became increasingly difficult, the Providence farm served to place white families elsewhere.

Although Providence farm initially housed only white families, it also experienced racial conflict. In 1941 a controversy over the work of the farm's staff with neighboring African Americans broke out. A northern couple working at the farm had stepped up outreach work with African Americans, leading local whites to attack the farm and its inhabitants. At a council meeting, one white cooperator stated "that because of the social work among the Negroes the surrounding white people look down on us and our children 'like we are dogs.'"[94] White families were particularly concerned that their children were bullied for having contact with African Americans. The Providence council recommended that local Black sharecroppers have only very limited access to the community house on the farm, which they had been using extensively. They also wanted to end any interracial socializing or meetings. In response Eddy stated, "This will probably force us in the end to a fresh effort for Negroes but we cannot force them down the throats of our white members."[95] The trustees suggested that the white families might give up the cooperative altogether, dividing the land into individual farms. Faced with this prospect, the Providence council relented. "They indicated that they were quite willing to have us go ahead on the old plan using the present community building," reported Franklin, "and that they would rather bear the onus of public criticism because of this Negro relationship than to give up the collective."[96] For their part, the trustees promised, "We shall always refuse to work for one race only, we shall count it our greatest duty to work for the Negroes in that county and to get some educational and practical work opened on their behalf."[97] When World War II began, many white Providence farmers left to fight in the military or obtain work in war industries. African American farmers took their place, finally creating an interracial community in Providence that matched the one created at Delta.

The momentary crisis at Providence farm suggests the limitations of a whites-only cooperative that simultaneously sought racial justice. It also points to the constant threats and harassments experienced on both farms. Given that the former sharecroppers had already been terrorized in Arkansas in retaliation for their support of the STFU, the continuation of white terror in Mississippi was scarring. The limited segregation practiced at Delta did not protect it from the "threats of horsewhippings and shootings" by neighboring whites.[98] During their first winter, Franklin described tensions with neighbors as a "volcano" that "smolders underneath." Giving one example, he described a white female bus driver who "became very angry when two Negroes on our place, not hearing her at first, did not come promptly enough to her demand of 'You niggers come and move this car!' She went off with threats that she would have her husband come down and beat up a lot of them."[99] At Providence this white hostility was directed at neighboring African Americans who made use of the farm's facilities. Landowners threatened to cut off their credit or displace them if they continued their affiliation with Providence.[100] After World War II, this hostility and threatened violence came to a head, ending the experiment in labor interracialism, if not the utopian ideals of racial brotherhood.

The war years disrupted the workings of both Providence and Delta farms. In 1942 the trustees decided to sell the Delta farm and focus their energies on the more profitable and productive Providence farm. Some of the Delta farmers moved to Providence, increasing the Black population there. By 1943, ten of the fifteen families at Providence were African American. By 1947, the land on Providence was divided among individual families, ending the producers' cooperative. Although collective production ended, equipment continued to be collectively owned, and purchasing and marketing were also collective.[101] Most significantly, Providence continued to serve as a center for the surrounding sharecroppers and tenant farmers, almost all of them Black. White farmers at Providence, working with the local community, built a large community center in 1941 that was used by Black families. Many neighboring African Americans also belonged to the Providence Cooperative Association, which offered a variety of educational and economic programs. They also shopped at the cooperative store, which continued after the demise of the producers' cooperative. The farm added an African American teacher, Fannie Booker, to its staff to offer continuation instruction for children and adults. Booker also ran highly popular summer schools for local residents. In addition, the summer health clinic run by the Black sorority Alpha Kappa Alpha proved highly successful, providing care to thousands of Black patients in the county. All of these programs threatened white supremacy in a county demographically dominated by African Americans.[102]

From the outset, some whites labeled those at Delta and Providence farms as communists. Sherwood Eddy's memoir, *Eighty Adventurous Years*, was prominently displayed in a town store near Providence as evidence of the founder's radicalism. Sam Franklin was routinely called a "god-damned communist" by local whites. But white supremacists reserved their most vicious attacks for African Americans, and it was this white terror that ended the cooperative experiment in the 1950s. A brutal white sheriff in Holmes County had terrorized the Black population for years. When he stopped a car with a Black driver, for example, he would have the driver stick his head out the window for "identification." At that point he would beat the man with his nightstick.[103] And sixty miles from Providence farm, a group of white men lynched a young African American teenager visiting relatives from Chicago in 1955. His name was Emmett Till.

The year before Till's lynching, Mississippi birthed the notorious Citizens' Councils in Indianola. White southerners, many of them respectable businessmen, created Citizens' Councils in the wake of the 1954 *Brown v. Board of Education* case to foster massive resistance against any move toward racial equality or integration. This was the context for an explosive incident at Providence in the fall of 1955. A white girl who lived on the farm reported to her school bus driver that some African American boys had whistled at her from a passing truck. The driver reported the incident to the school principal, who called the sheriff. He rounded up four African American teenage boys and threw them in jail. Although the girl's family insisted they were not pressing charges and asked for the boys to be set free, the sheriff ignored their pleas. The sheriff and members of the local Citizens' Council interrogated the boys, who were active at Providence, about any potential "communist" activities there. As one of the interrogators told a journalist, "They were practicing social equality out there, and we won't have that. We have been trying to get in on the inside of it for a great long time, and this was the break."[104] Terrified that they would share Emmett Till's fate, the boys provided information they thought their tormentors wanted.

Armed with a recording of the boys' false confession, local officials called Dr. David Minter, the farm's longtime physician, and its director, A. E. Cox, to a mass meeting at the local high school. When Minter and Cox arrived, they were met by over five hundred angry whites who listened to the interrogation tape. It contained questions such as "Did you see colored children swimming with whites out there?" and "Did they tell you can go to white schools?" Turning to the two farm leaders, they were asked about their attitudes toward segregation. Cox replied, "I believe it is unchristian," to a chorus of boos. The meeting overwhelmingly voted to force Cox and Minter from the county. When Cox and Minter did not immediately desert the farm, their phone lines were cut, insurance policies canceled, and a roadblock set before Minter's health clinic with a threatening fire burning at night. After months of this treatment, the staff decided to end the project in the summer of 1956. Some farmers stayed on tracts now owned by individual families, while others moved on. The trustees liquidated Cooperative Farms, Inc., and created the Delta Foundation, which continued to run summer camps on the property run by Fannie Booker.[105]

In the decade before its demise, Providence farm, much like Highlander, shifted its activism away from the labor movement toward civil rights. As the STFU declined, ties to organized labor became frayed and labor interracialism became more focused on the cooperatives. When Sam Franklin, who could be a controlling leader, left to work for the navy as a chaplain in Japan in 1943, decision making on Providence farm became more democratic and communal.[106] And the educational institutes for African Americans brought leading figures, like cooperative expert Jacob L. Reddix, to this rural Mississippi community. Providence teacher Booker remarked on the importance of this work. "Well it's like when the Yankees came through," she noted. "They was tired of people living in slavery and they was trying to let you come out on your own."[107] Many reformers viewed sharecropping as a form of slavery. The cooperative, then, offered a kind of emancipation. Booker continued running summer camps at Providence until the 1970s. She also promoted Black-owned businesses, ran the cooperative store, led voter registration drives, and worked with Head Start.[108] Thousands of African Americans and whites from the South and around the world visited or lived at Delta and Providence farms. There they learned the practical advantages of cooperatives and the spiritual possibilities of a racial brotherhood.

Planned Utopias

Racial terror ended the experiment of cooperation and racial equality in rural Mississippi for a time, but its existence had profound effects for New Deal government programs and the long civil rights movement. While the Agricultural Adjustment Act exacerbated the crisis of Delta sharecroppers, other New Deal programs sought to resolve that crisis. Much as Brookwood and Highlander influenced the New Deal's Workers' Education Project and the CIO, the STFU and Delta and Providence farms had a direct impact on a wide-scale attempt to resettle displaced sharecroppers on cooperative farms. Roosevelt's secretary of agriculture, Henry Wallace, was a racial liberal who sought to address the South's agricultural crisis in any way possible, including setting up cooperatives. In the early years of the New Deal, the Federal Emergency Relief Administration and the Department of the Interior's Division of Subsistence Homesteads carried out a tentative agricultural policy to address the growing crisis. These agencies primarily gave loans to small farmers, but they also bought submarginal land and created a small number of communities for displaced farmers and workers. In 1935 Wallace created the Resettlement Administration (RA) under the directorship of New Deal liberal Rexford G. Tugwell.[109] In a signal that he would not strictly follow the racial conservatism of the white South, Wallace hired Will Alexander, who had spent sixteen years running the Commission on Interracial Cooperation out of Atlanta and was the first president of the historically Black Dillard University. Alexander was also one of the authors of the important 1935 study *The Collapse of Cotton Tenancy*, which raised the profile of evicted sharecroppers.[110] His commitment to interracialism and firsthand knowledge of sharecroppers' plight made Alexander a compassionate and effective advocate.

At the same time that the STFU was carrying out its most successful mobilizations in 1936, Roosevelt instructed Wallace to spearhead a President's Committee on Farm Tenancy to seek viable solutions to the crisis of displaced sharecroppers and tenant farmers.[111] Despite vehement opposition from southern Democratic congressmen, Roosevelt was able to push through the Bankhead-Jones Act, which created the Farm Security Administration (FSA). Although the act itself was relatively modest, the FSA under the leadership of Alexander had significant independence. The testimony of STFU organizers, including H. L. Mitchell and Howard Kester, proved important for the FSA's creation and its ongoing operation. It was the STFU members who most encouraged the FSA to create large-scale cooperative communities. "For the union," writes historian Donald Holley, "only one of the FSA's major activities aroused any genuine enthusiasm: the resettlement communities."[112] And the labor leaders considered Alexander among the STFU's most sympathetic Washington allies. Alexander shifted the FSA's work away from the greenbelt cities that had preoccupied Tugwell's RA and insisted on hiring African American advisers in its southern regional offices. By 1941 the FSA had fifty-five Black home management supervisors and forty-one Black farm advisers. Despite this track record, the majority of the cooperative farms created by the FSA followed the norms of racial segregation, with only a few exceptions.[113]

FSA officers visited Delta farm to generate ideas about how a fully cooperative community could be formed and remain viable. Sam Franklin remembered that "high officials in the Department of Agriculture, especially in the Farm Security Administration, watched our experiment and kept in close touch with it."[114] In fact, FSA communities explicitly modeled themselves after utopian communities. Planners studied the nineteenth-century Shaker, Rappite, and Oneida colonies. And they visited one of few remaining communal utopias, the Amana Colonies in Iowa.[115] Writing in 1959, historian Paul Conkin argues that "the many architects of the New Deal communities, despite varying philosophies, were all striving to create, within the conducive environment of their planned villages, a new society, with altered values and new institutions."[116] To facilitate such a transformation, the communities were comprehensive, particularly the fully cooperative ones. Tenants had access to schools, community buildings, cooperative stores, and a variety of entertainment and educational resources. As at the Delta and Providence farms, visitors traveled to the FSA communities to view this new society at work. But the utopian and collectivist vision of the FSA administrators left the communities vulnerable to attack from southern white Democrats and the Republican Party. Even the relatively moderate *Washington Post* ran a series of articles entitled "Utopia Unlimited," criticizing the experiment in communal and cooperative living.[117] Compared to other New Deal programs, such as the Works Progress Administration, the RA and FSA communities were relatively small in scale. Yet the challenge they presented to mainstream economic and social mores made them a tempting target for conservatives.

New Deal agencies built nearly one hundred communities, from suburban greenbelt towns to southern rural cooperatives, that housed approximately ten thousand families. Of those communities, fifty-two were fully cooperative and the majority of these were in Arkansas and Louisiana.[118] Although Tugwell and Alexander were racial liberals, the FSA communities did not directly challenge the southern Jim Crow system. There were only nine all-Black projects built, and a scattering of Black families could be found in twenty-six predominately white communities, but they lived separately within these projects. W. E. B. Du Bois found some hope in these segregated cooperative farms, urging Blacks to "take advantage of it [segregation] by planning secure centers of Negro cooperative effort and particularly of economic power to make us spiritually free for initiative and creation in other and wider fields, and for eventually breaking down all segregation based on color or curl of hair."[119] For Du Bois, segregation, even if mandated by the government, could be a pragmatic solution to building a Black cooperative society. Despite this policy of segregation, both the Resettlement Administration and the FSA worked to accept African American job applicants on the same basis as whites, hiring more than one hundred staff members.[120] The FSA hired Jacob L. Reddix, the African American cooperative leader and frequent visitor to Delta farm, as "advisor on cooperatives" in 1939. And overall 20 percent of the client families were African American.[121] But the labor interracialism that was central to STFU and the Delta and Providence cooperative farms was sublimated in the New Deal communities as they bowed to political pressure. These projects were also less egalitarian in their management than Delta and Providence. Managers carefully screened families and controlled all aspects of their lives. These limitations did not go unnoticed by those at Delta and Providence farms.

While Franklin and Eddy pointed with pride to the Delta and Providence farms as models for the New Deal experiments, they also identified important differences. During his fundraising remarks, Eddy liked to contrast Delta with the less democratic RA and later FSA farms. Eddy pointed to the flexibility that they could exercise compared to the federal government. "Could the Government, for instance, under a confessedly capitalist economy promote such a Cooperative movement as frankly as we are doing; could it officially uphold the Southern Tenant Farmers' Union or any other similar organization; could it officially organize inter-racial cooperation with the object of giving equal economic justice to both races; or, with the complete separation of Church and State to which it is committed, could it apply the principles of realistic religion as a social dynamic?"[122] The answer was clearly no, and Eddy accurately pointed out the constraints on government resettlement farms in a South dominated by white supremacists.

Eddy's staff also worked to contrast the relative success of their cooperative farms with government efforts. Dorothy Irene Helms, who moved to Delta from a resettlement farm, spoke at a social reform meeting in Cleveland, Mississippi, in 1938 to do just this. She argued, "On the Delta Cooperative Farm the people make the rules, agree on them and abide by them. On the Resettlement farm the people have no authority other than to do as told by people that do not understand the situation at all." She also contrasted the housing conditions. "I lived there three years in a two-room house, and am now living on the Delta Cooperative Farm in a four-room house nicely sealed and with screened porches."[123] The cooperative farmers at Delta and Providence, then, were simultaneously proud of their connection to the New Deal farms while viewing their experiment in creating a new society as more advanced and potentially more successful than those run by the state.

The public support for the STFU, Delta farm, and the New Deal resettlement communities was closely tied to an outpouring of cultural production that focused on the plight of sharecroppers and small farmers. Like the workers' theater that helped legitimize the CIO, a series of novels—including Erskine Caldwell's *Tobacco Road* (1932) and *God's Little Acre* (1933), John Steinbeck's *Grapes of Wrath* (1939), and the photographic essay by James Agee with Walker Evans, *Let Us Now Praise Famous Men* (1940)—all placed these men and women in the public eye. Upton Sinclair's 1936 novel, *Co-op: A Novel of Living Together*, also celebrates cooperatives as a viable solution to grinding poverty.[124] Historian Michael Denning argues that the cultural front was a "documentary" culture, and intellectuals and writers found that documenting the lives of displaced farmers and sharecroppers made for stirring stories.[125] In particular, the plight of the "Okies," largely white migrants from the dust bowl who settled in California, dominated the genre. Most stirringly told in Steinbeck's *Grapes of Wrath*, the story of this migration was also captured by the Resettlement Administration's documentary film-maker, Pare Lorentz, in his 1936 film *The Plow Which Broke the Plains* and the songs of Woody Guthrie on his 1940 *Dust Bowl Ballads*. However, African American intellectuals also made use of the treasure trove of photographs captured by the Farm Security Administration. In 1941 Richard Wright and Edward Rosskam published *Twelve Million Black Voices* as a counterpoint to *Let Us Now Praise Famous Men*. The book documented the lives of southern Blacks displaced by the ravages of the Depression.[126] The New Deal agencies' commitment to collect documentary evidence proved invaluable to artists and brought needed attention and support to the most vulnerable victims of the Depression.

Like other New Deal programs, the FSA fell victim to the growing congressional conservatism during and after the war years. Although conservatives had always attacked the FSA as radical, the patriotism behind the war effort escalated this rhetoric. Conservative congressmen claimed the communities were copies of Soviet kolkhozy, collective farms built in Russia. Bowing to this pressure, during the war Congress ordered the liquidation of the FSA. The cooperative associations canceled their leases and gave farm families a mortgage to their land and homes. In 1946 President Truman abolished the FSA and replaced it with the Farmers Home Administration, which subsidized private land ownership rather than communal and cooperative projects.[127]

The STFU met a similar fate. In its final years, the STFU became embroiled in ideological struggles between the communist and socialist factions and its relationship to the mainstream union movement. By 1937 the STFU was 80 percent Black, but the union's leadership was largely white. This clear failing of labor interracialism led to further factionalism. While many African Americans favored affiliating with the CIO's United Cannery, Agricultural, Packing, and Allied Workers of America (UCAPAWA), some of the white leaders were concerned that communists controlled the union and disliked the CIO's dues, which placed a burden on their impoverished members. In 1939 the STFU split, with the largely Black faction moving to the UCAPAWA and the white socialists remaining independent. By World War II, the STFU was largely defunct. The postwar world was not a friendly place for the comprehensive civil rights unions promoted by the STFU and cooperative farms. However, their legacy lived within the broader civil rights movement.[128]

Conclusion

Reflecting back on Delta and Providence farms, Sam Franklin called them a "feeder" for the "human rights revolution."[129] Some of the most significant battles in that revolution were fought in the Mississippi Delta. In the summer of 1964, a coalition of civil rights organizations trained fifteen hundred volunteers, including white northern college students, to carry out voter registration and other campaigns throughout Mississippi.[130] Although much has been written about Freedom Summer, there has been little acknowledgment that recruiting and training white college students to work in Mississippi was not without precedent. Starting in the mid-1930s, hundreds of white and Black students spent hot summer months building and improving the Delta and Providence farms. In 1965 Mississippi was also the site of a revival of interest in cooperative farming as a solution to the crisis of rural Black poverty. Mechanization of agriculture had largely taken away the few agricultural jobs left. In response, many of the African American activists from CORE and other organizations began to organize agricultural workers. One such project was the Mississippi Freedom Labor Union (MFLU) founded in 1965 to help cotton choppers and tractor drivers demand higher wages from plantation owners. They soon attracted the support of hundreds of workers and their families. When a dozen families on a single plantation demanded higher wages, the plantation owner swiftly evicted them. In an echo of the STFU, the MFLU set up a small community for displaced families that became known as "Strike City." White plantation owners remained united and defeated the MFLU, which historian John Dittmer calls a "bold and romantic venture," if "anachronistic."[131]

If civil rights unionism was anachronistic, rural cooperatives had more success in Mississippi. Activists coordinated a series of ventures in 1965. The successor to the FSA, the Farmers Home Administration, funded the start-up costs for a group of Black farmers in Panola County to purchase land and equipment and develop a successful cooperative. In a similar venture, an African American activist from Boston, Owen Brooks, worked to develop the North Bolivar County Farm Cooperative, which housed nine hundred families producing food for themselves and the market. The legendary Mississippi activist Fannie Lou Hamer also built a cooperative she named Freedom Farm, which included a "pig bank" that poor families could use to begin to raise their own livestock. In 1966 another civil rights legend, John Lewis, began to work with the Southern Regional Council's Community Organizing Project to run cooperatives. This organization was a direct descendant of the Commission on Interracial Cooperation, which the FSA's William Alexander had run for many years.[132] Today the Mississippi Association of Cooperatives includes ten cooperatives with a largely Black membership, "building from a tradition steeped in the civil rights movement."[133] From the English Rochdale Weavers to Rochdale, Mississippi, cooperation had long been an essential tool for the labor movement. In Mississippi and elsewhere, it also became a tool in both Black self-sufficiency and labor interracialism. The most prosperous cooperatives in the country, however, were not in Mississippi. They were in Harlem and rural New York, the products of the most successful twentieth-century utopian community, Father Divine's Peace Mission.

3
The Divinites

With the same intensity that they have rejected their sky-God for
Father, they have given up thought of integration for Negroes in
some distant future. They would rather have Father's fantasy today.

SARA HARRIS[1]

Away down in Texas and in the farthest parts of the South
We shall eat and drink together, racism shall be wiped out
There will be no more race riots and lynchings,
There will be no more division or strife
When they recognize God's Body, they will value each other's life.

FATHER DIVINE[2]

The steamboat approached the dock midmorning filled with Black and
white families eager for a day in the countryside. They had each paid a
dollar for the excursion, with children riding for free. On the boat they sang,
clapped, and celebrated as they saw the dock ahead. Awaiting them was lavish spreads of food, games on the lush lawn of Krum Elbow, a manor house
and estate on the Hudson River owned by Father Divine's Peace Mission. The
steamboat passengers eagerly awaited the appearance of Father Divine, who
offered messages of peace, love, and interracial fellowship. While lingering
on the dock awaiting their return trip, they could peer across the Hudson
River to view President Roosevelt's mansion, Hyde Park.

For all their success as cooperative experiments, the Delta and Providence
farms were, from their inception, not self-sufficient. The cooperators depended on outside funding from sympathetic Protestant pacifists. The New
Deal resettlement farms, funded by the government, never achieved the inter-

racial ideals hoped for by liberal administrators. But there were interracial cooperatives, both rural and urban, that were fully independent and remarkably prosperous. Led by a charismatic African American man, Father Divine (born George Baker Jr.), the International Peace Mission was the most successful utopian community in the twentieth century.

Both during his lifetime and in later works of sociologists and historians, Father Divine has been dismissed as a cult leader and a charlatan. But his religious movement was both significant and successful. Divine's network of urban and rural cooperatives thrived into the 1950s. They drew from multiple legacies, including the entrepreneurship promoted by Booker T. Washington and white socialist cooperatives such as Llano del Rio. Similarly, Divine's religious teachings are an amalgamation of white Protestant beliefs, most importantly New Thought, and charismatic African American religions. These beliefs fostered a profoundly disruptive politics as Divine preached that all humans were fully equal and should live this reality in interracial homes and communities. Divinites who enacted these beliefs challenged racial mores from New York to California and engaged in political work from anti-lynching campaigns to the use of nonviolent direct action to desegregate public accommodations. Divine moved from the labor and liberal interracialism of his peers to embrace a fully utopian interracialism, blurring boundaries of race and gender in a cooperative society.

Building a Movement

Like many charismatic religious leaders, Father Divine's origins were not well known during his lifetime. Although many assumed he was born in the Deep South, in fact he was born in Maryland in 1876 and spent his formative years on a small impoverished farm outside of Baltimore. In 1899 Divine, then called George Baker, moved to Baltimore and worked as a gardener. But his real calling was as a preacher. In Baltimore he encountered a range of religious institutions from staid Catholic churches to Black storefront congregations. As a teenager, Baker began teaching Sunday school at a Black Baptist church and gave informal sermons in the evenings, soon drawing a following. When he left the city, he followed the path of many Black preachers by traveling from small town to small town. Baker carried his religious teachings throughout the South. He also traveled West, and in 1906 participated in one of the most significant events in modern American religious history, the Azusa Street Revival in Los Angeles, which sparked the spread of Pentecostalism and Holiness churches in Black and white communities nationwide. This event was transformative for Baker, who assumed a divine identity while in the emotional throes of the revival and rededicated himself to a religious life.[3]

When he returned to Baltimore after this period of itinerant preaching, Baker was further influenced by a group of Black evangelicals. John A. Hickerson, who became the Reverend Bishop Saint John the Divine, preached and studied alongside Baker in the city. Baker also boarded with a Black female evangelist, Anna Snowden, and worshipped alongside Samuel Morris. These Baltimore evangelicals preached that God dwelled inside individuals, including themselves. In 1912 Baker, who now called himself the Messenger, set out again to work as an itinerant preacher throughout the South. For the next five years, Baker honed his sermons and began to develop a set of teachings that would guide his twentieth-century Peace Mission. In 1917 he settled in Brooklyn, New York, with a small group of followers. It was there that his movement took shape.[4]

In Brooklyn, Baker's interracial followers lived communally and pooled their wages. This practice allowed them to accumulate a significant amount of money that they could invest in cooperative businesses and property. At this point the Messenger renamed himself Father Divine and declared his community a "Peace Mission." Divinites committed themselves to a strict set of ascetic practices, including abstaining from alcohol and cigarettes. Followers were cautious even with their language, greeting each other with "Peace" rather than the problematic "Hello," which contained the word "hell."[5] In 1919 Father Divine expanded his movement, purchasing property in the all-white community of Sayville, Long Island. Sayville was the first of a long string of real estate ventures Divinites deliberately used to challenge the color line. As they prospered, Divinites also bought property in Harlem. In both Sayville and in Harlem, the Peace Mission offered lavish banquets for its followers and community members. By the mid-1940s, the Peace Mission had extensions in twenty-six states and several countries, including England, Switzerland, and Australia. Because they kept no membership lists, the exact number of followers remains unknown, but it numbered at least in the tens of thousands. And as early as 1936, the Peace Mission had become the largest realty holder in Harlem. Divinites living in Harlem could claim 3 apartment houses, 9 private houses, 15–20 apartments and meeting halls, 25 restaurants, 6 groceries, 10 barber shops, 10 cleaning stores, 24 wagons, and a coal business.[6]

What accounts for the rapid growth of Divine's movement? Historian Judith Weisenfeld classifies the Peace Mission as a "religio-racial" movement, one of many that flourished in Black communities during the Great Migration. These groups "held in common a conviction that only through embrace of a true and divinely ordained identity could people of African descent achieve their collective salvation."[7] While the Moorish Science Temple and the Nation of Islam, flourishing Black religious groups during the interwar period, imagined a glorious Black past, the Divinites embraced a present and future entirely free of racial categories. This re-creation had profound physical and psychological impacts on Divinites. Divine's followers changed their names, many practiced celibacy, and their physical health was often transformed by the abundance of healthy food and renouncing of tobacco and alcohol. The Peace Mission teachings were laid out in the manual on church discipline: "It shall be a violation of the Discipline of this Church for any Member to smoke, chew tobacco, gamble, use profane language, indulge in intoxicating liquors, indulge in the lusts of the flesh, or participate in any of the vices, fancies, tendencies and unwholesome pleasures of the world."[8] There was plenty of food, music, and dancing at Peace Mission settlements, but "the vices of the world" were set aside in this earthly heaven.

Nevertheless, the appeal of rejecting an oppressive racial identity, central to religio-racial movements, does not explain the approximately one-third of Father Divine's Peace Mission who were white.[9] Instead, it is his commonality with other utopian communities that resonated with many white seekers. The Father Divine movement is the premiere example of the economic efficiency of utopian communalism. In the nineteenth century, utopianists in Owenite communities such as New Harmony had success as farmers and small-scale industrialists. The Oneida community achieved prosperity manufacturing silverware and other products in the mid- to late nineteenth century. But at its height the Peace Mission boasted thousands of properties and supplied low-cost housing and food for hundreds of thousands. The Peace Mission also shared the pacifist and cooperative goals of white socialist communities. And Father Divine's followers found his teaching on positive thinking and health appealing. Divinites lived communally, embraced celibacy, preached pacifism, and built a cooperative empire. These practices brought white and Black followers into the fold. And this utopian interracialism directly impacted civil rights work in the late 1930s and beyond.

New Thought and Religious Identity

Scholars and observers have categorized the Father Divine movement as one of many "sects and cults" that populated storefronts in growing Black neighborhoods during the interwar period.[10] Groups like the Moorish Science Temple or the Nation of Islam seemed outlandish to outsiders who ventured into growing Black communities such as Harlem. Followers often wore different clothing and invoked unfamiliar religious practices based loosely on

Islam and Judaism. Unlike these Black Nationalist religious groups, Father Divine's religion grew primarily out of a nineteenth-century white Protestant movement, New Thought.[11] New Thought's founder was a mid-nineteenth-century mesmerist, Phineas P. Quimby, who lectured and wrote extensively on the ability of positive thinking to heal and elevate individuals. His most famous student, Mary Baker Eddy, went on to found Christian Science. In 1895 Harvard University's Metaphysical Club, a highly influential philosophical club that laid the foundation for Pragmatism, defined New Thought's goals: "To promote interest in and the practice of a true philosophy of life and happiness, to show that through right thinking, one's loftiest ideals may be brought into present realization; and to advance intelligent and systematic treatment of disease by spiritual and mental methods."[12] New Thought was also influential for Edward Bellamy, author of the utopian novel *Looking Backward*, and Christian socialist leaders like A. J. Muste.[13] In the twentieth century, the teachings of Norman Vincent Peale, who wrote the best-selling 1952 book *The Power of Positive Thinking*, brought New Thought into the mainstream of American life. For utopianists, New Thought could be a blueprint for societal change because it emphasized the ability of individuals and groups to take "one's loftiest ideals" and bring them "into present realization."

It was Father Divine who most successfully harnessed New Thought for African Americans and translated its teachings to his flourishing interracial utopian communities. The Peace Mission newspaper, *New Day*, and Father Divine's lengthy sermons were filled with New Thought rhetoric. A 1945 sermon reprinted in *New Day* promised, "You will not even feel like you once felt; you will have New Characteristics and a New Disposition; you will be a New Person!"[14] This transformation, suggested Divine, could be enacted through the power of the mind. Father Divine also borrowed from secular New Thought works that were enormously popular in the twentieth century. For example, he drew from Robert Collier's 1926 best seller, *The Secret of the Ages*, which argues that prosperity could be manifested through positive thinking.[15] In the early years of his ministry, Father Divine distributed New Thought books to his followers. In addition to Collier, these included Bruce Barton's *The Man Nobody Knows*, which depicts Jesus as a successful businessman, and Baird Spalding's *The Life and Teaching of the Masters of the Far East*, which relates tales of Buddhist "masters" of enlightenment.[16]

Reflecting these New Thought teachings, in a 1934 meeting in Detroit, Divine urged his followers to "visualize the perfect, the pure, the positive, the true, the real and refuse to visualize the negative, the impractical, the improfitable [*sic*], the undesirable and the untrue, for 'as a man thinketh in his heart, so is he.'"[17] The Peace Mission's overflowing banquets were an outward manifestation of this positive thinking. The abundant food was a miraculous manifestation of what hungry people most desired during the depths of the Great Depression. Like all New Thought acolytes, Divinites were unfailingly optimistic about their own self-worth and the possibility of a perfect future. Between nearly every line of his sermons, Divine intoned the word "wonderful."[18] This emphasis on happiness through prosperity and positive thinking is replete in New Thought religion and secular teaching, and it was central to the Peace Mission.

Perhaps the most attractive aspect of New Thought was the belief that individuals could maintain good health through positive thinking. This message drew many suffering from ill health to the Peace Mission. Father Divine claimed the power of healing, much as Mary Baker Eddy claimed to heal her Christian Scientist followers. Similarly, the Unity Church, which influenced Father Divine and also came out of the New Thought movement, preached spiritual healing. Early in his career, Father Divine circulated Unity Church publications and expressed admiration for the white minister Charles Fillmore, the founder of Unity. "It is nothing strange with us to hear of the different individuals being abundantly healed physically," preached Father Divine in a 1933 sermon. "It comes through and by the mental contact."[19]

Like all New Thought churches, Divine's teaching and practice centered on the connection between body and mind. Divinites treated their bodies with care, eating well and not poisoning themselves with pollutants. And when they did become ill, they relied on Father Divine to cure them. Divinites repeatedly testified to his healing powers at banquets and in the pages of *New Day*. Charles Braden reported one such testimony from a "sister" who professed, "I love you, Father, because you healed me of a leaky heart."[20] Others claimed they were healed of addiction, obesity, and numerous other ailments. Journalist John Hoshor wrote in 1936 that Divinites testified about "how they had been cured of all diseases and sin by Father Divine, God Almighty. This one of the wasting disease, this one of T.B., another of a broken back, still others of syphilis, deafness, rheumatism, swelling of the feet, and so on, almost ad infinitum."[21] The promise of good health, like the promise of prosperity, was deeply attractive to utopianists who sought to prefigure a perfect life.

Spiritual healing was not limited to the white-dominated New Thought churches such as Christian Science and Unity. There was also a strong strain of spiritual healing in African American religious movements during the interwar period. The African American Spiritualist church, which thrived during the Great Migration era, practiced healing as did some of the sanctified churches that dotted the storefronts in urban centers.[22] Many of these churches were headed by Black women. In Chicago, one such congregation deeply resembled the Father Divine movement, the All Nations Pentecostal Church led by an African American woman, Elder Lucy Smith. Like Father Divine, Smith provided food to Chicago residents during the Great Depression. She also had a fully interracial congregation, which included white Appalachian migrants to Chicago. And like Divine, she used modern media, primarily radio, to reach out to her followers. But it was her faith healing, part of the church's "Divine healing" services, that drew many of her followers. "I heal with prayers," said Smith, "jus' lay my hand on the troubled place and pray, and it all goes away."[23] The All Nations church, like the Peace Mission, had a congregation that was majority Black and female. Elder Lucy Smith did not achieve the same level of success as Father Divine, but she asserted her own authority as a Black woman while building an interracial fellowship.

Father Divine also used the body in a metaphorical sense. One of the Divinites' popular songs, sung to the tune of "We Shall Overcome," has the lyric: "Here in America / Is the Kingdom of Heaven / Here in the land of the Free / We have the body of God."[24] An America free of racial prejudice was a healthy America, just as a body filled with the spirit of God was a healthy body. By paying attention to their own physical bodies Divinites helped to manifest a perfect society. This belief is also seen in the bodily practices of many pacifists, including the founders of the Congress of Racial Equality (CORE). Radical pacifists routinely fasted as part of their ascetic practices, particularly those who sought to follow Gandhi's example of satyagraha (nonviolent resistance). Indeed, Divine was also influenced by Gandhi's ascetic practices. A contemporary observer noted, "Father Divine is much in agreement with Gandhi, who declares that 'disease is the result of our thoughts as much as our acts,' and that all disease springs from the same origin, the neglect of natural laws of health."[25] A purified body could most effectively purify the surrounding community.

But Divinites' lavish feasts were the mirror to radical pacifists' fasting. Feasting also conflicted with New Thought teaching. "Where his New Thought forebears had looked ahead to a bodiless future, fasting vigorously in search of a way to sustain life without food," argues historian R. Marie Griffith, "Divine's paradise was precisely the opposite: a world in which nothing was more real than steaming hot, sumptuous meals, available virtually around the clock."[26] These meals were visible manifestations of prosperity and love that brought the hungry into the fold and provided needed nourishment to thousands.

Peace mission banquets were the most distinctive aspect of the Father Divine movement. Father Divine claimed to have fed nearly three thousand people a day at his large Harlem banquets during the height of the Great Depression.[27] As the diners filed into the banquet room, a group of young

FIGURE 3.1 Father Divine at a Peace Mission Banquet, c. 1935. Credit: Photographs and Prints Division, Schomburg Center for Research in Black Culture, The New York Public Library.

women, both white and Black, serenaded them. These were the Rosebuds, who dressed in matching blue skirts, white blouses, and red jackets embroidered with the letter "V" for "virtue." Father Divine sat at the center of the tables, which were adorned with white tablecloths and china. The first courses were vegetables, often a dozen kinds, passed family style. Next came platters of meat, both cold cuts such as ham, and hot roast beef, fried chicken, and roasted fowl. Next were salads and breads followed by an assortment of desserts. Iced and hot coffee and tea accompanied the meal, often served by Father Divine himself. During the feast, Divinites gave testimony and spoke of the need for racial harmony. At the meal's end, Father Divine rose and delivered a short sermon. These were reprinted verbatim in the Peace Mission publications after being assiduously recorded by his secretaries. At the movement's height, women and men waited patiently behind the chairs of diners for their own turn at the feast, which would be repeated three or four times in an evening.[28]

While Father Divine's feasting contrasted with Gandhi's fasting, the two shared a common belief in the power of celibacy. Claude McKay reported that in Father Divine's "Kingdom" there is "(1) no sex, (2) no race, (3) no color, (4) no money."[29] Divinites lived in sex-segregated rooms and the most devoted followers were celibate. As one Divinite wrote, "Men and women should not marry each other, but should marry GOD."[30] Father Divine told his followers to "rid yourselves of all selfish tendencies, of selfish human affection."[31] This gendered arrangement was also based partly on the Catholic monastic tradition. "Women live separately in convents . . . and men in monasteries," preached Divine, "So likewise I separate the male angels from the female angels in my Kingdom."[32] Father Divine's admiration for the celibate Shakers also strengthened his belief in celibacy. Couples who wished to remain together could still participate in the Peace Mission, but the most devout lived separately.

Gender division, however, did not reflect a gender hierarchy. In fact, Father Divine often challenged gender norms. Father Divine extended his unorthodox ideas of gender to God, occasionally referring to the deity as female. In a 1932 sermon he stated, "God is your Mother and you never had another."[33] At other times he suggested God was neither male nor female. One contemporary observer noted Father Divine preached that "GOD is both female and male."[34] This blurring of gender extended to the Divinites themselves. Women in the movement had prominent voices in running cooperative businesses and jointly owned many of the Peace Mission properties. And some Divinites took names that were either gender neutral or associated with the opposite gender. Names such as Peace, Wonderful, and Love had no immediately identifiable gender associated with them. And some women, such as "Joshua Love," took male angelic names.[35]

This relative gender equality may have accounted for the large numbers of Black women drawn to the movement. The Peace Mission offered relative safety from domestic violence and economic security for women facing the double bind of race and gender discrimination. Indeed, historian Beryl Satter labels the Peace Mission as a "Black women's movement" because African American women made up at least 75 percent of the following.[36] Divine gave these women equal responsibilities in running properties and businesses. In a particularly dramatic example, Father Divine hired an African American woman, Flying Determination, as his personal pilot.[37] Even those women who were not among the most devout followers, but lived in the low-cost housing provided by the Peace Mission, achieved some autonomy and stability through the movement. This was the case with "Nellie," as described by Sarah Harris, a sympathetic chronicler of Father Divine:

> She no longer had to struggle to pay forty-five dollars a month rent. She had only to pay $1.25 a week for a clean, comfortable bed in Father's heaven. When she came home from work, there was no housework for her to do, and she could rest and then eat a hot dinner for fifteen cents. . . . Best of all, though, was Nellie's knowledge that

"nobody could wipe their feet on me again." She could say that she wouldn't wash windows or "get down to scrub until my knees gave way under me." If the lady of the house did not approve, Nellie could leave and find a better job. Meanwhile, her savings could carry her at Father Divine's.[38]

During the depths of the Great Depression, Nellie was able to escape the "slave market" of Black female domestic workers.[39] While other women waited on street corners to be picked up for long days of arduous low-paying labor, she had gained independence and comfort within the Peace Mission.

It was the rejection of racial categories, even more than the blurring of gender lines, that formed the foundation of Divinites' utopian interracialism. And it was this social aspect that set Father Divine's Peace Mission apart from the more individualistic New Thought religions, which promised individual rather than societal transformation. Divinites refused to use any racial language, and Father Divine opposed the use of hair straighteners or skin lighteners. Church teachings stated, "It shall be a violation of the Discipline of this Church for Members to excessively use cosmetics, have their hair straightened or curled, or to use beauty preparations or other devices unnecessarily to make themselves appear what they are not."[40] If they had to refer to someone's appearance, Divinites would use the terms "light complected" or "dark complected." Black and white followers slept side by side in rooming houses and sat interspersed at banquet tables. When they marched down Harlem's streets, the Peace Mission alternated white and Black Divinites to the extent feasible. Father Divine—a dark-skinned, short, and heavyset man—was a living angel, even a living god, to his followers. William Pickens, a NAACP leader, remarked, "Father Divine has not simply made God Black; he has made a Black man God—and a humble American lynchable Black man at that."[41] The Divinites' utopian interracialism was guided by a Black man. Divine wrote in 1938, "The abolition of every tendency of races, creeds and colors and divisions among us, has been brought to fruition, and established once and forever."[42] Together Divinites were living "angelic" lives by creating heaven on earth. "We recognize and declare that the Kingdom of Heaven is here and now," read a 1941 church document, "and not somewhere above the sky, to be reached only after death."[43] But perfecting heaven on earth required changing the society around them.

The Promised Land

For some Americans during the 1930s, heaven could not be found in cities, where unemployment and poverty wreaked havoc on families. Instead they sought economic and social sustainability in the countryside, where they could grow their own food and live in relative safety. The Great Depression led to the confluence of two powerful social reform impulses: back-to-the-land campaigns and the cooperative movement. Although we often associate rural communes with the romantic ideals of middle-class whites, African Americans had a deep connection to the land. The ability to grow one's own food and live independently has been a goal stretching from Booker T. Washington in the late nineteenth century to Black Nationalists in the late twentieth century.[44] As African Americans became increasingly urbanized during the era of the Great Migration, their previous rural homes could be an alluring alternative when faced with the housing and employment discrimination of the urban North. Historian Russell Rickford, writing about agrarian Black Nationalism, notes, "Arcadian territories possessed the power to restore emotionally damaged urbanites and nurture politically desirable traits."[45] Father Divine drew from the legacy of Black agrarianism to create a matrix of rural cooperatives he called the Promised Land, a rural community designed to nurture and heal his angels, regardless of race or gender.

The back-to-the-land movement in the early twentieth century overlapped with utopian experimentation and the rise of cooperatives. For example, in the 1880s, anarchists and socialists founded numerous Jewish agricultural communities with utopian leanings. And some workers' education institutions, like Brookwood and Highlander, took workers from overcrowded cities into bucolic landscapes. But most Blacks before the Great Migration, unlike their immigrant counterparts in cities, remained very much "on the land." The Great Migration changed that reality, and for weary urbanites a return to the land on their own terms, free of enslavement or sharecropping, could be highly attractive. Nationwide the Great Depression saw a resurgence of interest in back-to-the-land communities, which the New Deal resettlement projects reinforced.[46] Combined with a growing cooperative movement and the promise of economic autonomy, moving from crowded Harlem to an upstate cooperative farm might well be attractive for a Black southern migrant. Together with the religious teachings and practices of the Peace Mission, it could even be utopian.

Divine established his Promised Land in Ulster County, New York, about one hundred miles due north of Harlem and accessible by steamboat, train, or car. Ulster County was an overwhelming white area, but for Divine this was an asset rather than a drawback. As he built his cooperative empire, he deliberately sought out opportunities to racially integrate communities, despite threats of violence. Divinites first challenged the color line in Sayville, Long Island, and now they challenged it in upstate New York. Divine bought his first cooperative farm in 1935 and put an African American woman, Mother Sarah Love, in charge. At its height, Promised Land consisted of thirty communities that housed twenty-three hundred people and was spread across about two thousand acres. All of the cooperatives were women-run and interracial. In addition to farms with cows, chickens, and garden vegetables, the Promised Land boasted cooperative gas stations, restaurants, and tourist residences. Two large docks with lavish boathouses welcomed excursion steamers from the city. As with his urban cooperatives, the Promised Land ran only on cash and Divinites sold all their goods at below-market rate. They lived communally, sharing the labor and the profit from their farms. Although initially dismayed by the influx of newcomers, white Ulster residents found that the flourishing cooperatives improved the local economy, raised property values, and attracted new businesses.[47]

Much of the food grown in Promised Land farms ended up on the banquet tables and restaurants of Harlem. It was an early example of a farm-to-table movement, and it enabled the Divinites to feed impoverished city dwellers economically. African American women's agricultural skills, honed in the South prior to migration to the North, proved invaluable to the farms' success and provided goods for cooperative businesses.[48] While commentators generally view Father Divine's movement as an urban phenomenon, the success and popularity of the Promised Land was integral to the movement's growth. Growing food and raising livestock provided abundant and healthy vegetables and meat to an urban population flocking to Divine's banquets and restaurants. It also provided a livelihood for hundreds of Divinites running the rural cooperatives and small businesses. And the interracial communities challenged the white domination of upstate New York, bringing racial integration to the rural North.

Perhaps the most audacious act of integration through property acquisition in the Promised Land was Divine's luxurious Hudson River estate, Krum Elbow. Directly across the river was an equally luxurious estate, Hyde Park, the home of Franklin and Eleanor Roosevelt. Divine bought the property in 1938 from Howland Spencer, a white socialite who detested Roosevelt. This led to speculation that Spencer may have sold to Divine to anger the president, but Spencer insisted he was impressed by the productivity of other Promised Land properties and approved of the Divinites' ascetic lifestyle. As a critic of the New Deal, Spencer also liked the Divinites' policy of accepting no relief from the government. In a "March of Time" newsreel, Spencer said, "I am backing the Divine deal against the New Deal."[49] Twenty-one Divinites, nearly all women, signed Krum Elbow's deed and held the property jointly. The mansion became a popular vacation spot for Divinites living in the city. They often traveled by boat up the Hudson River to picnic and swim. About

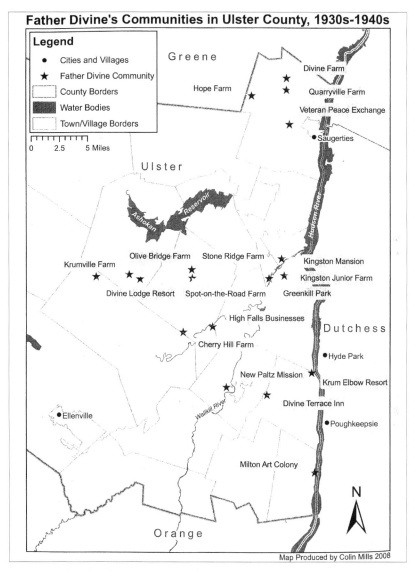

Father Divine's Communities in Ulster County, 1930s-1940s

Legend

- Cities and Villages
- ★ Father Divine Community
- County Borders
- Water Bodies
- Town/Village Borders

0   2.5   5 Miles

G r e e n e

Divine Farm

Hope Farm

Quarryville Farm

Veteran Peace Exchange

Saugerties

U l s t e r

Ashokan Reservoir

Hudson River

Krumville Farm

Olive Bridge Farm   Stone Ridge Farm

Kingston Mansion

Kingston Junior Farm

Divine Lodge Resort   Spot-on-the-Road Farm   Greenkill Park

High Falls Businesses

D u t c h e s s

Cherry Hill Farm

Hyde Park

New Paltz Mission

Krum Elbow Resort

Divine Terrace Inn

Ellenville

Wallkill River

Poughkeepsie

Milton Art Colony

N

Orange

Map Produced by Colin Mills 2008

MAP 3.1 Father Divine's Communities in Ulster County, 1930s–1940s. Map produced by Colin Mills, 2008, in Carleton Mabee, *Promised Land: Father Divine's Interracial Communities in Ulster County, New York* (New York: Purple Mountain Press, 2008), 80.

sixty Divinites lived there year-round, growing food and tending stock as well as maintaining the buildings. Orchards and vineyards surrounded the estate's twenty-eight buildings.[50]

A year after purchasing Krum Elbow, Father Divine attempted to purchase another estate adjoining the Roosevelts' home to use as a private residence

TABLE 3.1. Major Peace Missions in Ulster County: Dates Bought and Features

NAME	DATE	FEATURES
New Paltz Farm	1935	First property acquired in the county; quality river-bottom farm land; auditorium; served dinners to public
Stone Ridge Farm	1935	A productive farm, with old stone house overlooking Esopus Creed; served dinners to public
Kingston Mansion	1935	Divine headquarter for county; offered swimming pond; many children living there attended Kingston High School
Olive Bridge and Krumville Farms	1935–36	Substantial farms; included old stone house; mountain views; children attended one-room Krumville School
Divine Lodge, near Samsonville	1936	Resort high in the Catskills; westernmost Divine property in county; offered fishing, hiking, horseback riding
Hope Farm, in West Saugerties	1936	Farm; much expanded main house; fishing; children attended nearby Blue Mountain School
Divine Farm, in Saxton	1936	Farm, rooms for tourists, restaurants, gas stations; northernmost Divine property in county
Elting Corners, in Town of Lloyd	1936	Boarding house; fire destroyed its main building in 1937, but thereafter followers lived in its barns
High Falls Businesses	1936–39	Included a hotel, grocery, department store, shoe shop, dress shop, barber shop, garage, bakery, and restaurant. These businesses dominated the High Falls economy.
Greenkill Park, near Kingston	1937	Resort on Rondout Creek; hotel burned in 1937, but many bungalows remained; open-air auditorium; offered swimming pond, fishing, boating; served public dinners
Art Colony, Milton	1938	Moorish-style main building on Hudson River, with dock for river steamers; offered swimming and boating in the Hudson; southernmost Divine property in county
Krum Elbow, near Highland	1938	Estate on Hudson River, with dock for river steamers, farm, and views across the river of Pres. F. D. Roosevelt's house in Hyde Park

Source: Carleton Mabee, *Promised Land: Father Divine's Interracial Communities in Ulster County, New York* (New York: Purple Mountain Press, 2008), 81.

where he could entertain dignitaries. The *New York Times* reprinted the correspondence between Divine and the Roosevelts about this transaction. Clearly the reading public was intrigued by a dialogue between the white president and a Black charismatic religious leader. Eleanor Roosevelt replied to Divine's polite inquiry about purchasing the property, saying, "There can be no reason against any citizen of our country buying such property as he wishes to acquire." Her husband reaffirmed this sentiment. In reply Divine wrote, "It has been my aim and purpose to lift up a standard of moral betterment for social justice by the act of the cooperative system, in cooperation together with others to improve the economic system, to encourage and promote the brotherhood of man and the love for this democracy." Unfortunately for Father Divine, the estate's owner was unaware of his attempts to purchase the property and refused to enter into negotiations. Nevertheless, this remarkable correspondence suggests some of the power that Divine had accumulated by the late 1930s.[51]

Krum Elbow's proximity to the president elevated the Divine movement's public profile. In 1938, for example, Hearst Metrotone News produced a newsreel, "Father Divine and 2,500 Angels Inspect Their New Land at Krum Elbow, New York."[52] And the *New York Times* reported in 1939, "In this huge community that has facilities for feeding and lodging perhaps 10,000 persons at one time, where no person may smoke, drink or curse, there are cultivated farms, resort hotels, country clubs, estates, scores of houses and dormitories, all manner of restaurants, stores, gasoline stations, tailor shops, barber shops, garages and even two large docks with boathouses on the Hudson River, capable of accommodating the largest excursion steamers."[53] Divinites welcomed such publicity and staged elaborate, large-scale events to draw the press. In 1937, for example, they commissioned an oversized steamer to bring approximately two thousand Harlemites to a Promised Land resort in Kingston, New York. Thousands more joined them by rail or automobile. "It mattered not what color the angel's skin," reported the *Chicago Defender*, "they rejoiced, sang, raced, played and ate together. To the advocate of interracial harmony this was truly Utopian, heavenly."[54]

Visitors not associated with the Peace Mission also came to vacation in the Promised Land for a reasonable price. One of them was W. E. B. Du Bois, who visited in 1942. Du Bois was impressed with what he saw, noting that "the Father Divine movement differs from numbers of religious cults." He lauded the charity work done by the movement and was struck that it was "interracial among people of the laboring and middle class."[55] Most of the prominent activists in the 1930s and 1940s would have interacted with Divine's movement in some way. Ella Baker, for example, routinely ate at Father

Divine's Harlem restaurants.[56] Radical pacifists who resided at the Harlem Ashram or worked with the Fellowship of Reconciliation (FOR) were living on very small salaries and likely used the low-cost food and housing that the Father Divine cooperatives provided. Baker and others frequented these cooperatives, encountered Divinites on urban streets, and read about the movement's attempts to integrate numerous communities. It was the Promised Land, however, an interracial oasis in a white rural community, that most captured the public's imagination.

A Society of Utopians

The Promised Land's rural location was reminiscent of nineteenth-century utopian communities, a fact Father Divine often acknowledged. Father Divine had long felt a connection to Mother Ann Lee, the founder of the Shakers. He invoked Lee in his messages as a spiritual leader who spoke the truth, a legacy he followed in his own teachings. The fact that the Promised Land was adjacent to a Shaker community was no accident. Divine believed that Promised Land's success was at least partially due to her "spiritual legacy."[57] And Lee, like Divine, was considered by Shakers to be a reincarnation of Christ. She practiced faith healing, preached nonresistance, and established celibacy in her communities, all practices Father Divine embraced. The Peace Mission also shared a love of music with Shaker communities. Singing together was a powerful communal experience that drew outsiders to Peace Mission banquets. The Shaker community in Sabbathday Lake, Maine, which had survived into the twentieth century, incorporated Peace Mission songs into their repertoire.[58] In addition to the Shaker influence, Divine's cooperative movement drew directly from the Owenite and Rochdale cooperatives of the nineteenth century. These deep resonances with a spectrum of utopian communities attracted more followers as the Divine movement grew exponentially in the late 1930s.

Most Peace Mission observers focused on Divine's African American followers. But the relatively large numbers of white followers suggest how Father Divine built his movement on the legacy of utopian socialism and New Thought ideas. This was particularly true on the West Coast, long a hotbed of utopian communalism. In the first half of the twentieth century, California saw the establishment of more utopian communities than any other state in the union. And these communities helped shape pacifist and socialist movements. Llano del Rio, to name just one, was deeply influential for Highlanders. In addition to socialist communities, Californians were engaged with new religions such as Theosophy, a nineteenth-century religious movement that combined Western esotericism with Eastern religion. This combination of religious and secular interest in utopia helped build the number of Peace Mission extensions in California to twenty in 1935, the largest concentration outside of New York and Pennsylvania.[59]

In California many white Divinites migrated from the Utopian Society of America, an interracial organization that promoted economic and racial equality. Los Angeles reformers created the society in 1933 and promoted Edward Bellamy's socialist ideas, as well as opposing segregation and working for anti-discrimination legislation.[60] They met in secret and, much like the Brookwood Players, wrote dramas to illustrate their teachings. According to one of the founders, the performances epitomized "man's struggle for economic security and general well-being, tracing the progress of that struggle up thru past centuries, and looking into the near future for the attainment of its goal."[61] Like the clandestine southern sharecroppers unions, the Utopian Society also drew on Masonic rituals and encouraged interracial mixing. By 1934 they claimed to have initiated six hundred thousand members and had spread into six additional states. That year a meeting at the Hollywood Bowl reportedly attracted twenty thousand, eager to hear explanations for the Great Depression's economic crisis and solutions from the Bellamyites. Also fueling the movement was the socialist writer and politician Upton Sinclair's run for governor and his promotion of the End Poverty in California (EPIC) program. Along with the Utopian Society, EPIC called for large-scale public works programs, redistribution of resources, and cooperatives.[62]

Sinclair's election failure and concerns about the group's secrecy led to the Utopian Society's decline. But some percentage of the movement's followers then gravitated to Father Divine's Peace Mission, making up their largest white constituency. By the 1930s New Thought and utopian religious groups flourished from the Pacific Northwest to San Diego. These included Divine Science churches, Vedanta and Theosophical groups, Rosicrucian societies, Unity churches, and Absolute Science centers. This proved to be rich soil for the Father Divine movement, whose teachings were publicized in New Thought periodicals throughout the region. White West Coast followers also traveled to Sayville in the early 1930s to meet with Divine and his followers in person, returning to lecture on Divine's message.[63]

One of the most remarkable West Coast groups settled in the remote Vendovi Island off the coast of Washington State, which Father Divine called his "Peaceful Paradise of the Pacific." It served primarily as a retreat for Divine followers, much as Krum Elbow did in the East, but also housed a full-time interracial staff, including African Americans from Newark, Chicago, and Oakland. One Divinite argued that, much like in the Promised Land, "life of the Vendovi settlers is somewhat reminiscent of the Shakers . . . who established substantial, rural societies."[64] Like many Peace Mission extensions, Vendovi fell into decline after World War II, but during the 1930s it demonstrated the power and reach of Divine's teachings. And for some African Americans such as Wonderful Joy, a Black woman from Newark who resided in Vendovi, it provided a respite from the Great Depression's hardship. Although small in size, Vendovi suggests the centrality of Father Divine in utopian history nationwide.

A Righteous Government

Vendovi and the retreats at Promised Land and Sayville might imply that the Father Divine's Peace Mission, like other utopian communities, was isolated from political struggles. But that was not the case. The very existence of interracial cooperatives, rooming houses, and properties challenged spatial segregation and sparked white backlash. The Father Divine movement also began to engage with the realm of formal politics, particularly in Harlem, by the second half of the 1930s. And Peace Mission activists were among the earliest groups to deploy Gandhian nonviolence to combat racial segregation.

Both the Utopian Society and the Father Divine movement had strong anti-statist leanings. They were suspicious of the growing New Deal welfare programs and preferred the cooperative system as an economic solution to rapacious capitalism, rather than a centralized state. In fact, many of the most successful interracial communities, such as Highlander and the Fellowship Houses, were independent from state control. Similarly, Catholic Workers declined any state assistance and advocated for a decentralized society outside of government control.[65] Father Divine took this stance to an extreme by forbidding his followers to accept government welfare. In a 1939 sermon, Father Divine described his followers as "self-supporting and independent, expressing the spirit of independence such as I am stressing, and not a one is on the Welfare."[66] Divinites also paid off any debts when they joined the movement, making them entirely independent from banks. Father Divine pointed out in 1938: "My followers by the influence of MY Spirit, have not only saved the city twenty million dollars by MY taking them off of the welfares [*sic*], but they have returned to the city and state and the United States thousands and millions of dollars, by paying all of their old bills that were even outlawed, and by returning all stolen goods."[67] Father Divine worked to encourage poor Harlemites to avoid installment buying and chastised banks for exploiting African Americans who fell into debt. "I am concerned about the great mass of poor people," said Divine at a community meeting, "the chief

FIGURE 3.2 Peace Mission Parade in Harlem, 1938. Credit: Granger Historical Picture Archive.

victims of this form of exploitation."[68] To live entirely debt-free, the Peace Mission also paid for all of its properties in cash. These cash payments made the Peace Mission popular with sellers. And Father Divine did not accept any donations or speaking fees, which allowed him to deny corruption charges.[69]

As the Peace Mission grew in size, politicians began to take notice. And despite his suspicions of government, Father Divine and his followers responded. Clearly, Divine could harness large numbers of votes on the local level. In 1933 Fiorello La Guardia came to Divine to ask for his support for his successful mayoral run. He attended a Harlem banquet and implored Father Divine to support him. "I say, Father Divine," said the future mayor, "no matter what you want, I will support you. I am going to clean up this city and I came here tonight to ask Father Divine's help and counsel."[70] After La Guardia's election, Father Divine corresponded with him throughout his term as mayor, demanding that more Black public officials be appointed. And the Peace Mission worked in coalition with activist groups. In 1936, for example, the Consolidated Tenants League persuaded Divine to join a major rent strike in Harlem. The *New York Times* reported that three thousand Divinite "angels" attended a mass strike meeting. While there, Father Divine said in a speech, "We shall have a Utopia and we will do it by the ballot, not the bullet." Divinites, dressed in their characteristic white dresses and neat suits, outnumbered other protesters in a massive parade down the streets of Harlem in support of the strike.[71]

This visibility and voting power attracted other activist organizations staging mass protests. The same year that he joined the tenant's organization, Father Divine threw his support behind the All People's Party (APP), a coalition of eighty-nine secular and religious organizations demanding lower rents, higher wages, and better living conditions for Harlem residents. The APP epitomized the popular-front politics of the 1930s, when the Communist Party worked in coalition with a variety of political organizations to defeat fascism. The Communist Party first reached out to Father Divine in 1934 when they invited Divinites to join mass parades in support of the Scottsboro Boys, African American teenagers who were falsely convicted of rape in Alabama. The Peace Mission members responded enthusiastically, marching with militant African Americans and whites on the streets of Harlem, although they held their own signs proclaiming "Father Divine is God." The APP also ran a white communist, Vito Marcantonio, and a Black communist, Angelo Herndon, for office.[72] Father Divine was willing to align his followers with any political coalition that was working for racial justice, including the Communist Party. "But," suggested Claude McKay, "what the Communists were trying to do he was actually doing, by bringing people of different races and nations to live together and work in peace under his will."[73] The Divinites did not need to wait for a revolution to experience utopian interracialism.

Voting, however, raised legal issues for the Divinites, who had changed their names to reflect their rebirth in the Peace Mission. The board of elections refused to allow them to register their new names, insisting that they sign their birth names, despite a 1935 State Supreme Court decision that allowed them to use any names they wished. Three hundred Divinites staged a sit-in at the Harlem registration center in 1936 to demand their voting rights. And in 1937 over two thousand members filed petitions to vote under their "heavenly" names.[74] They also refused to state their race on registration forms, leading to conflict with registration officials in several cities. As late as 1944, Father Divine's secretary, John Lamp, reported that "in several cities registration officials have requested the Divine followers to identify themselves by color or by race," and "in various places registration boards have refused permission for the cultists to register under such unusual names as George Honesty, Sincerity Faith, and Dorcas Love."[75] The spiritual names that Divinites adopted were deeply meaningful to them, chosen through dreams and meditation. A name like "Peaceful Love" was aspirational and marked an accession into a new life and a new identity. Thus, their determination to have their names accepted in voter registration rolls asserted both their citizenship rights and their religio-racial identities.

Voting also was important to Divinites because it was a means to address racial injustice. Father Divine spoke openly and often about leading civil rights causes during the 1930s and 1940s. He supported the campaign to release the Scottsboro Boys, and when police in Georgia arrested Angelo Herndon while he was organizing Black workers, sentencing him to eighteen years, Father Divine was outspoken in his defense. The Peace Mission also consistently called for passage of a federal anti-lynching bill, gathering thousands of signatures to petition Congress.[76] Reflecting these political stances, a large poster at one of his banquets read, "Father Divine's Peace Mission is in sympathy with any movement which seeks to abolish racial discrimination, eradicate prejudice and establish the fundamentals which stand for the good of Humanity. We are against War and Fascism. We believe in and practice the principle of the Brotherhood of all Mankind."[77] Father Divine also published letters he wrote to public officials. In a 1935 article, Claude McKay quotes one such letter: "We the Inter-racial, International, Inter-denominational and Inter-religious Coworkers . . . do demand the release through commutation of the life sentence of the Scottsboro boys. . . . And also we demand freedom, and extermination of the mistreatment of the Jews in Germany and all other countries, and we demand the equal rights and religious liberty according to our Constitution."[78]

Father Divine's political thought found its fullest articulation at his Righteous Government convention in 1936. Attended by six thousand followers, the convention was held at Rockland Palace in Harlem. Attendees drafted the "Righteous Government Platform," which was widely circulated in the decade that followed the convention. Peace Mission extensions also held Righteous Government forums to discuss the document and develop plans to institute its goals. The platform called for sweeping civil rights legislation, including the end of all segregation, voting rights for African Americans, and the use of nonviolent direct action to challenge discrimination. The first demand was "Immediate Legislation . . . making it a crime to discriminate in any public place against any individual on account of race, creed, or color; abolishing all segregated neighborhoods in Cities and Towns, making it a crime for landlords or hotels to refuse tenants on such grounds; abolishing all segregated schools and colleges, and all segregated areas in Churches, theatres, public conveyances, and other public places."[79] The platform went on to demand an end to lynching and all forms of capital punishment.

The Righteous Government Platform was also addressed to other institutions, including organized labor. Father Divine was hostile to unions, which he described as corrupt and racially discriminatory. The platform demanded that labor unions "accept all qualified applicants and give them equal privileges regardless of race, creed, color or classification."[80] Rather than union-

ization, Father Divine's economic solutions were based on his highly successful cooperative plans, government control of "idle plants and machinery,"
and full employment. These demands could also be found in Sinclair's EPIC
program and in California's Utopian Society. In a 1939 speech, Father Divine
argued that "labor and capital should be unified together that all might enjoy
the actual blessings of each other." This was very much a socialist and cooperative vision, shared by those in the workers' education movement and cooperative enterprises. "Why not come together in the unity of the spirit,"
proposed Father Divine, "of mind, of aim and of purpose."[81] Labor unions that
excluded Black workers did not fit into this vision, and Divine was skeptical
that labor interracialism would fulfill its promise.

The Righteous Government Platform also called for free education to be
made available to all citizens.[82] The Peace Mission had made education, by
the late 1930s, a major goal of the movement, and Father Divine encouraged
his followers to attend night school. Divinites made use of the adult education classes provided by the WPA to learn the skills they needed to run Peace
Mission extensions. These are the schools that Floria Pinkney, Ella Baker,
and Pauli Murray, all graduates of Brookwood, developed in Harlem during
the New Deal.[83] This was one instance when Divinites embraced a New Deal
program that fit with their own priorities. In this case it was an extension
of the idealistic workers' education program developed in the 1920s by A. J.
Muste and Fannia Cohn. In those Harlem classrooms, Brookwood graduates
interacted directly with Divinites, all working toward the goal of racial justice.

Even before Father Divine drafted the Righteous Government Platform,
the Peace Mission fought segregation by creating highly visible integrated
communities. That was the case in his first large mansion in Sayville, Long
Island, and the Promised Land. In 1942 Father Divine purchased a large
hotel in Brigantine, New Jersey, so his followers could break the color barrier on Atlantic City's beaches and boardwalks.[84] And in 1943 Father Divine
helped fight the Metropolitan Life Insurance Company, whose Stuyvesant
Town apartments were racially exclusive. "When you segregate . . . in a state
that has passed the Fair Employment Practices Committee Bill and the Civil
Rights Bill," wrote Father Divine to the company, "all evidences reflect as if
though you desire to endorse segregation and discrimination, which bring
on such disasters as have claimed the lives of millions in recent years."[85] As
both property owners and through persuasion, Father Divine and his followers sought integration, gaining publicity and popular support along the way.

The Peace Mission movement also took on the segregation of public accommodations. All of the Peace Mission cooperative businesses welcomed
whites and Blacks, and at the public banquets white and Black visitors sat in

alternate seats to reinforce utopian interracialism. According to one follower, in the Divinite hotels, "white and colored non-followers must sleep side by side just as followers do. Every double bed must be shared where proportions permit by one white and one colored person."[86] These hotels, the retreats in the mountains of upstate New York, and the resorts on the New Jersey coast offered African Americans low-cost and safe travel. City dwellers could stay at the Brigantine beach resort near Atlantic City for only two dollars per week. Or they could stay at the Pine Brook Hotel in the rural hills near Newark, New Jersey, for even less.[87] Because they forbade tipping and charged low rates, these retreats were affordable for working-class Blacks and whites alike. As sociologist Arthur Huff Fauset points out, "Here we have a functional transformation with regard to a very vital need of American Negroes growing out of the general practice of American hostelries to refuse to receive them."[88] There was no racial harassment, uncertainty, or restrictions in the Peace Mission accommodations. In an era when *The Negro Motorist Green Book* was necessary to guide Black travelers to safe and secure accommodations, Father Divine provided reliable and accessible recreational facilities.

Black and white Divinites also deliberately frequented segregated establishments to directly challenge segregation, risking arrest and harassment. Father Divine boasted about these escapades in his sermons, and Divinites sang about them in their communal worship. Historian Charles S. Braden noted that "white and Black sing with apparently equal enthusiasm the crusading songs in which racial discrimination is condemned and the ideal of racial brotherhood proclaimed."[89] One such hymn went:

We shall have the Same Rights
Not only Equal but the Same
Side by side, we shall ride
The Same car, bus and train
We shall play in the Same parks
Study our lessons in the Same schools.
There shall be the Same Equal Rights
For you, and you, and you![90]

In their housing, property ownership, transportation, and small businesses, Divinites practiced utopian interracialism daily. They had an absolute and uncompromising commitment to full racial equality.

In the 1930s, Father Divine also drew from Gandhi's teachings to create his heaven on earth. Gandhi's satyagraha practices included celibacy, and although Father Divine's large banquets contrasted with the periodic fasting practiced at Gandhi's ashrams, the two men shared a similar worldview. Gandhi taught that "man tends to become a slave of his own body, and engages in many activities and commits many sins for the sake of physical enjoyment."[91] Divinites eschewed tobacco, sex, and alcohol for similar reasons, although they also viewed the body as a source of pleasure through food and music. Thus, Gandhi's ashrams and the Peace Mission extensions had many parallel practices: simple clothing, celibacy, nonviolence, and other ascetic practices. But perhaps most important was their shared commitment to nonviolence in both daily life and political practice.

As reflected in the term "Peace Mission" and Divinites' invariable greeting of "Peace," nonviolence was central to the movement's teaching.[92] The Peace Mission followers also used nonviolent direct-action tactics in the 1940s and 1950s to combat segregation. This is the same period in which CORE and FOR began to develop nonviolent tactics, training activists across the country in this vital form of resistance. Divinites' use of nonviolent direct action accelerated after Father Divine and many of his closest followers moved to Philadelphia in the 1940s. For example, the American Civil Liberties Union (ACLU) and the NAACP in Philadelphia had received dozens of complaints from African Americans who had been harassed and beaten at public facilities. In the face of prevalent segregation, Father Divine attempted to purchase the segregated Crystal Pool at the Woodside Amusement Park in order to open it to all races in the late 1940s. In 1952, after a Black Korean War veteran was turned away from Northeast Philadelphia's lavish Boulevard Pools, Father Divine responded by using his interracial congregation to test pool policies, following the CORE model. Using photographs and testimonies, Father Divine's followers documented their exclusion from Boulevard Pools—the park's owners claimed that the group was not a member of the Boulevard Swimming and Tennis Club. The Peace Mission activists turned their evidence over to the city's Commission of Human Relations (CHR), which had compiled an extensive record of pool discrimination in Philadelphia. A group of African Americans, who had been part of a string of demonstrations, filed a successful class-action suit against Boulevard Pools.[93]

In the case of Philadelphia's pools, an eclectic mix of civil rights groups, religious organizations, and ordinary citizens forced the city and private operators to abide by the law. The Divinites were an essential part of this coalition. Marching alongside communists in Harlem, forcibly integrating recreational facilities, or visibly living in interracial communities, Divinites were persistently politically engaged utopians. In a 1941 document, Father Divine declared, "This church will endeavor to provide wholesome food, and comfortable, clean, respectable sleeping accommodations for those among our neighbors who have fallen victim to the thieves of today . . . the thieves of economic slavery occasioned by race segregation and discrimination."[94] Divinites lived under the Righteous Government in the here and now, and they sought to bring others, Black and white, under its protection.

Backlash and Decline

Father Divine's forceful indictment of racial segregation came at a cost. White backlash to Father Divine's ministry occurred at nearly every location where he set up an extension. Although such conflicts often led to legal trouble, they also generated significant publicity and sympathy among his Black and progressive white followers. Perhaps this was no more so than in his first major extension, in the all-white community of Sayville, Long Island. White neighbors there complained of the "noisy" crowds coming from the city to join in the Peace Mission's banquets and worship. But, as Claude McKay suggested, the real motivation was likely the interracial mixing. "It appeared that the major disturbing factor was that considerable numbers of white pilgrims began to join with the Blacks in the rampant revels and the worship of Father Divine." The *Chicago Defender* maintained that a mass meeting of white business leaders and professionals in 1931 "to object to the cult of 'Father Divine' as a nuisance" was inspired by "jealousy coupled with prejudice against the many first-class white followers who unashamedly avow their faith in the philosophy of the Colored leader." McKay pointed out that even Black elites, who frowned on the "cultists" of the interwar period, came to Father Divine's defense and championed his cause after he was arrested for "disturbing the peace." Black newspapers covered his trial, and Harlemites held mass meetings in support of Father Divine.[95] The white backlash to his interracial community inadvertently led to his growing fame.

That fame rose to even greater proportions when, three days following Judge Smith's verdict that Father Divine receive the maximum penalty, the judge died of an apparent heart attack. Father Divine reportedly said in his jail cell, "I hated to do it." His followers rejoiced that the judge "sentenced God to prison and God sentenced him to death."[96] Father Divine later claimed that he "did not desire Judge Smith to die." "I did desire that my spirit would touch his heart and change his mind," he reported in a message to followers, "that he might repent and believe and be saved from the grave." After Divine was released on bail, the New York State Supreme Court overturned the verdict because it had been marred "by gross prejudice" on the part of the judge. "Like wild fire, the news of the reversal and the death of the convicting judge spread," reported the *Chicago Defender*. "Kingdoms sprang up with dizzying duplication."[97] The fame and publicity that followed Father Divine's release drew more members to the Peace Mission, but its expansion also created more backlash.

New extensions in white neighborhoods were consistently met with hostility. In 1936 in Ivywild, a suburb of Colorado Springs, Colorado, a white mob attacked a newly established "heaven." They set a fire in the street and hurled rocks through the windows until a local sheriff regained control. The KKK, who had a stronghold in upstate New York, frequently targeted Promised Land properties. The Klan also burned crosses and attempted to oust Divinites at its New Jersey and Rhode Island extensions.[98] Access to beaches and swimming pools often created the strongest backlash, as segregated recreation was pervasive in the mid-twentieth century. In 1939 the Peace Mission obtained a large and luxurious home at the Sutton Manor estates, in a white area of New Rochelle, New York. This purchase, which was carried out by white followers, allowed Divinites access to a nearby beach and yacht club. Predictably the white residents erupted in anger and disgust when they realized that a large interracial group was moving into the property. But despite their best efforts to oust the offending neighbors, the Divinites remained.[99] This pattern of white violence following new Peace Mission extensions was reminiscent of the threats and violence experienced by the Highlander Folk School and the Delta Cooperative Farm. Utopian interracial communities profoundly challenged the mores of American life, from rural Mississippi to suburban New York.

But it was not only white racist backlash that burdened the movement. The most often heard criticism of the Peace Mission was that Father Divine was a charlatan who exploited his followers and lived a lavish lifestyle. Newsreel images of him in Rolls-Royces or flying over Harlem in a private airplane reinforced this image. However, academics who have closely studied his movement, such as Charles S. Braden and Arthur Huff Fauset, found little evidence of corruption. Some followers who worked outside of the extensions contributed their salaries to the movement, but Father Divine himself refused all direct donations. And there was little evidence that followers had to turn over their savings when joining the movement. Rather, it was the cooperative system itself and the economy of communal living that proved profitable over the long term. The cars, airplane, and homes used by Father Divine and his personal secretaries were owned by the Peace Mission communally and were not personal possessions. And the businesses were run not for profit, but for service to the community.[100] Father Divine preached in 1932 that "the love of money is the root of all evil."[101] Living with no debt and charging wholesale prices at their businesses helped spread this gospel. However, the Peace Mission certainly used public displays of wealth, even if communally owned, to bring more attention to the movement. Such displays, including the abundant banquets, also reinforced Divinites' belief that Father Divine was God, who had created a "heaven" on earth.

The white mainstream press often ridiculed the movement and was especially critical of its interracial mixing. The *Forum and Century* said in 1934, "In the adherence given Father Divine there is much that is comic, not a little that is tragic, and some elements bordering on the sinister."[102] Within the African American community, there was a mixed response to Father Divine's success. Claude McKay pointed out, "The Negro intelligentsia may be skeptical of the cult, but they admire the Divine courage and cleverness in circumventing the great American taboo and bringing white and colored people together in intimate collaboration."[103] Some Black religious leaders felt threatened by Father Divine's success and saw him as manipulative. Adam Clayton Powell Jr., the pastor of Harlem's large Abyssinian Baptist Church, led the charge, lashing out in 1936 that Father Divine was "the colossal farce of the twentieth century."[104] Others from the Black bourgeoisie agreed with this assessment and often lumped Divine in with other "cult" leaders such as the charismatic preachers Daddy Grace and Elder Michaux. These criticisms also came from Divine's religious peers. Father Divine's religious partner in Baltimore, Reverend Bishop Saint John the Divine (formerly John A. Hickerson), turned against him with accusations that Father Divine had stolen his teachings and was an impostor.[105] Overall, however, many in the Black community admired both Father Divine's politics and his cooperative business practices.

Ongoing legal battles eventually took their toll on Father Divine's Peace Mission movement. Most significantly, a 1937 lawsuit filed by a former follower, Verinda Brown, dragged on for years and led Father Divine to leave Harlem and take up residency in Philadelphia in 1942. One of his most devout followers, Faithful Mary, left the movement in the mid-1930s to start her own sect in the Promised Land. Although she returned to the fold several years later, her defection led to negative publicity and turmoil among Divinites.[106] These defections and legal struggles were all highlighted in both the Black and white press. William Randolph Hearst, the newspaper tycoon, became obsessed with taking down Father Divine's empire and closely followed the scandals and lawsuits. In California the Utopian Society had been outspoken critics of Hearst, further strengthening his wish to "expose" the movement.[107] The Peace Mission movement, however, largely weathered the negative publicity and occasional defections.

In 1941 Father Divine incorporated his Northeast centers to allow him greater legal stability and the opportunity to purchase property in the church's name. This led to greater bureaucracy and hierarchy in the Peace Mission, in contrast to the more egalitarian, if somewhat anarchistic, organization of the interwar years. In this hierarchical system, it was more difficult for followers to establish new extensions or cooperative businesses, and the banquets were no longer completely open to the public. Wartime employment largely ended the Great Depression, which also lessened the movement's appeal. Fewer people needed the low-cost cooperative housing, restaurants, and resorts. Greater prosperity also lessened the appeal of the cooperative life. The farms and businesses in the Promised Land began to close as some followers joined Father Divine in Pennsylvania or left the movement altogether. Ulster County Peace Mission properties declined in number from twenty-five in 1942 to nine in 1950.[108] The remaining cooperative businesses were concentrated in Philadelphia, Newark, and Harlem.

Larger events also made the Peace Mission a more cautious and conservative movement. Throughout his ministry, Father Divine embraced nonviolence; however, World War II posed a challenge to this teaching. In the end he told his followers that they should fight if so inspired, and he supported the selling of war bonds.[109] However, he also supported those who became conscientious objectors. Father Divine consistently spoke out against totalitarianism and was horrified by the Nazis' racial beliefs. This wartime nationalism merged into a cold war politics, as he became increasingly strident in his anti-communist and anti-union rhetoric after World War II. During the cold war, he called for a "one-world" government that would replicate American democracy on a global scale.[110] And as he grew more conservative, his postwar teachings on gender lacked the fluidity and flexibility of earlier decades. Divine increasingly emphasized the need for female modesty and respectability.[111] Although commentators have pointed to his growing anti-communism after the war, they have overlooked the Divinites' continued work against racial segregation in Philadelphia and elsewhere. Divinites' political activism in this period paralleled the work of CORE and FOR. In the 1950s, Father Divine also called for international reparations for the descendants of African American slaves.[112] Therefore, his general move toward a cold war conservatism was mitigated by his continued support of the civil rights movement's goals.

The ultimate test of any utopian movement is the demise of its charismatic leader, particularly a movement in which illness and death were anathema. As he aged, Father Divine adjusted his teachings about death, viewing it not as a failure of a sinful mind but as the passage into a more perfect body. This was particularly convenient after the death of the first Mother Divine, Peninnah, in 1943. In 1946 he married, although only spiritually, a young white woman from Canada, Edna Rose Ritchings. This new Mother Divine was said to be a reincarnation of his first wife. Over time she grew to be a capable leader of the movement as her husband's health declined.[113] By that point, Father and Mother Divine had retreated to a mansion on the outskirts of Philadelphia, the Woodmont estate, as their cooperative empire continued to shrink. Despite the movement's diminished visibility, religious and civil rights leaders continued to visit Father Divine until his death in 1965.[114] At the time of his death, Mother Divine and the remaining followers argued that although his body was no longer on earth, he was present. "Father Divine sacrificed his body so as to prove to his followers," argued one Divinite, "that they could carry on his work and be independent without his body being visible to the world."[115] To this day, the remaining Divinites set a place for him at their meals and keep his room with all his belongings in place. It was fitting that the Woodmont estate was located in an exclusive white neighborhood in the Philadelphia suburbs, yet another blow to segregation.

While living and working at Woodmont, Father Divine witnessed the major civil rights battles of the postwar period. He supported the movement, although from afar. After President Lyndon Johnson signed the Voting Rights Act, just months before his death, Father Divine sent him a telegram, which read, "There is nothing that can prevent the establishment of a universal Utopian democracy in which all men, everywhere, shall enjoy the reality of life, liberty and happiness."[116] The Peace Mission may not have played a direct role in creating that utopian democracy in the postwar period, but the movement's success in the 1930s and 1940s suggests that many African Americans and a smaller number of idealistic whites were ready for its arrival.

Conclusion

The Father Divine Peace Mission's prefigurative politics touched many thousands of Black and white Divinites in ways that Myles Horton or A. Philip Randolph could only dream of. As Sarah Harris reported, "Father Divine's Negro followers get more immediate satisfaction from the way their leader attacks discriminatory patterns than the followers of more down-to-earth Negro leaders can ever get from theirs."[117] It is difficult to evaluate the impact of this political work, although the economic value of Divine cooperatives and the food and lodging provided are evident. And the ability to travel with access to hotels and resorts was a profound expression of freedom for African Americans. In addition to access to recreation and a life free of discrimination, the Father Divine movement offered a utopian interracialism that challenged American racial mores. And although Father Divine was indisputably its charismatic leader, African American women made up the majority of Divinites, maintaining scores of urban and rural cooperatives and sharing decision-making power. For Divinites, the Peace Mission offered heaven on earth and ample opportunities to express the political, social, and economic ambitions of its followers.

Father Divine's complete rejection of racial categories and his utopian teachings appeared extreme to both contemporaries and to later historians. Indeed, his utopian interracialism is at the far end of a spectrum of civil rights movement activism. The Peace Mission movement did more than Brookwood or the Delta and Providence farms to promote cooperatives and demonstrate how they could revive both individual fortunes and whole communities. We don't know how many people suffering from hunger and ill health in the midst of the Great Depression were aided by the cooperative businesses and extensions run by the movement, but it was in the thousands. Nor did Father Divine retreat from politics in developing his movement. Divinites marched in support of the Scottsboro Boys, submitted petitions for anti-lynching legislation, and practiced nonviolent direct action to desegregate public accommodations. While it is difficult to gauge the long-term impact of this work on the civil rights movement, to ignore its utopian aims entirely would be a mistake.

Father Divine's lack of respectability and his marginalization from mainstream African American denominations, however, has made his political strivings marginal in this broader narrative. More "respectable" religious leaders, in contrast, have been given credit for shaping the movement. During the years Father Divine was reading and teaching about Gandhi, another African American spiritual leader, Howard Thurman, traveled to India and met with Gandhi in person. Like Father Divine, he helped create an interracial church. But despite being smaller than the Peace Mission, this church would garner the attention and praise of the Christian Left, from A. J. Muste to Martin Luther King Jr.

4

The Fellowshippers

The God of the Fellowship Church is neither male nor female, Black nor white, Protestant nor Catholic nor Buddhist nor Hindu.

HOWARD THURMAN[1]

Fellowship isn't an organization; it's a movement.

MARJORIE PENNEY[2]

The teenagers clustered around a long table in a sprawling Philadelphia house planning their next campaign to desegregate neighborhood roller-skating rinks. Black and white youths discussed which of the white teens would approach the rink first, establishing that white teenagers were welcome. Then they choose which Black teens would follow, risking assault or arrest. Many had grown up in the comfortable and familiar surroundings of Fellowship House, singing in the interracial choir and playing with multicultural dolls in the library. Now approaching maturity, they were taking their convictions to the city streets and would soon carry their training and their principles with them as they traveled South to join the mass civil rights movement. These were the fellowshippers, whose religious and political foundations played a key role in the long civil rights movement.

Fellowshippers were part of the broader Christian Left, committed to the linked civil rights and pacifist movements. For Father Divine, the road to utopia required a profound internal transformation that allowed his followers to connect to a spiritual sense of oneness. Divinites changed their names to symbolize their renouncing of strict racial and gender codes and embraced a full utopian interracialism. While their practices may seem extreme, they were not so far removed from mainstream Protestantism. By the early 1940s, some on the Christian Left developed a theology and set of practices that resembled those of Father Divine. Theologians such as Howard Thurman and institution builders like Marjorie Penney fostered a liberal interracialism that emphasized polite interactions to promote interracial understanding. But like Father Divine, they also embraced forms of mysticism and Eastern religion, and they supported nonviolent direct action many years before it was embraced by moderate civil rights organizations.

In the Church for the Fellowship of All Peoples, founded in San Francisco in the early 1940s, and in Philadelphia's Fellowship House founded a decade before, Blacks and whites met and worshipped together. The physical spaces of these interracial experiments provided much-needed safety where activists could share their experiences on the picket lines and in city halls and state capitals, as they sought to move the needle toward racial equality. They called themselves "fellowshippers," to mark their commitment to a fully realized intercultural and interracial fellowship. Through the late 1940s, these institutions echoed the liberal interracialism of the YMCA and YWCA movement. However, they were also where Gandhian ideas were communicated to, among others, Martin Luther King Jr. And they were where a new generation of radical pacifists, including the founders of the Congress of Racial Equality (CORE), received much of their religious as well as their political training. By the late 1950s, fellowshippers were actively engaged in nonviolent direct action, supporting the growing civil rights movement in multiple ways. Thus, two interracial experiments, on opposite coasts but with similar goals, were grounded in liberal interracialism but bolstered the utopian strain in the long civil rights movement.

Howard Thurman and Mahatma Gandhi

Howard Thurman came of age just as Gandhi's teachings began to influence the Christian Left. Born in 1899, Thurman grew up in the starkly segregated community of Daytona Beach, Florida, where he witnessed brutal racial violence and saw the impact of disenfranchisement on the Black community. From there he attended Morehouse College in Atlanta, graduating as valedictorian in 1923. Atlanta introduced him to the teachings of pacifism, and at Morehouse he became active in the Fellowship of Reconciliation (FOR).

After his ordination as a Baptist minister, Thurman continued his studies at Rochester Theological Seminary, where he was the only African American student. In western New York, he encountered an active KKK presence, disabusing him of the belief that racism was regionally limited. He remembered later that in Rochester "within the Christian church, the pattern of segregation was effective without regard particularly to the section of the country in which the church was located. North or South, it made no difference. *This was new to me.*"[3] The extent of religious segregation and virulent racism in the North was a stunning blow to the young minister.[4]

Thurman left Rochester to accept a position as pastor at a Baptist church in the liberal enclave of Oberlin, Ohio. After a number of years in this position, Mordecai Johnson, Dean of Howard University, hired the young man as a faculty member and Dean of Rankin Chapel at Howard. As his world widened, Thurman's politics evolved during this formative period. Like most of his fellow pacifists, by the late 1920s Thurman was an avowed socialist and supporter of Norman Thomas.[5] Throughout the late 1920s and 1930s, Thurman became more deeply involved with FOR, eventually serving on its steering committee and helping to shift the organization toward a focus on civil rights. His ascendancy as a leading pacifist thinker is evident in one of his early essays, "Relaxation and Race Conflict," which was published in FOR's periodical *The World Tomorrow* and reprinted in *Pacifism in the Modern World*, a 1929 edited collection by the prominent white pacifist Devere Allen. This essay, from the collection's sole Black author, calls on pacifists to acknowledge the differential in power between Blacks and whites, and advises that whites should exercise a "relaxation of the will to dominate."[6] The process of "relaxation" reflects Thurman's interest in mysticism, which ideally would allow individuals to escape power relations and view one another as fully equal. Overall, the volume, which includes an essay by A. J. Muste on "class war," called for a more engaged and worldly form of pacifism, which would take on a variety of issues outside of warfare. This was a welcome development for Black pacifists.

The same year that Devere Allen published Thurman's influential essay, W. E. B. Du Bois introduced Gandhi to an African American public by publishing Gandhi's short piece "To the American Negro," in *Crisis* magazine. Gandhi, claimed Du Bois, was the "greatest colored man in the world." "Let us realize," wrote Gandhi to the Black community, "that the future is with those who would be truthful, pure and loving."[7] This message of love and unity resonated with a young Howard Thurman, who was fascinated by mystical writers, such as the South African author Olive Schreiner.[8] Wanting to explore this religious teaching in greater depth, Thurman sought out the most prominent mystic in the United States, the white Quaker theologian Rufus Jones. He traveled to Pendle Hill, Pennsylvania, a Quaker retreat that also played a key role in the foundation of the Fellowship House, to meet with Jones in 1929. Jones agreed to take him on as a student, and Thurman studied with him at nearby Haverford College for six months. There he explored a form of spirituality that emphasized the unity of life and the belief that God is love, similar in many ways to Father Divine's worldview.[9] In his work as a preacher, Thurman introduced periods of meditation, liturgical dance, and other practices to bring this heightened spirituality to his congregants.

Because of Thurman's prominence in pacifist circles, as well as his growing reputation as a religious thinker, the YMCA's Student Christian Movement gave him the opportunity to travel to India in 1935. There he and his wife were the first African Americans to meet face-to-face with Gandhi. The delegation was made up of Thurman; his second wife, Sue Bailey Thurman, an accomplished YWCA activist; and another African American couple, the Rev. Edward G. Carroll and his wife, Phenola Carroll. The four visited fifty-three cities, and Thurman spoke at dozens of colleges and other public venues. During these appearances, South Asian audiences repeatedly challenged Thurman to defend Christianity's teachings given the reality of racial segregation and white violence.[10] These conversations inspired Thurman to later write his most famous book, *Jesus and the Disinherited*. But the trip's most memorable moment was a three-hour private meeting with Gandhi at his retreat in Bardoli, India. In an article recalling the visit, Gandhi's assistant wrote about their dialogue. Thurman asked, "How are we to train individuals or communities in this difficult art?" Gandhi replied, "Through living the creed in your life which must be a living sermon." And in his most famous message to Thurman, Gandhi declared, "It may be through the Negroes that the unadulterated message of non-violence will be delivered to the world."[11] Decades later Bayard Rustin reported that when he and Martin Luther King Jr. left the founding meeting of the Southern Christian Leadership Conference (SCLC) in 1957, they discussed this "prophetic statement" by Gandhi.[12] And, with the help of a mass movement, they struggled to make it true.

After his meeting with Gandhi, Thurman continued his travels in South Asia and experienced a vision while gazing at the Khyber Pass from Pakistan. Being a student of mysticism and already profoundly moved by his meeting with Gandhi, Thurman was open to mystical revelations. At this place of great beauty, overlooking the site of the ancient Silk Road connecting Central Asia to the Indian subcontinent, Thurman was overcome with the power of history and religion. It was there that Thurman and his wife "knew that we must test whether a religious fellowship could be developed in America that was capable

FIGURE 4.1 Howard Thurman, Sue Bailey Thurman, Phenola Carroll, and Edward G. Carroll in India, 1935. Credit: Howard Thurman and Sue Bailey Thurman Collections, Howard Gotlieb Archival Research Center at Boston University.

of cutting across all racial barriers, with a carry-over into the common life, a fellowship that would alter the behavior patterns of those involved."[13] He spent the rest of the decade searching for this opportunity and seeking to make his religious leadership at Howard University a model of ecumenical and mystical fellowship.

Upon his return to the United States in 1936, Thurman became increasingly frustrated with the limits of liberal interracialism. Writing to John Nevin Sayre, then serving as chairman of FOR, he criticized the Commission for Interracial Cooperation (CIC) and liberal "church groups" for their gradualism. "They are trying by slow processes of education and cultivation to bring about reconciliation and harmony," Thurman complained.[14] But in his experience, these were not enough. Thurman had encountered the CIC while at Morehouse. Writing years later, he remembered one of their meetings: "At the end of the morning session, I was beside myself with disgust. It seemed to me to be a waste of time and I could not accept the honesty and

FIGURE 4.2 Sue Bailey Thurman and Mahatma Gandhi, 1936. Credit: Howard Thurman and Sue Bailey Thurman Collections, Howard Gotlieb Archival Research Center at Boston University.

integrity of the Southern white people at the meeting."[15] Thurman embraced aspects of liberal interracialism, particularly the use of education and institution building. But he sought to quicken the pace of change by challenging the segregated churches he encountered nationwide.

Thurman spread Gandhi's message of nonviolence and his own commitment to interracialism through speaking tours after his trip to India. He regularly left Howard's campus in the 1930s and early 1940s to travel to Philadelphia where he became a frequent visitor to Philadelphia's Fellowship House as a guest preacher and adviser.[16] He and Marjorie Penney, who became a close friend, even corresponded about the possibility of him taking a permanent position at the Fellowship House and running a new Fellowship Church. Writing in 1942 after a visit, Penney said, "Certainly the congregation was deeply impressed with your words. . . . Believe me, if and when the Fellowship Church becomes more than a series of services, we shall be seriously thinking of what you said regarding your interest in it."[17] Although Fellowship House never created an established church, Penney's vision served as a model of how Thurman might fulfill his Khyber Pass epiphany in his own church.

In 1940 Thurman was unanimously selected by FOR leadership to be one of its three vice chairmen, a recognition of his increased prominence in pacifist circles and FOR's growing interest in race relations.[18] During the early 1940s, he frequently spoke and wrote about his visit to India, spreading the teachings of Gandhi and enthralling his large audiences. Gandhi and Thurman became so closely linked that in a 1942 *Pittsburgh Courier* article, journalist Peter Dana reported, "He is perhaps one of the few Black men in this country around whom a great, conscious, national movement of Negroes could be built, not unlike the great Indian movement with which Gandhi and Nehru are associated."[19] Soon an invitation to lead an interracial church allowed Thurman a partial expression of this vision.

San Francisco

It was Howard Thurman's relationship with A. J. Muste that led him to accept the co-pastorate of San Francisco's Church for the Fellowship of All Peoples in 1944. In October 1943, Muste wrote to Thurman, saying he had been contacted by a progressive white minister, Alfred G. Fisk, asking for suggestions for a co-pastor of a new interracial church. Fisk also contacted Thurman directly, describing a city transformed by African American mass migration and the resettlement of Japanese Americans during World War II. "New Negroes are pouring into this area in the tens of thousands; tension rising to the breaking point," wrote Fisk. He also alerted Muste that fellow pacifist Bayard Rustin, who had recently helped organize CORE, was in the city working on desegregation efforts. "Bayard Rustin has also been here for a month directing a group, in which I have participated, in the use of non-violent direct action in situations of race tension."[20] Rustin's campaign focused on the desegregation of recreational facilities in the city, bringing the tactics of Gandhian nonviolent direct action to the West Coast.[21] Because of his responsibilities at Howard, Thurman could not immediately accept the position of assistant pastorate. But his correspondence with Fisk continued, and he began preparations to take up the challenge. Fisk was impatient but hopeful. "San Francisco," he wrote in November 1943, "is doomed if you do not come!"[22]

Also in San Francisco working with Rustin in 1943 was a "female collective" of white women who formed a pacifist community based on the teachings of a white British activist, Muriel Lester. Lester had spent a significant amount of time with Gandhi and was a leader in the International Fellowship of Reconciliation. She was a charismatic figure who disseminated Gandhi's teachings widely and helped popularize a more aggressive and engaged pacifist politics. Writing in 1940, Lester argued: "Our business is to stop war, to purify the world, to get it saved from poverty *and* riches, to make people like each other, to heal the sick, and comfort the sad, to wake up those who have not yet found God, to create joy and beauty wherever we go, to find God in everything and in everyone."[23] She carried out this work in her London settlement house, Kingsley Hall, which historian Seth Koven describes as "a utopian enterprise deeply rooted in the gritty materiality of slum life, not some Arcadian flight into an ideal world of their own making."[24] Because of his alliance and friendship with Lester, when Gandhi visited London in 1931, he chose to stay at Kingsley Hall. In San Francisco, a group of women sought to replicate Lester's experiment by creating a communal pacifist enclave.

The Lester acolytes became known as the Sakai group, after they took the home of a Japanese American family who had been relocated to an internment camp. Like the Harlem Ashram during the same period, the Sakai group reached out to their African American neighbors, who had replaced the relocated Japanese, and began to hold informal religious services. Thurman remembered, "They sought to share a common life among these Negroes and to help them with their individual and collective needs."[25] Given that California generally was a hotbed of utopianism—for example, having the largest number of white Divinites—it is not surprising that the Sakai group found fertile ground in San Francisco. In fact, it was the Sakai women who contacted Fisk about creating an Interracial Fellowship Church, most likely through their shared affiliation with FOR.[26] Once the church opened its doors, the Sakai group was among its most active members.

Fisk agreed to take on the project and began his recruitment of Thurman. In the meantime, he invited a Black minister, Albert Cleage Jr., to be his assistant pastor. Cleage had been recommended by the Black sociologist Charles S. Johnson. But from the beginning, Cleage, who went on to be the pastor of the Shrine of the Black Madonna Church in Detroit, was an uneasy fit. Cleage's emerging Black Nationalism made him uncomfortable with the liberal interracialism of the church. Historian Angela Dillard notes, "Cleage saw an artificiality in the style and substance of fellowship worship and a lack of concrete involvement in social problems." But Cleage did incorporate some of Thurman's teachings on spirituality in his evolving Black liberation theology. "In a Thurmanesque move," explains Dillard, "Cleage came to see the experience of God and love as the basis of revolutionary transformation and a program of self- and communal actualization as ultimately more important than institutional strategy and tactics."[27] Cleage was also impressed by the church's support for CORE's San Francisco nonviolent direct-action campaigns under Rustin's leadership. "They brought a freshness of spirit and a sincerity of conviction which made of Fellowship something more than just another church," he wrote in 1944. However, his general unease with the interracial project led him to leave only six months after his arrival.[28]

Only days after Cleage's departure, Thurman, his wife, Sue Baily Thurman, and their two daughters arrived in the city. Before leaving Washington, DC, Thurman led a major fundraising campaign for the church that culminated in a farewell dinner with Eleanor Roosevelt in attendance.[29] Roosevelt was a supporter of the Delta and Providence farms, Highlander, FOR, and the Fellowship Church. Thurman immediately sought to apply his theological and social ideals to the church, which he saw as "a creative experiment in interracial and in cultural communion, deriving its inspiration from a spiritual interpretation of the meaning of life and the dignity of man."[30] Initially the church served the surrounding neighborhood, which was primarily made up of African American migrants—indeed, it was known as the "Neighborhood Church." But after moving twice to accommodate the growing congregation, in 1949 they settled in a relatively large building on Larkin Street, where the church remains today. The initial congregation numbered only thirty; five years later, two hundred congregants attended the weekly services.[31] In addition to the two pastors, an interracial committee with three whites, three African Americans, two Japanese, and one Chinese oversaw church affairs. Together they drafted "The Declaration," a statement of principle that read, in part, "The Church for the Fellowship of All Peoples is a creative venture in interracial, intercultural, and interdenominational communion. It believes that human dignity is inherent in man as a creature of God, and it interprets the meaning of human life as essentially spiritual."[32] The rapid growth of the Fellowship Church suggests this ecumenical message found fertile ground in San Francisco.

Although initially a branch of the Presbyterian Church, which was Fisk's denomination, in 1945 the Fellowship Church became entirely independent. This required them to rely on a broad network of members-at-large for financial support. Thurman made a particular point to not accept funds from white philanthropic foundations, not wanting the church to be viewed as an object of white charity. Therefore, most of the funding came from like-minded Christian socialists, pacifists, and civil rights activists. By 1952 the list of at-large members who supported the church had grown to over one thousand, including Mary McLeod Bethune, Pauli Murray, Josephine Baker, A. J. Muste, and other leading pacifists and civil rights activists.[33] The church's non-affiliation with any established denomination, then, helped spread the message of fellowship to a large group of like-minded reformers.

As the church grew, its programs became increasingly experimental. While still at Howard University, Thurman had developed liturgical forms that he hoped would help connect congregants with a spiritual force that united humanity. He began services with a half hour of silent meditation, a practice that reflected the teachings of Rufus Jones and other mystics, as well

as Eastern religious teachings. The church also set aside a room for meditation, supplied with books and figures from a variety of religious traditions.[34]
At Howard, Thurman experimented with using alternative forms of worship
such as reproducing living tableaus of religious paintings and incorporating
modern dance interpretations of spiritual teachings into services. He brought
these practices with him to San Francisco and encouraged his congregants
to explore the aesthetics of spirituality beyond reading scripture or studying traditional theology. The church also boasted an interracial choir and a
traveling theater to spread these ideas throughout the San Francisco area.
And every summer they held a "children's workshop in international living,"
essentially a summer camp for interracial ecumenical worship.[35] Congregants
also met in private homes to study mysticism and the teachings of Gandhi,
and the church held a weekly discussion group for young people.[36] Like Father
Divine, Thurman's goal was to create an environment in which congregants
could experience mysticism and the presence of God outside the constraints
of mainstream Protestantism.

The church summarized its beliefs in a document called "The Commitment," first drafted in 1944 and revised three additional times. It read, in part:

> I affirm my need for a growing understanding of all men as sons of God, and seek
> after a vital interpretation of God as revealed in Jesus of Nazareth whose fellowship
> with God was the foundation of his fellowship with men. I desire to have a part in the
> unfolding of the ideal of Christian fellowship through the union of men and women
> of varying national, cultural, racial, or creedal heritage in Church communion.
> I desire the strength of corporate worship through membership in this Church for the
> Fellowship of All Peoples with the imperative of personal dedication to the working
> out of God's purposes here and in all places.[37]

Here the emphasis was on fellowship and brotherhood, the full equality of
women and men under God. Given the diversity of congregants, which included Mexican, Chinese, and Filipino immigrants, Thurman and Fisk always
emphasized the theme of unity and brotherhood. "Such unity has taken place
here," they wrote in a 1944 fundraising letter, "that individuals in the church
community are not conscious of race or nationality distinctions except when
called upon to articulate contributions or interpret problems pertaining to a
particular group." Events such as the monthly all-Fellowship dinners sought
to celebrate a "composite experience of the life of the group."[38] Church members did not believe in the literal absence of race, as did Father Divine, but
they worked toward a similar goal of full equality and brotherhood.

Thus, through church ritual and writings, Thurman sought to spread a message of love and fellowship. Muriel Lester, who knew Thurman well and helped prepare him for his trip to South Asia, wrote in 1937: "There is nothing more illumining, more ennobling, than to be one of a company of people who have come together in order to free their spirit from entangling personal bonds, quiet their soul by silence, release their aspiration by music and poetry, concentrate their mind on spoken wisdom, open their heart to all that is good, true, and beautiful, thus to tune themselves to God and to come into touch with Jesus Christ."[39] The interracial church's services sought to bring this experience to many. "I believe that the elimination of barriers between man and man," wrote one admirer, "and the freedom from denominational bias in Fellowship Church have prepared the way for more effective access to God."[40] This was more of a spiritual than an overtly political message, but it was a spirituality conducive to building a broad civil rights coalition as it celebrated full equality and brotherhood.

Curious reformers and activists routinely visited the Fellowship Church, often becoming part of a growing network of affiliates who did not live in the city. In 1945, for example, W. E. B. Du Bois visited and spoke at the church while in the city for a United Nations conference on the topic "The World Peace and the Darker Peoples." Soon after, he devoted his "Winds of Time" column in the *Chicago Defender* to praising the work that Thurman was doing. Mordecai Johnson, Thurman's former boss at Howard University and a frequent speaker at Philadelphia's Fellowship House, traveled to the West Coast and preached at the Fellowship Church in 1945. Josephine Baker, the performer and international civil rights activist, also visited, as did the South African novelist Alan Paton.[41] The international nature of this support reflected the global scope of pacifism and the Christian Left. These dignitaries could also follow news of the Fellowship Church in the press, which was fascinated with this interracial experiment. *Time* magazine did a major story on the church in 1948, and other major publications, including *Ebony* and *Life*, followed with feature articles.[42]

On the local level, the church became a hub and a resource for labor and civil rights organizations. Thurman, for example, attended and spoke at the constitutional convention of the Cooks and Stewards Union International, and he worked with the San Francisco Labor School. A "Community Bulletin" newsletter published at the church reported on NAACP and CORE campaigns as well as neighborhood study groups and lectures. In 1944, for example, the bulletin urged congregants to work closely with the NAACP to investigate restrictive covenants, agreements on housing deeds that restricted the sale or rental of property only to whites. The church also helped to mobilize a crowd of two thousand to attend A. Philip Randolph's 1944 speech in the city. In his speech, Randolph denounced segregation and called for the formation of cooperatives, positions supported by the church. And in the early 1950s, the church actively promoted FOR and CORE's "Brotherhood Month," which encouraged individuals to "demonstrate" their "belief in brotherhood by at least one new act that challenges the pattern of segregation and discrimination."[43] Therefore, although the church did not train activists in the same way as Highlander or Brookwood, they did actively support progressive causes in the 1940s and beyond.

In addition to fighting racial segregation and discrimination, the church was eager to work with Japanese Americans as they returned to the city after internment. Given the history of the Sakai house and the fact that the church's first location was in a former Japanese Presbyterian church, Thurman and Fisk were compelled to aid these victims of discrimination. They made the church a hub for Japanese Americans to obtain employment and housing after losing so much during the war. And the president of the Japanese American Citizens League was an early member of the church board of trustees after returning from internment.[44] Thurman recalled that during his time in San Francisco, "It was not infrequent that one saw billboard caricatures of the Japanese: grotesque faces, huge buck teeth, large dark-rimmed thick-lensed eyeglasses. The point was, in effect, to read the Japanese out of the human race."[45] He sought to challenge these stereotypes and offer a safe haven for the persecuted.

As a Black minister, Thurman found serving his white congregants could prove problematic in a segregated city. Segregated hospitals often barred Thurman from visiting white congregants. And he had difficulties holding funeral services at white cemeteries.[46] An integrated congregation was often in conflict with a segregated city, and the obstacles Thurman encountered in his ministry reflected this reality.

As it grew in popularity, the Fellowship Church spawned imitators in several cities. Homer A. Jack, a white Unitarian minister and one of CORE's founding members, declared "the emergence of the interracial church" by 1947.[47] In Detroit the white Unitarian minister Ellsworth M. Smith opened an interracial Church of All Peoples in 1945. In addition to the Detroit church, Jack cited the Fellowship House's religious services in Philadelphia and its imitators in Baltimore, New York, and Washington, DC. Congregational churches in Berkeley and Chicago were also explicitly interracial. Another large church, and the one most resembling Thurman's congregation, was the Church of All Peoples in Los Angeles. Like Thurman's church, this congregation was located in a former Japanese church, vacated by its parishioners due to internment. Its founder, Dan B. Genung, wrote to Thurman upon hearing that he accepted the position in San Francisco. "Our primary motive," wrote

Genung, "is to build a church, where all men can worship together as broth-ers."[48] Homer A. Jack, however, wanted these churches to promote pacifists' political program as well providing a space for interracial fellowship. "For while the interracial church is a critic of the white or the Negro church," concluded Jack, "to function in a sustained manner it must also be a critic of the capitalistic church, the militaristic church, the isolationist church, the secular church."[49] These connections, from spirituality to the social world, would push the Fellowship movement from liberal interracialism toward utopian interracialism in the postwar years.

"An Activator of Activists"

Like other liberal interracialists, Thurman stopped short of direct involve-ment with more radical movement activity. The Fellowship Church was never used for nonviolent direct-action training, and Thurman was not involved in formal labor and political campaigns, although he encouraged congregants to be educated on these issues. But he had a profound impact on the long civil rights movement, nonetheless. In a 1978 *Ebony* profile, famed journal-ist Lerone Bennett argued that Thurman "was *more than* an activist, he was an activator of activists a mover of movers."[50] This dynamic began with his work at Howard University, where he became a mentor for some of the leading movement figures. Prentice Thomas, who ran the Delta Cooperative Farm for many years, was a student at Howard and worked closely with Thurman. In 1938 Thurman recommended him to Sherwood Eddy for the position at the farm. A co-founder of CORE, James Farmer, launched his activist career at FOR after Thurman recommended him to John Nevin Sayre.[51] Although Thur-man was not directly engaged in CORE's nonviolent campaigns, he strongly supported them, showing none of the skepticism and criticism of more mod-erate civil rights leaders and organizations. And his popularization of Gandhi proved crucial to CORE's early work.

Pauli Murray also studied with Thurman at Howard, and the two became close friends, corresponding often. When Murray and fellow female Howard students launched a series of sit-ins in 1943 and 1944, for example, Thurman stood firmly behind them.[52] And when the university's administrators refused to support the students, Murray went to Thurman for "spiritual guidance." He advised her, "A characteristic of evil is that we never fully destroy it. When we beat it down in one place, it pops up in another."[53] Murray continued to seek support and advice from Thurman throughout her long career, and her decision to be ordained as an Episcopal priest later in life reflected her ad-miration and engagement with Thurman's theological teachings.

After Thurman's widely publicized 1935 trip to India, he influenced Black and white activists beyond the university through his lectures and writing. Bernice Fisher, a white woman from Rochester, New York, contacted Thurman in 1943 after working with James Farmer and Bayard Rustin to establish CORE in Chicago. She, like so many, sought advice on how to most effectively use Gandhi's teachings on nonviolent direct action in the American context. Another white co-founder of CORE, George Houser, corresponded with Thurman about CORE's work. In 1945 Thurman agreed to serve on CORE's advisory board, writing, "I think that the fundamental program to which CORE is dedicated is of primary importance, both for democracy and for Christianity." In this correspondence, as well as in his writing, Thurman strongly endorsed nonviolent direct action. He continued to advise CORE activists, including Bayard Rustin, into the 1960s.[54]

Thurman's most profound impact on the long civil rights movement, however, was his best-selling book, *Jesus and the Disinherited*, which he wrote while serving as pastor of the Church of All Peoples. This work was by far Thurman's most popular; one historian calls it a "midcentury classic" and another a "manual for resistance."[55] Thurman wrote this short and elegant book as a response to the South Asian Muslims and Hindus who challenged him to explain how he could reconcile Christianity with racial oppression and segregation. Drawing from his work at the Fellowship Church, he concluded that "the segregated church as such was a reaction response to the environment, and not inherent in the genius of the Christian faith itself."[56] He urged readers to follow the life of Jesus, who was marginalized in his own time but reacted to that injustice with love, not anger. "If we dare take the position that in Jesus there was at work some radical destiny," argued Thurman, "it would be safe to say that in his poverty he was more truly Son of man than he would have been if the incident of family or birth had made him a rich son of Israel." And most significantly, Jesus "was a member of a minority group in the midst of a larger dominant and controlling group." By making "the love-ethic central," Jesus had a clear message for others who are disinherited, including African Americans. "They must recognize fear, deception, hatred, each for what it is," explained Thurman. "Once having done this, they must learn how to destroy these or to render themselves immune to their domination."[57] Thurman's message spoke directly to those activists facing the hatred of white supremacy while attempting to enact radical change.

Thurman's most impactful reader was Martin Luther King Jr., who encountered the book in his second year at Crozer Theological Seminary, near Philadelphia. This was 1949, just before he heard Mordecai Johnson's sermon at the Fellowship House and began reading Gandhi and his interpreters. King drew on Thurman's work in preparing sermons and speeches throughout his career.[58] He also developed a personal friendship with the theologian. In fact, Thurman had attended Morehouse College with King's father, Martin Luther King Sr. and remained friends with the family after graduation. When Thurman left San Francisco and moved to Boston, where King was completing his doctoral work at Boston University, the two formed a close relationship, reportedly watching baseball together as well as engaging in theological discussions.[59] After his departure for Montgomery, King returned often to *Jesus and the Disinherited* for guidance, reportedly keeping a tattered copy of the book with him at all times during the height of the civil rights movement. As the movement ballooned, Thurman and King corresponded regularly throughout all the major civil rights campaigns.[60]

Thurman's friendship with King blossomed when Thurman left his San Francisco pastorate to become Dean of the Chapel at Boston University. It was the tenth anniversary of the church's founding and a promising moment for the civil rights movement. Thurman felt that his work in San Francisco had neared a natural end and was ready to take on a new challenge. "By 1954 not only was the United Nations established and at work on many of its problems," wrote Thurman in his autobiography, "but in that very year a scant sixty days before the celebration of our Tenth Anniversary, the historic decision of the United States Supreme Court on integration in public education was handed down. All of this is to indicate that the origin and development of Fellowship Church were part of a world-wide ferment of which many people were increasingly aware."[61] Thurman had succeeded in creating the church he first envisioned while gazing at the Khyber Pass nearly two decades before. And he was optimistic that this vision of racial equality was resonating on a global scale.

Thurman hoped that the Fellowship Church would help create a unified society. "The degree to which in our deliberative living of life as individuals and as groups that we are able to project in our religion the kind of wholeness and synthesis that the experience of the living God implies, we shall become like Him and our world will be whole, free, one."[62] But despite his influence on the movement, he was also hesitant to directly engage white supremacy, arguing that "a heavy-handed attack against those who harbor prejudice will achieve no good purpose and will probably do great harm." Instead, he continued to rely on a form of liberal interracialism, emphasizing education and moral suasion. "Prejudice yields most readily when prejudiced people are brought together in friendly and natural ways under religious auspices," wrote Thurman in 1946.[63] But Thurman's teachings were deeply influential in the Christian Left and sustained a generation of activists, particularly those in CORE, as they developed a new set of tactics to defeat segregation. And the people of San Francisco continued to support the church Thurman helped build long after he left for Boston. Indeed, it remains today, serving an interracial congregation in a city that has become a global symbol of inequality.

Pendle Hill

Three years before Thurman met with Gandhi, a young white Quaker woman made a much shorter trip, which had a similar revelatory outcome. In 1932 Marjorie Penney traveled from Philadelphia to Pendle Hill, a Quaker school and retreat center outside of the city where Howard Thurman studied with Rufus Jones. She was invited by a friend she had met in college. "I was very foggy about the purpose of going there," remembered Penney years later. "I did know that a weekend in the country sounded good."[64] In fact, this was the second interracial youth conference convened by a group of elderly white Quaker women who reached out to a progressive white minister, Dr. Fred Wentzel of the Evangelical Lutheran Church, and several Black ministers in Philadelphia to organize the event. Prior to the Pendle Hill meeting, dozens of Black and white youths had met monthly to survey and discuss Philadelphia's racial problems.[65] They brought these stories to the rural retreat. "It was traumatic," remembered Penney. "I've never been the same since. I heard and met blacks whom I shared a city with and about whom I knew less than nothing tell about what it was like to grow up black in Philadelphia."[66] Pendle Hill was Penney's Khyber Pass, where she came to the realization that she must dedicate the rest of her life to the cause of interracial fellowship.

At Pendle Hill, remembered Penney, "they talked to one another," much as the Brookwooders and Highlanders did at their retreats. Penney returned to her home having "decided that 'City of Brotherly Love' was the worst possible name for a city thoroughly Jim Crow and badly segmented along a lot of other racial and religious and nationality lines."[67] After the meeting the activists formed the Young People's Interracial Fellowship, now directed by Penney, and worked to find a Philadelphia church where they could hold their discussion meetings. However, the established denominations repeatedly rebuffed the fellowshippers. They finally located a worn-down hotel to hold biweekly meetings, which they did from 1931 to 1941.[68] In 1941 the fellowshippers located and purchased a permanent home at 1431 Brown Street, a "contact neighborhood" between Black and white communities in the growing city, similar to the Fellowship Church's San Francisco location. This Fellowship House became a center of political mobilization and prefigurative practices

FIGURE 4.3 Marjorie Penney, c. 1946. Philadelphia Award Records. Digital Library record 451. Credit: Reproduced with permission from the Historical Society of Pennsylvania.

into the late twentieth century. "In its higher stage of development," declared one 1955 report on the Fellowship House movement, "it further stresses the idea and practice of starting with oneself, and with the Fellowship group it-self, as a living demonstration to the community that this approach is good and works." The Fellowship Houses became experiments in utopian life, living their future hopes in the present. "It has developed the 'Fellowship' concept to a point where to many of its staff and most active membership it has be-come a total way of life—an experiment in family and community living and of relating oneself more meaningfully to people in all kinds of situations."[69] Fellowshippers embodied the change they sought to create and built the com-munity they hoped to foster.

Philadelphia's Fellowship House is remembered primarily for its role in shaping Martin Luther King Jr.'s intellectual development by introducing him to the works of Gandhi. It was there in 1950 that he listened to a sermon by Mordecai Johnson, the president of Howard University who had hired How-ard Thurman. "His message was so profound and electrifying," remembered King, "that I left the meeting and bought a half-dozen books on Gandhi's life

FIGURE 4.4 Fellowship House Seder, 1944. Philadelphia Record Photograph Morgue [V07]. Digital Library record 12097. Credit: Reproduced with permission from the Historical Society of Pennsylvania.

and works."[70] But there was more to that encounter than a passive student listening to an illustrious Black leader. After Johnson's talk, King and other seminary students followed him into the Fellowship House dining room, where the group sat and talked until midnight.[71] Having a physical space, a home, to meet and work through ideas and strategies was a key role for Fellowship Houses. It was what Highlander offered in Tennessee, Father Divine in New York's Promised Land, the Delta and Providence cooperative farms in Mississippi, and Brookwood in New York.

It is also telling that King spent time in the Fellowship House sharing food with fellow students. The Fellowship House was known for feeding masses of visitors. In 1946 alone, they fed more than five hundred monthly at the house.[72] "Breaking bread together," argued the organizers, "is a powerful help in drawing people across racial barriers."[73] It's possible that Father Divine influenced this linking of food and fellowship. During the 1940s, fellowshippers frequented Father Divine's Philadelphia banquets and restaurants.[74] The power of plentiful food in fellowship was clearly a lesson they learned well.

This space of sociability was also an educational institution for young activists and reformers. A 1950 pamphlet listed all the ways in which the Fellowship House served as "a training center for social justice," "a training center for democratic living," "a training center for the fight against prejudice and discrimination and for equal rights and equal opportunities," and "a training center for making Brotherhood real in American life."[75] Fellowship House training went beyond the education espoused by racial liberals, although it did not go as far as the direct-action campaigns pioneered by Father Divine, FOR, and CORE. Historian Matthew Countryman writes that Fellowship House's "emphasis on intergroup dialogue and study was rooted in the liberal Protestant belief that the roots of prejudice lay in ignorance and that education was the key to building intergroup harmony and understanding."[76] However, it would be a mistake to dismiss this training as mere education, not only for its impact on King, but for its national reach and the range of programs that its activists organized. Many of these activities predated the 1941 establishment of the house, but that space accelerated what fellowshippers could accomplish. In the first year of Fellowship House alone, Penney and her African American associate director, Gladys Rawlins, estimated that more than six thousand people had made use of the space.[77] Some of those individuals were key to the launching of a mass civil rights movement.

Fellowship House resembled another interracial movement for justice with an undercurrent of religious commitment. In 1938 Catherine de Hueck, a Russian émigré and Catholic convert, opened Friendship House in Harlem. Her first Friendship House was in Toronto and served working-class immigrants in that city. De Hueck was also a frequent speaker on the Chautauqua circuit, which offered middle-class audiences religious and intellectual lectures, and she had grown increasingly troubled by American race relations in her travels. She frequently criticized Catholic institutions, particularly universities and hospitals, for their segregation policies. Her Harlem Friendship House served primarily as a study center for Black Catholics, staffed by white volunteers. It contained a library, donated clothing and other goods, and had a childcare facility. Staffers also worked to document incidents of racial discrimination, lobbied for civil rights legislation, and participated in demonstrations. They tested existing anti-discrimination laws by having interracial groups eat at restaurants and reporting those that refused to serve them. This testing was a method the Fellowship House staffers would also deploy. But the voluntary poverty that Friendship House workers adopted, like that of the Catholic Worker Movement, was not attractive to many Blacks, whose experience with poverty was decidedly not voluntary.[78]

In 1941 the renowned Catholic thinker Thomas Merton heard de Hueck

lecture at Saint Bonaventure University and subsequently visited Harlem's
Friendship House. "She had a strong voice, and strong convictions, and strong
things to say," remembered Merton, "and she was saying them in the sim-
plest, most unvarnished, bluntest possible kind of talk, and with such uncompromising directness that it stunned."[79] Merton's descriptions of de Hueck's
work reached a large audience when he published *The Seven Storey Mountain* in 1948. Dorothy Day also kept in touch with de Hueck and admired the
work she was doing. Unlike Day's Catholic Worker houses of hospitality, the
Friendship Houses engaged in more overt civil rights work similar to Penney's Fellowship Houses. De Hueck opened a third Friendship House in Chicago in 1942, but left that city soon after to a retreat in rural Canada. A small
number of new houses emerged in the early 1950s, but de Hueck's movement
never had the reach of Penney's Fellowship Houses. For some white Catholics
like de Hueck and Protestants like Penney, establishing a physical center in
African American or mixed neighborhoods was a key way to promote liberal
interracialism. The Fellowship House movement, however, also proved a vital training ground for civil rights activists.

Training for Action

The Philadelphia Fellowship House's primary training group was Units for
Unity, which offered comprehensive courses for activists "so that they may
work effectively in the community relations field and build racial and religious understanding."[80] This group offered a series of eight lectures three
times per year, which proved enormously popular from their outset in 1941.
In 1945, for example, two hundred Philadelphians signed up for the courses,
and sixty of those became active members of the Fellowship House.[81] By 1950
fellowshippers estimated that "thousands of people, both young and old, have
learned the techniques of democracy and have gone back to their own neighborhoods . . . and have helped their neighbors to understand the importance
of regarding one another as equals regardless of race, color, or creed." To further this goal, the Units for Unity distributed thousands of Fellowship House
pamphlets, as well as printed material from other organizations. Similar to
Myles Horton's philosophy at Highlander, organizers focused these efforts
on empowering ordinary people to take on issues of racial and religious discrimination in their communities. "Fellowship believes that commonplace
people can be strong fighters for racial and religious justice," they argued
in 1946, "if they are trained." Philadelphia's Fellowship House was known
as a "laboratory in racial and religious understanding." The Units for Unity
courses were the primary vehicle for that experimentation.[82]

Much of this training happened within the house, which contained a Fellowship Library and also served as the rehearsal space for the Fellowship players. Like the Brookwood Labor Players during the Great Depression, the Fellowship players traveled throughout the 1930s, 1940s, and 1950s to present works on racial harmony. They began this work in 1933, while fellowshippers were still without a permanent building. Singing City, a Fellowship House innovation, played a similar role, bringing interracial choirs to numerous houses of worship, much as the San Francisco Fellowship Church did on the West Coast. Fellowshippers declared that the choirs were "designed to promote brotherhood and understanding through singing songs of democracy." By the early 1950s, multiple choirs performed dozens of concerts citywide every year. Temple University teamed up with the Fellowship House to offer a degree in choral conducting to Singing City students. In order to be eligible as a Singing City choir, groups had to be interracial and "believe they must play a part in the steady growth of democracy." At its height in the 1940s and 1950s, the success of this message was apparent as the Philadelphia Fellowship House boasted two thousand members, individuals who had completed the Units for Unity training course and contributed time and money to the organization.[83]

Those who successfully completed the Fellowship House training often joined a large speakers' bureau, consisting of over one hundred people by 1943. These women and men gave hundreds of speeches every year and often traveled outside the city to speak in communities nationwide. They generally worked in "trios," with one African American, one white Protestant, and one Jewish speaker. The Fellowship House also targeted young children with a doll program, where dolls of different nationalities visited local schools and community centers accompanied by a doll "librarian."[84] All of these educational endeavors reflected the racial liberalism of the 1940s, which focused on education and moral suasion to persuade white Americans that Black people were worthy and deserving of full citizenship rights. Such liberal interracialism could have an impact on a small scale, but depended on the belief that gradual change would eventually lead to racial equality.

But the Fellowship House pushed at the boundaries of liberal interracialism by engaging in overt political work. Well before Penney opened the permanent house, the fellowshippers launched lobbying campaigns in Pennsylvania's capital of Harrisburg and in Washington, DC. Much of this work was done by the Cooperative Council, which sent out Fellowship House representatives to other civil rights organizations and coordinated lobbying campaigns. They were "cooperative" in the sense of working with national and local agencies. From its inception, the fellowshippers also worked closely with the NAACP and the more radical National Negro Congress (NNC) to coordinate their campaigns. Starting in 1934, fellowshippers' major focus was testing Pennsylvania's Civil Rights Bill by investigating restaurants, theaters, and other public accommodations. This was a tactic that the Catholic activists in Harlem's Friendship House also deployed. The NAACP used the evidence they gathered to file civil rights cases. This testing stopped short of nonviolent direct action; fellowshippers retreated when confronted, but it was the first crucial step in what would develop as the primary civil rights strategy to address public accommodation segregation by the 1940s. Fellowshippers also assisted the state legislature in carrying out community surveys on "the urban Negro" starting in 1940.[85] Indeed, the Cooperative Council became a touchpoint when there was a crisis in race relations in the city, given their extensive contacts. In 1940, for example, they came to the aid of hundreds of African Americans whom police arrested on charges of being "suspicious characters."[86]

The testing of public accommodations for compliance to Pennsylvania law in the mid-1930s escalated in the 1940s. By that point CORE and the Father Divine movement were using nonviolent direct action in Philadelphia and other cities. A major focus of this work was recreational facilities, particularly swimming pools, which remained segregated in Philadelphia in the mid-twentieth century. In the summer of 1954, for example, fellowshippers repeatedly tested Boulevard Pools, setting up a case for the ACLU to prosecute.[87] As these cases proliferated, activists created the Committee on Integration in Recreation and started to branch out to other facilities. In the case of bowling alleys and skating rinks, activists carried out the "sandwich" method of testing. A small group of whites would enter first, followed by a group of African Americans, and ending with another group of whites. Often the manager denied entry to Black testers, saying all the lanes were taken at the bowling alley or the rink was too crowded. If they then allowed white testers to enter, this discrimination provided valuable evidence for lawyers. In the winter of 1954–55, for example, the committee tested eight bowling alleys, three of which discriminated against the Black groups. This evidence was given to the Commission on Human Relations, the city agency responsible for enforcing civil rights statutes. High school students were particularly enthusiastic about the testing, which could be entertaining as well as politically relevant. They targeted rinks on nights that had formally been restricted only to whites, showing up in large integrated numbers to skate.[88]

In addition to aiding legal cases, fellowshippers organized marches and pickets. In 1935, for example, fellowshippers worked with the NAACP to organize a mass meeting against lynching. In 1937 Penney traveled with Dorothy

Bristol to Washington, DC, to lobby Congress and deliver the many signatures they had collected on anti-lynching petitions. The anti-lynching mass meetings became an annual event, and the Fellowship Houses continued to lobby for an anti-lynching bill well into the postwar period.[89] Fellowshippers also frequently traveled to Washington, DC, to march in civil rights protests. In 1948, for example, they demonstrated against the separation of African American blood in the nation's blood banks. While in the nation's capital, they lobbied for the continuation of national Fair Employment Practices Committee and for the passage of an anti-lynching bill.[90]

Fellowshippers were part of a larger network of activists on the Christian Left advocating for greater racial and class equality. Like many other reformers, Marjorie Penney traveled to Mississippi to spend a summer at the Delta Cooperative Farm in 1937. Howard Kester had sent the fellowshippers an appeal to help the Southern Tenants Farmers' Union (STFU) in 1935, and they responded enthusiastically. Penney was clearly curious about the interracial experiment and sought to learn more about its operation. After her Mississippi trip, the Fellowship House eagerly participated in "national sharecroppers week," a fundraising effort to support the STFU. Writing to a cooperative member after returning home, Penney noted, "Racial prejudice—of a sort I have never imagined—is the common order of affairs. Against this background, the Fellowship seems more important than ever before."[91] Penney's work at Delta shaped her desire not only to pursue fellowship in Philadelphia, but to support the sharecroppers in the Deep South.

Closer to home, the Fellowship House worked with city agencies to foster racial peace in the city, particularly during the volatile World War II years. This work was emblematic of the moderate interracial commissions that characterized racial liberalism in the 1940s. In Philadelphia the most significant of these was the Fellowship Commission, made up of the Jewish Community Relations Council, Fellowship House, the Philadelphia Council of Churches, and the Friends Committee on Race Relations. Over the next two decades, numerous other cooperating agencies joined this effort to foster positive intergroup relations and racial peace.[92] The Fellowship Commission's work reflected a broader, international effort on the part of the Federal Council of Churches (FCC), which called for nonsegregated churches in 1946 and used international human rights discourse to challenge domestic racism. But, unlike the Fellowship House, the FCC refused to work with CORE and radical pacifists.[93] Similarly, the Fellowship Commission's focus on education and forestalling conflict limited its effectiveness in advancing racial equality. Ecumenical Protestants' reform efforts reflected liberal interracialism and did not embrace the more radical direct-action campaigns of utopian interracialists. The Fellowship House and San Francisco's Fellowship Church stood in the middle of these two poles, assisting more radical activists by providing space and resources while not actively participating in their tactics until the 1950s.

One reflection of how mainstream liberal interracialism had become by World War II was Hollywood's embrace of its rhetoric. In 1945 a group of young fellowshippers, mostly high school students, were in the house singing together. To their shock, Frank Sinatra appeared at the door. Sinatra was in town on business and was interested in visiting Fellowship House. He had grown up in poverty in Hoboken, New Jersey, and during the 1940s worked to advance racial tolerance and liberal causes. That same year he released a short anti-racist film, *The House I Live In*, which depicts Sinatra stopping a gang of youths from taunting a Jewish boy with stories of racial and religious tolerance and, of course, a song. The scene at the Fellowship House must have resembled the idealized film he had just released. He reportedly joined the children for a time and took a tour of the house. Sinatra also sent an $8,000 check to Marjorie Penney soon after.[94] Most of the Fellowship House visitors and speakers, however, were not as illustrious as Sinatra. Generally they were stalwarts of the Christian Left, such as A. J. Muste and Norman Thomas, who both routinely visited the Fellowship House.[95]

Fellowshippers strongly identified with the Christian Left from the inception of the group; however, by 1935 they decided to form a more explicitly religious organization, an Interracial Fellowship Church. This was launched with a sermon by Mordecai Johnson at the First Baptist Church. Penney and others were concerned that the audience would be small, but to their surprise fifteen hundred people filled the church and spilled into the surrounding streets. After that initial meeting, an interracial congregation met monthly in different churches and synagogues around Philadelphia.[96] At times fellowshippers debated setting up a separate Fellowship Church, as Howard Thurman had done in San Francisco. However, they were never able to locate a permanent building and eventually abandoned the idea, instead creating a Religious Fellowship as an offset of the Fellowship House. San Francisco's Fellowship Church was deeply influenced by the Philadelphia experiment, as were the offshoots of that church in Detroit and Los Angeles. "Howard Thurman," remembered Penney, "set up his own 'round-the-clock Black and white church and admitted very frankly it was all built on what he had seen in his visit to Philadelphia." Penney was in constant communication with Thurman, who frequently returned to Philadelphia to give sermons and strategize about how best to foster liberal interracialism.[97]

In addition to their monthly meetings at various congregations, the Religious Fellowship was engaged in overt political work. In 1957, for example, they brought a large contingent to Washington, DC, for a "prayer pilgrimage" in support of civil rights. One of the Fellowship House choirs performed at the event, which was designed to "arouse the conscience of the nation" in the wake of the Montgomery Bus Boycott. Fellowshippers instructed those accepted in the Religious Fellowship, who had completed a Units for Unity course, to form a "community unit" in their neighborhood. Approximately twenty people who met periodically to "study the community for discriminatory trends and influences in order to bring about counter-action" made up these groups.[98] "Neither a new sect for a new religion is proposed," reassured Fellowship leaders. "Rather, Religious Fellowshippers believe that a fresh understanding of the ancient Judeo-Christian tradition, plus disciplines of devotion, meditation, study, worship, and service, are needed if changed individuals are to be available for changing the community."[99] These Neighborhood Fellowships extended the reach of Fellowship House throughout the city. "Each one," reported Penney, "is a miniature of the whole religious fellowship, representing the same sort of satisfactory cross section of the community."[100] The Religious Fellowship was typical of the Fellowship movement in seeking to replicate its interracial experiments in education and worship as widely as possible.

As the movement outgrew its urban location, in 1951 fellowshippers expanded their work to a nearby farm, "to serve as a country retreat for families and training center in methods of non-violent social change." As Fellowship Houses proliferated in other cities, the original Fellowship House could only provide "one hot, crowded week each summer," to meet and train the new fellowshippers. The Fellowship Farm, 126 acres of Pennsylvania countryside, offered the retreat and training ground that the growing movement needed.[101] The activities at Fellowship Farm included daily classes, periods of meditation, manual labor, and group singing. Explaining these activities, one brochure noted, "It is a proven fact that we learn thru our hands what we never to thru our heads, so that manual labor is a part of each day." Furthermore, "real Fellowship is not dependent upon 'much speaking' but is often strengthened by silence."[102] In addition to hosting summer interns, generally students, the farm brought in activists for weeklong training, weekend workshops, or day trips. In 1956 alone, Fellowship Farm hosted four thousand visitors. Dorothy Day was one of the many activist leaders who taught at the farm, connecting her Catholic Worker Movement to fellowshippers' civil rights and pacifist work.[103] This rural retreat was yet one more protected space where Black and white reformers could meet and strategize while living out an interracial future in the present.

Radicalizing Interracialism

From the Fellowship House's inception, Penney received correspondence and visits from those seeking to replicate her experiment in other cities. To help the movement grow, the Fellowship House held an annual weeklong "house party" that brought these activists together. In 1948 they decided to create an umbrella organization, a Federation of Fellowship Houses, that would "allow them to share continually through the year the inspiration and valuable exchange of ideas."[104] Their founding document stated that "Fellowship Groups across the country are linked by a strong bond-belief in an dedication to the task of seeking out and overcoming the causes of prejudice and discrimination and creating communities in which there are opportunities and equal rights for all."[105] By the early 1950s, fifteen cities hosted a Fellowship House that replicated Philadelphia's work. They continued to meet in Philadelphia annually and exchanged literature, curricula, and desegregation strategies. Baltimore, for example, launched a campaign to desegregate its theaters, and Kansas City, working with its FOR chapter, tested a variety of public accommodations. Knoxville, Tennessee, had the only southern Fellowship House, which ran an interracial day camp and formed the city's first interracial choir. One of Highlander's residents, Henry Shipperd, visited the Knoxville Fellowship House in 1955 and reported that it "is doing the foremost job throughout the South."[106] Thus, the federation spread liberal interracialism across the nation and provided both spaces and resources for the burgeoning civil rights movement.

In 1950 the federation added another Fellowship House to its roster in the nation's capital. The DC Fellowship House, a six-room rental, offered training modeled after the Units for Unity courses in Philadelphia. Activists first conceived of the house in 1943, when a number of them attended a FOR conference in Philadelphia that highlighted the work of the Fellowship House. The group, "composed of those persons who are personal friends of Miss Penney, others who have worked with the Philadelphia Center, and addressed the Interracial Fellowship Church services," returned to DC determined to create a similar program.[107] One of those activists was Pauli Murray, who had just graduated from Howard University's law school, where she came to know and befriend Howard Thurman. At Howard, Murray had become increasingly interested in the role that "interracial college-trained youth" could play in advancing civil rights. She was inspired, in part, by frequent Fellowship House speaker Mordecai Johnson's baccalaureate address at her graduation.[108] Given her connection with Thurman and Johnson, her participation in the establishment of DC's Fellowship House was an outgrowth of her commitment to both liberal and utopian interracialism. In a few short years, Johnson would also inspire a young Martin Luther King Jr. to take up nonviolent direct action in the cause of civil rights.

Pauli Murray was not the only young activist to fall under the Fellowship movement's influence. Marjorie Penney was a key ally to the founding members of CORE, who were the kind of idealistic students who gravitated to the Fellowship Houses. CORE's first chapter in Chicago, an interracial home, was a residential version of Philadelphia's Fellowship House, although it was not officially part of the federation. One of CORE's founders, George Houser, was a frequent correspondent with Penney, sharing information about the interracial work he was doing and its relationship to the Fellowship House mission. He also corresponded with the Fellowship House in Toledo, Ohio, about setting up an interracial house and church in Chicago.[109] The Fellowship House in Denver, Colorado, actively supported the work of their CORE chapter, which carried out a major nonviolent direct-action campaign there in the mid-1940s.[110] Thus, the Fellowship Houses offered a physical and organizational base for utopian interracialists who sought to create a new society immediately, rather than relying on education and moral suasion alone.

By the mid-1950s, fellowshippers began to support and even practice nonviolent direct action in greater numbers. During and after the 1955–56 Montgomery Bus Boycott, Fellowship Houses quickly mobilized to support the southern movement. The Friends Peace Committee, for example, drafted a guide to nonviolence for use by activists who would soon travel to join southern protests. And fellowshippers organized pickets at downtown chain stores as the sit-in movement escalated in early 1960.[111] In April 1960, Penney, accompanied by three other fellowshippers, attended the Raleigh conference at Shaw University, which saw the formation of the Student Nonviolent Coordinating Committee (SNCC) in the wake of mass sit-ins. While in the South, the Philadelphia fellowshippers also visited a number of historically Black colleges where the sit-in movement had emerged that spring. Penney later reported that "a number of the young people planned to visit the House and Farm this summer."[112] Not satisfied with remaining in a supportive role, northern fellowshippers soon traveled south, including to Mississippi during the Freedom Summer of 1964.

Perhaps the most dramatic story of a fellowshipper who became a central actor in the southern struggle was that of Prathia Hall, whom white supremacists shot while she was volunteering for a SNCC project in southwest Georgia in the fall of 1962. Hall remembered that while in high school and college, she "was active with students from across Philadelphia" at the Fellowship House, which she characterized as "a place of advocacy for peace and interracial human relations." Hall attended speeches by both King and Thurman at the Fellowship House, and after 1954 she participated in "workshops on nonviolent direct action as preparation for our campaign to support the southern student sit-ins as we had supported the Montgomery Bus Boycott."[113] In 1962 Hall began full-time work with SNCC in the heart of the southern campaign. She was organizing alongside legendary activist Charles Sherrod near Albany, Georgia, when white supremacists sprayed the home she and other SNCC activists were staying with gunfire, hitting her lower extremities. Even after this terrifying incident, Hall continued her work with SNCC, becoming known as a powerful orator and earning the respect of Dr. King. After her eventual return north, she earned a PhD from Princeton Theological Seminary and became an ordained Baptist preacher in Philadelphia.[114]

Fellowship Houses provided crucial spaces to train nonviolent activists like Prathia Hall. Pauli Murray's work establishing a Washington, DC, Fellowship House paid off when the house played a key role in two major Freedom Rides. The first, CORE and FOR's 1947 Journey of Reconciliation, used the Washington Fellowship House to train for the risky bus ride south to test a new Supreme Court decision desegregating interstate transportation. The activists engaged in seminars and role-playing to prepare them for the dangerous southern venture.[115] In 1961 activists again convened at the Washington Fellowship House to prepare for a new round of Freedom Rides. It was there that John Lewis and his fellow Freedom Riders engaged in three days of nonviolence training and preparation. Lewis remembered, "Inside was room after room filled with books and posters and pieces of art all centered around the themes of peace and community." "I'd never been in a building like this," recollected Lewis, "I'd never been among people like this."[116] James Farmer, a seasoned CORE activist long affiliated with FOR and the Fellowship House movement, trained the young Freedom Riders. He helped direct the sociodramas where activists played the roles of police officers, white hoodlums, and nonviolent participants.[117] This tactic was honed in the 1940s by fellowshippers who used "incident" training to ensure that activists were prepared for what confronted them when challenging segregated accommodations. The Washington House, like those in other cities, provided a safe and supportive space for activists embarking on life-threatening campaigns.

The centrality of Fellowship Houses to the growing civil rights movement was also apparent in Penney's ongoing relationship with Martin Luther King Jr. after his initial introduction to Fellowship House while attending Crozer in 1949. In 1961 Penney returned to the South, traveling to Atlanta to meet with King and other Southern Christian Leadership Conference (SCLC) activists. While there, she remembered, "I sat for an hour with Dr. King and

Coretta and the children, and he felt that his place was in the South; he didn't want to come to the North."[118] Penney reports that Coretta convinced Martin to come back to Philadelphia, as part of a northern urban tour. King arrived in the city by train on October 21 for a four-day visit. Upon arrival at the station, he was met by a motorcade, which escorted him to the Fellowship House, where he held a press conference. He spent much of his Philadelphia trip at the Fellowship House, giving smaller lectures and dining with civic leaders. King also met with high school Fellowship Clubs at the house, speaking with them about the role of nonviolence for interracial and interethnic peace in schools.[119]

The Fellowship House organizers called King's Philadelphia trip the "King's way" and had him speak at multiple venues. King delivered a stirring early version of his "I Have a Dream" speech, for example, at the Academy of Music in front of thirty-four hundred people. At Penney's invitation, King returned to Philadelphia in 1965 for a two-day visit, as part of a tour of six northern cities that sought to jump-start a northern protest campaign. Staying true to her ideals of fellowship, and recognizing the changing political landscape, Penney was careful to include emerging Black Power leaders in the city, including Cecil Moore, the radical head of Philadelphia's NAACP. King began his visit with a welcome breakfast at Fellowship House, attended by nine hundred people. At a large rally later that day, King called for a broad coalition of civil rights organizations in the city, echoing Penney's wish to bring Black Power critics of nonviolence into that coalition.[120] The fact that the Fellowship House remained the locus of civil rights work three decades after Penney first went to Pendle Hill was a testament to the fellowship ideal. And during those decades, organizers shifted from a liberal interracialism, which emphasized cooperation and brotherhood through education, to a utopian interracialism that embraced nonviolent direct action and interracial living.

Conclusion

"We can create little islands of goodwill and fellowship in the seeming sea of hatred," Howard Thurman wrote in the mid-1940s. "The islands will grow and become linked together until a veritable continent is born. The tiniest island is important."[121] The Fellowship Church of All Peoples was one such island, and the dozens of Fellowship Houses and their imitators that spread out from Philadelphia were an archipelago. Most of the major figures of the civil rights movement interacted with these institutions. Like John Lewis in the days before embarking on a perilous Freedom Ride, they received training and support from seasoned activists. Young African Americans such as

Prathia Hall grew up as part of the fellowship community and dedicated their lives to the movement. And the intercultural and interdenominational religious worship communicated a powerful message of unity and peace. Some of those fellowshippers went on to form new interracial utopian communities, such as the Harlem Ashram or the Koinonia Farm. Others took utopian ideas of cooperation, brotherhood, and peace into the center of the burgeoning civil rights movement.

5

The Pacifists

Today, as the Gandhian forces in India face their critical test, we can add to world justice by placing in the hands of thirteen million black Americans a workable and Christian technique for the righting of injustice and the solution of conflict.

BAYARD RUSTIN[1]

Moral suasion having proved ineffective the Satyagrahis do not hesitate to shift their technique to compulsive force.

KRISHNALAL SHRIDHARANI[2]

The group of young activists crowded into Inspiration House's overheated living room in the summer following World War II. Wallace Nelson, an African American veteran of nonviolent direct-action campaigns, led them in a discussion of how to combat the pervasive segregation of the nation's capital. After extensive conversation, a half dozen Black and white activists set out to eat together at a local restaurant, challenging the management's segregation policies. Over the weeks that followed, interracial teams streamed out across the city. Networking with the local African American community, they swam in segregated pools, attended segregated theaters, and picketed segregated hotels. Some were arrested and many beaten, but these women and men challenged the nation's capital to live up to the ideals of equality and brotherhood.

In 1941 James Farmer, an African American pacifist working as race relations secretary for the Fellowship of Reconciliation (FOR), penned a doc-

ument entitled "A Provisional Plan for Brotherhood Mobilization." Farmer
called for immediate action to end racial segregation in America. "Not to
make housing in ghettos more tolerable, but to destroy residential segregation; not to make Jim Crow facilities the equal of others, but to abolish Jim
Crow; not to make racial discrimination more bearable, but to wipe it out."
Participants in such a mobilization, declared Farmer, would live in "interracial housing cooperatives."[3] While the memorandum was in the mail to
FOR's director, Brookwood founder A. J. Muste, Farmer moved into an interracial Fellowship House, modeled after Philadelphia's Fellowship House, in
a white Chicago neighborhood, putting into practice his call for immediate
action. In that house, Black and white activists assiduously studied Krishnalal Shridharani's *War without Violence* (1939), a handbook of Gandhian
nonviolence they used to attack segregation in the city's coffee shops and
roller-skating rinks. Shridharani advised his readers across the globe, "Racial and political minorities, as well as relatively weaker economic groups,
are better off with Satyagraha [nonviolence] than with violence."[4] Acting on
these ideas Farmer, Bayard Rustin, and white activists George Houser and
James Peck founded the Congress of Racial Equality (CORE) and called for
the proliferation of cooperative interracial communities across the country.[5]

Farmer and Rustin were part of a generation of African Americans who
believed that utopian interracialism would bring racial justice. They were
products of the ecumenical Student Christian Movement of the interwar
period, coming out of the YMCA and YWCA's student divisions, FOR, and
mainstream Protestant denominations.[6] These vibrant circles had been de-
bating the relevancy of Gandhian teachings to the Black Freedom struggle
since the 1920s. But they were limited by their liberal interracial beliefs,
stopping short of calling for immediate and revolutionary change. The CORE
founders pushed their teachings toward a more radical conclusion. They circulated among small interracial communities who practiced prefigurative
politics, living the life they envisioned for a future society. Central to this
concept was the creation of "counter-institutions," like the cooperatives, ashrams, and interracial churches that activists founded in the late 1930s and
1940s.[7] Radical pacifists demanded "freedom now," rejecting the gradualism
of racial liberals. They were socialists who believed in building cooperatives
as an alternative to capitalism while rejecting the Communist Party's sectarian politics. They practiced utopian interracialism in their religious worship, social activism, and communal housing. And they developed a form of
Gandhian nonviolent direct action that was more aggressive than the passive
resistance promoted by the traditional pacifist peace churches. Using distinctly military language, for example, Shridharani called for "direct action

just short of war."[8] At times these tenets were embodied in utopian communities, such as the Harlem Ashram; at other moments activists taught them in short-term workshops or places of worship. But in all these cases, activists promoted utopian interracialism and were integral in building a powerful civil rights movement.

Ahimsa and the Harlem Ashram

By 1940 pacifists were reading and discussing Shridharani's works, Muste had taken charge of a newly invigorated FOR at a moment of heightened militarism, and experiments in communal and cooperative living proliferated. Individual and small group actions had applied nonviolence to segregation prior to the 1940s. Police arrested white pacifist David Dellinger, for example, in 1937 "for a nonviolent action against racial segregation in a northern movie house."[9] But in 1940, a group of college students established a communal ashram that would be widely influential, if not long lasting. Their experimentation helped initiate a fuller mobilization of nonviolent direct action and utopian interracialism.

In June 1940, six white students from the progressive Antioch College established Ahimsa Farm in Yellow Springs, Ohio.[10] Modeled after Gandhian ashrams, Ahimsa was a cooperative community about thirty miles outside of Cleveland. An Indian professor at Antioch, Manmatha Chatterjee, introduced the students to Gandhi's teachings and financed the ashram. The students grew vegetables, raised chickens, milked goats, and engaged in nightly study sessions that attracted fellow travelers from around the country. At Ahimsa they sought to prefigure the world they envisioned. "The members of the project have committed themselves to work for a society where violence and war will be replaced by techniques of non-violent direct action," stated their foundational document, "where race prejudice and class hatred will give way to tolerance and a common basis of understanding; and finally to build a society founded not upon exploitation, but upon cooperation."[11] Their chosen name, "Ahimsa," Sanskrit for "non-harming," reflected both their admiration for Gandhi and their belief in a society based on cooperation rather than competition.

Every evening the Ahimsa residents and visitors spent hours discussing politics in what they referred to as "the manner of the Friends." These freewheeling discussions, without a clear leader or hierarchy, would become a hallmark of the participatory culture of the New Left in decades to come.[12] Folk dancing, singing, and daily meditation also supplemented the physical labor of running the farm. These practices reflected the culture of Highlander, the Fellowship Farm, and other interracial experiments. Like those institutions, Ahimsa was not an isolated commune. Residents were avid students of Shridharani and sought to practice what they termed "aggressive pacifism." This form of pacifism would be "an effective, workable, substitute for the war method."[13]

Racial segregation, prevalent in nearby Cleveland, was an ideal battlefield for such nonviolent aggression. Although Ahimsa never had the opportunity to integrate its experiment, despite stating that the community was open "to young people of all races and religious affiliations," they were committed to racial equality and eager to use nonviolent direct action to challenge segregation.[14] One of the residents, Lee Stern, was involved with a Quaker group in the city, Cleveland Young Friends, and began to meet with local African American youths in 1941 to discuss the racial segregation and violence at a segregated swimming pool in Garfield Park. A large municipal pool in Garfield Heights, a suburb of Cleveland, had become a racial battleground. Although Black Clevelanders used the surrounding picnic grove, groups of white youth stymied their attempts to swim by chasing them out of the water. On July 4, 1941, Black teenagers retaliated by taking over the pool using sheer numbers, ignoring the racial epithets of whites. But this was a temporary victory. After meeting with Stern and members of the local FOR chapter, the youths agreed to use nonviolent direct action to permanently desegregate the pool. Twelve whites entered the pool with four Black swimmers, intending to form a protective ring around them if white swimmers attacked. When challenged by a group of whites, they explained their position and left the pool area. They continued this protest throughout the summer, with varying results. In the following year, a newly formed CORE chapter took over the nonviolent protests at Garfield Park, which continued until 1948, when the pool was successfully desegregated.[15]

The Garfield Park campaign was not a clear-cut success, but it marked the beginning of pacifists' embrace of nonviolent direct action as a primary tactic in the fight against segregation. "Because this was our first experiment of this type," reported the Ahimsa members, "we know . . . we didn't accomplish all that we might have. But the experience was splendid and we are certain that we will be able to record real progress each week until there is a good fellowship among all who inhabit the pool."[16] That fall Stern and other Ahimsa members presented this project at the annual FOR conference. James Farmer was reportedly "elated." As historian Charles Chatfield recounts, "Here, it seemed was proof of a conviction he had held for some time, that nonviolence could be applied profitably to the American civil-rights struggle."[17] George Houser included a lively description of the campaign in his

1945 booklet, *Erasing the Color Line*, which narrated the early desegregation work of pacifist groups and CORE. Ahimsa broke up in 1942 as its members struggled with the outbreak of World War II and resistance to the draft. But this utopian community had a lasting impact on midcentury activism and the honing of a novel tactic in the freedom struggle.

As suggested by the influence of Manmatha Chatterjee, the Ahimsa residents viewed their work as part of a global struggle. Increasingly, historians have uncovered African Americans' connections to Asia, in particular India. This broad perspective posits a "Black globality" that deeply informed radical pacifists and went beyond the study groups of Sherwood Eddy's American seminar.[18] They were most engaged with the ongoing anti-colonial struggle in India, but also worked on Puerto Rican independence and European trauma in the face of both World War II and the cold war. Many of those who lived in or founded radical pacifist utopian communities were themselves international figures, having, in some cases, resided with Gandhi in his Indian ashram. And the ideas and tactics of leading pacifist thinkers circulated widely. This international perspective among radical pacifists, or "colored cosmopolitanism" as historian Nico Slate terms it, illustrates pacifists' transnational reach. And it demonstrates that anti-colonial campaigns were a significant preoccupation of the anti-communist Left.[19]

Ahimsa residents sought to imitate Gandhi's ashrams by deploying another tactic, the long march. Before its breakup, Ahimsa engaged in a series of marches with FOR members and like-minded activists. They carried out two "Feed Europe" marches to raise awareness about the plight of civilians in German-occupied Europe. These marches were modeled after Gandhi's famous 1930 Salt March to the sea, which protested the British ban on Indians collecting and selling salt. Pacifists sought to highlight the plight of continental Europeans during the Allied blockade of humanitarian aid in the early years of World War II. The first march lasted from December 21 to 25 in 1940, and stretched from Lancaster, Pennsylvania, to New York City. The following Easter a second march began in Wilmington, Delaware, and culminated in Washington, DC. In both, pilgrims pulled handcarts laden with canned goods for starving Europeans. And they dressed as refugees in "an assortment of green and red stocking hats, leather lumber jackets and soft khaki shirts."[20]

Although the founders of Ahimsa did not meet their long-term goal of a "permanent community and educational institution" with cooperative housing and labor, their work was influential among civil rights activists.[21] James Farmer was one of many prominent pacifists to visit the farm. And Ahimsa activists traveled to New York City to visit with Muste and Shridharani and to nearby Cleveland to meet with Socialist Party leader Norman Thomas.[22] Most significantly, Ahimsa's Garfield Park protest served as a model for CORE's use of nonviolent direct action in desegregation campaigns. Other pacifists followed the lead of the Antioch students during and after World War II. Their communities sought to follow Gandhi's teachings and provide a safe haven during the tumult of the war years. And although many were in rural idylls like the Ahimsa Farm, others choose to locate in urban centers to better address the problems of racial inequality and poverty. It was in Harlem that the most celebrated of these experiments thrived in the 1940s.

Shridharani, author of *War without Violence*, was in the United States when Houser and Farmer were meeting in Chicago and following the work of the Ahimsa students. He was living with two white Methodist missionaries, Jay Holmes Smith and Ralph Templin, who had spent time with Gandhi in his Indian ashram and were now attempting to replicate that experience in a modest Harlem brownstone on Fifth Avenue near 125th Street. A few years earlier, Catherine de Hueck had opened her Friendship House in the same neighborhood. They hoped the Harlem Ashram would fulfill the oft-quoted words of Gandhi to Howard Thurman: "If it comes true it may be through the Negroes that the unadulterated message of non-violence will be delivered to the world."[23] By January 1941, eleven members of the ashram (Shridharani, three African Americans, and seven whites) began an experiment in cooperative living and utopian interracialism. "We Live in Harlem," they proclaimed in a pamphlet, "because we regard the problem of racial justice as America's No. 1 problem in reconciliation." As "the Negro capital of the nation," Harlem was the logical location for an interracial ashram, they believed. And somewhat naively, they believed that "living here helps us who are white to get something of the 'feel' of being Negro in America."[24] Racial reconciliation, ashram residents argued, required an experiment in interracial cooperative living and the implementation of nonviolent direct action as taught by Shridharani, Smith, and Templin.

The ashram's religious teachings, although nominally open to all faiths, were guided by FOR's commitment to the "Christian nonviolent tradition."[25] Smith, the spiritual leader of the ashram, focused much of his teaching on the "genius of original Christianity."[26] This fascination with the "primitive" church parallels the early nineteenth-century utopian communities that traced their lineage through the Pietists and Puritans of the Protestant Reformation. Members of these communities, such as the Ephratans and the Shakers, lived cooperatively and communally. Writing about the Harlem Ashram in its infancy, Smith suggested that "our surest foundation lies in the fact that living in real day-to-day community is integral to the Hebrew-

Christian purpose. Studies of original Christianity, as of Hebrew prophetism, convinced us that in trying live as a Kingdom-of-God family, or family of reconciliation, we are in line with our religious foundations."[27] More recently, the Social Gospel movement of the early twentieth century pushed Protestants toward an engagement with the social and political world, and the "lived religion" of Howard Kester and other southern radicals pervaded civil rights unionism during the 1930s. Smith summarized these worldviews: "The dominant purpose in our ashram groups in India and Harlem has been the rediscovery of original Christianity and its application to such problems as war and racial justice in our time."[28]

In *War without Violence*, Shridharani warned, "Like war, Satyagraha demands public spirit, self-sacrifice, organization, endurance and discipline for its successful operation."[29] In order to practice the true brotherhood of "original Christianity" and foster utopian interracialism, ashram members sought to erase social class by pooling their resources, much as Father Divine followers did. Living cooperatively in austere conditions had pragmatic, as well as religious, advantages. "The strength of comrades working in the same cause is a constant help," read the ashram brochure. And, as the Divinites knew well, it was much cheaper to live together and share resources.[30] Austerity, however, required discipline, and like many utopian communal experiments that preceded it, this discipline would eventually become the ashram's undoing.

Despite its reliance on earlier experiments in communal living, the Harlem Ashram was among the first communities to have as its primary purpose the practice of nonviolent direct action. "Whenever the pacifist who has been living in the ordinary way," wrote Smith, "helps to form a 'family of reconciliation,' which deliberately crosses lines of race and class and unites its members in a disciplined and deeply-sharing fellowship, he is making possible a strong base for non-violent action campaigns."[31] It was in the communal ashram that radical nonviolence could be nurtured and perfected. For this reason, historian Aldon Morris grouped the Harlem Ashram with the Highlander Folk School as a "movement halfway house" that could provide a "battery of social change resources."[32]

FOR established a nonviolent direct-action group in December 1940 that began to meet weekly at the ashram when it opened in the spring of 1941. By that summer, the ashram was leading a "summer training school in total pacifism."[33] Participants studied prominent pacifists' works and surveyed neighborhood African Americans about the racial discrimination they experienced. In response to repeated complaints about "the practice of the downtown YMCAs in excluding Negroes from their dormitories and facilities in general," they began a campaign to challenge segregation at YMCAs. Homer Nichols, a Black ashram member and president of the Harlem Christian Youth Conference, experienced this discrimination firsthand. When he requested a room at the downtown Sloane House YMCA, the reply was: "We send you fellows up to the Harlem Y." Thus, the ashram's first major campaign challenged the city's segregated YMCAs.[34] Given that reformers viewed the YMCAs as promoters of liberal interracialism, this campaign highlighted the gap between racial liberals and radical pacifists.

Utilizing nonviolent direct action to challenge racial segregation, rather than depending on moral suasion, was also the mission of the newly formed CORE. Both James Farmer and Bayard Rustin were in close contact with the Harlem Ashram and stayed with the community when visiting the New York FOR offices. By 1942 Farmer and Rustin actively pushed FOR to place racial reconciliation at the center of its work. Writing in the organization's periodical, *Fellowship*, Farmer argued that mainstream civil rights organizations' support of the war in their Double V campaign, which called for victory against fascism abroad and victory against racism at home, was misguided. "It is extremely doubtful whether they can creditably pursue their primary task of struggling for racial equality within the framework of a war program which denied the validity of their struggle. It is quite impossible to ride two horses which are increasingly moving in opposite directions." Instead Farmer called for "a cooperative endeavor recognizing no distinctions of race and mobilizing men of conscience of every race in a comprehensive program to resist racism."[35] Rustin echoed Farmer's call to resistance in the same publication, lamenting the increase of racial violence and discrimination during the war years and calling repeatedly for an immediate response through nonviolence.

One way to carry out such a campaign was to foster a close alliance with A. Philip Randolph's March on Washington Movement (MOWM), established in 1941 to pressure the Roosevelt administration to desegregate the military and war industries. The MOWM's 1943 "We Are Americans Too" Chicago convention included Rustin and Farmer, as well as prominent white pacifist E. Stanley Jones and Harlem Ashram leader, Jay Holmes Smith, as speakers. At that meeting, MOWM activists adopted nonviolent direct action as their primary tactic.[36] Reflecting on the successful convention, Charles Wesley Burton, a Congregationalist minister and friend of Randolph, noted, "I think the conference did a great deal to awaken the people to the possibilities of non-violent, good-will direct action as a technique in the solution of the Negro's major problems."[37]

Despite their alliance with Randolph, CORE and FOR members were more critical of the war effort than the MOWM and never embraced the Double V campaign. Instead, in 1942 pacifists organized a march to Washington, DC, to protest the poll tax, racial segregation, and racial violence.[38] A well-publicized march to Washington was an appealing project for a group of committed nonviolent activists. Smith and Shridharani had both participated in Gandhi's original Salt March and supported the earlier Ahimsa marches in support of starving Europeans. A march was also a performative form of activism, which was a key characteristic of Gandhian nonviolence.[39] In addition, it is notable that Randolph called off his planned March on Washington in the summer of 1941, after Franklin Roosevelt issued his executive order 8802 creating the Fair Employment Practices Committee. FOR leaders and Harlem Ashram members were frustrated by Randolph's cancellation of the march, given the ongoing segregation of the military and the increasing levels of white racial violence nationwide.[40] These pacifists signaled their unwillingness to cooperate with the war effort as well as their commitment to racial equality by organizing their own march. This was not a public showing of Double V sentiment, but a protest against the linked violence of war and racial discrimination. However, its relatively small size was not the mass march planned by Randolph in 1941, or in 1963 by Bayard Rustin. Like the relatively small pacifist utopian communities, this was a prefiguring of larger changes to come.

The protesters left Harlem on June 3, 1942, after a sendoff at the Abyssinian Baptist Church led by Adam Clayton Powell Jr. The core of sixteen marchers walked fifteen miles per day, carrying signs and handing out literature to curious bystanders, and were often joined by sympathetic locals. At their destinations, activists organized open mass meetings for the marchers and housed them overnight. Every evening interracial pairs tested restaurants, hotels, theaters, and YMCAs. The marchers designed this testing to give local activists an agenda for future acts of nonviolent direct action.[41] The journey was peaceful until they reached Havre de Grace in Maryland, where two white soldiers accosted one of the pilgrims when they objected to his sign that read, "Take the 'Mock' Out of Democracy." At a toll bridge in the same town, a guard inspected the male members' draft cards, took names and addresses, and copied the text of each sign before allowing them to move on. And a driver of a car with Virginia license plates called out a warning not to come to his state because "we'll lynch you there." Just outside of Baltimore, five white men threw stones at the marchers and ripped apart their placards. One man reportedly broke a bottle on the pavement and threatened the marchers with the jagged end, declaring, "You're south of the Mason-Dixon line now, and we don't stand for that stuff down here." Throughout these ordeals, pilgrims employed the Gandhian techniques they had been trained in, speaking quietly with the attackers about the nature of democracy and even trying to bandage the injured hand of the bottle breaker. When police finally arrived, they refused to press charges.[42]

The climax of the march was a rousing rally at the Lincoln Memorial, where they proclaimed their "rededication to the unfinished task of emancipation." Activists had gathered petitions with over three thousand signatures on a range of issues including discrimination in the armed forces and industry, the repeal of the poll tax and Jim Crow laws, the anti-lynching bill, the Sojourner Truth riots in Detroit protesting segregated public housing, and the imminent execution of Odell Waller, a sharecropper who was sentence to death in Virginia. They hoped to present the petition to the president, who, unsurprisingly, refused to meet with them. But Smith and Conrad Lynn, an African American lawyer who would go on to play a key role in the civil rights movement, did manage to meet with one of Roosevelt's secretaries in the White House, Marvin McIntyre. It did not go well. When Smith and Lynn complained about the administration's reluctance to work with Walter White, president of the NAACP, and A. Philip Randolph, McIntyre referred to them as "Randolph, White and the boys," and dismissed their demands for greater attention to the poll tax and anti-lynching bills.[43] What, then, did the pilgrimage accomplish? Compared to the monumental March on Washington in 1963 very little. But this 1942 march marked a call to arms on the part of pacifists to focus on the violence of racial apartheid in America. These pacifists were young, militant, and central to the foundations of the mass civil rights movement.

When the pilgrims returned to New York City, they engaged in a variety of projects organized by the Harlem Ashram, many of which had a powerful transnational reach. One of the major "action projects" focused on the independence struggle in Puerto Rico. Appealing to ashram residents because of its parallel to the independence struggle in India, the Puerto Rican movement also had a leader who claimed to be committed to nonviolence. Don Pedro Albizu Campos was, Smith proclaimed, the "Gandhi of Puerto Rico."[44] Campos had served seven years in prison for his political work. When the authorities released him, ashram members came to his aid as he was very frail. Intrigued by the anti-colonial struggle, Rustin spent the summer of 1941 on the island investigating "Yankee imperialism, economic, cultural, and political" on behalf of the ashram.[45] Their opposition to colonialism also led Ralph Templin and Smith to organize a "Free India" committee headquartered at the ashram. The committee designed a "Gandhi Cap" with the slogan "Free India Now" embroidered on the front. They wore these caps during "poster walks" in New York City, Philadelphia, and Washington, DC, publicizing the colonized nation's plight. When the colonial government imprisoned Gandhi and Nehru in 1943, Templin, Smith, and other protesters traveled to Washington, DC, on Indian Independence Day and picketed the British embassy. In response, Congress passed a law forbidding picketing foreign embassies and consulates. Undeterred, during the summer of 1943, protesters picketed the British embassy and consulates throughout the East Coast weekly, resulting in multiple arrests and prison sentences.[46]

As well as engaging in anti-colonial protests, ashram members became deeply involved in their surrounding neighborhood. In 1941 they identified a vacant lot on 113th Street between Fifth and Madison Avenues, a largely Puerto Rican neighborhood, to run a Play Co-Op. The ashram residents worked with the Police Athletic League to declare the block a "play street" reserved for organized games under the direction of trained "recreational workers." Black and Puerto Rican residents of the street were initially suspicious of the largely white workers who began to organize games every afternoon. Following the spirit of the ashram, the workers rented an apartment on the block so they could fully engage in interracial organizing and gain the community's trust. By the end of the summer, the ashram workers organized a successful block party with a twelve-piece "Spanish" band and over a thousand attendees. The ashram abandoned Play Street in 1943, in part because the war created a "manpower shortage" as conscientious objectors (COs) left for prison or camps, but they felt it was a success during its two years in operation.[47]

Members of the ashram and fellow travelers also continued their work for racial justice, both within the confines of the city and nationally. One of their central projects was an attempt to pressure Congress to revoke the southern poll taxes created to disenfranchise Black voters. Following up on contacts they made during the pilgrimage, ashram members converged on the capital in May 1944 joined by "eighteen Negro ministers from Washington" with two hundred protesters from their congregation joining in the "poster walk." Every summer and over Christmas holidays, the ashram also ran training courses for pacifists interested in learning the techniques of nonviolent direct action and the advantages of living in an ashram.[48]

In addition to being a model of utopian interracialism, the Harlem Ashram became a "home" that welcomed COs released from camps or prison around the country. The male members of FOR, CORE, and ashrams declared themselves conscientious objectors when the draft began. Most reported to service camps, but others made the choice to face prison rather than aid the war effort in any way. Authorities classified Rustin, for example, as a CO in 1940, but he refused to comply with an order to report to a CO camp in November 1943. Rustin returned his draft cards to the local board on Amsterdam

Avenue in New York City. In a letter to the board explaining his decision, he wrote, "The conscription act denies brotherhood—most basic New Testament teaching. Its design and purpose is to set men apart—German against American, American against Japanese—that ends justify means, that, from unfriendly acts a new and friendly world can emerge."[49] The price for this stand was two years in prison. COs' lives were in constant turmoil as they were in and out of courtrooms, camps, and prisons for much of the duration of the 1940s. Their families also became itinerant as they often followed COs to camps, and women worked to supply a basic income deprived by their husbands' imprisonments.[50] As a result, the Harlem Ashram, as well as other cooperative communities, offered a welcome respite, companionship, and legal advice during the war years.

Cooperative communities also offered a safe space for activists whose work was, by nature, itinerant. Rustin, Houser, and Farmer traveled widely as FOR race relations secretaries and founding members of CORE. While in New York City, they stayed at the Harlem Ashram and worked closely with its members on their desegregation campaigns. CORE's New York chapter used the ashram as its primary meeting place to plan desegregation campaigns at local restaurants, YMCAs, and recreational facilities. The civil rights activist and feminist Pauli Murray, then a young law student at Howard University, was a charter member and frequent visitor at the ashram. Murray also participated in a MOWM conference in 1942 that developed a plan for wide-scale nonviolent direct-action campaigns.[51] Muriel Lester, who had inspired San Francisco's Sakai group, was an adviser to the ashram and stayed there while in America. The African American educator Wilson Head also roomed at the ashram while in New York.[52] The Harlem Ashram then, like Fellowship Houses, provided space for those committed to radical interracialism to meet, live, play, and plan for the future.

But within the history of all utopian communal settlements lay tension around daily practices, economics, and leadership. The Harlem Ashram was no different. Commitment to radical nonviolence required discipline, a lesson often taught by Gandhi and his interpreters. As Lester said, "We must out-train the totalitarians, outmatch their intrepidity, contempt for comfort, surrender of private interest, obedience to command, with a superior courage, frugality, loyalty and selflessness. Our job is bigger than theirs."[53] This was a call to arms, a "war without violence," for pacifists who rejected the revolutionary tactics of communism and the militarism of World War II. Training for war at the Harlem Ashram required multiple periods of prayer and daily meditation, "alertness to the constant need of self-purification," manual arts, "honest effort to examine questions of smoking, drinking etc.," limiting personal expenditures, and submitting to the discipline of the ashram leaders.[54] The permanent members of the ashram committed to these practices, choosing to "voluntarily require of ourselves a finer discipline and a deeper sacrifice than are expected of the soldier."[55] Part of that discipline was voluntary poverty and a pooling of economic resources. Food was plain; according to Daniel Zwickel, it consisted mostly of "soy beans and kale." And Farmer described it as "an inducement to fasting."[56]

By establishing such discipline, the ashram was following the "ascetic impulse" inherent in Christian nonviolence, as well as the teachings of Gandhi, who required obedience from his followers.[57] This asceticism alienated some activists, particularly Black pacifists. Farmer, who spent an extended stay at the ashram in 1943, criticized the "voluntary poverty" required of residents. "My poverty was wholly involuntary," he pointed out.[58] After being told she could not smoke, Murray wrote in her diary, "If the ashram is to become a convent or a monastery, then I have no place there."[59] In addition, the folk dancing and singing that constituted their recreational time were drawn from the white-dominated "peace churches," rather than African American culture.[60] This reliance on white countercultural practices limited the possibilities of utopian interracialism. And an ongoing problem that emerged at the Harlem Ashram was the leadership of Smith. A. J. Muste expressed his concern about Smith's "inflexibility" and the lack of an African American co-leader in the ashram as early as 1942.[61] For his part, Smith had become frustrated by 1946 with what he perceived as a lack of discipline among the ashram members. "There are those of us who seem to feel that they should be a cooperative fellowship with a minimum of group discipline and with a preoccupation with immediate community service. . . . There are others of us who feel that we must become as fully and rapidly as possible an American ashram."[62] In the end Smith lost this argument, and the ashram broke up in 1947.

Peace Cells and Communes

Ahimsa and the Harlem Ashram were not isolated communal experiments. During the 1940s, similar radical pacifist groups proliferated in urban, suburban, and rural areas. Writing in FOR's publication, *Fellowship*, in 1941, John Swomley urged young pacifists to "establish a Fellowship House in the city where members can live cooperatively and inter-racially."[63] These group homes, modeled after Philadelphia's Fellowship House but with permanent residents living in the homes, formed peace cells. Small groups of pacifists made up these cells and spent their time studying, discussing tactics, and training in nonviolent direct action. Those affiliated with CORE, the secular

War Resisters League, or FOR were overtly political. Others were more cultural in orientation, such as Almanac House, an interracial commune in the West Village of New York City where white folk singers such as Pete Seeger and Woody Guthrie lived and performed with African American performers such as Josh White and Brownie McGhee. The house was largely funded by the Almanac Singers, a folk group organized in 1941 with Pete Seeger, Woody Guthrie, and Lee Hays. They opened it to all, with large communal meals and visitors sleeping wherever there was room. The African American blues musician Josh White joined them to produce the Almanac Singers' first album, *Songs for John Doe*, which was filled with antiwar tracks on the eve of World War II. "The Ballad of October 16," which referred to the passage of the peacetime conscription act, had this chorus: "Oh, Franklin Roosevelt told the people how he felt / We damn near believed what he said / He said, 'I hate war, and so does Eleanor' / 'But we won't be safe 'till everybody's dead.'"[64]

The Almanac Singers established their commune in 1941, the same year that pacifists established the Harlem Ashram. The year before also saw a group of radical pacifists, most notably the white activist David Dellinger, set up an ashram in Newark, New Jersey. These men and their families had met in Union Theological Seminary and spent most of the war years in jail, leaving their families to run the ashram. Black pacifist Bill Sutherland's wartime experience was typical. After joining the Newark Ashram in the fall of 1940, authorities imprisoned Sutherland with Dellinger at Lewisburg maximum security prison for resisting conscription. While in prison the men worked with other inmates to desegregate the cafeteria and challenged racist prison practices. In all, eight seminarians at Union Theological Seminary, including Dellinger and George Houser, served time in jail. The Newark Ashram, also known as the Newark Christian Colony, was similar to its Harlem counterpart, serving as a safe haven and a launching pad for interracial activism. The ten or so members (numbers fluctuated depending on prison sentences) carried out neighborhood programs and challenged racial segregation in the city. Ashram participants, both Black and white, leafleted and picketed Newark's segregated restaurants, stores, and movie theaters.[65]

The ashram attracted draft resisters and fellow activists, particularly those in the Catholic Worker Movement, throughout the war years. Dellinger remembered, "Besides endless discussions on the nonviolent way of life, they could participate in community work that served as a laboratory in which to test the practicality of their ideas about moral alternatives to society's ceaseless wars between races, classes, and nation-states." One small group of activists broke off to create a separate commune in "another depressed area of Newark."[66] The Newark Ashram became known for its open hospitality, sharing food and clothing to any who knocked on their door, much like the West Village's Almanac House and the Catholic Worker's houses of hospitality. Similar to Father Divine's Promised Land, which supplied fresh food to urban banquet halls and restaurants, the ashram ran a small farm outside of the city and sold their surplus produce at a cooperative store. Ashram members donated anything left unsold to the poor.[67]

The Newark Ashram disbanded in 1943, but many of its members moved to a rural New Jersey community in 1947. According to historian Andrew Cornell, "Dellinger hoped that communal life could be balanced with confrontational organizing campaigns—indeed, that the two practices might support and amplify the impact of each other."[68] To accomplish this, Dellinger and other radical pacifists created the Glen Gardner intentional community, which ran a printing cooperative and a workshop that manufactured children's toys. The nineteen inhabitants of Glen Gardner designated themselves as the first "world's citizens community" and carried out protests against growing cold war militarization, including launching a hunger strike at the outset of the Korean War in 1950. The group rejected individual land ownership, holding the land in common, and many remained until 1968. Beyond fasting and other political actions, the Glen Gardner community's primary contribution was its publication of a series of periodicals, which were highly influential among pacifists and civil rights activists. They called the printing cooperative Libertarian Press and from 1947 to 1977 produced the journals *Direct Action*, *Alternative*, *Individual Action*, and *Liberation*. This last periodical, printed from 1956 to 1977, was particularly significant, publishing works by Martin Luther King Jr., C. Wright Mills, and leading New Left thinkers alongside older pacifist thinkers such as A. J. Muste and Bayard Rustin.[69]

In the 1940s the audience for anti-communist Left literature was small but dedicated. And their lively debates led to several splinter groups that worked closely with the mass civil rights movement as it grew in the mid-1950s. In 1948 Dellinger and Houser, along with dozens of other pacifists, met in Chicago for the "Conference on Non-violent Revolutionary Socialism." There they formed the Committee for Non-Violent Revolution. This short-lived organization morphed into the Peacemakers, a radical pacifist organization that took its name from the Bible's Beatitudes, "Blessed are the Peacemakers, for they will be called children of God" (Matt. 5:9). As befitting their name, the Peacemakers embraced Christian nonviolence, but with more radical tactics than FOR and an emphasis on utopian interracialism. They were committed to communal living, ascetic practices such as fasting, nonpayment of taxes, and total nonresistance upon arrest. Like other peace cells, they were nonhierarchical and they formed small interracial communities that organized on a local level and modeled egalitarian living. Muste, Dellinger, Rustin, Houser, and the anarchist intellectual Dwight Macdonald were among its most visible members.[70]

In a 1952 document, the Peacemakers stated:

We will live in communities because we can no longer remain apart from our brothers; because we want to share with them, to live in love and brotherhood. We will not register for war because we could not possibly sign up to become murderers or in any way sanction that process. We will not pay taxes because we could not possibly pay others to do that which we ourselves could not do. We will not accept society's pattern of segregation and discrimination against any group, this most obscene and cruel denial of brotherhood daily before us.[71]

As this statement suggests, Peacemakers were explicitly committed to a prefigurative politics that was communal, cooperative, and resistant to any form of militarism or inequality. The Glen Gardner community was a Peacemaker cell, and others existed across the country. Like Glen Gardner, many of these intentional pacifist communities resided not in inner cities or rural idylls, but in postwar suburbia. In Gano, Ohio, for example, two Peacemaker couples, the Bromleys and the Nelsons, led a major campaign to desegregate businesses in Cincinnati.[72] Perhaps the best known suburban pacifist community was Skyview Acres, thirty miles northwest of New York City in Rockland County. Nine families, many of them Peacemakers, joined together in 1946 to build an interracial and interfaith cooperative community. The residents—which included Houser, who joined in 1949—sought "close community, racial integration, and semirural life."[73] Thus in the heart of postwar suburbia, often unknown to their neighbors, interracial peace cells by their very existence refuted cold war conformity and practiced utopian interracialism.

As they traveled the country, Rustin, Houser, and others found like-minded Peacemakers willing to deploy nonviolent direct action to attack segregation. In Kansas, for example, a Peacemaker member and local Mennonite, Selma Platt, escorted Rustin to local meetings and actions. After the tour, Platt wrote to him, "I believe we have to get used to the idea of being told that we must be careful and that we should not act lest we create more harm than good.... You and I believe that ... the radical who insists upon far-reaching and immediate change has throughout history been proved the gadfly which has stirred men into action."[74] Radicals like Platt believed in immediate change, not gradualism. And increasingly they spread throughout the country to create the society they envisioned. Dorothy Day's Catholic Worker Movement also had a close alliance with the Peacemakers, working with them on projects such as the 1950 Fast for Peace after Truman's announcement of plans to develop a hydrogen bomb. During Easter Week, Day joined Muste, the Nelsons, and other Peacemakers on a weeklong fast in Washington, DC. Pacifists both in the United States and abroad joined them in fifty-one other cities. And in 1955 the Catholic Workers allied with the Peacemakers and FOR to protest civil defense drills in New York City.[75] Indeed, it was pacifism, rather than civil rights, that most closely tied the Catholic Worker Movement with the Peacemakers, an alliance that would prove generative during the Vietnam War as Catholic resistance to militarization escalated.

While Peacemaker cells and Catholic Worker mobilizations predominated in cities, in rural areas utopian interracial communities resembled the Delta Cooperative Farm, Highlander, Brookwood, and the Promised Land. Southern farms provided crucial havens for exhausted activists recovering from violent civil rights campaigns.[76] In 1942, for example, pacifists founded the interracial Koinonia Farm in rural Georgia, which played a central role in fostering civil rights below the Mason-Dixon Line. Koinonia settlers modeled themselves after the early Christian church and, like Highlander, were influenced by the Danish folk schools.[77] As in other pacifist communities, residents of these interracial farms were at times in conflict. Historian Tracy K'Meyer points out that, in a similar dynamic as that of the Harlem Ashram, Koinonia's Black residents were reluctant to become full communal members "because they would not accept voluntary poverty."[78] And like the Providence Cooperative Farm, white supremacists increasingly targeted Koinonia by the mid-1950s. The Ku Klux Klan terrorized the farm in 1956 and 1957, and local businesses boycotted their products. During this period, community members kept watch at night, with only flashlights in hand, hoping to discourage attacks.[79]

Koinonia managed to survive this violent period and served as a safe haven for young activists exhausted from brutal civil rights campaigns beginning in 1960. Hundreds of these civil rights workers flocked to the farm for communal meals and serenity.[80] Macedonia Cooperative Community in Clarkesville, Georgia, was another haven for pacifists and civil rights activists. Founded in 1937 in a similar spirit as the Delta Cooperative Farm, as an attempt to aid struggling sharecroppers, by World War II Macedonia had become a sanctuary for radical pacifists and civil rights workers seeking to both learn and teach about cooperative living. White pacifists and promoters of utopian communities, Staughton and Alice Lynd, for example, lived in Macedonia for many years until moving to the Glen Gardner community in the mid-1950s.[81] The Catholic Worker Movement also established a network of farms by the 1940s. Day's co-founder, Peter Maurin, championed these farming communes and established at least twenty-five during the 1930s. Like Father Divine, Maurin preferred to offer destitute Catholics agricultural labor rather than have them depend on the state for welfare. Although the Catholic Workers preached pacifism, the farms were less political than the pacifist communes, and the utopian interracialism of Koinonia and Macedonia was not prioritized. Instead, the farms became houses of hospitality in the countryside.[82]

The utopian interracialism practiced at pacifist farms, urban ashrams, and suburban enclaves countered an early cold war culture that valorized individual nuclear families. They nurtured and spread cooperative economics, first promulgated by workers' education program, and applied nonviolent direct action to American race relations on a large scale. Thus, ashrams and cooperative farms did not represent an isolated or withdrawn utopianism, although some back-to-the-land communes did.[83] In 1949 the Peacemakers recommended, as part of their "Communal and Cooperative Living Plans," "that, although we do form communal or cooperative groups, we emphasize the necessity of playing an active social role—in other words that we do not withdraw from society."[84] While living in their peace cells, these activists created and supported a variety of organizations, including the Peacemakers, Committee for Nonviolent Revolution, Committee for Nonviolent Action, the War Resisters League, CORE, and FOR. All called for immediate change and sought to model a new society, practicing prefigurative politics well before the New Left.

Teaching and Practicing Radical Nonviolence

Living in ashrams and cooperative farms reflected a demand for immediacy that separated radical pacifists from the gradualism of mainstream civil rights organizations. The Commission on Interracial Cooperation, the National Urban League, and the NAACP had made little headway on racial progress during the 1930s and early 1940s. Most radical pacifists, who generally defined themselves as socialists or anarchists, were equally critical of communists, particularly after the 1939 Hitler-Stalin pact. Writing in the 1944 collection *What the Negro Wants*, A. Philip Randolph noted, "The history and record of this political cult shows that it conforms with rigid fidelity to the rapidly changing, unpredictable climate of Soviet Russia, without regard to the national interests of any other group."[85] Historian Nikhil Pal Singh argues that radical pacifists opposed the Communist Party "not because they sought the political mainstream, but because they felt the party was not radical enough and believed it had betrayed a consistent and principled commitment to Black self-determination and the primacy of struggles against racism and colonialism."[86] Thus, by forging a new path using nonviolent direct action, radical pacifists challenged both racial liberals and the communist Left.

During the 1940s and 1950s, moderate organizations such as the NAACP and some Black leaders denounced the use of nonviolent direct action and viewed pacifists as dangerously radical. W. E. B. Du Bois, for example, was highly skeptical that nonviolent direct action would be effective in an American context, and in 1943 he spoke out against the MOWM's embrace of nonviolence.[87] In 1946 Thurgood Marshall wrote, "A disobedience movement on the part of Negroes and their white allies, if employed in the South, would result in wholesale slaughter with no good achieved."[88] Many in the Black press also opposed nonviolent direct action in the early 1940s. The *Pittsburgh Courier,* for example, called civil disobedience "suicidal."[89] Instead, moderates embraced the Double V campaign during the war and, afterward, campaigns that sought to educate whites through moral suasion that did little to directly challenge the status quo. The latter strategy reflected Swedish sociologist Gunnar Myrdal's highly influential book, *An American Dilemma*, which argued that racial liberals needed to transform the "hearts and minds" of white Americans.[90] CORE activists also wanted to change hearts and minds, but they were willing to put themselves at immediate risk and call for rapid change rather than a gradual evolution toward racial harmony.

Myrdal's call for moral suasion embodied a liberal interracialism that held out hope for the power of government institutions to institute real change. But the major figures in FOR and CORE embraced a very different vision of transformation. Bayard Rustin wrote to A. J. Muste in 1942 that "Negroes have generally lost faith in the 'pink tea social methods' which I have heard described as 'well-meanin' but getting us nowhere." He also wrote in the periodical *Fellowship* that same year, "Those who argue for an extended educational plan are not wrong, but there must also be a plan for facing *immediate* conflicts."[91] Randolph called attempts to educate whites at "good-will, interracial conferences . . . chloroform for the masses." "When the chloroform wears off," he argued, "the passions of the beast of race prejudice flare up again."[92] Randolph and CORE's founding members sought more immediate and direct change. They studied and taught the works of Richard Gregg, Krishnalal Shridharani, Gandhi, and other pacifist thinkers. But their interracial institutes went beyond education and moral suasion. Instead, they engaged in numerous demonstrations and trained a generation of activists who, in turn, would train the walkers in Montgomery, the students in SNCC, and influence anti-colonial movements on a global scale.

In the 1940s George Houser and James Farmer, along with Rustin, developed an innovative plan to bring nonviolent direct action to as many interested activists as possible. Rather than simply educating whites and Blacks about racial equality, a strategy promoted by racial liberals, they challenged businesses to hire Blacks, fought against segregated housing, and deployed radical nonviolence at segregated public accommodations. The first institutes in 1940 came solely out of FOR and were organized by Farmer, Rustin, and white activists Houser and John Swomley, the race relations secretaries for the organization.[93] They organized these early institutes as weekend retreats for committed activists and interested community members, similar to the programs innovated by workers' education institutions such as Brookwood and Highlander. Fridays commenced with religious and scientific discussions about race relations in American cities. Institute leaders, for example, encouraged participants to read the works of anthropologists, who argued against the notion that race was biologically fixed, and they often invited local faculty to speak.[94] But institute organizers insisted that education was not enough. "The seriousness of the times," argued Houser in a 1945 publication, "would seem to demand more virile action to supplement personal conversion and enlightenment by education." That "virile" action was nonviolent direct action. CORE activists deployed their actions on Saturdays, when interracial groups tested public accommodations in the cities. Organizers argued that these "action projects" were the institutes' "most unique characteristic."[95]

Facilities that denied service to interracial groups became the scene of sit-ins and picketing by institute participants. Institute leaders left behind an organized group of local activists to continue this work, affiliated either with FOR or CORE or acting independently. This method could be highly effective. Swomley remembered that in Denver "every theater and restaurant in the downtown area was opened on a nondiscriminatory basis within six months by a FOR group in 1943."[96] Muste estimated that the average attendance at institutes was between 150 and 250 people, with one institute drawing 600. With approximately ten institutes held per year through FOR and CORE between 1943 and 1955, activists exposed many thousands of Blacks and whites to the teachings of radical nonviolence, and these recruits then carried out direct-action campaigns in their neighborhoods.[97] In the summer of 1942, Rustin reported to Muste that he estimated he had spoken before more than five thousand people. "I have visited 8 CPS camps, 10 denominational conferences for high school youth. I have spoken in 17 colleges; conducted classes in four historic peace church summer camps; counseled with numerous men and boys considering the CO position; visited 4 work camps; and traveled among Negro groups, attempting to create an interest in nonviolent direct action."[98] Training institutes launched campaigns that were instrumental in desegregating public accommodations outside the South.

In the spring of 1943 alone, activists organized eight institutes in cities across the North and West. The action projects varied from city to city, but the most common targets were theaters, department stores, restaurants, and recreational facilities. In the case of stores, activists demanded increased African American employment in addition to desegregation. Stores in Cleveland, Pittsburgh, and Chicago, for example, agreed to change their hiring policy after institute participants picketed and pressured them. While interracial commissions, which proliferated during the 1940s, studied employment discrimination, FOR and CORE demanded immediate change. Most local CORE chapters challenged restrictive covenants and housing segregation as well.[99]

The action projects taken on by activists in the April 1943 race relations institute in Detroit are indicative of the range of targets, usually selected by members of the local community. Two restaurants known to discriminate were the sites of sit-ins; activists tested other restaurants and interviewed managers. Participants also targeted a bowling alley and roller-skating rink. Another group visited the editors of the three major white newspapers, requesting editors not specify race in their want ads and stories about crime. Activists investigated discrimination at the Willow Run housing project. Finally, an interracial group of picketers engaged in a downtown "poster walk" to publicize the anti-poll tax bill then being debated in the House of Representatives.[100] The poll tax was a barrier to southern African Americans' voting power, and therefore was a central target for northern activists. Long meetings followed the action projects, dissecting the level of success and drawing up plans for follow-up to be undertaken by groups in Detroit.

At the end of the war, as male pacifists were slowly being released from prison or returning home from camps, plans for institutes and workshops accelerated. In 1946, for example, activists organized six institutes in cities across the East Coast and Midwest.[101] They were geared toward individuals who "wish to take a direct part in the struggle for racial justice." In addition to the weekend institutes, FOR now also offered weeklong workshops, which one participant termed "a magnificent laboratory of action."[102] During these workshops, participants spent mornings in discussion and afternoons carrying out action projects. High drama often ensued. At a 1947 workshop in Toledo, Ohio, for example, Rustin and Houser went to a restaurant for a bite to eat before the evening session. When they were refused service, they staged an impromptu sit-in. They then phoned the workshoppers, who immediately joined them, taking up all the seats in the restaurant. The manager called the police, who declined to intervene. After long negotiations, the manager agreed to change his policy.[103] At times institutes sparked strong negative reactions from white business owners. During a 1946 institute in Bloomington, Indiana, signs appeared in restaurant windows announcing "We Cater to White Trade."[104] Such incidents helped inform the public about the extent of racial segregation in states that had civil rights laws on the books and galvanized the local Black community to protest discrimination.

In 1947 an interracial group of men, most of whom had passed through the Harlem Ashram's doors and were Peacemakers, carried out the Journey of Reconciliation. CORE and FOR organized the early Freedom Ride jointly to test the 1946 Supreme Court ruling *Morgan v. Virginia*, which stated that interstate travel could not be segregated. It was an important precursor to the 1961 and 1963 Freedom Rides and, in a highly dramatic fashion, signaled a wedding of the Black freedom struggle to pacifism. After meeting at the Washington Fellowship House for training, the group traveled through several southern states on public buses. Local police jailed a number of riders, and Rustin spent thirty days on a chain gang.[105] Riding together on the buses, Black and white pacifists gained significant publicity during the campaign and learned vital lessons for the future Freedom Rides of the early 1960s. Rustin noted in a speech the following year, "The Journey of Reconciliation was organized not only to devise techniques for eliminating Jim Crow in travel, but also as a training ground for similar peaceful projects against discrimination in such major areas as employment and in the armed services. Central to that training would be the organization of disciplined cells across the nation to advise resistance and to provide spiritual, financial, and legal aid to resisters."[106] The Journey of Reconciliation was the only major campaign during this period that ventured below the Mason-Dixon Line. However, by 1949 Rustin advocated that the "time had arrived for CORE to begin working organizationally in the South."[107] When the Montgomery Bus Boycott began in 1955, that time finally came.

Not all communities that held institutes went on to establish CORE or FOR chapters; existing interracial organizations or newly formed ones often committed themselves to radical nonviolence. One group that worked closely with CORE in several Ohio cities during the 1940s was the Vanguard League. Founded in 1940 and committed to nonviolent direct action, the Vanguard League trained members at interracial workshops and addressed restrictive covenants, police brutality, and segregated accommodations. In Washington, DC, CORE worked closely with the Committee for Racial Democracy in the Nation's Capital, which carried out picketing and sit-ins at public accommodations. In Lawrence, Kansas, the League for the Practice of Democracy took on the cause of desegregation. Similarly, CORE workshops helped form the Intercultural Fellowship in Fresno, California, and the Christian Friends for Racial Equality in Seattle.[108] These organizations, along with the Fellowship Houses and churches and Father Divine's Peace Mission, challenged more

FIGURE 5.1 Journey of Reconciliation participants: Worth Randle, Wallace Nelson, Ernest Bromley, Jim Peck, Igal Roodenko, Bayard Rustin, Joe Felmet, George Houser, and Andy Johnson, 1947. Credit: Library of Congress, Prints and Photographs Division, NYWT&S Collection, LC-USZ62-120215.

mainstream civil rights organizations and played an instrumental role in the burgeoning civil rights movement.

The 1940s and early 1950s institutes allowed activists to refine their tactics and publish "how to" guides that could be followed by others. These publications included detailed descriptions of actual desegregation campaigns. Activists gave institute participants instructions for nearly every possible reaction they might encounter. For example, when trying to get served at segregated restaurants, they had a variety of scripts to follow. If they were told, "You may take your sandwich in a bag," they were to reply, "Thank you, but I really don't want to take it out" and proceed to order a cup of coffee. If told, "You may sit at the counter in the back," activists were to ask questions such as "If I came back disguised as a white person could I sit where I want?" When offered a rusty tin cup, apparently a common occurrence, they were to threaten to call the board of health. Throughout, activists were to be polite but firm and have full knowledge of the existing civil rights laws. In 1949 Houser reported that CORE had distributed ten thousand pieces of literature. In addition to the literature, the *CORE-Lator* newsletter reported on campaigns nationwide. By 1953 the CORE mailing list for their newsletter had grown to over sixteen hundred. CORE fieldworkers also distributed literature and held meetings throughout the country. Black CORE activist and Peacemaker Wallace Nelson, for example, reported that between 1950 and 1953, he had "met with 128 groups in 52 cities and towns in 13 states."[109]

CORE activists expended the most energy on revising and perfecting their central blueprint on nonviolent direct action, "CORE Action Discipline." This short booklet outlined the steps that activists would take to carry out campaigns, beginning with investigation and ending with nonviolent action. CORE emphasized the need for discipline in the instructions, both the discipline of nonviolence and the group discipline of following orders. It also explained in clear terms what the group was attempting to accomplish, and activists distributed the booklet to adversaries at picket lines and sit-ins. In 1946, for example, the Evanston, Illinois, chapter of CORE requested fifteen hundred copies to use in their campaigns.[110] Activists updated "CORE Action Discipline" yearly at annual CORE conventions and conferences, where activists from around the country met to compare their experiences. During these meetings, participants also engaged in large-scale nonviolent action. "Each year," reported Houser, "the CORE convention has as a part of its program the very practical task of 'practicing what it preaches,' of resisting unjust racial practices on the spot."[111] City by city these activists took on the contradictions of segregated accommodations and employment discrimination in states with existing civil rights laws.

Building on FOR institutes and workshops, which were relatively brief in duration, after the war CORE sponsored monthlong programs to train activists in nonviolence and to foster utopian interracialism. Starting in the summer of 1945, activists held workshops in Chicago, Los Angeles, and Washington, DC.[112] During the summers of 1945 and 1946, activists in Chicago challenged restrictive covenants and called attention to realtors who practiced block busting. They also pressured department stores to hire African Americans and protested segregation at YMCAs and discrimination at the University of Chicago. Volunteers lived communally, following Farmer's vision of Fellowship Houses across the country. One observer noted, "A small interracial group of young people fought on more fronts and got more accomplished than most of the professional high-salaried race relations experts in Chicago." A volunteer who participated in the 1945 workshop called the experience "a magnificent laboratory of action."[113] White participants praised the focus on action rather than education. One wrote, "In our direct action we assume that civil rights exist in this city and act as naturally as possible in the circumstances—being sure to act instead of merely theorizing and reading books on the subject."[114] Experiencing the reality of racism firsthand and directly challenging the status quo through nonviolent direct action was a life-changing experience for many.

By the late 1940s, CORE began to focus its efforts on Washington, DC, creating a permanent interracial workshop there every summer between 1947 and 1954, with a smaller group organizing during the year.[115] Washington had no official Jim Crow laws but was a deeply segregated city. Pauli Murray noted that when she arrived in Washington to study law at Howard University in 1943, "Union Station was the only place in downtown Washington where a Negro could get a meal or use rest room facilities."[116] Washington, DC, also held symbolic importance as the nation's capital. A group of female students at Howard University, led by Murray, had already deployed nonviolent direct action to desegregate restaurants in the city.[117] The first summer workshop in 1947 followed up on this earlier activism by testing restaurants throughout the city and targeting those that resisted interracial groups being served. Often staff seated the activists in the back of a restaurant, ignoring them. Indeed, out of the twenty-five restaurants visited, only two served the interracial groups. In addition to their work in public accommodations, activists handed out five thousand leaflets titled "You Don't Have to Ride Jim Crow" at interstate bus and train stations, informing passengers of the recent Supreme Court decision outlawing segregation in interstate transportation. The leaflet included specific advice on how to deal with conflicts with bus drivers and police, in part drawn from the 1947 Journey of Reconciliation.[118]

A radio interview with some of the participants suggests the range of backgrounds and motivations that spurred them to travel to Washington. A Japanese American student hitchhiked from Illinois to join the workshop because "as a member of a minority group I have always known the bitter taste of prejudice." A mother of two said she "found it is inadequate just to teach the ideals of brotherhood and democracy to young people." A white woman from Miami noted, "We think that discrimination isn't just a problem for the colored people of America." All expressed their desire to "carry back to our home communities new ideas and methods."[119] Workshoppers in Washington stayed at Inspiration House, a large well-appointed home in an African American neighborhood and the headquarters of the permanent interracial workshop. They reported that the experience of interracial living in a communal setting was transformative. "If we had done nothing else, simply living in an interracial group for that period of time would have been worth the time for me," noted one participant. "Living in an interracial group," testified another, "has made the problems of segregation and discrimination seem less intellectual and more human." Others described the "rich fellowship" and "feeling of accomplishment" their summer experience offered.[120] In addition to the planning and execution of work projects, the students participated in social activities and long meetings, reminiscent of Ahimsa and the work of SNCC fifteen years in the future.[121] During the summer months, Inspiration House functioned much as other pacifist intentional communities, fostering utopian interracialism and providing a laboratory for practicing radical nonviolence.

Participants in the interracial workshops were also nimble, responding to spontaneous challenges to segregated facilities by local African Americans. For example, the 1949 workshop coincided with a riot at the Anacostia pool, when a white mob stormed a group of young African Americans attempting to desegregate the pool, which the city then closed. The workshoppers investigated the causes of the riot and offered their assistance to the Department of the Interior, which oversaw the city's pools, to reopen it as a desegregated facility.[122] That summer, workshoppers also worked to desegregate the Greyhound bus station restaurant, the YMCA coffee shop, and a downtown theater. By the mid-1950s, the ongoing work of the interracial workshop had created wholesale change in the city, as downtown theaters and restaurants increasingly opened their doors to African Americans in response to the unrelenting pressure from radical pacifists and local Black residents.[123]

But these victories came at a cost. Those involved in the summer workshops always risked being victimized by police and onlookers. Wilson Head remembered, "Many participants in Chicago sit-ins were physically assaulted. Many were burned, kicked, struck and otherwise harassed."[124] During the 1951 workshop, an attempt to desegregate a Maryland nightclub ended in a riot with CORE members badly beaten.[125] More violence followed during a campaign that CORE spearheaded to desegregate Rosedale playground, located in a mixed neighborhood in the nation's capital, but open only to whites. The first summer the project worked to secure neighborhood support by forming the all-Black Rosedale Citizens Committee. These community members, mostly women and children, picketed the playground accompanied by interracial groups of CORE activists. Local whites attacked them viciously, and there were several incidents of beatings.

On a hot June evening in 1952, the second summer of protests at Rosedale, a thirteen-year-old Black boy climbed the playground fence during the night, wanting to cool off in the restricted pool. Denied the swimming lessons given his white neighbors, the boy drowned in the unattended pool, and his death galvanized the local Black community to engage in a full-on assault on the playground. Ten members of the interracial workshop, five white and five

Black, blocked the entrance to the playground. When police apprehended them, they immediately fell to the ground and police carried them into a wagon and then into the patrol house. There they refused to give their names or post bond at the jail. While imprisoned the group went on a hunger strike. The workshop leader and Peacemaker, Wallace Nelson, later reported that while in custody an officer kicked him to the floor, ground a lit cigarette into his skin, and twisted his arm with a metal clamp that left permanent scars on his wrist. Now emboldened, community members began to routinely defy the segregation policy, as young Blacks climbed over the playground fence daily. Under intense pressure, the Recreation Board finally declared it a desegregated facility, and it reopened that October to African American and white children.[126]

The struggle for access to Rosedale playground was brutal but ultimately successful. And it took place precisely at the moment that historians consider the civil rights movement to be at its lowest ebb. There is no doubt that by 1954 CORE had lost momentum, and debates within the organization about practicing total noncooperation—for example, carrying out hunger strikes when arrested—inspired some, including Nelson, to resign. But this was, in part, a reflection of radical nonviolence's success in the North and West. The groups were most successful in cities where they encountered a significant amount of segregation. Houser argued, "They grow if there is a courageous leadership and challenging campaign. But they also die if no major project asserts itself."[127] He noted in 1952 that in a ten-year period, thirty-two different chapters were affiliated with CORE. But he also pointed out, "Because CORE groups are youthful, not staid and conservative[,] they may be unstable." In addition, CORE was deliberately planned to be "small, interracial action units."[128] Therefore, judging the impact of radical pacifists' work purely on membership numbers is misguided. The twelve years of institutes and workshops had trained a new generation of radical activists in the tactics of nonviolence. They did so to educate and promote interracialism, but also to challenge segregation directly and bring revolutionary pacifism to American activists. The ramifications of this training would unfold quickly in the years to come. Looking back on this era, Swomley identified the institutes as the "forerunners of the civil rights campaigns of the 1960s."[129] Their direct-action projects refined the teachings of Gandhi and Shridharani for a distinctly American context, and their communal peace cells modeled utopian interracialism.

One reason that civil rights historians have largely overlooked this early radical nonviolent movement was its location in northern and border states. Although organizers reached out to southern activists and FOR had a south-

ern secretary, they did not launch major campaigns there. "Non-violent direct action will not work successfully in the South," argued Houser, "until
there is a substantially large group of persons who are willing to take group
action and suffer punishment non-violently."[130] The civil rights unionism of
the Southern Tenant Farmers' Union did pursue economic and racial equality nonviolently. But its eventual failure, like the failure of the CIO's Operation Dixie following World War II, suggests that Houser was correct. Indeed,
many considered radical nonviolence in the South "suicidal" in the 1940s,
and the Journey of Reconciliation was the only major campaign that ventured below the Mason-Dixon Line. But this does not mean that the success
of radical nonviolence outside the South should be ignored. One of the key
advances of the long civil rights movement historiography is the geographic
expansion of the field to include the North and West. For African Americans
facing daily humiliations at hotels, restaurants, and amusement parks, challenging that racism directly and gaining access to urban spaces was a significant accomplishment.

In 1945 Houser identified one of the key strengths of radical nonviolence as
"cause-consciousness." "Legal action will not arouse this cause-consciousness
to the same extent that group direct action will, for the simple reason that
action in a legal case is left in the hands of a lawyer and a few witnesses. But
in non-violent direct action, a group must unitedly discuss its strategy, decide
what course to follow, and then pursue the course unfalteringly." The "masses
of Negroes," Houser emphasized, needed to embrace such a consciousness to
enact "racial democracy."[131] The midcentury direct-action movement did not
successfully arouse cause-consciousness among the masses. Nevertheless,
the connection between radical pacifists and the successful mass movement
is direct. In 1955, hearing of the outbreak of the Montgomery Bus Boycott,
Rustin and fellow pacifist Glenn Smiley quickly traveled to Alabama to advise Martin Luther King Jr.[132] They went on to travel throughout the South,
training and advising activists.[133] Black radical pacifist James Lawson, for
example, was first introduced to the works of Gandhi in college when he read
about Howard Thurman's encounter and heard Muste speak. Inspired, he
worked with both FOR and CORE and did missionary work in India, studying
nonviolence. In 1950, at the outset of the Korean War, Lawson spent time in
prison for resisting the draft. And he became FOR's southern secretary and
trained African American students in Nashville, Tennessee, while he was
attending divinity school at Vanderbilt University. Many of those students
became the vanguard of SNCC, and Lawson drafted the group's statement
of purpose in 1960.[134] Students took the lead in this movement, and older
activists like Lawson were careful to give them the most prominent voices.

But their experiences in the 1940s and 1950s institutes proved invaluable. By 1961 CORE was running training institutes in nonviolent direct action every summer, one in the South and one in the North.[135]

The Montgomery Bus Boycott did not mark the start of nonviolent direct action in the Jim Crow South; there had been sporadic sit-ins and other demonstrations prior to 1955. And there were enclaves such as Highlander, Delta and Providence farms, Macedonia, and Koinonia that provided training and models of utopian interracialism. However, the size and visibility of the mass movement, particularly between 1960 and 1965, was distinct. Indeed, an important critique of the long civil rights narrative is its potential for flattening out change by narrating an extensive period of continual activism.[136] But if there was something distinctive about the scale and success of the classical phase of the movement, its "cause-consciousness," then we should identify its major influences. Radical pacifism shaped the tactics of SCLC, SNCC, and CORE and offered an alternative to the NAACP's legalism and racial liberals' gradualism. And those methods grew out of relatively small groups of activists committed to utopian interracialism.

Indeed, the work carried out by radical pacifists in the 1940s and early 1950s was significant in its own right. For African Americans facing daily humiliations at hotels, restaurants, and amusement parks, challenging that racism directly and gaining access to urban spaces was a significant accomplishment. Their freedom dreams were impatient ones, and a generation of activists emerging from the linked workers' education, cooperative, and fellowship movements were poised to make them come true.

Conclusion

As organized labor turned away from its most democratic impulses in the 1930s, the appeal and success of radical nonviolence in the North was attractive to Black and white activists impatient with the slow pace of change. Although activists' shift away from labor has been understood primarily within the context of the cold war, CORE's founding, the establishment of interracial utopian communities, and the interracial institutes and workshops all preceded the outbreak of the cold war. The application of radical nonviolence to the freedom struggle created dramatic changes outside the South prior to 1955, and with SNCC's founding in 1960, this tactic became central to the mass civil rights movement. But radical nonviolence was not simply a tactic—it involved a prefigurative utopian politics that sought to create a new society based on cooperation, peace, and equality. That politics was nurtured in peace cells, communes, and ashrams at midcentury. The students of SNCC held up these ideals as models, as they brought the movement to a new level in 1960. The utopian interracialism promoted within the Harlem Ashram, FOR, and CORE did not reflect the gradual and polite politics of liberal interracialism and went beyond the purely class politics of labor interracialism. In contrast, utopian interracialism demanded a fundamental break from the past and immediate, even revolutionary, change. This racial revolution took decades to complete, but on 125th Street in Harlem and at Inspiration House in Washington, DC, it had already begun.

Afterword

All the great turning points of history have been made by small, determined groups.

MARTIN LUTHER KING JR.[1]

Freedom . . . is to stop living the lie.

SNCC[2]

In April 1960 Marjorie Penney traveled from the Philadelphia Fellowship House to Shaw University in North Carolina for a meeting of the Southern Christian Leadership Conference (SCLC), formed after the Montgomery Bus Boycott under the leadership of Martin Luther King Jr. At a mass rally in downtown Raleigh, she heard King praise "small determined groups" as history makers. Hundreds of African American students who had been engaging in sit-ins for the previous six weeks, expanding the use of nonviolent direct action throughout the South, joined King for the meeting.[3] Penney was part of a small northern contingent, experienced in nonviolent direct action and eager to help grow the movement. Ella Baker, alumna of Brookwood and Highlander and SCLC's executive director, organized the meeting and urged the young activists to maintain their autonomy. She was joined by James Lawson, who brought his experience with radical pacifism to Black students in Nashville, Tennessee, where he was attending Vanderbilt University. Lawson trained those students to withstand the taunts and violence of racist whites during their lunch counter protests and introduced them to philosophical and political writings of Howard Thurman, Gandhi, A. J. Muste, and others.

By the time of the Raleigh meeting, Vanderbilt had expelled Lawson for his activism. This left him free to work with the politicized and energized young students, who decided to form their own organization, the Student Nonviolent Coordinating Committee (SNCC). Lawson drafted SNCC's statement of purpose. "The redemptive community supersedes systems of gross social immorality," wrote Lawson. "Love is the central motif of nonviolence." The Raleigh conference and a second conference in Atlanta a month later drew from the decades of democratic and experimental meetings at Highlander, in Fellowship Houses, and in CORE meetings held at ashrams and peace farms. Under Baker's tutelage and Lawson's guidance, the students resisted the more hierarchical structure of SCLC and the NAACP's moderate politics.[4] They engaged in participatory decision making, welcoming opinions from all present and attempting to reach a broad consensus, which would become the primary mode of organizing in the New Left. And like Muste and Krishnalal Shridharani during the 1940s, SNCC called for a "nonviolent revolution." In preparing for a "nonviolent army," Lawson recommended establishing "work camps for training, study, reading, meditation and constructive work in voting, repairing neighborhood slums, community centers."[5] Such a call had a clear precedent in the workers' education colleges, cooperatives, and interracial churches of the previous three decades.

In an April 1960 issue of *Liberation*, the periodical printed out of the utopian Glen Gardner community, the editors, thrilled at the rising tide of southern activism, wrote: "It was pacifist organizations immediately after World War II . . . that carried out projects in nonviolent direct action in the racial field, circulated Gandhian and other literature on the subject, and quietly trained a considerable number of people, all of which is now bearing fruit."[6] SNCC's founding proved that these strategies had purchase outside of the mid-twentieth-century utopian socialist circles. The decade that followed would be one of almost constant struggle from the Mississippi Delta to Chicago's segregated neighborhoods. The utopian strategy of forming small groups to prefigure and help enact change was only one part of the overall success of the Black freedom movement. Without mass marches, Black Nationalist strategies, and political mobilization, among other elements, the major successes of the movement would not have been achieved. But it is striking how little known utopian practices and ideas are in the civil rights movement's public image and in many scholarly works. And the charismatic Father Divine movement, which touched so many in the 1930s and 1940s, has been entirely marginalized in these narratives. Utopian socialists and radical pacifists rejected the gradualism of liberal politics and demanded immediate and profound societal changes. The Raleigh meeting was the fruition of this strategy and demonstrated how a deep and meaningful reservoir of practical politics emerged from prefigurative utopian experimentation.

Raleigh also marked a resurgence of utopian thought, which was marginalized during the height of the cold war in the 1950s. The liberal consensus of that decade found utopianism suspect, unrealistic, and potentially reinforcing totalitarian tendencies. The rise of the New Left brought utopianism back to center stage. The influential sociologist David Riesman, frustrated with the liberal consensus, called for a "revival of the tradition of utopian thinking" in his 1954 work *Individualism Reconsidered*. "Without great plans," wrote Riesman, "it is hard, and often self-defeating to make little ones."[7] Utopianism suggested a way out of the cold war's ideological binds, a view increasingly appealing to a progressive baby boom generation forging a new political path. After SNCC's stirring call for revolutionary nonviolence, white college students formed the Students for a Democratic Society (SDS) and drafted the Port Huron Statement in 1962. "The decline of utopia and hope is in fact one of the defining features of social life today," wrote the young activists. "To be idealistic is to be considered apocalyptic, deluded."[8] Thus, the New Left coalition revived the utopian idealism of an earlier generation.

With the escalation of the Vietnam War in 1965, the linked civil rights and peace movements became a major force on the American Left.[9] Catholic Workers, for example, allied with a coalition of peace activists to fight against nuclear proliferation and the Vietnam War. The "movement of movements" that emerged by the second half of the 1960s was discordant, with sometimes contradictory goals and unintended outcomes. While the utopian socialists and radical pacifists had in common a commitment to interracialism, cooperation, and nonviolence, the New Left lacked the same coherence. But many New Left activists, from radical feminist communitarians to antiwar protesters, shared a basic commitment to honor ends and means equally and practice prefigurative politics. And some sought to replicate the pacifist communes of midcentury. In the mid-1950s, white pacifists and socialists Helen Nearing and Scott Nearing published *Living the Good Life: How to Live Sanely and Simply in a Troubled World*, which became a guidebook for countercultural communes.[10] The two radicals left 1930s New York City to homestead in rural Vermont, later moving to a larger homestead in Maine. They had long traveled in pacifist and socialist circles; Scott Nearing, for example, lectured at Brookwood Labor College.[11] Pacifists, including Richard Gregg, author of *The Power of Nonviolence*, spent time at the homestead, and it became a major attraction during the Vietnam War as young activists sought to hear the Nearings' teachings on pacifism, vegetarianism, and self-sustaining living.[12] While many of the communes that imitated the Nearings were nearly all white, Macedonia and Koinonia continued to propagate utopian interracialism in the new era.[13] Both Georgia farms sheltered SNCC and other civil rights workers, offering them respite during brutal southern campaigns.

The communal and cooperative experiments that were most political and innovative in the post-1964 landscape were run not by interracialists, but by Black Nationalists. These projects, however, also had a utopian inflection. African Americans have a long tradition of creating collective spaces separate from the dominant white power structure. All-Black towns in the nineteenth century, where freedpeople built safe and relatively prosperous communities, are perhaps the best examples. In the 1920s, the Garvey movement promoted economic nationalism through Black-owned businesses that catered to the Black community, a model that the Nation of Islam followed in later decades. But it was in the late 1960s and 1970s that Black Nationalism was at its most utopian as activists developed a myriad of economic, cultural, and political worlds where they could live out their freedom dreams.

One can see echoes of the Father Divine movement in the Black Nationalist groups of the 1960s and 1970s, despite the fact that Divine fully embraced interracialism. Both the Revolutionary Action Movement and the Black Panther Party (BPP) had platforms that echoed parts of Divine's Righteous Government Platform. The BPP, like Father Divine's Peace Mission, called for an end to capital punishment and lynching. Both groups advocated for economic reparations and universal education free from racial bias.[14] There is no evidence of a direct link between these groups; however, these similarities suggest how the power to imagine a more just future drove social activism. Black Power advocates who were strident critics of capitalism also embraced cooperatives as a central aspect of economic nationalism. Historian Joshua Clark Davis notes that in the 1960s and 1970s "activist entrepreneurs," including Black Power activists running bookstores and other businesses, "viewed their businesses as 'prefigurative institutions' that served as models for the democratic society that social movements hoped to build."[15] Many embraced the term *ujamaa*, a Kiswahili word popularized by Tanzania's first Black president Julius K. Nyerere, which promoted socialism through community. Maulana Karenga, the leader of the Black Power US Organization and creator of the Kwanzaa holiday, popularized the term in America. Karenga explained that *ujamaa* reflected a "commitment to the practice of shared social wealth," which included a cooperative economic model that would benefit the Black community.[16] Activist entrepreneurs designed Black Nationalist cooperatives to serve their community, rather than model a utopian interracialism, but the overlap in terms of visionary reach is clear.

Black utopian thought reached its apex during the Afrofuturist movement in the 1970s, a social and cultural movement that projected a Black aesthetic into an imagined future. From the futurist jazz artist Sun Ra, who explored space travel with his Arkestra, to the pathbreaking science fiction writers Samuel Delany and Octavia Butler, Afrofuturism infused the 1970s Black Arts movement with its utopian dreaming. In recent years, Afrofuturism has experienced a revival, perhaps most familiar in the 2018 release of the film *Black Panther*. The blockbuster is based on the Marvel Comics of the same name and posits a utopian African republic, Wakanda, where technology and Afrocentric practices merge in a near-perfect society.[17] Today Afrofuturists continue to create speculative fiction, art, and music that look to this rich past while envisioning a future of Black empowerment and freedom.

Black Power activists also created real utopian communities, in both rural and urban areas, that built on the ideals of *ujamaa* and the legacies of all-Black towns and communes. These resembled Father Divine's Promised Land's cooperative farms and businesses and built on the legacy of the Delta and Providence farms. Agrarian nationalists sought to create safe and productive land in rural areas, particularly in the South. The Federation of Southern Cooperatives, founded in 1967 in Mississippi, brought together numerous Black cooperative experiments, many organized by civil rights veterans such as Fannie Lou Hamer, James Forman, and Charles Sherrod. A decade later the federation was coordinating over thirty agricultural cooperatives and providing educational support to low-income rural families.[18]

A central theme in Black Power ideology was political nationalism, the creation of physical spaces that could be controlled by a fully autonomous Black community. Some Black thinkers, influenced by the Caribbean author Frantz Fanon, viewed African Americans as a colonized people. Creating physical enclaves free from the colonizer was necessary to experience freedom and autonomy. In Detroit, the Republic of New Africa (RNA) argued for the creation of such a state in the Deep South, the territory that had once held the Delta and Providence cooperative farms. In a 1972 manifesto, the RNA proclaimed that the new nation would be run under "Ujamaa," which would bring about "a revolution for a better life, a better station for mankind, a surer harmony with the forces of life in the universe."[19] Like the Father Divine movement, RNA followers chose new names, marking their inclusion into the community and making a decisive break from a more oppressive past. The RNA's plan did not materialize—the group was a prime target of the FBI and police, who jailed many of its leaders. But their legacy remains. Two of the RNA founders moved to Mississippi in 1970 and established the "Provisional Government of the Republic of New Afrika," which they envisioned as a "a *new society* built with no color, class, gender and physical ability discrimination."[20]

Although their efforts were stymied by local law enforcement and white resistance, in 2013 one of the RNA activists, Chokwe Lumumba, was elected as mayor of Jackson, Mississippi, and helped to spearhead a project known as Cooperation Jackson. Under Lumumba's leadership, the citizens of Jackson engage in participatory democracy to determine the city's budget and priorities. And, cognizant of the long history of Black cooperatives, they launched a series of cooperatives that include agriculture, commerce, arts, and culture. Jackson's Community Land Trust also laid the groundwork for cooperative housing developments.[21] In the poorest state of the union, Cooperation Jackson is building *ujamaa* to provide a more equitable world for its inhabitants. This is the direct outgrowth of the RNA's utopian vision of a Black southern nation, as well as a broad and international cooperative and socialist movement.

A less successful attempt to create a Black intentional community based on Black Power principals was the establishment of Soul City in North Carolina. This was the brainchild of civil rights activist and lawyer Floyd B. McKissick, who headed CORE from 1966 to 1968 before leaving to build his southern utopian community. In contrast to the independent Father Divine Peace Mission or Delta Cooperative Farm, McKissick sought out federal funding for his utopia, which was to be built from scratch in a sparsely populated and economically depressed region. In 1972 he obtained a $14 million guarantee from the Department of Housing and Urban Development to build the community, working closely with the Nixon administration to obtain the funding. Because of this alliance with leading Republicans, McKissick did not openly state that the community was separatist. "Soul City is intended to be a town open to all," he claimed in 1974, "but placing a special emphasis on providing opportunities for poor and minority groups." However, it is clear that his intention was to create a separate Black nation. "My primary concern is not with saving white America," wrote McKissick in 1969, "I am concerned with liberating Black America."[22] His plans were ambitious, including eight residential villages with schools, recreational facilities, and light industry. But only one of the villages was built, and McKissick struggled to get capital investment in the community. By 1979 the federal government withdrew all support for Soul City, and McKissick's plans never reached full fruition.[23]

The RNA and McKissick were not alone in their aspirations. Black Panther Party members and the Congress of African People (CAP), led by poet and artist Amiri Baraka, developed cooperative businesses in numerous cities during the late 1960s and 1970s.[24] In 1972 Philadelphia saw the emergence of another cooperative and communal Black Power organization, MOVE. MOVE members embraced an environmental and anarchist philosophy, combining Black Power ideas with the communalism and back-to-the-land ethos of the counterculture. They are best known, however, for a series of escalating conflicts with Philadelphia police that shockingly culminated in the 1985 bombing of MOVE's headquarters. Eleven people, including five children, died in the bombing and ensuing fire.[25] The FBI surveillance and police violence suffered by these organizations might be explained by their embrace of self-defense rather than nonviolence. However, such surveillance and white supremacist attacks also terrorized Highlander Folk School, the Delta and Providence farms, and agricultural communes such as Koinonia. Police and white mobs brutally beat CORE activists when they challenged the color line. Only more moderate liberal interracialist organizations, such as Howard Thurman's interracial church, were spared from this brutality. Clearly Black Power organizations suffered the most unrelenting state violence; however, practicing nonviolence did not protect activists from bombings, beatings, and imprisonment.

Beyond nonviolence there are other distinctions between the Black Nationalist communities and the utopian socialists and pacifists of midcentury. Black Nationalism was generally more patriarchal than institutions such as Brookwood Labor College, whose foundation in workers' education arising from feminist labor unions helped nurture female activists such as Ella Baker and Pauli Murray.[26] And Black Nationalist groups rejected interracialism, although they did ally with radical white organizations. But Black Power activists were not the only ones to reject interracialism as a primary goal. During the Black Power era, it is striking that the countercultural communes were largely white and did not place interracialism at the forefront of their prefigurative teaching. These white groups, for the most part, also did not experience the state-sponsored violence that their Black counterparts did. But despite their differences, in the 1960s and 1970s many Black and white activists practiced a prefigurative politics that would have been familiar to Father Divine, A. J. Muste, and Pauli Murray.

In recent decades, interracialism has become more central to political dreaming and many new social movements resemble the midcentury activism explored in this work. Activist and author Chris Dixon, for example, points to a thriving "anti-authoritarian, anti-capitalist, nonsectarian left" that embraces prefigurative politics in which activists are "trying to manifest and build . . . the egalitarian and deeply democratic world we would like to see through our means of fighting in this one."[27] These activists embrace a decentered and democratic politics that mirrors a larger practice of twentieth-century utopian communities. And their interracialism recognizes ethnic and racial groups' unique challenges, rather than positing a conservative colorblindness that erases these distinctions. The extent to which these "small determined groups" that Martin Luther King Jr. identified can enact transformative change will be found in their ability to connect to grander visions of a transformed future. A future that tackles climate change, income inequality, and racial equity through a nonviolent revolution.

In the summer of 2020, this connection between engaged political activism and a utopian vision for the future could be seen in the massive uprisings in the wake of George Floyd's brutal murder by a Minneapolis police officer. In the months that followed, the Black Lives Matter movement reached unprecedented heights and large interracial crowds demanded wholesale transformation in the criminal justice system. They also transformed urban landscapes by demanding the removal of white supremacist statues that celebrated the Confederacy. What set these demonstrations apart from those of the long civil rights movement was the large number of white participants. And these rallies and marches were not limited to residents of progressive cities, but spread into small towns in more conservative states. In fact, the majority of white Americans, 60 percent, supported the Black Lives Matter movement at the height of the summer.[28] Corporations, sports franchises, and academic institutions launched racial diversity and inclusion programs in response to the mass movement. Importantly, like the strongest experiments in utopian interracialism, the movement's primary organizers were African American. The long-term impacts of Black Lives Matter's mass interracial movement are still playing out. But the vision of a more equitable future is more widely shared as a result of this mobilization.[29]

Indeed, in the new millennium, utopianism has mounted something of a comeback. Sociologist Erik Olin Wright, for example, has called for "real utopias" that will reflect "our deepest aspirations" while recognizing problems of "unintended consequences and self-destructive dynamics."[30] In *Becoming Utopian*, the cultural critic Tom Moylan calls for a "politics of radical transformation." The Dutch historian Rutger Bregman's best-selling book, *Utopia for Realists*, has helped popularize universal income and open borders.[31] The alter-globalization and Occupy movements have taken up the strategy of prefigurative politics. Anthropologist and anarchist David Graeber, in particular, has promoted this form of activism. "It's one thing to say, 'Another world is possible,'" writes Graeber. "It's another to experience it, however momentarily."[32] And visionary policies—such as prison abolition,

Universal Basic Income, and the New Green Deal—have a utopian strain as they envision a future without mass incarceration, searing poverty, or an escalating climate crisis.

Nonviolent direct action was appealing to activists engaged in prefigurative politics in the 1930s, 1960s, and today. This is most powerfully demonstrated by the interracial activists in the Black Lives Matter movement who have used nonviolent direct action to bring attention to police brutality and mass incarceration.[33] Even workers' education is making a comeback. In 2019 the New Brookwood Labor College opened in St. Paul, Minnesota, as an explicit effort to revive the work of the original Brookwood. "We are creating an inclusive labor movement," state the founders, "that uses the power of organization not merely to lift individual workers or worksites, but to create a more just world."[34] The Highlander Research and Education Center continues the legacy of the Highlander Folk School by training interracial activists in Tennessee.[35] And in the wake of George Floyd's murder, a group of African American women established "The Freedom Georgia Initiative," an intentional community in rural Georgia that was established "out of an extreme sense of urgency to create a thriving safe haven for Black families in the midst of racial trauma, a global pandemic, and economic instabilities across the United States of America brought on by COVID-19."[36] The freedom dreams of early civil rights activists helped fuel a mass social movement. In this current moment of crises, social dreaming may show us the way to a transformed future.

What is less visible in contemporary movements is religion, which was so central to the activists this work explores. However, the Christian Left remains a vibrant part of inclusive progressive movements. Often overlooked because of the political dominance of the more cohesive Evangelical Right, numerous progressive religious groups have taken on social justice campaigns. To take one particularly visible example, since 2013 the African American religious leader Rev. William J. Barber has led a "Moral Mondays" movement to protest North Carolina's draconian cuts to education and welfare programs. Those protests have since expanded to a broader interracial Poor People's Campaign, modeled after King's 1968 Poor People's March. Religious activists have also worked on the front lines of the immigrant rights movement and in anti-poverty groups nationwide.[37] And Catholic Workers continue their advocacy for social justice and run hospitality houses throughout the country.[38] These groups carry on the legacy of the twentieth-century Christian Left in their calls for unity, morality, and nonviolence.

The city in which I wrote this book, Buffalo, New York, exemplifies the possibilities of multi-racial, inclusive social movements. In the summer of

1956, after testifying at the Democratic National Convention, King came to Buffalo to give a speech. "We stand today between two worlds," he said, "the dying old and the emerging new." King then invoked the "beloved community," a phrase and an ideal that fueled the movement for the next decade. "The end is the creation of a beloved community. The end is the creation of a society where men will live together as brothers."[39] Today Buffalo is home to myriad of social movement organizations that reflect many of King's priorities and the utopian socialists he admired. Cooperation Buffalo, for example, promotes and supports the creation of worker-owned cooperatives in the city. People United for Sustainable Housing (PUSH) works on the interconnected issues of affordable housing, employment, and environmental justice. Much like the Fellowship Houses, PUSH has refurbished an abandoned school to create affordable housing, a theater, and meeting spaces for community groups. Nearby the West Side Bazaar harbors a new generation of activist entrepreneurs—refugees and immigrants who have opened small businesses celebrating their native cultures. And in a quickly gentrifying neighborhood known as the Fruit Belt, residents have formed a community land trust to ensure that housing remains affordable. Despite the efforts of these organizations, Buffalo remains an impoverished and segregated city, but it is also a city in which the freedom dreams of refugees, low-income Black families, and the LGBTQ community have flourished.[40]

Robin D. G. Kelley's invocation of "freedom dreams" also has contemporary resonances across the modern world. In Hong Kong, journalist Yi-Ling Liu notes that for the country's activists, "The act of protest itself is referred to as 'dreaming.' 'Let's decide on a meeting point for the dreaming,' a protester might say. 'I dreamed I was out on the streets last night,' another might write."[41] The metaphor of dreams opens up the imagination, which allows protesters to envision and enact a different future. Writing about utopia, Howard Thurman noted, "Even when men are sure that what they seek is a dream that can never be realized in their lifetime or in the lifetime of all who live at the present moment, they dare to say, nevertheless, that it will come to pass, sometime, somewhere."[42] The dreams of civil rights activists invested in utopian ideas and practices were only partially realized, but the dreaming itself was part of the point. For utopian dreamers, the means and ends work together seamlessly. Their counter-institutions and movements are those dreams manifested, not in the imagined future but in the very real present.

Acknowledgments

I could not have predicted that my final months of writing and revising this book would take place during a global pandemic. That fact has deepened my sense of gratitude profoundly. The ability to travel to archives, talk with colleagues over a cup of coffee, or to dwell on small problems rather than cataclysmic ones were all gifts I had taken for granted. More positively, the uprising of social protests around police brutality and racial equality during the summer of 2020 has brought an optimism that undergirds this book project. Black and white protesters together challenged the status quo in unprecedented numbers, a message that spread globally. Their linked freedom dreams shine a light into the hopes of the women and men who populate these pages. At the same time, the tumultuous final months of the Trump presidency underscored how white supremacists have long sought to undermine this utopian future. But this chaos has also demonstrated the need for utopian thinking as we all move forward.

My first debt of gratitude goes to the archivists and librarians whom I relied on to pull together the threads of my book. These include Cornell University's Kheel Center for Labor-Management Documentation and Archives; Temple University's Urban Archives; Boston University's Howard Gotlieb Archival Research Center; the Library of Congress and National Archives; New York Public Library's Schomburg Center for Research in Black Culture; Swarthmore College's Peace Collection; the University of North Carolina's Southern Historical Collection; and Wayne State University's Walter P. Reuther Library. A small army of archivists at these myriad institutions pulled boxes, found obscure records, and provided all that I needed to make my research pleasurable and fruitful. When the pandemic hit, the librarians at the University at Buffalo went to heroic lengths to ensure that I had access to my sources, even mailing books to my home address. And the interlibrary loan staff tirelessly tracked down microfilm collections and obscure publications. A special thank-you to Michael Kicey, the humanities librarian at the University at Buffalo, for his professionalism and dedication during these difficult times.

The University of Chicago Press was enormously supportive throughout the publication process. I must thank my friend and colleague Amanda Seligman for convincing me that the Press would be an ideal place to publish this work. She was absolutely right. I am particularly indebted to executive editor Timothy Mennel for ushering the book through the publication process and providing insightful editorial advice. Editorial associate Susannah Engstrom has also been an invaluable resource and supporter of the project, and Erin DeWitt expertly copyedited the book. I owe the Press's external reviewers a debt of gratitude for their insightful comments on the manuscript. Two journal editors also played a part in developing ideas for the book when I published articles for them. Michael Ezra, editor of the *Journal of Civil and Human Rights*, was strongly supportive of my article about the significance of the Congress of Racial Equality's early work and helped me refine my ideas at a key moment. And Pero G. Dagbovie, editor of the *Journal of African American History*, is a model editor, both challenging and encouraging. Publishing my article on Floria Pinkney in his journal allowed me to rethink the category of interracialism as I was revising the manuscript.

I have been blessed to workshop my writing with a group of historians in western New York for nearly two decades, the Rochester Area U.S. Historians (RUSH). They read multiple chapters of this book and gave me invaluable insights. A particular debt of gratitude goes to Alison Parker and Tamar Carroll, who have both led RUSH and whose scholarship served as a model for me. I am so grateful for their friendship and support. In 2019–20 I was also fortunate to be part of a remarkable cohort of scholars at the University at Buffalo's Humanities Institute. Thank you to David Castillo, Christina Milletti, Neil Coffee, Meredith Conti, Christian Flaugh, Andrew Lison, Ariel Nereson, Michael Rembis, and Bill Solomon for your intellectual companionship and insights. The National Endowment for the Humanities, a true national treasure, awarded me a fellowship in 2016 that gave me the momentum I needed to tackle the project. Peter Eisenstadt, whose masterful new biography *Against the Hounds of Hell: A Life of Howard Thurman* came out after this book went to press, gave me invaluable leads linking Thurman to other utopian projects explored in this book. And a special thank-you to Howard Thurman's granddaughter, Suzanne M. Chiarenza, who gave me permission to reproduce photographs of Howard and Sue Bailey Thurman. Conversations with a larger group of scholars at conferences, events, and on social media have shaped my work in profound ways. These scholars include Thomas Sugrue, Tracy K'Meyer, Jay Driskell, Heather Thompson, David Freund, Walter Greason, Julian Chambliss, Clare Corbould, Nathan Connolly, Andrew Sandoval-Strausz, Anastasia Curwood, Andrew Kahrl,

Donna Murch, Nancy Kwak, and Suzanne Smith, among others. I am looking forward to the day when we can share our work in person.

My colleagues at the University at Buffalo have been supportive and model scholars. A particular thank-you to my fellow twentieth-century Americanists: Gail Radford, Susan Cahn, Michael Rembis, and David Herzberg. Through dozens of comprehensive exams and dissertation defenses, not to mention your published work, I have learned so much from you about history and academic citizenship. Other Buffalo colleagues—including Carl Nightingale, Elizabeth Otto, Marla Segol, Gwynn Thomas, Henry Louis Taylor, Margarita Vargas, Rachel Ablow, Carole Emberton, Hal Langfur, Camillo Trumper, Dalia Muller, Patrick McDevitt, and Kristin Stapleton—have made working at the University at Buffalo a deeply fulfilling experience. Over the years the friendship and support of fellow historians Georgina Hickey, Robin Bachin, and Alison Isenberg have bolstered me. Alison's own work on Philadelphia's Fellowship House helped me enormously as I revised chapter 4. May we meet again for a long dinner at a conference venue in the future.

My family—parents Nancy, Jeff and Peter, and siblings Joel, Jennifer, and Lauren—have grown even more precious to me during the pandemic. They have all been unfailingly enthusiastic about this book and supportive of my work. My wonderful in-laws, Ray and Gail, have showered me with affection and support. They never fail to lift my spirits. My daughters, Nora and Maya, were teenagers when this adventure began and are now young adults who make me both proud and a little awed on a daily basis. This book is dedicated to them because, like the many students I teach, they are shaping the future. My husband, Erik, is my first reader. He has commented on every sentence I wrote and supported all of my endeavors. And his own remarkable scholarship serves as an inspiration. Together we live in our own little utopia.

Notes

INTRODUCTION

1. Martin Luther King Jr., "Who Speaks for the South," *Liberation*, March 1958, 13.

2. Martin Luther King Jr., *The Papers of Martin Luther King, Jr.*, vol. 6, ed. Clayborne Carson (Oakland: University of California Press, 2007), 123–24.

3. Lyman Tower Sargent, *Utopianism: A Very Short Introduction* (New York: Oxford University Press, 2010), 2. Western concepts of utopia predated More, dating back to at least Plato's *Republic*. There are also powerful non-Western traditions of utopia. Other overviews of utopia include Howard P. Segal, *Utopias: A Brief History from Ancient Writings to Virtual Communities* (London: John Wiley & Sons, 2012); Russell Jacoby, *Picture Imperfect: Utopian Thought for an Anti-Utopian Age* (New York: Columbia University Press, 2005); and Ruth Levitas, *The Concept of Utopia* (London: Philip Allan, 1990).

4. As a result some proponents of utopian thought and practice have preferred the term "eutopia." In his 1922 work, *The Story of Utopias* (repr., Gloucester, MA: Peter Smith, 1959), for example, the urbanist Lewis Mumford wrote about possible eutopias, planned communities like the garden cities of England and later America. On Mumford's use of "eutopia," see Donald L. Miller, *Lewis Mumford: A Life* (New York: Weidenfeld & Nicolson, 1989), 167; Robert Wojtowicz, *Lewis Mumford and American Modernism: Eutopian Theories for Architecture and Urban Planning* (New York: Cambridge University Press, 1996), 35–40; and Casey Nelson Blake, *Beloved Community: The Cultural Criticism of Randolph Bourne, Van Wyck Brooks, Waldo Frank, and Lewis Mumford* (Chapel Hill: University of North Carolina Press, 1990), 207–11.

5. In *The Quest for Utopia in Twentieth-Century America* (Syracuse, NY: Syracuse University Press, 1998), Timothy Miller argues that intentional communities are "not so much an episodic series of isolated occurrences as [they are] a continuous, if small, ongoing theme in American life" (xiii). Lyman Tower Sargent defines intentional communities as "a group of five or more adults and their children, if any, who come from more than one nuclear family and who have chosen to live together to enhance their shared values or for some other mutually agreed upon purpose." Sargent, "The Three Faces of Utopianism Revisited," *Utopian Studies* 5, no. 1 (1994): 15. In "Second-Wave Cohousing: A Modern Utopia?" *Utopian Studies* 23, no. 1 (2012): 28–56, Lucy Sargisson argues that intentional communities are a form of "practical utopian experiments" that "create distance by establishing bounded

spaces *in which* to try something better and *from which* critically to regard life in the mainstream" (30).

6. Sargent, "The Three Faces of Utopianism Revisited," 3.

7. Robin D. G. Kelley, *Freedom Dreams: The Black Radical Imagination* (New York: Beacon Press, 2002), 12. Similarly, Ruth Levitas views utopia as the "the expression of the desire for a better way of being." She goes on to say, "We learn a lot about the experience of living under any set of conditions by reflecting upon the desires which those conditions generate and yet leave unfulfilled. For that is the space which utopia occupies." Levitas, *The Concept of Utopia*, 9.

8. Friedrich Engels, *Socialism: Utopian and Scientific* (1892). For a discussion of the relationship between scientific and utopian socialism, see Levitas, *The Concept of Utopia*, 41–67; and Barbara Goodwin and Keith Taylor, *The Politics of Utopia: A Study in Theory and Practice* (London: Hutchinson, 1982), 72–77, 163–68. Marx and Engels were primarily reacting to the popular mid-nineteenth-century Owenite and Fourier movements.

9. Csaba Toth, "Resisting Bellamy: How Kautsky and Bebel Read *Looking Backward*," *Utopian Studies* 23, no. 1 (2012): 57–78. Toth argues, "The immediatism of this American utopia flagrantly violated the stagist view of history" (63).

10. Marc Stears, *Demanding Democracy: American Radicals in Search of a New Politics* (Princeton, NJ: Princeton University Press, 2010), 13. Stears identifies A. J. Muste, Reinhold Niebuhr, and Bayard Rustin as three such utopianists.

11. A. J. Muste, *Non-Violence in an Aggressive World* (New York: Harper & Brothers, 1940), 51.

12. Aldous Huxley, *Island* (New York: Harper & Brothers, 1962). Huxley wrote several books on pacifism including *An Encyclopedia of Pacifism* (London: Chatto & Windus, 1937). For a discussion of India's influence on Huxley, see Sumita Roy, Annie Pothen, and K. S. Sunita, eds., *Aldous Huxley and Indian Thought* (New Delhi: Sterling, 2003).

13. Aldous Huxley, *Ends and Means: An Inquiry into the Nature of Ideals* (1937; repr., New Brunswick, NJ: Transaction, 2012), 96.

14. Carl Boggs, "Marxism, Prefigurative Communism, and the Problem of Workers' Control," *Radical America* 11 (November 1977): 100.

15. Wini Breines, *The Great Refusal: Community and Organization in the New Left, 1962–1968* (New York: Praeger, 1982), xiv. The historian Sheila Rowbotham uses the term in her 1979 essay "The Women's Movement and Organizing for Socialism," in *Beyond the Fragments: Feminism and the Making of Socialism* (Newcastle: Socialist Center, 1979). See also Stears, *Demanding Democracy*, 185; and Francesca Polletta, *Freedom Is an Endless Meeting: Democracy in American Social Movements* (Chicago: University of Chicago Press, 2002), 6–8.

16. Breines argues that older activists such as Muste and David Dellinger were direct precursors of the New Left. "Their ethically oriented criticism of capitalism, emphasis on the activism of moral witness and distrust of hierarchical organizations distinguished them from the old left parties and organizations proper." Breines, *The Great Refusal*, 14.

17. See Arthur M. Schlesinger Jr., *The Vital Center: The Politics of Freedom* (Boston: Houghton Mifflin, 1949); Daniel Bell, *The End of Ideology: On the Exhaustion of Political Ideas in the Fifties* (New York: Free Press, 1960), esp. "The Exhaustion of Utopia," 275–409;

Judith N. Shklar, *After Utopia: The Decline of Political Faith* (Princeton, NJ: Princeton University Press, 1957); Hannah Arendt, *Origins of Totalitarianism* (Cleveland: World Publishing, 1958); Karl Popper, *The Origins of Totalitarian Democracy* (New York: Praeger, 1960); and J. L. Tallmon, *The Origins of Totalitarian Democracy* (New York: Praeger, 1960). In *Picture Imperfect*, historian Russell Jacoby insists that totalitarian regimes should not be considered utopian. "Utopia has lost its ties with alluring visions of harmony and has turned into a threat. Conventional and scholarly wisdom associates utopian ideas with violence and dictatorship" (81). See also Stears, *Demanding Democracy*, 123–30; and Goodwin and Taylor, *The Politics of Utopia*, 18–19. Goodwin and Taylor argue that true utopias should benefit everyone within a society, which excludes totalitarian societies.

18. On "blueprint" utopias, see Jacoby, *Picture Imperfect*, x–xv.

19. Shklar, *After Utopia*, vii.

20. Schlesinger, *The Vital Center*, 159, 190.

21. Krishnalal Shridharani, *My India, My America* (New York: Duell, Sloan and Pearce, 1941), 278–79. On liberal interracialism, see Lauren Kientz Anderson, "A Nauseating Sentiment, a Magical Device, or Real Insight? Interracialism at Fisk University in 1930," *Perspectives on the History of Higher Education* 29 (August 2012): 75–112; Glenda Elizabeth Gilmore, *Defying Dixie: The Radical Roots of Civil Rights, 1919–1950* (New York: Norton, 2008), 235; Thomas J. Sugrue, *Sweet Land of Liberty: The Forgotten Struggle for Civil Rights in the North* (New York: Random House, 2008), 7; Jacquelyn Dowd Hall, *Sisters and Rebels: A Struggle for the Soul of America* (New York: Norton, 2019), 162–66; Amanda L. Izzo, *Liberal Christianity and Women's Global Activism: The YWCA of the USA and the Maryknoll Sisters* (New Brunswick, NJ: Rutgers University Press, 2018), 101–4.

22. Robin D. G. Kelley, *Hammer and Hoe: Alabama Communists during the Great Depression* (Chapel Hill: University of North Carolina Press, 1990); Gerald Horne, *Black Liberation/Red Scare: Ben Davis and the Communist Party* (Wilmington: University of Delaware Press, 1994); Gilmore, *Defying Dixie*. On Black communist women, see Erik S. McDuffie, *Sojourning for Freedom: Black Women, American Communism, and the Making of Black Left Feminism* (Durham, NC: Duke University Press, 2011); Carole Boyce Davies, *Left of Karl Marx: The Political Life of Black Communist Claudia Jones* (Durham, NC: Duke University Press, 2008); and Dayo F. Gore, *Radicalism at the Crossroads: African American Women Activists in the Cold War* (New York: New York University Press, 2012).

23. Quoted in Christopher Strain, "Soul City, North Carolina: Black Power, Utopia, and the African American Dream," *Journal of African American History* 89, no. 1 (Winter 2004): 57.

24. Jessica Gordon Nembhard, *Collective Courage: A History of African American Cooperative Economic Thought and Practice* (University Park: Pennsylvania State University Press, 2014), 49, 71–77; John Curl, *For All the People: Uncovering the Hidden History of Cooperation, Cooperative Movements, and Communalism in America* (Oakland: PM Press, 2009), 56–180; Thomas I. Brown, ed., *Economic Co-operation among the Negroes of Georgia* (Atlanta: Atlanta University Press, 1917).

25. Upton Sinclair, *Co-op: A Novel of Living Together* (Pasadena, CA: printed by the author, 1936), 43.

26. Myles Horton, *The Long Haul: An Autobiography* (New York: Doubleday, 1990), 38–40, 142.

27. Studies on radical pacifism's religious culture include Patricia Appelbaum, *Kingdom to Commune: Protestant Pacifist Culture between World War I and the Vietnam Era* (Chapel Hill: University of North Carolina Press, 2009); Joseph Kip Kosek, *Acts of Conscience: Christian Nonviolence and Modern American Democracy* (New York: Columbia University Press, 2009); Leilah Danielson, "'It Is a Day of Judgement': The Peacemakers, Religion, and Radicalism in Cold War America," *Religion and American Culture: A Journal of Interpretation* 18, no. 2 (Summer 2008): 215–48; Vaneesa Cook, *Spiritual Socialists: Religion and the American Left* (Philadelphia: University of Pennsylvania Press, 2019); Gary Dorrien, *Breaking White Supremacy: Martin Luther King Jr. and the Black Social Gospel* (New Haven, CT: Yale University Press, 2018); Leilah Danielson, Marian Mollin, and Doug Rossinow, eds., *The Religious Left in Modern America: Doorkeepers of a Radical Faith* (New York: Palgrave Macmillan, 2018).

28. Niebuhr was deeply influential in utopian socialist and radical pacifist circles, but with the rise of fascism in the late 1930s, he renounced pacifism and split from FOR, becoming a leading member of the "Christian realists." See Danielson, *American Gandhi*, 213; Richard Wightman Fox, *Reinhold Niebuhr: A Biography* (New York: Pantheon, 1985), 167–68; Heather A. Warren, *Theologians of a New World Order: Reinhold Niebuhr and the Christian Realists, 1920–1948* (New York: Oxford University Press, 1997), 129–31; and Kosek, *Acts of Conscience*, 130–32.

29. On the role of prophetic religion in the early civil rights movement, see David L. Chappell, *A Stone of Hope: Prophetic Religion and the Death of Jim Crow* (Chapel Hill: University of North Carolina Press, 2004); Danielson, *American Gandhi*; Ansley L. Quiros, *God with Us: Lived Theology and the Freedom Struggle in Americus, Georgia, 1942–1976* (Chapel Hill: University of North Carolina Press, 2018); Dan McKanan, *Prophetic Encounters: Religion and the American Radical Tradition* (Boston: Beacon Press, 2011); David S. Gutterman, *Prophetic Politics: Christian Social Movements and American Democracy* (Ithaca, NY: Cornell University Press, 2005), esp. 69–93; and Albert J. Raboteau, *American Prophets: Seven Religious Radicals and Their Struggle for Social and Political Justice* (Princeton, NJ: Princeton University Press, 2016).

30. Muste, *Non-Violence in an Aggressive World*, 172. Radical pacifists who were more secular often joined the War Resisters League, which worked closely with FOR and CORE. See Scott H. Bennett, *Radical Pacifism: The War Resisters League and Gandhian Nonviolence in America, 1915–1963* (Syracuse, NY: Syracuse University Press, 2003).

31. Dorrien, *Breaking White Supremacy*, 2. See also Dennis Dickerson, "African American Religious Intellectuals and the Theological Foundations of the Civil Rights Movement," *Church History* 74, no. 2 (June 2005): 217–35.

32. Warren, *Theologians of a New World Order*; Michael G. Thompson, *For God and Globe: Christian Internationalism in the United States between the Great War and the Cold War* (Ithaca, NY: Cornell University Press, 2015); Sarah Azaransky, *This Worldwide Struggle: Religion and the International Roots of the Civil Rights Movement* (New York: Oxford University Press, 2017); Brent Edwards, "Black Globality: The International Shape of Black Intellectual Culture" (PhD diss., Columbia University, 1998); Gerald Horne, *The End of Empires:*

African Americans and India (Philadelphia: Temple University Press, 2008); Sean Scalmer, *Gandhi in the West: The Mahatma and the Rise of Radical Protest* (Cambridge: Cambridge University Press, 2011), esp. 107–36; Sean Chabot, *Transnational Roots of the Civil Rights Movement: African American Explorations of the Gandhian Repertoire* (New York: Lexington Books, 2012); Sudharsan Kapur, *Raising Up a Prophet: The African-American Encounter with Gandhi* (Boston: Beacon Press, 1992); Bill Mullen, *Afro Orientalism* (Minneapolis: University of Minnesota Press, 2004); Gene Zubovich, "For Human Rights Abroad, against Jim Crow at Home: The Political Mobilization of American Ecumenical Protestants in the World War II Era," *Journal of American History*, September 2018, 267–90; and Nico Slate, *Colored Cosmopolitanism: The Shared Struggle for Freedom in the United States and India* (Cambridge, MA: Harvard University Press, 2012).

33. Dorothy Day, *The Long Loneliness: An Autobiography of Dorothy Day* (New York: Harper and Row, 1952), 62.

34. On the Catholic Worker Movement, see Patricia McNeal, *Harder Than War: Catholic Peacemaking in Twentieth-Century America* (New Brunswick, NJ: Rutgers University Press, 1992); Mel Piehl, *Breaking Bread: The Catholic Worker and the Origin of Catholic Radicalism in America* (Philadelphia: Temple University Press, 1982); Dan McKanan, "Inventing the Catholic Worker Family," *Church History* 76, no. 1 (March 2007): 84–113; Cook, *Spiritual Socialists*, esp. 69–91; Patrick G. Coy, ed., *A Revolution of the Heart: Essays on the Catholic Worker* (Philadelphia: Temple University Press, 1988); James Terence Fisher, *The Catholic Counterculture in America, 1933–1962* (Chapel Hill: University of North Carolina Press, 1989), esp. 1–100; and Robert Coles, *Dorothy Day: A Radical Devotion* (Boston: Da Capo Press, 1987).

35. Thomas C. Cornell and James H. Forest, eds., *A Penny a Copy: Readings from "The Catholic Worker"* (New York: Macmillan, 1968), 16.

36. Karen Johnson, *One in Christ: Chicago Catholics and the Quest for Interracial Justice* (New York: Oxford University Press, 2018), 49–50, 60–66, 91–97; Francis Sicius, "The Chicago Catholic Worker," in *A Revolution of the Heart: Essays on the Catholic Worker*, ed. Patrick G. Coy (Philadelphia: Temple University Press, 1988), 337–59. On African American Catholics in Chicago, see Matthew Cressler, *Authentically Black and Truly Catholic: The Rise of Black Catholicism in the Great Migration* (New York: New York University Press, 2017). The Catholic Workers' focus on poverty and labor was influential for the progressive thinker Michael Harrington. As an editor of the *Catholic Worker* in the 1950s, he gathered the ideas and data used to publish his pathbreaking *The Other America: Poverty in the United States*, a book that deeply influenced President Lyndon Johnson's War on Poverty. See Nancy L. Roberts, *Dorothy Day and the Catholic Workers* (Albany: SUNY Press, 1984), 4; McKanan, *Prophetic Encounters*, 161; and Michael Harrington, *The Other America: Poverty in the United States* (New York: Macmillan, 1962).

37. Danielson, "'It Is a Day of Judgement,'" 220; Cook, *Spiritual Socialists*, 57–58, 69–102; Angie O'Gorman and Patrick G. Coy, "Houses of Hospitality: A Pilgrimage into Nonviolence," in *A Revolution of the Heart*, ed. Coy, 217–38.

38. Appelbaum, *Kingdom to Commune*, 151; Bennett, *Radical Pacifism*, 127–28; Danielson, "'It Is a Day of Judgement.'"

39. On the influence of anarchism in the Catholic Worker Movement, see Andrew Cor-

nell, *Unruly Equality: U.S. Anarchism in the 20th Century* (Oakland: University of California Press, 2016), esp. 133–37, 169–71; Cook, *Spiritual Socialists*, 86; Nicholas Rademacher, "Dorothy Day, Religion, and the Left," in *The Religious Left in Modern America: Doorkeepers of a Radical Faith*, edited by Leilah Danielson, Marian Mollin, and Doug Rossinow (New York: Palgrave Macmillan, 2018), 81–100.

40. Douglas V. Steere, *A Manual on the Need, the Organization, and the Discipline of Cells for Peace* (Fellowship of Reconciliation, 1947), 15.

41. Kelley, *Freedom Dreams*. Works that explore Black traditions of utopia include Alex Zamalin, *Black Utopia: The History of an Idea from Black Nationalism to Afrofuturism* (New York: Columbia University Press, 2019); William H. Pease and Jane Pease, *Black Utopia: Negro Communal Experiments in America* (Madison: University of Wisconsin Press, 1963); and Wilson J. Moses, *Afrotopia: The Roots of African American Popular History* (New York: Cambridge University Press, 1998).

42. Major works in the field of Peace Studies include Peter Brock and Nigel Young, *Pacifism in the Twentieth Century* (Toronto: University of Toronto Press, 1999); Bennett, *Radical Pacifism*; Charles Chatfield, *For Peace and Justice: Pacifism in America* (Knoxville: University of Tennessee Press, 1971); Marian Mollin, *Radical Pacifism in Modern America: Egalitarianism and Protest* (Philadelphia: University of Pennsylvania Press, 2006); Lawrence S. Wittner, *Rebels against War: The American Peace Movement, 1941–60* (New York: Columbia University Press, 1969); and Robbie Lieberman, *The Strangest Dream: Communism, Anticommunism, and the U.S. Peace Movement, 1945–1963* (Syracuse, NY: Syracuse University Press, 2000). Biographical studies include Alton B. Pollard III, *Mysticism and Social Change: The Social Witness of Howard Thurman* (New York: Peter Lang, 1992); Quinton H. Dixie and Peter Eisenstadt, *Visions of a Better World: Howard Thurman's Pilgrimage to India and the Origins of African American Nonviolence* (Boston: Beacon Press, 2011); and Danielson, *American Gandhi*.

43. There is a rapidly growing literature on the long civil rights movement. The best overview of the field remains Jacquelyn Dowd Hall, "The Long Civil Rights Movement and the Political Uses of the Past," *Journal of American History* 91, no. 4 (March 2005): 1–28. A key contribution of the long civil rights movement historiography has been works that focus on the North and West, where radical pacifism was strongest. Yet Jeanne F. Theoharis and Komozi Woodward's groundbreaking book *Freedom North: Black Freedom Struggles Outside the South, 1940–1980* (New York: Palgrave Macmillan, 2003) includes no essays on radical pacifism, and the topic is absent in most other works. Two exceptions include Sugrue, *Sweet Land of Liberty*, esp. 42–58, 130–62; and Martha Biondi, *To Stand and Fight: The Struggle for Civil Rights in Postwar New York City* (Cambridge, MA: Harvard University Press, 2003), esp. 79–89.

Civil Rights historians have also underestimated nonviolent direct action's radical potential, as practiced in CORE, FOR, and Father Divine's Peace Mission. For example, Kevin M. Kruse and Stephen Tuck argue, "CORE's nonviolent direct action techniques were, in fact, neither innovative nor inspirational." Kevin M. Kruse and Stephen Tuck, *Fog of War: The Second World War and the Civil Rights Movement* (New York: Oxford University Press, 2012), 5–6. Clarence Lang labels the 1940s, when widespread training in nonviolent direct action occurred, as the "nadir of Black radicalism." Lang, "Freedom Train Derailed: The National Negro Labor Council and the Nadir of Black Radicalism," in *Anticommunism and the African American Freedom Movement: "Another Side of the Story,"* ed. Robbie Lieberman and Clarence Lang (New York: Palgrave Macmillan, 2009), 164. The downplaying of CORE's work in the 1940s may reflect August Meier and Elliott Rudwick's negative evaluation of the early years of CORE in their seminal book *CORE: A Study in the Civil Rights Movement* (Chicago: University of Illinois Press, 1975). Meier and Rudwick argue that CORE's accomplishments were "relatively modest" and by the early 1950s the organization was "a shambles" (57, 70). This characterization fits into the more traditional master narrative of the civil rights movement, which downplays activism before 1954. In *Up South: Civil Rights and Black Power in Philadelphia* (Philadelphia: University of Pennsylvania Press, 2006), Matthew J. Countryman claims, "CORE only grew into a major national civil rights organization after it initiated Freedom Rides on interstate buses across the South in 1961" (132). He also fails to examine the role of radical nonviolence in desegregating Philadelphia's public accommodations. Similarly, in his work *Fighting Jim Crow in the County of Kings: The Congress of Racial Equality in Brooklyn* (Louisville: University Press of Kentucky, 2013), Brian Purnell highlights the importance of interracialism and nonviolent direct action for the northern civil rights movement, but largely dismisses CORE activism in the 1940s and early 1950s as ineffective. In *American Gandhi*, Leilah Danielson also relies on Meier and Rudwick to downplay the impact of CORE's early work (224–29).

44. Works that emphasize the decline of labor in the civil rights movement include Risa L. Goluboff, *The Lost Promise of Civil Rights* (Cambridge, MA: Harvard University Press, 2007); Kruse and Tuck, *Fog of War*; Lieberman and Lang, eds., *Anticommunism and the African American Freedom Movement*; and Lieberman, *The Strangest Dream*. Works that argue for the persistence of labor in the movement include Robert H. Zieger, *For Jobs and Freedom: Race and Labor in America since 1865* (Lexington: University Press of Kentucky, 2007); William P. Jones, *The March on Washington: Jobs, Freedom, and the Forgotten History of Civil Rights* (New York: Norton, 2013); Nancy MacLean, *Freedom Is Not Enough: The Opening of the American Workplace* (Cambridge, MA: Harvard University Press, 2006); Michael Ezra, ed., *The Economic Civil Rights Movement: African Americans and the Struggle for Economic Power* (New York: Routledge, 2013); Gavin Wright, *Sharing the Prize: The Economics of the Civil Rights Revolution in the American South* (Cambridge, MA: Belknap Press of Harvard University Press, 2013); and Thomas F. Jackson, *From Civil Rights to Human Rights: Martin Luther King, Jr., and the Struggle for Economic Justice* (Philadelphia: University of Pennsylvania Press, 2007).

45. Bold in the original. "CORE Comments," May 1944, microfilm, reel 10, series 3, CORE Papers (Sanford, NC: Microfilming Corporation of America, 1980).

46. John M. Swomley, *Confronting Systems of Violence: Memoirs of a Peace Activist* (New York: Fellowship Publications, 1998), 4.

47. Bell, *The End of Ideology*, 405. Bell titles one section of his work "The Exhaustion of Utopia," 275–409.

48. Fredric Jameson, *An American Utopia: Dual Power and the Universal Army* (New York: Verso, 2016); David Graeber, "The New Anarchists," *New Left Review* 13 (January–

February 2002), 12. See also his reflections on the Occupy movement and prefigurative politics in *The Democracy Project: A History, a Crisis, a Movement* (New York: Random House, 2013); Erik Olin Wright, "Transforming Capitalism through Real Utopias," *American Sociological Review* 78, no. 1 (2013): 1–25; and Erik Olin Wright, *Envisioning Real Utopias* (New York: Verso, 2010).

49. On Jackson, Mississippi, see Kali Akuno and Ajamu Nangwaya, *Jackson Rising: The Struggle for Economic Democracy and Black Self-Determination in Jackson, Mississippi* (Ottawa: Daraja Press, 2017). On contemporary movements, see Rutger Bregman, *Utopia for Realists: How We Can Build the Ideal World* (New York: Little, Brown, 2017); and Geoffrey Pleyers, *Alter-Globalization: Becoming Actors in the Global Age* (Cambridge: Polity Press, 2010). On the World Social Forum, see "Charter of Principles," World Social Forum of Transformative Economies, https://transformadora.org/en/about/principles (accessed June 11, 2019).

CHAPTER ONE

1. A. J. Muste, *The Essays of A. J. Muste*, ed. Nat Hentoff (New York: Simon and Schuster, 1970), 136.

2. Myles Horton, *The Long Haul: An Autobiography* (New York: Doubleday, 1990), 227.

3. See Ralph E. Luker, *The Social Gospel in Black and White: American Racial Reform, 1885–1912* (Chapel Hill: University of North Carolina Press, 1991); Gary Dorrien, *The New Abolition: W. E. B. Du Bois and the Black Social Gospel* (New Haven, CT: Yale University Press, 2015); Ronald C. White, C. Howard Hopkins, and John C. Bennett, *Social Gospel: Religion and Reform in Changing America* (Philadelphia: Temple University Press, 1976).

4. Staughton Lynd, "Can Men Live as Brothers?" *Fellowship*, February 1958, 12–14; Timothy Miller, *The Quest for Utopia in Twentieth-Century America* (Syracuse, NY: Syracuse University Press, 1998), 36, 99.

5. Lewis Mumford, "Reeducating the Worker," *Survey* 47 (January 7, 1922): 568. For an overview of Brookwood, see Charles F. Howlett, *Brookwood Labor College and the Struggle for Peace and Social Justice in America* (Lewiston, NY: Edwin Mellen Press, 1993); Leilah Danielson, *American Gandhi: A. J. Muste and the History of Radicalism in the Twentieth Century* (Philadelphia: University of Pennsylvania Press, 2014), 84–125; and Vaneesa Cook, *Spiritual Socialists: Religion and the American Left* (Philadelphia: University of Pennsylvania Press, 2019), 31–39. Cook argues that Brookwood "operated as an intentional community, a place where idealists could practice their values of cooperative living" (32).

6. Robin Miller Jacoby, "The Women's Trade Union League Training School for Women Organizers, 1914–1926," in *Sisterhood and Solidarity: Workers' Education for Women, 1914–1984*, ed. Joyce L. Kornbluh and Mary Frederickson (Philadelphia: Temple University Press, 1984), 4–21.

7. *Training School for Women Organizers of the National Women's Trade Union League* (Chicago: NTUL, 1914), 1.

8. Ruth Milkman, *Women, Work, and Protest: A Century of U.S. Women's Labor History* (New York: Routledge, 2013), 34–35; Richard J. Altenbaugh, *Education for Struggle: The American Labor Colleges of the 1920s and 1930s* (Philadelphia: Temple University Press, 1990), 26–27.

9. Daniel Katz, *All Together Different: Yiddish Socialists, Garment Workers, and the Labor Roots of Multiculturalism* (New York: New York University Press, 2011), 20; Susan Stone Wong, "From Soul to Strawberries: The International Ladies' Garment Workers' Union and Workers' Education, 1914–1950," in *Sisterhood and Solidarity*, ed. Kornbluh and Frederickson, 43; Janette Elice Gayle, "Sewing Change: Black Dressmakers, Garment Workers and the Struggle for Rights in Early Twentieth Century New York City" (PhD diss., University of Chicago, 2015), 191. See also the special issue on workers' education in *International Labor and Working-Class History* 90 (Fall 2016).

10. Fannia Cohn, "Our Educational Work—A Survey," report submitted to the Conference of the Workers' Education Bureau of America held in New York City, April 2–3, 1921, folder 20, box 5, ILGWU Papers, Kheel Center for Labor Management Documentation and Archives, Cornell University, Cornell, New York. On unity centers, see Kornbluh and Frederickson, eds., *Sisterhood and Solidarity*, 40–44; Annelise Orleck, *Common Sense and a Little Fire: Women and Working-Class Politics in the United States, 1900–1965* (Chapel Hill: University of North Carolina Press, 1995), 178, 186; Katz, *All Together Different*, 81–82.

11. Cohn, "Our Educational Work—A Survey." On Cohn, see Orleck, *Common Sense and a Little Fire*; and Katz, *All Together Different*, 76–79.

12. Orleck, *Common Sense and a Little Fire*, 170.

13. Len De Caux, *Labor Radical: From the Wobblies to CIO* (Boston: Beacon Press, 1970), 25.

14. Rita Heller, "Blue Collars and Bluestockings: The Bryn Mawr Summer School for Women Workers, 1921–1938," in *Sisterhood and Solidarity*, ed. Kornbluh and Frederickson, 108–45. In contrast, the Southern Summer School for Women Workers only accepted white students. See Mary Frederickson, "Recognizing Regional Differences: The Southern Summer School for Women Workers," in *Sisterhood and Solidarity*, ed. Kornbluh and Frederickson, 148–86. On the connection between Bryn Mawr, Brookwood, and Highlander, see Francesca Polletta, *Freedom Is an Endless Meeting: Democracy in American Social Movements* (Chicago: University of Chicago Press, 2002), 34–37.

15. H. B. Brougham, "The New Brookwood," in *Workers Education in the United States: Report of Proceedings First National Conference on Workers Education in the United States* (New York: Workers Education Bureau of America, 1921), 52.

16. Muste, *The Essays of A. J. Muste*, 85, 86, 88. Later in life Muste was critical of intentional communities, noting that they could not on their own challenge society's ills (88). On the Comradeship, see Howlett, *Brookwood Labor College*, 129; and Danielson, *American Gandhi*, 63–64.

17. Howlett, *Brookwood Labor College*, 3.

18. "Organization of Brookwood: A Memo, 1924," folder 4, box 12, series 1, Brookwood Labor College Papers, Walter Reuther Library, Wayne State University, Detroit, Michigan (hereafter cited as Brookwood Labor College Papers).

19. Altenbaugh, *Education for Struggle*, 158; Helen G. Norton, "Brookwood—Where the Students Work," folder 11, box 12, series 1, Brookwood Labor College Papers.

20. "Report of Brookwood Executive Committee," April 18, 1931, folder 1, box 1, series 1, Brookwood Labor College Papers.

21. Helen G. Norton, "A Survey of Brookwood Students, 1921–31," folder 11, box 96, se-

ries 4, Brookwood Labor College Papers. In 1931 Brookwood stopped admitting communist students, a policy that alienated some students and faculty. "Admission of Communist Students," n.d., folder 10, box 96, series 4, Brookwood Labor College Papers.

22. Joyce L. Kornbluh, *A New Deal for Workers' Education: The Workers' Service Program, 1933–1942* (Chicago: University of Illinois Press, 1987), 13. John Dewey's most influential book was *Democracy and Education: An Introduction to the Philosophy of Education* (New York: Macmillan, 1916). When the AFL attacked Brookwood, John Dewey came to their defense, publishing a rebuttal in the *New Republic* that called the attack a "scholastic lynching." See Dewey, "Labor Politics and Labor Education," *New Republic*, January 9, 1929, 211.

23. "Memo on Curriculum," 1929, folder 1, box 1, series 1, Brookwood Labor College Papers.

24. A. J. Muste, "Some Questions about the Cooperative Movement," 1926, folder 26, box 29, series 2, Brookwood Labor College Papers; "Brookwood Community Cooperative Constitution," n.d., folder 13, box 1, series 1, Brookwood Labor College Papers; "Program of the First Consumers Cooperative Institute," July 28–August 3, 1929, folder 24, box 29, series 2, Brookwood Labor College Papers.

25. "Schuyler Heard at Brookwood College," *New York Amsterdam News*, August 5, 1931, 11.

26. Jessica Gordon Nembhard, *Collective Courage: A History of African American Cooperative Economic Thought and Practice* (University Park: Pennsylvania State University Press, 2014), 89–91; Barbara Ransby, *Ella Baker and the Black Freedom Movement: A Radical Democratic Vision* (Chapel Hill: University of North Carolina Press, 2003), 73–74, 82–91; "Co-operative League Awards Scholarship," *New York Amsterdam News*, July 29, 1931, 20; Ransby, *Ella Baker*, 74.

27. Ransby, *Ella Baker*, 85. Ransby argues that the YNCL foreshadowed the Student Nonviolent Coordinating Committee (SNCC) in its democratic idealism and youth leadership (90). See also Lizabeth Cohen, *A Consumers' Republic: The Politics of Mass Consumption in Postwar America* (New York: Vintage, 2003), 49.

28. "Courses of Study," pamphlet, 1937, p. 2, folder: "Miscellaneous Material, 1936–39," box 22, Records of the Works Progress Administration, National Archives, College Park, Maryland (hereafter cited as Records of the WPA).

29. Pauli Murray, *Song in a Weary Throat: An American Pilgrimage* (New York: Harper and Row, 1987), 105; Glenda Elizabeth Gilmore, *Defying Dixie: The Radical Roots of Civil Rights, 1919–1950* (New York: Norton, 2008), 254; Rosalind Rosenberg, *Jane Crow: The Life of Pauli Murray* (New York: Oxford University Press, 2017), 54–55, 76.

30. Murray, *Song in a Weary Throat*, 105, 106–7.

31. Altenbaugh, *Education for Struggle*, 46–49; Alice Kessler-Harris, *Out to Work: A History of Wage-Earning Women in the United States* (New York: Oxford University Press, 1982), 243–44; Heller, "Blue Collars and Bluestockings," 108–45.

32. On M. Carey Thomas's racism and anti-Semitism, see Helen Lefkowitz Horowitz, *The Power and Passion of M. Carey Thomas* (New York: Knopf, 1994), 341. Horowitz notes that when the African American writer Jessie Fauset won a scholarship to Bryn Mawr, Thomas "diverted" the young woman to Cornell University, keeping the university segregated (342–43).

33. Horowitz, 434–35; Heller, "Blue Collars and Bluestockings," 116.

34. "Twelfth Anniversary Review," 1933, p. 6, folder 17, box 1, Brookwood Labor College Collection, Kheel Center for Labor Management Documentation and Archives, Cornell University, Cornell, New York (hereafter cited as Brookwood Labor College Collection).

35. Gertrude Wilson to A. J. Muste, March 8, 1927, folder 18, box 13, series 1, Brookwood Labor College Papers.

36. "P" to A. J. Muste, March 28, 1927, folder 18, box 13, series 1, Brookwood Labor College Papers.

37. "NAACP 16th Annual Report," 1925, p. 28, folder 2, box 44, series 2, Brookwood Labor College Papers; Katz, *All Together Different*, 126; Gayle, "Sewing Change," 182. The NAACP awarded Floria Pinkney and Thomas L. Dabney the first two scholarships in 1925. On Pinkney, see Victoria W. Wolcott, "Networks of Resistance: Floria Pinkney and Labor Interracialism in Interwar America," *Journal of African American History* 105, no. 4 (Fall 2020): 567–92.

38. "Accepted Student Form for Floria Pinkney," 1925, folder 29, box 63, series 4, Brookwood Labor College Papers; "Brooklyn YWCA," *Chicago Defender*, September 26, 1925, A6.

39. A. J. Muste to James Weldon Johnson, June 24, 1926, folder 18, box 13, series 1, Brookwood Labor College Papers.

40. Floria Pinkney to A. J. Muste, September 9, 1926, folder 18, box 13, series 1, Brookwood Labor College Papers.

41. A. J. Muste to I. L. Burgess, June 9, 1927, and A. J. Muste to James Weldon Johnson, September 26, 1927, folder 18, box 13, series 1, Brookwood Labor College Papers; Shannon King, *Whose Harlem Is This, Anyway?: Community Politics and Grassroots Activism during the New Negro Era* (New York: New York University Press, 2015), 208; Katz, *All Together Different*, 125–26; "International Organizes Negro Dressmakers," *Justice* 11, no. 19 (September 27, 1929): 1, 2; Joseph Spielman, "With the New York Dressmakers," *Justice* 11, no. 19 (September 27, 1929): 3; "Negro Group Plan to Aid Dress Strike," *New York Times*, December 18, 1929, 55.

42. Floria Pinkney to A. J. Muste, July 25, 1930, folder 31, box 89, series 4, Brookwood Labor College Papers; "Two Go Abroad on Scholarships," *New York Amsterdam News*, April 9, 1930, 8. Another African American woman, Wenonah Bond, joined Pinkney on the trip.

43. Nancy Marie Robertson, *Christian Sisterhood, Race Relations, and the YWCA, 1906–46* (Chicago: University of Illinois Press, 2007), 130. See also Judith Weisenfeld, *African American Women and Christian Activism: New York's Black YWCA, 1905–1945* (New York: Cambridge University Press, 1997).

44. Leila J. Rupp, *Worlds of Women: The Making of an International Women's Movement* (Princeton, NJ: Princeton University Press, 1997), 120; "World YWCA," in "Report to Twelfth National Convention, Part 1," 1932, p. 81, microfilm, reel 31, YWCA National Board, YWCA USA Records.

45. "Proceedings of the Twelfth National Convention of the Young Women's Christian Associations of the United States of America," May 5–11, 1932, p. 100, microfilm, reel 31, YWCA National Board, YWCA USA Records; Annabel M. Stewart, *The Industrial Work of the Y.W.C.A.* (New York: The Womans Press, 1937), 101–3; Robertson, *Christian Sisterhood*, 125; Amanda L. Izzo, *Liberal Christianity and Women's Global Activism: The YWCA of the USA and the Maryknoll Sisters* (New Brunswick, NJ: Rutgers University Press, 2018), 96–103;

Adrienne Lash Jones, "Struggle among Saints: African American Women and the YWCA, 1870–1920," in *Men and Women Adrift: The YMCA and the YWCA in the City*, ed. Nina Mjagkij and Margaret Spratt (New York: New York University Press, 1997), 160–87.

46. Martin Luther King Jr., "The Bravest Man I Ever Met," *Pageant*, June 1965, 23–29; Anthony P. Dunbar, *Against the Grain: Southern Radicals and Prophets, 1929–1959* (Charlottesville: University Press of Virginia, 1981), 84–86.

47. Thomas J. Sugrue, *Sweet Land of Liberty: The Forgotten Struggle for Civil Rights in the North* (New York: Random House, 2008), 42; Gilmore, *Defying Dixie*, 315. The WDL was designed as a counter to the Communist Party's International Defense League.

48. Charlotte T. Morgan, "Finding a Way Out: Adult Education in Harlem during the Great Depression," *Afro-Americans in New York Life and History* 8, no. 1 (January 31, 1984): 20; "Courses of Study," pamphlet, 1937, p. 2, folder: "Miscellaneous Material, 1936–39," box 22, Records of the WPA.

49. A. J. Muste to James Weldon Johnson, June 24, 1926, folder 18, box 13, series 1, Brookwood Labor College Papers; "Labor School Has 2 Negro Students," *New York Amsterdam News*, December 9, 1925, 9.

50. Thomas Dabney to A. J. Muste, September 25, 1926, folder 1, box 81, series 4, Brookwood Labor College Papers.

51. Thomas Dabney to A. J. Muste, c. 1927, folder 2, box 81, series 4, Brookwood Labor College Papers. Muste told Dabney that he was concerned that Dabney's work with the ANLC would "cut you off from much chance to do anything through more regular channels," including the Brotherhood of Sleeping Car Porters. Muste to Dabney, August 5, 1927, folder 2, box 81, series 4, Brookwood Labor College Papers.

52. Thomas Dabney to A. J. Muste, December 16, 1927, folder 4, box 81, series 4, Brookwood Labor College Papers; Dabney to Muste, December 1928, and Dabney to Muste, n.d., folder 5, box 81, series 4, Brookwood Labor College Papers.

53. Thomas Dabney to A. J. Muste, July 6, 1932, folder 5, box 81, series 4, Brookwood Labor College Papers.

54. Thomas Dabney to A. J. Muste, June 29, 1932, folder 5, box 81, series 4, Brookwood Labor College Papers.

55. Sugrue, *Sweet Land of Liberty*, 87.

56. Sugrue, *Sweet Land of Liberty*, 87–90, 101–2; Gilmore, *Defying Dixie*, 136; Thomas Dabney to A. J. Muste, January 15, 1936, folder 8, box 81, series 4, Brookwood Labor College Papers; Howlett, *Brookwood Labor College*, xii. The Soviet film was never made. See Gilmore, *Defying Dixie*, 133–54.

57. Ben McLaurin to A. Philip Randolph, September 28, 1935, folder: "General Correspondence: B-T, 1926–1941," box 1, A. Philip Randolph Papers, Library of Congress, Washington, DC.

58. Howlett, *Brookwood Labor College*, 60; "B. F. McLaurin, 83, An Ex-Labor Leader and Rights Official," *New York Times*, March 24, 1989.

59. Thomas Dabney to A. J. Muste, January 15, 1936, folder 8, box 81, series 4, Brookwood Labor College Papers.

60. Thomas Dabney to A. J. Muste, September 13, 1927, folder 2, box 81, series 4, Brookwood Labor College Papers. The ILGWU was also a pioneer in establishing workers' education

by creating an Education Department in 1914. See Richard J. Altenbaugh, "'The Children and the Instruments of a Militant Labor Progressivism': Brookwood Labor College and the American Labor College Movement of the 1920s and 1930s," *History of Education Quarterly* 23, no. 4 (Winter 1983): 396.

61. A. J. Muste, "Trends in Labor Organization," April 14, 1928, pp. 5–6, folder 10, box 43, series 2, Brookwood Labor College Papers. For a discussion of the institutes on Black workers, see Howlett, *Brookwood Labor College*, 246–49; Altenbaugh, *Education for Struggle*, 142.

62. A. Philip Randolph, "Negro Symposium," n.d., folder 11, box 44, series 2, Brookwood Labor College Papers; Abram L. Harris, "Brookwood's Symposium on Negro Labor," *The Crisis* 34 (September 1927): 226.

63. Rienzi B. Lemus, "Negro Symposium," p. 2, folder 9, box 44, series 2, Brookwood Labor College Papers.

64. Beulah Camden to A. J. Muste, June 6, 1927, and A. J. Muste to Ben Stolberg, June 9, 1927, folder 7, box 44, series 2, Brookwood Labor College Papers.

65. "Labor Withdraws Support of College," *New York Times*, October 31, 1928, 32.

66. "Leaders Open Fight on Labor College," *New York Times*, April 6, 1929, 9.

67. Du Bois quoted in *Economic Co-operation among the Negroes of Georgia*, ed. Thomas I. Brown (Atlanta: Atlanta University Press, 1917), 10.

68. Nembhard, *Collective Courage*, 103; Cohen, *A Consumers' Republic*, 49; Ransby, *Ella Baker*, 88.

69. A. J. Muste to Friend, December 16, 1930, folder 17, box 56, series 2, Brookwood Labor College Papers.

70. "Persons Invited to Conference on Workers Education among Negroes," December 27, 1930, folder 18, box 56, series 2, Brookwood Labor College Papers; "To Air Labor Problems of Negro at Brookwood," *New York Amsterdam News*, December 24, 1930, 5; "Make Plan for Unity of Workers of All Races at Big Labor Confab," *Pittsburgh Courier*, January 10, 1931, A2. On Abram Harris's participation, see Jonathan Scott Holloway, *Confronting the Veil: Abram Harris Jr., E. Franklin Frazier, and Ralph Bunche, 1919–1941* (Chapel Hill: University of North Carolina Press, 2002), 62.

71. Howlett, *Brookwood Labor College*, 255; Altenbaugh, *Education for Struggle*, 205–19.

72. "Press Release," n.d., p. 2, folder 18, box 56, series 2, Brookwood Labor College Papers.

73. "Statement of Conference on Negro Labor and Worker Education at Brookwood Labor College," December 27, 1930, p. 1, folder 18, box 56, series 2, Brookwood Labor College Papers.

74. Michael Denning, *The Cultural Front: The Laboring of American Culture in the Twentieth Century* (New York: Verso, 1997), xv. See also Colette A. Hyman, *Staging Strikes: Workers' Theatre and the American Labor Movement* (Philadelphia: Temple University Press, 1997), 10.

75. Hyman, *Staging Strikes*, 10–11; Karen J. Blair, "Pageantry for Women's Rights: The Career of Hazel Mackaye," *Theatre Survey* 31 (May 1990): 23–46; Karen J. Blair, *The Torchbearers: Women and Their Amateur Arts Associations in America, 1890–1930* (Bloomington: Indiana University Press, 1994); Mary Mcavoy, "The Variegated Shoots: Hazel MacKaye and the Advent of Pedagogical Drama at Brookwood Labor College, 1925–1926," *Youth Theatre Journal* 29 (2015): 45–61.

76. Quoted in Mcavoy, "The Variegated Shoots," 45.

77. Clyde W. Barrow, "Playing Workers: Proletarian Drama in the Curriculum of American Labor Colleges, 1921–1937," *Journal of Arts Management and Law* 20, no. 4 (1991): 5–29; Richard Altenbaugh, "Proletarian Drama: An Educational Tool of the American Labor College Movement," *Theatre Journal* 34, no. 2 (1982): 197–210; Danielson, *American Gandhi*, 94–95.

78. Charles F. Howlett, "Brookwood Labor College and Peace Education," *Encyclopedia of Peace Education* (New York: Columbia University, Teachers College, 2008), 3.

79. Altenbaugh, "'The Children and the Instruments of a Militant Labor Progressivism,'" 405.

80. "Twelfth Anniversary Review," 1933, pp. 4–5, folder 17, box 1, Brookwood Labor College Collection; Altenbaugh, "'The Children and the Instruments of a Militant Labor Progressivism,'" 401.

81. Helen G. Norton, "Drama at Brookwood," *Labor Age* 15 (May 1926): 15.

82. Hyman, *Staging Strikes*, 24.

83. Hyman, 125–26.

84. Howlett, "Brookwood Labor College and Peace Education," 3.

85. Richard B. Gregg, *The Power of Nonviolence* (New York: Schocken, 1934), 26. On Gregg, see Joseph Kip Kosek, "Richard Gregg, Mohandas Gandhi, and the Strategy of Nonviolence," *Journal of American History*, March 2005, 1318–48. See also Joseph Kip Kosek, *Acts of Conscience: Christian Nonviolence and Modern American Democracy* (New York: Columbia University Press, 2009); and Howlett, *Brookwood Labor College*, 303.

86. Howlett, *Brookwood Labor College*, 306.

87. Victor G. Reuther, *The Brothers Reuther and the Story of the UAW* (Boston: Houghton Mifflin, 1976), 125.

88. Howlett, *Brookwood Labor College*, 294. Brookwood also shaped the Reuther brothers' personal lives. While at Brookwood, Victor fell in love with a young student, Sophia Goodlavich. As part of the Brookwood Players, she traveled that summer performing labor plays for workers nationwide. Victor caught up with her in Pennsylvania and they married in Peekskill, New York, near the school later that summer. Roy would also marry a Brookwood student, Fania Sasonkin. See Reuther, *The Brothers Reuther*, 126–27, 130–31, 196.

89. Sidney Fine, *Sit-Down: The General Motors Strike of 1936–1937* (Ann Arbor: University of Michigan Press, 1970), 121–22.

90. Howlett, *Brookwood Labor College*, 299, 302–3; Fine, *Sit-Down*, 95, 113, 162; Hyman, *Staging Strikes*, 125. Fine notes that Merlin Bishop "had learned at Brookwood Labor College that music could play an important part in building a union" (163).

91. Sugrue, *Sweet Land of Liberty*, 298–99; William P. Jones, *The March on Washington: Jobs, Freedom, and the Forgotten History of Civil Rights* (New York: Norton, 2013), 168–69.

92. Quoted in Jones, *The March on Washington*, xii.

93. Muste, *The Essays of A. J. Muste*, 150; Howlett, *Brookwood Labor College*, 270–74; Albert J. Raboteau, *American Prophets: Seven Religious Radicals and Their Struggle for Social and Political Justice* (Princeton, NJ: Princeton University Press, 2016), 39–42.

94. Howlett, *Brookwood Labor College*, vi.

95. Howlett, "Brookwood Labor College and Peace Education," 4.

96. Kornbluh, *A New Deal for Workers' Education*. The program was initially run under the Federal Emergency Relief Administration and in 1935 taken over by the Works Progress Administration. In 1939 it was renamed the Workers' Service Program.

97. Wong, "From Soul to Strawberries," 39. See also Theodore Brameld, *Ends and Means in Education: A Midcentury Appraisal* (New York: Harper Brothers, 1950).

98. Quoted in Francis Robert Shor, *Utopianism and Radicalism in a Reforming America, 1888–1918* (Westport, CT: Greenwood Press, 1997), 166. On Llano del Rio and New Llano, see Robert V. Hine, "California's Socialist Utopias," in *America's Communal Utopias*, ed. Donald E. Pitzer (Chapel Hill: University of North Carolina Press, 1997), 419–31; William H. Cobb, *Radical Education in the Rural South* (Detroit: Wayne State University Press, 2000), 25–75; and Miller, *The Quest for Utopia*, 98–100. Mark Fannin, in *Labor's Promised Land: Radical Visions of Gender, Race, and Religion in the South* (Knoxville: University of Tennessee Press, 2003), points out that local African Americans did participate in New Llano's cooperative (76).

99. Cobb, *Radical Education*, 34.

100. Cobb, 113.

101. Cobb, 213.

102. Altenbaugh, "'The Children and the Instruments of a Militant Labor Progressivism,'" 400–403; Cobb, *Radical Education*; Miller, *The Quest for Utopia*, 123–25; John Egerton, *Speak Now against the Day: The Generation before the Civil Rights Movement in the South* (Chapel Hill: University of North Carolina Press, 1995), 156–59; Fannin, *Labor's Promised Land*, 78–79.

103. Roy Reed, "Orval E. Faubus: Out of Socialism into Realism," *Arkansas Historical Quarterly* 54, no. 1 (Spring 1995): 13–29.

104. Aldon D. Morris, *The Origins of the Civil Rights Movement: Black Communities Organizing for Change* (New York: Free Press, 1984), 157.

105. Aimee Isgrig Horton, *The Highlander Folk School: A History of Its Major Programs* (New York: Carlson, 1971), 22; John M. Glen, *Highlander: No Ordinary School* (Knoxville: University of Tennessee Press, 1996), 13.

106. Horton, *The Long Haul*, 30. On the Ruskin colonies, see W. Fitzhugh Brundage, *A Socialist Utopia in the New South: The Ruskin Colonies in Tennessee and Georgia, 1894–1901* (Urbana: University of Illinois Press, 1996).

107. Frank Adams and Myles Horton, *Unearthing the Seeds of Fire: The Idea of Highlander* (Winston-Salem, NC: John F. Blair, 1975), 16–19.

108. Glen, *Highlander*, 5–6; Adams and Horton, *Unearthing the Seeds of Fire*, 20–24; Horton, *The Highlander Folk School*, 25–32; Horton, *The Long Haul*, 52–57.

109. Joseph K. Hart, *Light from the North: The Danish Folk High Schools—Their Meaning for America* (New York: Henry Holt, 1926), 144.

110. Horton, *The Long Haul*, 53; Adams and Horton, *Unearthing the Seeds of Fire*, 26; Horton, *The Highlander Folk School*, 38. West left Highlander within a year due to conflicts with Horton.

111. Myles Horton, "The Program at Highlander," *New World Commentator*, December 1949, 12, in folder 2, Highlander Folk School Collection, Kheel Center for Labor Manage-

ment Documentation and Archives, Cornell University, Cornell, New York (hereafter cited as Highlander Folk School Collection).

112. Michael K. Honey, *Southern Labor and Black Civil Rights: Organizing Memphis Workers* (Urbana: University of Illinois Press, 1993), 52.

113. Eliot Wigginton, ed., *Refuse to Stand Silently By: An Oral History of Grass Roots Social Activism in America, 1921–64* (New York: Doubleday, 1991), 94.

114. Adams and Horton, *Unearthing the Seeds of Fire*, 36.

115. Horton, *The Highlander Folk School*, 97; Egerton, *Speak Now against the Day*, 162. On the 1934 general strike, see Janet Irons, *Testing the New Deal: The General Textile Strike of 1934 in the American South* (Urbana: University of Illinois Press, 2000); and John A. Salmond, *The General Textile Strike of 1934: From Maine to Alabama* (Columbia: University of Missouri Press, 2002).

116. Quoted in Glen, *Highlander*, 84. See also Dunbar, *Against the Grain*, 145–51.

117. Horton, *The Highlander Folk School*, 92; Glen, *Highlander*, 38; Adams and Horton, *Unearthing the Seeds of Fire*, 91. Noted Black sociologist Charles S. Johnson was also a frequent visitor to Highlander as were faculty from Fisk University and Tennessee A&I College, both historically Black universities.

118. Quoted in Horton, *The Highlander Folk School*, 124.

119. Horton, *The Long Haul*, 38.

120. Sudarshan Kapur, *Raising Up a Prophet: The African-American Encounter with Gandhi* (Boston: Beacon Press, 1992), 151.

121. Horton, *The Highlander Folk School*, 70–71; Glen, *Highlander*, 62.

122. Egerton, *Speak Now against the Day*, 185–97, 292–301; Honey, *Southern Labor and Black Civil Rights*, 118–19; Adams and Horton, *Unearthing the Seeds of Fire*, 93–99; Gilmore, *Defying Dixie*, 269–72; Thomas A. Krueger, *And Promises to Keep: The Southern Conference for Human Welfare, 1938–48* (Nashville: Vanderbilt University Press, 1967); Dunbar, *Against the Grain*, 187–98; David L. Chappell, *Inside Agitators: White Southerners in the Civil Rights Movement* (Baltimore: Johns Hopkins University Press, 1994), 41–46.

123. Egerton, *Speak Now against the Day*, 197.

124. Horton, "The Program at Highlander," 14; Adams and Horton, *Unearthing the Seeds of Fire*, 100–101; Glen, *Highlander*, 113–14; Egerton, *Speak Now against the Day*, 161.

125. Horton, "The Program at Highlander," 16.

126. Honey, *Southern Labor and Black Civil Rights*, 216; Adams and Horton, *Unearthing the Seeds of Fire*, 167.

127. "The Highlander Fling," June 1948, and "Highlander's Program on Civil Rights," pp. 1–4, folder 2, Highlander Folk School Collection.

128. Glen, *Highlander*, 104, 121; Barbara S. Griffith, *The Crisis of American Labor: Operation Dixie and the Defeat of the CIO* (Philadelphia: Temple University Press, 1988), 67–76; Elizabeth Fones-Wolf and Ken Fones-Wolf, *Struggle for the Soul of the Postwar South: White Evangelical Protestants and Operation Dixie* (Chicago: University of Illinois Press, 2015); Honey, *Southern Labor and Black Civil Rights*, 243–45.

129. Highlander Folk School 21st Annual Report, October 1, 1952–September 30, 1953, p. 3, folder 1, Highlander Folk School Collection.

130. Horton, *The Highlander Folk School*, 160; Adams and Horton, *Unearthing the Seeds*

of Fire, 86–87; Martin Luther King Jr., *"All Labor Has Dignity,"* ed. Michael K. Honey (1963; repr., Boston: Beacon Press, 2011), 4; Fones-Wolf and Fones-Wolf, *Struggle for the Soul of the Postwar South*, 127–28.

131. "Highlander Folk School Statement of Purpose, Program and Policy," November 29, 1949, folder 2, Highlander Folk School Collection.

132. Highlander Executive Council Minutes, January 22–23, 1951, folder 2, Highlander Folk School Collection.

133. Morris, *The Origins of the Civil Rights Movement*, 147.

134. "Integration of the Public Schools, Check List," folder 1, Highlander Folk School Collection; Highlander Folk School 21st Annual Report, October 1, 1952–September 30, 1953, p. 4, folder 1, Highlander Folk School Collection; "Summary of Discussion on Goals and Procedures," document, June–July 1954, p. 1, folder 1, Highlander Folk School Collection.

135. Memo to potential funders, "Proposed Follow-Up on the Supreme Court Decisions and the Public Schools," August–September 1953, p. 2, folder 1, Highlander Folk School Collection.

136. Quoted in Jeanne Theoharis, *The Rebellious Life of Mrs. Rosa Parks* (Boston: Beacon Press, 2013), 38.

137. Adams and Horton, *Unearthing the Seeds of Fire*, 153.

138. Rosa Parks, Handwritten Notes on Highlander Folk School Meeting, 1955, folder 18, box 2, series 2, Rosa L. Parks Collection, Walter Reuther Archives, Wayne State University, Detroit, Michigan (hereafter cited as the Rosa L. Parks Collection).

139. Quoted in Theoharis, *The Rebellious Life*, 39.

140. Quoted in King, *"All Labor Has Dignity,"* 17.

141. Horton, *The Long Haul*, 126–27.

142. King, *"All Labor Has Dignity,"* 7; Adams and Horton, *Unearthing the Seeds of Fire*, 124; Horton, *The Highlander Folk School*, 213.

143. Ned Touchstone, "Rosa Admits to Editor That She Attended Notorious Training School," April 15, 1966, folder 17, box 2, series 2, Rosa L. Parks Collection.

144. Myles Horton, Memo, April 1, 1965, folder 17, box 2, series 2, Rosa L. Parks Collection.

145. Horton, *The Highlander Folk School*, 213–14.

146. Cynthia Stokes Brown, ed., *Ready from Within: Septima Clark and the Civil Rights Movement* (Navarro, CA: Wild Tree Press, 1986), 60. See also Adams and Horton, *Unearthing the Seeds of Fire*, 104–20; and Horton, *The Highlander Folk School*, 216–37.

147. Brown, *Ready from Within*, 78.

148. Adams and Horton, *Unearthing the Seeds of Fire*, 108; Horton, *The Highlander Folk School*, 218.

149. Brown, *Ready from Within*, 126.

150. "News from Highlander," September 1954, and "College Weekend Workshop on Human Relations," 1954, folder 1, Highlander Folk School Collection; Horton, *The Highlander Folk School*, 240. In earlier years, white college students from liberal universities such as Antioch attended the school in the summer. 18th Annual Report, 1932–1950, and "Highlander Folk School Executive Council Meeting Minutes, Nov. 29–30, 1950," folder 2, Highlander Folk School Collection.

151. Adams and Horton, *Unearthing the Seeds of Fire*, 143, 167; Horton, *The Highlander*

Folk School, 240–49; Wesley C. Hogan, *Many Minds, One Heart: SNCC's Dream for a New America* (Chapel Hill: University of North Carolina Press, 2007), 9, 79, 148; Clayborne Carson, *In Struggle: SNCC and the Black Awakening of the 1960s* (Cambridge, MA: Harvard University Press, 1981), 41–42, 50–51, 77–78; Ransby, *Ella Baker*, 267–68.

152. Adams and Horton, *Unearthing the Seeds of Fire*, 142; Horton, *The Highlander Folk School*, 237; Glen, *Highlander*, 243–50.

153. Adams and Horton, *Unearthing the Seeds of Fire*, 214. Highlander continues to face white racial terror. In March 2019, white supremacists set fire to Highlander, part of a contemporary upsurge of white racial violence.

154. Adams and Horton, 72.

155. Wigginton, *Refuse to Stand Silently By*, 115. See also Michael K. Honey, *Sharecropper's Troubadour: John L. Handcox, the Southern Tenant Farmers' Union, and the African American Song Tradition* (New York: Palgrave Macmillan, 2013).

156. Quoted in Kerran L. Sanger, *"When the Spirit Says Sing!": The Role of Freedom Songs in the Civil Rights Movement* (New York: Garland, 1995), 29.

157. Glen, *Highlander*, 176.

158. Sanger, *"When the Spirit Says Sing!,"* 47.

159. Brown, *Ready from Within*, 58.

160. King, *"All Labor Has Dignity,"* 14.

161. Wigginton, *Refuse to Stand Silently By*, 204. Seeger and famed folk musician Woody Guthrie visited Highlander in 1940.

CHAPTER TWO

1. Howard Kester, *Revolt among the Sharecroppers* (New York: J. J. Little and Ives, 1936), 96.

2. Sherwood Eddy, *A Door of Opportunity; or, An American Adventure in Cooperation with Sharecroppers* (New York: Eddy and Page, 1937), 58.

3. Eddy, 34. For a comprehensive history of the Delta and Providence Cooperative Farms, see Robert Hunt Ferguson, *Remaking the Rural South: Interracialism, Christian Socialism, and Cooperative Farming in Jim Crow Mississippi* (Athens: University of Georgia Press, 2018). See also Timothy Miller, *The Quest for Utopia in Twentieth-Century America* (Syracuse, NY: Syracuse University Press, 1998), 137–38; Mark Fannin, *Labor's Promised Land: Radical Visions of Gender, Race, and Religion in the South* (Knoxville: University of Tennessee Press, 2003), 123–25; Anthony P. Dunbar, *Against the Grain: Southern Radicals and Prophets, 1929–1959* (Charlottesville: University Press of Virginia, 1981), 114–20; Fred C. Smith, *Trouble in Goshen: Plain Folk, Roosevelt, Jesus, and Marx in the Great Depression South* (Oxford: University Press of Mississippi, 2014), 114–42; Vaneesa Cook, *Spiritual Socialists: Religion and the American Left* (Philadelphia: University of Pennsylvania Press, 2019), 56, 62–68; Rick L. Nutt, *The Whole Gospel for the Whole World: Sherwood Eddy and the American Protestant Mission* (Macon, GA: Mercer University Press, 1997), 275–80; and Jerry W. Dallas, "The Delta and Providence Farms: A Mississippi Experiment in Cooperative Farming and Racial Cooperation, 1936–1956," *Mississippi Quarterly* 40, no. 3 (Summer 1987): 283–308.

4. Jessica Gordon Nembhard, *Collective Courage: A History of African American Cooperative Economic Thought and Practice* (University Park: Pennsylvania State University Press, 2014), 53. See also Steven Hahn, *A Nation under Our Feet: Black Political Struggles in the Rural South from Slavery to the Great Migration* (Cambridge, MA: Harvard University Press, 2003), 177–98.

5. Samuel Lloyd Myers, "Consumers' Cooperation: A Plan for the Negro" (MA thesis, Boston University, 1942), 58; Aurelius P. Hood, *The Negro at Mound Bayou* (A.M.E. Sunday School Union, 1909).

6. Alethea H. Washington, "Section B: Rural Education—the Cooperative Movement," *Journal of Negro Education* 8, no. 1 (January 1939): 105.

7. Myers, "Consumers' Cooperation," 51; Jacob L. Reddix, *A Voice Crying in the Wilderness* (Jackson: University Press of Mississippi, 1974), 117–22. See also Lizabeth Cohen, *A Consumers' Republic: The Politics of Mass Consumption in Postwar America* (New York: Vintage, 2003), 49–50; and Barbara Ransby, *Ella Baker and the Black Freedom Movement: A Radical Democratic Vision* (Chapel Hill: University of North Carolina Press, 2003), 82–91.

8. Works on southern radicalism during this period include Erik S. Gellman and Jarod Roll, *The Gospel of the Working Class: Labor's Southern Prophets in New Deal America* (Chicago: University of Illinois, 2011); Dunbar, *Against the Grain*; Robert H. Craig, *Religion and Radical Politics: An Alternative Christian Tradition in the United States* (Philadelphia: Temple University Press, 1992); Fannin, *Labor's Promised Land*; and David L. Chappell, *Inside Agitators: White Southerners in the Civil Rights Movement* (Baltimore: Johns Hopkins University Press, 1994).

9. Dunbar, *Against the Grain*, vii, 73.

10. Quoted in Dunbar, 51.

11. Craig, *Religion and Radical Politics*, 144.

12. On Kester, see Dunbar, *Against the Grain*, 18–45; Craig, *Religion and Radical Politics*, 131–50; Joseph Kip Kosek, *Acts of Conscience: Christian Nonviolence and Modern American Democracy* (New York: Columbia University Press, 2009), 129–45; Robert F. Martin, *Howard Kester and the Struggle for Social Justice in the South, 1904–77* (Charlottesville: University Press of Virginia, 1991); and Elizabeth Fones-Wolf and Ken Fones-Wolf, *Struggle for the Soul of the Postwar South: White Evangelical Protestants and Operation Dixie* (Chicago: University of Illinois Press, 2015), 115–20.

13. On Claude Williams, see Craig, *Religion and Radical Politics*, 160–64; Gellman and Roll, *The Gospel of the Working Class*; Fannin, *Labor's Promised Land*, 294–95; Angela D. Dillard, *Faith in the City: Preaching Radical Social Change in Detroit* (Ann Arbor: University of Michigan Press, 2007), 140–52; and Fones-Wolf and Fones-Wolf, *Struggle for the Soul of the Postwar South*, 125–27.

14. Nembhard, *Collective Courage,* 52–53; Hahn, *A Nation under Our Feet*, 418–19.

15. On the Elaine massacre, see Nan Elizabeth Woodruff, *American Congo: The African American Freedom Struggle in the Delta* (Cambridge, MA: Harvard University Press, 2003), 83–109; Grif Stockley, *Blood in Their Eyes: The Elaine Race Massacres of 1919* (Fayetteville: University of Arkansas Press, 1994); and Richard Cortner, *A Mob Intent on Death: The NAACP and the Arkansas Riot Cases* (Middletown, CT: Wesleyan University Press, 1988).

16. Hahn, *A Nation under Our Feet*, 474; Woodruff, *American Congo*, 163.

17. Kester, *Revolt among the Sharecroppers*, iv.

18. Woodruff, *American Congo*, 153, 157–58; Craig, *Religion and Radical Politics*, 152–53; Fannin, *Labor's Promised Land*, 91; Kester, *Revolt among the Sharecroppers*, 27–54.

19. Kester, *Revolt among the Sharecroppers*, 54.

20. Nicholas Natanson, *The Black Image in the New Deal: The Politics of FSA Photography* (Knoxville: University of Tennessee Press, 1992).

21. Woodruff, *American Congo*, 83. On the role of religion in the STFU, see Dan McKanan, *Prophetic Encounters: Religion and the American Radical Tradition* (Boston: Beacon Press, 2011), 154–55.

22. The all-Black Alabama Sharecroppers Union existed from 1931 to 1936. See Robin D. G. Kelley, *Hammer and Hoe: Alabama Communists during the Great Depression* (Chapel Hill: University of North Carolina Press, 1990).

23. Kester, *Revolt among the Sharecroppers*, 34.

24. Eddy, *A Door of Opportunity*, 18, 20. On the STFU, see Donald H. Grubbs, *Cry from the Cotton: The Southern Tenant Farmers' Union and the New Deal* (Chapel Hill: University of North Carolina Press, 1971); Dunbar, *Against the Grain*, 83–185; Craig, *Religion and Radical Politics*, 130–75; Fannin, *Labor's Promised Land*, 71–129; Woodruff, *American Congo*, 152–90; and Kester, *Revolt among the Sharecroppers*.

25. Fannin, *Labor's Promised Land*, 155–81.

26. Michael K. Honey, *Sharecropper's Troubadour: John L. Handcox, the Southern Tenant Farmers' Union, and the African American Song Tradition* (New York: Palgrave Macmillan, 2013).

27. Dunbar, *Against the Grain*, 87.

28. Eddy, *A Door of Opportunity*, 30.

29. Eddy, 31.

30. Harvey P. Vaughn, "Outline for an Urban Agricultural-Industrial Cooperative Colony," Tennessee Valley Authority, June 24, 1934, p. 2, folder 1, box 1, Delta and Providence Cooperative Farm Papers, Southern Historical Collection, University of North Carolina, Chapel Hill, North Carolina (hereafter cited as Delta and Providence Cooperative Farm Papers).

31. Egerton, *Speak Now against the Day*, 94.

32. Quoted in Richard Wightman Fox, *Reinhold Niebuhr: A Biography* (New York: Pantheon, 1985), 176.

33. Eddy, *A Door of Opportunity*, 31–33; Sam Franklin to Eugene Sutherland, May 14, 1936, folder 5, box 1, Delta and Providence Cooperative Farm Papers.

34. Heather A. Warren, *Theologians of a New World Order: Reinhold Niebuhr and the Christian Realists, 1920–1948* (New York: Oxford University Press, 1997), 7. See also Michael G. Thompson, *For God and Globe: Christian Internationalism in the United States between the Great War and the Cold War* (Ithaca, NY: Cornell University Press, 2015); David L. Chappell, "Niebuhrisms and Myrdaleries: The Intellectual Roots of the Civil Rights Movement Reconsidered," in *The Role of Ideas in the Civil Rights South*, ed. Ted Ownby (Jackson: University Press of Mississippi, 2002), 3–18; and David L. Chappell, *A Stone of Hope: Prophetic Religion and the Death of Jim Crow* (Chapel Hill: University of North Carolina Press, 2004).

35. On the relationship between Eddy and Niebuhr, see Cook, *Spiritual Socialists*, 103–6. Niebuhr's pessimism and renunciation of pacifism also put him at odds with A. J. Muste. See Leilah Danielson, *American Gandhi: A. J. Muste and the History of Radicalism in the Twentieth Century* (Philadelphia: University of Pennsylvania Press, 2014), 206–9.

36. Nembhard, *Collective Courage*, 49, 71–77; John Curl, *For All the People: Uncovering the Hidden History of Cooperation, Cooperative Movements, and Communalism in America* (Oakland: PM Press, 2009), 56–180; Thomas I. Brown, ed., *Economic Co-operation among the Negroes of Georgia* (Atlanta: Atlanta University Press, 1917).

37. John Hope II, "Rochdale Cooperation among Negroes," *Phylon* 1, no. 1 (1940): 39.

38. Myers, "Consumers' Cooperation," 3, 87, 93.

39. Sam H. Franklin Jr. to Dr. Alfred Lee Wilson, September 24, 1937, folder 14, box 2, Delta and Providence Cooperative Farm Papers.

40. Hope, "Rochdale Cooperation," 48–49.

41. Eddy, *A Door of Opportunity*, 38. On production at the farm in its early years, see Eddy, 34–40; Alice Rex, "After Fourteen Months," *The Witness*, June 24, 1937, pp. 5–7, folder 36, box 4, Delta and Providence Cooperative Farm Papers; Sam H. Franklin Jr., "Early Years of the Delta Cooperative Farm and the Providence Cooperative Farm," n.d., folder 188, box 19, Delta and Providence Cooperative Farm Papers; and "Cooperative Farm in Mississippi Aids Sharecroppers of Both Races," *New Journal and Guide*, December 30, 1939, 3.

42. "Members Manual," n.d., p. 5, folder 177, box 17, Delta and Providence Cooperative Farm Papers.

43. Eddy, *A Door of Opportunity*, 50; "Members Manual," 22.

44. Report to Trustees, August 2, 1936, p. 2, folder 11, box 2, Delta and Providence Cooperative Farm Papers.

45. "Members Manual," 13–15. Initially the farm's trustees provided the money to start the credit cooperative. Over time a small percentage of the producers' cooperative dividends went to the credit cooperative.

46. Ferguson, *Remaking the Rural South*, 81–82. Delta residents evacuated to Memphis, where they stayed in the Rust Brothers' factory until it was safe to return. Ferguson notes the 1937 flood killed nearly four hundred people.

47. "Members Manual," 4; "Providence Plantation Sold to Delta Co-Operative Farms," February 6, 1938, clipping, folder 60, box 7, Delta and Providence Cooperative Farm Papers.

48. "Members Manual," 18.

49. Dot McPhail to Sherwood Eddy, July 22, 1936, folder 11, box 2, Delta and Providence Cooperative Farm Papers.

50. Copy of letter received from S. M. Magsby to Sherwood Eddy, May 25, 1936, folder 7, box 1, Delta and Providence Cooperative Farm Papers.

51. "Members Manual," 19.

52. Franklin, "Early Years of the Delta Cooperative Farm"; Robert Hunt Ferguson, "Race and the Remaking of the Rural South: Delta Cooperative Farm and Providence Farm in Jim Crow–Era Mississippi" (PhD diss., University of North Carolina, 2012), 102.

53. Sam Franklin to Sherwood Eddy, August 7, 1939, folder 105, box 11, Delta and Providence Cooperative Farm Papers.

54. Sam Franklin, manuscript, n.d., p. 14, folder 170, box 17; and "Delta Co-Op Call," June 19, 1937, folder 36, box 4: both in Delta and Providence Cooperative Farm Papers. Franklin insisted that the farm was not sectarian as it received aid from Catholic and Jewish sources as well as Protestants. Sam Franklin to Arthur Packard, November 5, 1936, folder 17, box 2, Delta and Providence Cooperative Farm Papers.

55. A. J. Muste, "The Eddy Farm Makes a Group," p. 2, November 1936, clipping, folder 18, box 2, Delta and Providence Cooperative Farm Papers.

56. Alice Rex, "After Fourteen Months," *The Witness*, June 24, 1937, p. 7, folder 36, box 4, Delta and Providence Cooperative Farm Papers.

57. "Members Manual," 20; Ferguson, "Race and the Remaking of the Rural South," 114. The Board of National Missions of the Presbyterian Church paid Hail's salary.

58. Rose to Dorothy Franklin, National Committee on Federal Legislation for Birth Control, October 5, 1936, folder 15, box 2, Delta and Providence Cooperative Farm Papers; Clarence Gamble to Sam Franklin, July 10, 1936, and Franklin to Gamble, December 17, 1936, folder 20, box 2, Delta and Providence Cooperative Farm Papers.

59. Document, c. 1938, p. 1, folder 57, box 7, Delta and Providence Cooperative Farm Papers; "Members Manual," 20; Sam Franklin to Sherwood Eddy, June 4, 1936, folder 6, box 1, Delta and Providence Cooperative Farm Papers; "Why a Doctor Is Needed," n.d., folder 20, box 2, Delta and Providence Cooperative Farm Papers; Sam Franklin to William Mercer Green, June 26, 1939, folder 102, box 11, Delta and Providence Cooperative Farm Papers; "Cooperative Farm in Mississippi Aids Sharecroppers of Both Races," *New Journal and Guide*, December 30, 1939, 3; Ferguson, *Remaking the Rural South*, 114–16.

60. Report on Providence Cooperative Farm, 1942–1943, p. 1, folder 157, box 16, Delta and Providence Cooperative Farm Papers; "A.K.A. Health Clinic Is Opened in Mississippi," *Pittsburgh Courier*, August 15, 1942, 8.

61. Crystal R. Sanders, *A Chance for Change: Head Start and Mississippi's Black Freedom Struggle* (Chapel Hill: University of North Carolina Press, 2016).

62. Kester, *Revolt among the Sharecroppers,* 45; "Agreement," 1937, p. 2, folder 6, box 1, Delta and Providence Cooperative Farm Papers.

63. Kester, *Revolt among the Sharecroppers*, 46.

64. "Memorandum of Request for an Educational Project," June 2, 1936, folder 6, box 1, Delta and Providence Cooperative Farm Papers; Letter to Daniel Howard, September 12, 1936, folder 15, box 2, Delta and Providence Cooperative Farm Papers; Sam Franklin to Dorothy Drescher, September 29, 1936, folder 11, box 2, Delta and Providence Cooperative Farm Papers.

65. "Children's Book," c. 1937, p. 1, folder 36, box 4, Delta and Providence Cooperative Farm Papers.

66. "Children's Book," 4.

67. "Children's Book," 6.

68. "Children's Book," 6.

69. "Social Survey Tour," brochure, n.d., folder 33, box 4, Delta and Providence Cooperative Farm Papers.

70. "Social Survey Tour"; "Delta Co-op Call," August 6, 1936, p. 3, folder 11, box 2, Delta and

Providence Cooperative Farm Papers; Kester, *Revolt among the Sharecroppers*, 86; George B. Ellenberg, *Mule South to Tractor South: Mules, Machines, and the Transformation of the Cotton South* (Tuscaloosa: University of Alabama Press, 2007); Smith, *Trouble in Goshen*, 123.

71. Sam Franklin to Arthur Packard, November 5, 1936, folder 17, box 2, Delta and Providence Cooperative Farm Papers; Robert Allen Rosevear, "Seek Judgment, Relieve the Oppressed," October 4, 1936, pp. 6–7, typewritten manuscript, folder 15, box 2, Delta and Providence Cooperative Farm Papers. On Kagawa, see Thomas John Hastings, *Seeing All Things Whole: The Scientific Mysticism and Art of Kagawa Toyohiko* (London: Pickwick, 2015).

72. Warren, *Theologians of a New World Order*, 28–30; Gary Dorrien, *Breaking White Supremacy: Martin Luther King Jr. and the Black Social Gospel* (New Haven, CT: Yale University Press, 2018), 59; Cook, *Spiritual Socialists*, 43; Nutt, *The Whole Gospel for the Whole World*, 3.

73. Franklin, "Early Years of the Delta Cooperative Farm," 59.

74. Marjorie Penney to "Friend," August 20, 1937, folder 29, box 2, series 1, Fellowship House Papers, Urban Archives, Temple University, Philadelphia, Pennsylvania. Penney raised money for the cooperative farms and the STFU into the 1940s.

75. "The Cooperative Farm Carries On," 1947, p. 8, folder 191, box 19, Delta and Providence Cooperative Farm Papers; Eddy, *A Door of Opportunity*, 50; Sam Franklin to Sherwood Eddy, August 3, 1936, folder 11, box 2, Delta and Providence Cooperative Farm Papers; Sam Franklin to James Myers, August 9, 1936, folder 11, box 2, Delta and Providence Cooperative Farm Papers; Report to the Trustees, p. 2, August 13, 1936, folder 11, box 2, Delta and Providence Cooperative Farm Papers; Ferguson, "Race and the Remaking of the Rural South," 103.

76. Sherwood Eddy to Fellowship of Socialist Christians, January 23, 1943, p. 1, folder 153, box 16, Delta and Providence Cooperative Farm Papers.

77. A. J. Muste, "The Eddy Farm Makes a Group," November 1936, folder 18, box 2, Delta and Providence Cooperative Farm Papers.

78. Postcard from F. E. Danner, May 10, 1936, folder 6, box 1, Delta and Providence Cooperative Farm Papers; William J. Ressell to Sam Franklin, June 9, 1936, p. 3, folder 7, box 1, Delta and Providence Cooperative Farm Papers; "Members Manual," n.d., p. 3, folder 170, box 17, Delta and Providence Cooperative Farm Papers.

79. Rosevear, "Seek Judgment, Relieve the Oppressed," 5.

80. Howard Thurman to Sherwood Eddy, November 9, 1936, reprinted in *The Papers of Howard Thurman*, vol. 2, ed. Walter Earl Fluker et al. (Columbia: University of South Carolina Press, 2012), 18–19. One of those students, Prentice Thomas, took a leadership position at the farm and went on to work with Thurgood Marshall at the NAACP. Quinton H. Dixie and Peter Eisenstadt, *Visions of a Better World: Howard Thurman's Pilgrimage to India and the Origins of African American Nonviolence* (Boston: Beacon Press, 2011), 159.

81. "Delta Co-Op Call," May 8, 1937, pp. 1, 2, folder 33, box 4, Delta and Providence Cooperative Farm Papers; Ferguson, *Remaking the Rural South*, 85–87.

82. Eddy, *A Door of Opportunity*, 43–44.

83. Eddy, 31.

84. Rose Terlin to Dorothy Franklin, June 14, 1936, folder 7, box 1, Delta and Providence Cooperative Farm Papers.

85. Sam Franklin to Winifred Wygal, November 23, 1936, folder 18, box 2, Delta and

Providence Cooperative Farm Papers; Eddy, *A Door of Opportunity*, 24; Dunbar, *Against the Grain*, 128–29.

86. "Case Histories," pp. 2–3, 5, folder 105, box 11, Delta and Providence Cooperative Farm Papers.

87. Sam Franklin to Ruth M. Pattison, June 25, 1936, folder 11, box 2, Delta and Providence Cooperative Farm Papers; Sam Franklin to George Lawrence Parker, June 22, 1937, folder 36, box 4, Delta and Providence Cooperative Farm Papers. The daughter seems to have decided against the visit.

88. Sherwood Eddy to Sam Franklin, June 11, 1936, folder 6, box 1, Delta and Providence Cooperative Farm Papers; Eddy to Franklin, June 15, 1936, folder 7, box 1, Delta and Providence Cooperative Farm Papers; Sherwood Eddy to Lucius Miles Tobin, June 7, 1937, folder 35, box 4, Delta and Providence Cooperative Farm Papers.

89. Celestine Smith to Rose Terlin, May 29, 1936, folder 8, box 1, Delta and Providence Cooperative Farm Papers. Smith recommended Howard Thurman as a possible representative. Ferguson, *Remaking the Rural South*, 98.

90. John J. Riggle to R. W. Hudgens, May 24, 1939, p. 4, folder 102, box 11, Delta and Providence Cooperative Farm Papers; Sherwood Eddy, "Report to the Trustees of the Cooperative Farm, Inc.," p. 1, folder 100, box 11, Delta and Providence Cooperative Farm Papers.

91. Report to the Trustees, August 13, 1936, p. 2, folder 11, box 2, Delta and Providence Cooperative Farm Papers; Sam Franklin to Sherwood Eddy, August 14, 1936, folder 11, box 2, Delta and Providence Cooperative Farm Papers; Smith, *Trouble in Goshen*, 134.

92. A. James McDonald to Frank Toothaker, February 12, 1938, folder 60, box 7, Delta and Providence Cooperative Farm Papers.

93. Sam Franklin to Trustees, December 28, 1936, p. 1, folder 20, box 2, Delta and Providence Cooperative Farm Papers. Some African Americans complained to the STFU about their treatment. See Sam Franklin to Howard Kester, June 14, 1937, folder 35, box 4, Delta and Providence Cooperative Farm Papers.

94. Sam Franklin to Sherwood Eddy and Arthur Raper, August 1, 1941, p. 2, folder 132, box 14, Delta and Providence Cooperative Farm Papers.

95. Sam Franklin to Sherwood Eddy and Arthur Raper, August 8, 1941, p. 1, and Eddy to Franklin, August 6, 1941, folder 132, box 14, Delta and Providence Cooperative Farm Papers.

96. Memo, Sam Franklin to Sherwood Eddy, Reinhold Niebuhr, and Arthur Raper, August 31, 1941, p. 4, folder 133, box 14, Delta and Providence Cooperative Farm Papers.

97. Sherwood Eddy to Mr. and Mrs. Hatch, September 30, 1941, folder 134, box 14, Delta and Providence Cooperative Farm Papers.

98. Rosevear, "Seek Judgment, Relieve the Oppressed," 5; and Sam Franklin to Clarence Senior, folder 11, box 2, Delta and Providence Cooperative Farm Papers.

99. Sam Franklin to Joseph Moody, December 16, 1936, p. 2, folder 19, box 2, Delta and Providence Cooperative Farm Papers.

100. Sherwood Eddy to Trustees, March 9, 1943, p. 2, folder 155, box 16, Delta and Providence Cooperative Farm Papers.

101. Ferguson, *Remaking the Rural South*, 125; "The Cooperative Farm Carries On," 1947, p. 5, folder 191, box 19, Delta and Providence Cooperative Farm Papers.

102. "The Cooperative Farm Carries On," 6–8; Ferguson, *Remaking the Rural South*, 89–91, 114–16.

103. Franklin, "Early Years of the Delta Cooperative Farm." Franklin speculates that Eddy's descriptions of Soviet Russia in the book raised suspicions. Sam Franklin to Sherwood Eddy, October 14, 1941, folder 135, box 14, Delta and Providence Cooperative Farm Papers.

104. Quoted in Franklin, "Early Years of the Delta Cooperative Farm," 86.

105. Franklin, 87, 88–89, 90–91.

106. Ferguson, *Remaking the Rural South*, 123.

107. Quoted in Ferguson, 130.

108. Ferguson, 129–34.

109. Donald Holley, *Uncle Sam's Farmers: The New Deal Communities in the Lower Mississippi Valley* (Chicago: University of Illinois Press, 1975), ix, 25–28. Works on the agencies that built New Deal communities include Sara M. Gregg, *Managing the Mountains: Land Use Planning, the New Deal, and the Creation of a Federal Landscape in Appalachia* (New Haven, CT: Yale University Press, 2010); Paul Conkin, *Tomorrow a New World: The New Deal Community Program* (Ithaca, NY: Cornell University Press, 1959); Brian Q. Cannon, *Remaking the Agrarian Dream: New Deal Rural Resettlement in the Mountain West* (Albuquerque: University of New Mexico Press, 1996); Sidney Baldwin, *Poverty and Politics: The Rise and Decline of the Farm Security Administration* (Chapel Hill: University of North Carolina Press, 1968); and Grubbs, *Cry from the Cotton*.

110. John B. Kirby, *Black Americans in the Roosevelt Era: Liberalism and Race* (Knoxville: University of Tennessee Press, 1980), 49–51; Donald Holley, "The Negro in the New Deal Resettlement Program," *Agricultural History* 45, no. 3 (July 1971): 183; John Egerton, *Speak Now against the Day: The Generation before the Civil Rights Movement in the South* (Chapel Hill: University of North Carolina Press, 1995), 94–97; Charles Spurgeon Johnson, Edwin Rogers Embree, and Will W. Alexander, *The Collapse of Cotton Tenancy: Summary of Field Studies and Statistical Surveys, 1933–35* (New York: Books for Libraries Press, 1935).

111. Dunbar, *Against the Grain*, 130; Grubbs, *Cry from the Cotton*, 141–44; Holley, *Uncle Sam's Farmers*, 99–104. When Wallace ran for president in 1948 with the Progressive Party, he campaigned throughout the South to interracial crowds. See Thomas W. Devine, *Henry Wallace's 1948 Presidential Campaign and the Future of Postwar Liberalism* (Chapel Hill: University of North Carolina Press, 2013), 233–61.

112. Holley, *Uncle Sam's Farmers*, 104. See also Grubbs, *Cry from the Cotton*, 141–44; and Baldwin, *Poverty and Politics*.

113. Kirby, *Black Americans in the Roosevelt Era*, 51; Holley, "The Negro in the New Deal Resettlement Program," 189.

114. Franklin, "Early Years of the Delta Cooperative Farm," 83.

115. Conkin, *Tomorrow a New World*, 13, 205.

116. Conkin, 186. Historian Sidney Baldwin similarly describes the FSA as a "plaything created for the diversion of utopian dreamers." Baldwin, *Poverty and Politics*, 4.

117. Felix Brunner, "Utopia Unlimited," *Washington Post*, February 10, 11, 12, 13, 1936.

118. Conkin, *Tomorrow a New World*, 331; Baldwin, *Poverty and Politics*, 205.

119. W. E. B. Du Bois, *Dusk of Dawn: An Essay toward an Autobiography of a Race Concept* (1940; repr., New York: Oxford University Press, 2007), 108.

120. Holley, "The Negro in the New Deal Resettlement Program," 184, 189; Holley, *Uncle Sam's Farmers*, 181–82. For a discussion of Mexican, Japanese, and white residents of FSA migrant camps in the West, see Veronica Martinez-Matsuda, "For Labor and Democracy: The Farm Security Administration's Competing Visions for Farm Workers' Socioeconomic Reform and Civil Rights in the 1940s," *Journal of American History*, September 2019, 338–61.

121. Reddix, *A Voice Crying in the Wilderness*, 122; Baldwin, *Poverty and Politics*, 297.

122. Eddy, *Door of Opportunity*, 35.

123. Dorothy Irene Helms, "Address," March 26, 1938, pp. 1, 2, folder 64, box 7, Delta and Providence Cooperative Farm Papers.

124. Holley, *Uncle Sam's Farmers*, 90; Grubbs, *Cry from the Cotton*, 145; Upton Sinclair, *Co-op: A Novel of Living Together* (Pasadena, CA: printed by the author, 1936).

125. Michael Denning, *The Cultural Front: The Laboring of American Culture in the Twentieth Century* (New York: Verso, 1997), 268.

126. Denning, *The Cultural Front*, 264. Richard Wright and Edward Rosskam, *Twelve Million Black Voices: A Folk History of the Negro in the United States* (New York: Viking Press, 1941).

127. Baldwin, *Poverty and Politics*, 3; Holley, *Uncle Sam's Farmers*, 137; Grubbs, *Cry from the Cotton*, 160.

128. Woodruff, *American Congo*, 184–86; Philip S. Foner, *American Socialism and Black Americans: From the Age of Jackson to World War II* (Westport, CT: Greenwood Press, 1977), 354–55; Fannin, *Labor's Promised Land*, 127.

129. Franklin, "Early Years of the Delta Cooperative Farm," 93.

130. Works on Freedom Summer include Clayborne Carson, *In Struggle: SNCC and the Black Awakening of the 1960s* (Cambridge, MA: Harvard University Press, 1981); Doug McAdam, *Freedom Summer* (New York: Oxford University Press, 1988); and Bruce Watson, *Freedom Summer: The Savage Season That Made Mississippi Burn and Made America a Democracy* (New York: Viking, 2010).

131. John Dittmer, *Local People: The Struggle for Civil Rights in Mississippi* (Chicago: University of Illinois Press, 1994), 365.

132. Dittmer, 365; Nembhard, *Collective Courage*, 178–80, 218; Monica M. White, *Freedom Farmers: Agricultural Resistance and the Black Freedom Movement* (Chapel Hill: University of North Carolina Press, 2018), 65–87. On the role of southern cooperatives for Black nationalists, see Russell Rickford, "'We Can't Grow Food on All This Concrete': The Land Question, Agrarianism, and Black Nationalist Thought in the Late 1960s and 1970s," *Journal of American History* 103, no. 4 (March 2017): 956–80.

133. http://www.mississippiassociation.coop/ (accessed May 18, 2021).

CHAPTER THREE

1. Sara Harris, *Father Divine: Holy Husband* (Garden City, NY: Doubleday, 1953), 191.

2. Quoted in Robert Weisbrot, *Father Divine and the Struggle for Racial Equality* (Chicago: University of Illinois Press, 1983), 158.

3. Biographical works on Father Divine include Weisbrot, *Father Divine*; Jill Watts, *God, Harlem U.S.A.* (Berkeley: University of California Press, 1992); Harris, *Father Divine*; and Kenneth E. Burnham, *God Comes to America: Father Divine and the Peace Mission Movement* (Boston: Lambeth Press, 1979). Father Divine's Peace Mission is recognized by scholars as a utopian community. See Timothy Miller, *The Quest for Utopia in Twentieth-Century America* (Syracuse, NY: Syracuse University Press, 1998), 83–84; Robert Weisbrot, "Father Divine and the Peace Mission," in *America's Communal Utopias*, ed. Donald E. Pitzer (Chapel Hill: University of North Carolina Press, 1997), 432–44; and Robert S. Fogarty, *Dictionary of American Communal and Utopian History* (Westport, CT: Greenwood Press, 1980), 31–32. On the influence of the Azusa Revivals, see Watts, *God, Harlem U.S.A.*, 25; and Clarence E. Hardy III, "Fauset's (Missing) Pentecostals: Church Mothers, Remaking Respectability, and Religious Modernism," in *The New Black Gods: Arthur Huff Fauset and the Study of African American Religions*, ed. Edward E. Curtis IV and Danielle Brune Sigler (Bloomington: Indiana University Press, 2009), 26.

4. Weisbrot, *Father Divine*, 18–20; Watts, *God, Harlem U.S.A.*, 26–28; Jacob S. Dorman, *Chosen People: The Rise of American Black Israelite Religions* (New York: Oxford University Press, 2013), 166.

5. Weisbrot, *Father Divine*, 26–28; Leonard Norman Primiano, "'The Consciousness of God's Presence Will Keep You Well, Healthy, Happy, and Singing': The Tradition of Innovation in the Music of Father Divine's Peace Mission Movement," in *The New Black Gods*, ed. Curtis and Sigler, 99. The Black Muslim religious leader Noble Drew Ali claimed that the greeting "Peace" originated from his religious teachings. See "'Peace'—Did Father Divine Borrow the Word from 'Prophet' Noble Drew Ali?" *Chicago Defender*, May 1, 1927, 1.

6. Weisbrot, "Father Divine and the Peace Mission," 436; Charles Samuel Braden, *"These Also Believe": A Study of Modern American Cults and Minority Religious Movements* (New York: Macmillan, 1956), 13–15; Weisbrot, *Father Divine*, 122.

7. Judith Weisenfeld, *New World A-Coming: Black Religion and Racial Identity during the Great Migration* (New York: New York University Press, 2016), 5.

8. "Church Discipline, Constitution and By-Laws," c. 1941, p. 8, folder 1: "Circle Mission, Inc.," box 1, Father Divine Collection, Schomburg Library, New York, New York (hereafter cited as Father Divine Collection).

9. The Peace Mission kept no membership list and did not recognize race. Therefore, we don't know the exact percentage of white followers.

10. Arthur Huff Fauset's seminal work, *Black Gods of the Metropolis: Negro Religious Cults of the Urban North* (New York: Octagon Books, 1944), uses the phrase "sects and cults." On Fauset, see Curtis and Sigler, *The New Black Gods*.

11. Works on New Thought include Beryl Satter, *Each Mind a Kingdom: American Women, Sexual Purity, and the New Thought Movement, 1875–1920* (Berkeley: University of California Press, 1999); Charles S. Braden, *Spirits in Rebellion: The Rise and Development of New Thought* (Dallas: Southern Methodist University Press, 1963); and Darnise C. Martin, *Beyond Christianity: African Americans in a New Thought Church* (New York: New York University Press, 2005).

12. Quoted in Braden, *Spirits in Rebellion*, 9.

13. Satter, *Each Mind a Kingdom*, 200–202.

14. Quoted in Braden, *"These Also Believe,"* 65; R. Marie Griffith, "Body Salvation: New Thought, Father Divine, and the Feast of Material Pleasures," *Religion and American Culture: A Journal of Interpretation* 11, no. 2 (2001): 119–53.

15. Weisbrot, *Father Divine*, 28–29; Claude McKay, *Harlem: Negro Metropolis* (New York: E. P. Dutton, 1940), 69. Collier's book was repackaged in the Rhonda Byrne 2006 best seller, *The Secret*. Charles Samuel Braden also emphasizes the importance of "unlimited abundance" in Father Divine's teachings as taken from New Thought. See Braden, *"These Also Believe,"* 73.

16. Lavere Belstrom, *Rediscovering God: Our International Treasure* (2005), 43, 102–3, http://peacemission.info/mission/books/book-rediscovering-god-our-international -treasure/ (accessed September 10, 2017). Belstrom reports that Bruce Barton attended a 1938 banquet and praised Father Divine (109–10).

17. No. 2, at Mrs. Bessie Roy's Home, April 11, 1934, Detroit, p. 1, folder 12: "Father Divine's Messages—Verbatim Transcripts, 1933–34," box 1, Father Divine Collection.

18. See, for example, "Father Divine's Messages, Copied Verbatum [*sic*], 1932," box 1, folder 11, Father Divine Collection.

19. "The Power of Positive Thinking," September 8, 1933, reprinted in the *New Day*, July 7, 1984, p. 2, folder 1, box 2, Father Divine Collection; Braden, *"These Also Believe,"* 75.

20. Quoted in Braden, *"These Also Believe,"* 68.

21. John Hoshor, *God in a Rolls Royce: The Rise of Father Divine, Madman, Menace, or Messiah* (New York: Hillman-Curl, 1936), 20.

22. Victoria W. Wolcott, *Remaking Respectability: African American Women in Interwar Detroit* (University of North Carolina Press, 2001), 113–15; Milton C. Sernett, *Bound for the Promised Land: African American Religion and the Great Migration* (Durham: Duke University Press, 1997); Anthea D. Butler, *Women in the Church of God in Christ: Making a Sanctified World* (Chapel Hill: University of North Carolina Press, 2007).

23. Quoted in St. Clair Drake and Horace R. Cayton, *Black Metropolis: A Study of Negro Life in a Northern City* (Chicago: University of Chicago Press, 1945), 645. Wallace D. Best, *Passionately Human, No Less Divine: Religion and Culture in Black Chicago, 1915–1952* (Princeton, NJ: Princeton University Press, 2015), 147–80. Best points out that Father Divine did not have a large following in Chicago, which may be because Elder Lucy Smith's congregation provided similar religious teachings (20). See also Sernett, *Bound for the Promised Land*, 195; Drake and Cayton, *Black Metropolis*, 643–45; and Davarian L. Baldwin, *Chicago's New Negroes: Modernity, the Great Migration, and Black Urban Life* (Chapel Hill: University of North Carolina Press, 2007), 168, 188–91.

24. Quoted in Primiano, "'The Consciousness of God's Presence,'" 108.

25. Hoshor, *God in a Rolls Royce*, 241.

26. Griffith, "Body Salvation," 146. See also R. Marie Griffith, *Born Again Bodies: Flesh and Spirit in American Christianity* (Berkeley: University of California Press, 2004), 140–55.

27. Harris, *Father Divine*, 51.

28. This description is primarily drawn from Braden, *"These Also Believe,"* 1–5. The banquets are described at length in all the major works on Father Divine. On the Rosebud's attire, see Weisenfeld, *New World A-Coming*, 125.

29. McKay, *Harlem*, 45.

30. Belstrom, *Rediscovering God*, 282.

31. "Father Divine's Messages—Verbatim Transcripts, 1933–34," No. 3, May 19, 1934, p. 12, folder 12, box 1, Father Divine Collection.

32. Quoted in McKay, *Harlem*, 46.

33. "Father Divine's Messages, Copied Verbatum [*sic*], 1932," 19.

34. Quoted in Belstrom, *Rediscovering God*, 277.

35. Beryl Satter, "Marcus Garvey, Father Divine and the Gender Politics of Race Difference," *American Quarterly* 48, no. 1 (March 1996): 584. See also Weisenfeld, *New World A-Coming*, 95–102.

36. Satter, "Marcus Garvey, Father Divine," 574. See also Weisenfeld, *New World A-Coming*, 182–99.

37. Satter, "Marcus Garvey, Father Divine," 600n47. The interwar period saw the rise of female pilots, or "aviatrixes," as popular figures.

38. Quoted in Harris, *Father Divine*, 63.

39. On the Bronx slave market, where African American domestic workers were hired for little money, see Ella Baker and Marvel Cooke, "The Bronx Slave Market," *Crisis* 42 (November 1935): 330, 340.

40. "Church Discipline, Constitution and By-Laws," c. 1941, 9; Weisbrot, *Father Divine*, 102.

41. Quoted in Weisbrot, *Father Divine*, 185.

42. "Here's the Answer," booklet, 1938, 14, folder 4: "Father Divine's Righteous Government Platform and Libel Suit," box 3, Father Divine Collection.

43. "Church Discipline, Constitution and By-Laws," c. 1941, 2.

44. On Booker T. Washington, see Dona Brown, *Back to the Land: The Enduring Dream of Self-Sufficiency in Modern America* (Madison: University of Wisconsin Press, 2011), 51; and Monica M. White, *Freedom Farmers: Agricultural Resistance and the Black Freedom Movement* (Chapel Hill: University of North Carolina Press, 2018), 28–62. On Black Nationalist agrarianism, see Russell Rickford, "'We Can't Grow Food on All This Concrete': The Land Question, Agrarianism, and Black Nationalist Thought in the Late 1960s and 1970s," *Journal of American History* 103, no. 4 (March 2017): 956–80; and Steven Conn, *Americans against the City: Anti-Urbanism in the Twentieth Century* (New York: Oxford University Press, 2014), 266–69. On the "whiteness" of nature, see Paul Outka, *Race and Nature: From Transcendentalism to the Harlem Renaissance* (New York: Palgrave Macmillan, 2008).

45. Rickford, "'We Can't Grow Food on All This Concrete,'" 971.

46. Brown, *Back to the Land*, 49, 141–71; Andrew Cornell, *Unruly Equality: U.S. Anarchism in the 20th Century* (Oakland: University of California Press, 2016), 84–100; Conn, *Americans against the City*.

47. Carleton Mabee, *Promised Land: Father Divine's Interracial Communities in Ulster County, New York* (Fleischmanns, NY: Purple Mountain Press, 2008); Weisbrot, *Father Divine*, 6, 124–34; Watts, *God, Harlem U.S.A.*, 137–38; McKay, *Harlem*, 50–53. See also "'Father Divine' Rides High: Angels Own $212,000 Worth of Real Estate," *Chicago Defender*, July 8, 1939, 2; and Robert S. Bird, "Father Divine's Movement Expands," *New York Times*, July 2, 1939, E10.

48. Satter, "Marcus Garvey, Father Divine," 585.

49. "Father Divine, The March of Times, Krum Elbow Estate, Part II," https://www.you tube.com/watch?v=dAYNxuMSLZY.

50. Mabee, *Promised Land*, 73–79; "Father Divine Group Buys 'Krum Elbow,'" *New York Times*, July 29, 1938, 1.

51. "Divine Gets President's Sanction to Buy Next-Door Estate but Owner Won't Sell," *New York Times*, August 17, 1939, 1.

52. "Father Divine and 2,500 Angels Inspect Their New Land at Krum Elbow, New York," Hearst Metrotone News, August 9, 1938, newsreel, UCLA Film Archives.

53. "Father Divine's Movement Expands," *New York Times*, July 2, 1939, E10.

54. "Father Divine Proves He Is Still 'God,'" *Chicago Defender*, July 17, 1937, 6. There was a similar gathering the previous summer, which also generated significant publicity. "Father Divine, Angels, Sail to 'Heaven,'" *Chicago Defender*, August 29, 1936, 20.

55. W. E. B. Du Bois, "As the Crow Flies," *New York Amsterdam News*, May 23, 1942.

56. Barbara Ransby, *Ella Baker and the Black Freedom Movement: A Radical Democratic Vision* (Chapel Hill: University of North Carolina Press, 2003), 78.

57. Watts, *God, Harlem U.S.A.*, 138; Mabee, *Promised Land*, 94–95.

58. Primiano, "'The Consciousness of God's Presence,'" 103.

59. Robert V. Hine, *California's Utopian Colonies* (Los Angeles: Henry E. Huntington Library, 1953), 6; Braden, *"These Also Believe,"* 15.

60. Douglas Flamming, *Bound for Freedom: Black Los Angeles in Jim Crow America* (Berkeley: University of California Press 2005), 300–308; Watts, *God, Harlem U.S.A.*, 127–28; Newton Van Dalsem, *History of the Utopian Society of America: An Authentic Account of its Origin and Development up to 1942* (Los Angeles: Board of Director of the Utopian Society, 1942). Hine discusses the importance of Bellamy's Nationalist clubs for numerous utopian groups in California. Hine, *California's Utopian Colonies*, 162. It is also significant that Charlotta Bass, the prominent African American publisher of the Los Angeles paper the *California Eagle*, was a strong supporter of Father Divine and often reprinted his sermons in her paper. Weisenfeld, *New World A-Coming*, 274).

61. Van Dalsem, *History of the Utopian Society*, 11.

62. Van Dalsem, 13–16, 39; James J. Kopp, "Edward Bellamy and the New Deal: The Revival of Bellamyism in the 1930s," *Utopian Studies* 4 (1991): 10–16.

63. Charles P. LeWarne, "Vendovi Island: Father Divine's 'Peaceful Paradise of the Pacific,'" *Pacific Northwest Quarterly* 75, no. 1 (January 1984): 12. See also Belstrom, *Rediscovering God*, 253–62. On the importance of utopian communities for the Pacific Northwest, see Charles P. LeWarne, *Utopias on the Puget Sound: 1885–1915* (Seattle: University of Washington Press, 1995). White westerners who traveled to Sayville included Thomas A. Hampton from San Francisco and Henry A. Joerns from Seattle. LeWarne, "Vendovi Island," 5.

64. LeWarne, "Vendovi Island," 8–11; Belstrom, *Rediscovering God*, 257.

65. Watts, *God, Harlem U.S.A.*, 127–28; Nancy L. Roberts, *Dorothy Day and the Catholic Workers* (Albany: SUNY Press, 1984), 8–9; Cornell, *Unruly Equality*, 136. Unlike the Divinites, the Catholic Workers preferred not to vote.

66. Reprinted in "The New Day," November 9, 1985, p. 14, folder 15: "Sermons (Copies) Published in 'The New Day' 1933–45," box 1, Father Divine Collection.

67. "Here's the Answer," booklet, pp. 24–25, folder 4: "Father Divine's Righteous Government Platform and Libel Suit," box 3, Father Divine Papers, Father Divine Collection.

68. Carolyn Dixon, "Father Divine Hits Credit Buying," *New York Amsterdam News*, January 28, 1950, 1.

69. Weisbrot, *Father Divine*, 91–92.

70. Quoted in Sutherland Denlinger, "Heaven Is in Harlem: And a Rolls-Royce the 'Sweet Chariot' of a Little Black God," *Forum and Century* 55, no. 4 (April 1936): 211. Father Divine did not give his full support to La Guardia but did encourage his followers to vote.

71. John Henrik Clarke, ed., *Harlem U.S.A.* (Brooklyn: A&B Books, 1964), 254; Weisbrot, *Father Divine*, 133, 146; "'Angels' Paraded by Father Divine," *New York Times*, September 14, 1936, 28; Joel Schwartz, "The Consolidated Tenants League of Harlem: Black Self-Help vs. White, Liberal Intervention in Ghetto Housing, 1934–1944," *Afro-Americans in New York Life and History* 10 (January 1986): 31–51. Mass parades by Divinites in Harlem were a common spectacle in the late 1930s. See, for example, "Father Divine Rides in Parade of 1,500," *New York Times*, August 1, 1938, 3.

72. Mark Naison, *Communists in Harlem during the Depression* (Chicago: University of Illinois Press, 1983), 129–30; Watts, *God, Harlem U.S.A.*, 119–20; Weisbrot, *Father Divine*, 145–46. See also Cheryl Lynn Greenberg, *"Or Does it Explode": Black Harlem in the Great Depression* (New York: Oxford University Press, 1991), 105–7. The Peace Mission was also part of the more moderate Harlem Political Union, founded in 1935.

73. McKay, "'There Goes God!'" 153.

74. "Father Divine Angels Stage Riot at Polls," *Chicago Defender*, October 16, 1937, 5; "Divine Orders Angels to Strike," *New York Amsterdam News*, April 6, 1946, 1; "Now Father Won't 'Low Voting Going on Around There," *New York Amsterdam News*, September 30, 1944, A1; Weisbrot, *Father Divine*, 165; Weisenfeld, *New World A-Coming*, 102–4.

75. "Now Father Won't 'Low Voting Going on Around There," A1.

76. Weisbrot, *Father Divine*, 147, 158; Watts, *God, Harlem U.S.A.*, 164.

77. Quoted in McKay, *Harlem*, 38–39.

78. Quoted in Claude McKay, "'There Goes God!' The Story of Father Divine and His Angels," *The Nation*, February 6, 1935, 152.

79. "Father Divine's Righteous Government Platform," pamphlet, n.d., p. 1, folder 4: "Father Divine's Righteous Government Platform" and Libel Suit, box 3, Father Divine Papers, Father Divine Collection; "Platform Drafted by Father Divine," *New York Times*, January 13, 1936, 19.

80. "Father Divine's Righteous Government Platform," 3.

81. "This Great Country," 1939, p. 1, folder 15, box 1, Father Divine Collection.

82. "Father Divine's Righteous Government Platform," 3–5; Weisbrot, *Father Divine*, 152–57; Watts, *God, Harlem U.S.A.*, 136–37; Fauset, *Black Gods of the Metropolis*, 55, 95; Hoshor, *God in a Rolls Royce*, 239–40.

83. McKay, *Harlem*, 67; Charlotte T. Morgan, "Finding a Way Out: Adult Education in Harlem during the Great Depression," *Afro-Americans in New York Life and History* 8, no. 1 (January 31, 1984): 17–29; Joyce L. Kornbluh, *A New Deal for Workers' Education: The Workers' Service Program, 1933–1942* (Chicago: University of Illinois Press, 1987); Ransby,

Ella Baker and the Black Freedom Movement, 85; Lizabeth Cohen, *A Consumers' Republic: The Politics of Mass Consumption in Postwar America* (New York: Vintage, 2003), 49; Pauli Murray, *Song in a Weary Throat: An American Pilgrimage* (New York: Harper and Row, 1987), 105; Glenda Elizabeth Gilmore, *Defying Dixie: The Radical Roots of Civil Rights, 1919–1950* (New York: Norton, 2008), 254; Rosalind Rosenberg, *Jane Crow: The Life of Pauli Murray* (New York: Oxford University Press, 2017), 54–55, 76.

84. Weisbrot, *Father Divine*, 115.

85. Quoted in Harris, *Father Divine*, 189–90.

86. Harris, 240.

87. Braden, *"These Also Believe,"* 28, 65.

88. Fauset, *Black Gods of the Metropolis*, 92. See also Sylvester A. Johnson, "Religion Proper and Proper Religion: Arthur Fauset and the Study of African American Religions," in *The New Black Gods*, ed. Curtis and Sigler, 149.

89. Braden, *"These Also Believe,"* 18.

90. Braden, 19.

91. M. K. Gandhi, *Ashram Observances in Action* (Ahmedabad: Navajivan, 1955), 16. There is no direct evidence that Father Divine read the most important works by interpreters of Gandhi that were so influential for early civil rights groups. But it is likely that he was familiar with them. See Krishnalal Shridharani, *War without Violence: A Study of Gandhi's Method and Its Accomplishments* (New York: Harcourt, Brace, 1939); and Richard B. Gregg, *The Power of Nonviolence* (New York: Schocken, 1934). By the 1930s, Black newspapers regularly covered Gandhi's campaigns. On African Americans' relationship with Gandhi, see Sudarshan Kapur, *Raising Up a Prophet: The African-American Encounter with Gandhi* (Boston: Beacon Press, 1992); Joseph Kip Kosek, *Acts of Conscience: Christian Nonviolence and Modern American Democracy* (New York: Columbia University Press, 2009); Sean Scalmer, *Gandhi in the West: The Mahatma and the Rise of Radical Protest* (Cambridge: Cambridge University Press, 2011); and Nico Slate, *Colored Cosmopolitanism: The Shared Struggle for Freedom in the United States and India* (Cambridge, MA: Harvard University Press, 2012).

92. Hoshor argues that the greeting "Peace" was taken from Gandhi's teachings. Hoshor, *God in a Rolls Royce*, 39.

93. "Father Divine May Buy Philly Woodside Swim Pool," *Billboard*, June 17, 1950, 68; Victoria W. Wolcott, *Race, Riots, and Roller Coasters: The Struggle over Segregated Recreation in America* (Philadelphia: University of Pennsylvania Press, 2012), 111–12. The Boulevard pools were in a large park with four pools and other facilities. The Court of Common Pleas initially ruled on the case in 1953. Memo from Sol Rabkin and Theodore Leskes to CRC Offices, ADS Regional Offices, AJC Area Offices, December 9, 1953, folder: "Discrimination, Beaches and Swimming Pools, 1953–55," group II, box A 234, NAACP Papers, Library of Congress, Washington, DC (hereafter cited as NAACP Papers); Memo to CRC Offices; ADL Regional Offices; AJC Area Offices from Sol Rabkin and Theodore Leskes, January 24, 1955, folder: "Discrimination, Beaches and Swimming Pools, 1953–55," group II, box A 234, NAACP Papers; "50G Suit Charges Discrimination by Philly Pool Ops," *Billboard*, September 22, 1951, 66; "Leo Everett et. al. v. Paul F. Harron et al.," *Race Relations Law Reporter* 1, no. 2 (April 1956): 366–70.

94. "Church Discipline, Constitution and By-Laws," c. 1941, 6.

95. McKay, *Harlem*, 34, 35; "'Messiah' Wants $30,000 to Move His Sayville 'Heaven,'" *Chicago Defender*, December 5, 1931, 2; Weisbrot, *Father Divine*, 49.

96. McKay, *Harlem*, 36. This infamous story is retold in all the major works about Father Divine. See, for example, Weisbrot, *Father Divine*, 46–55.

97. "Father Divine's Messages, Copied Verbatum [*sic*], 1932," 24; Weisbrot, *Father Divine*, 54; "The Truth about Father Divine," *Chicago Defender*, February 6, 1937, 1.

98. Denlinger, "Heaven Is in Harlem," 218; Weisbrot, *Father Divine*, 109; Weisenfeld, *New World A-Coming*, 233.

99. Weisbrot, *Father Divine*, 113–14; Weisenfeld, *New World A-Coming*, 233.

100. For a defense of Father Divine, see Braden, *"These Also Believe,"* 331–35. Negative portrayals include Hoshor, *God in a Rolls Royce*. This image of Father Divine as a charlatan can also be seen in contemporary historiography. Barbara Ransby, in *Ella Baker*, for example, claims that "Divine siphoned off a good chunk of the excess to support his own lavish lifestyle" (89).

101. Quoted in Belstrom, *Rediscovering God*, 279.

102. Lionel Levick, "Father Divine Is God," *Forum and Century* 92, no. 4 (October 1943): 218. See also Denlinger, "Heaven Is in Harlem," 211–18.

103. McKay, *Harlem*, 68.

104. Adam Clayton Powell Jr., "The Soapbox," *New York Amsterdam News*, June 6, 1936, 12. See also "'Father Divine' Does Duty of a God but Menaces Religion," *Chicago Defender*, January 4, 1936, 12.

105. *New York Amsterdam News*, November 23, 1932, 1; Watts, *God, Harlem U.S.A.*, 107.

106. Weisbrot, *Father Divine*, 209–10; Watts, *God, Harlem U.S.A.*, 152–55; Mabee, *Promised Land*, 199; Harris, *Father Divine*, 73–74.

107. Watts, *God, Harlem U.S.A.*, 156–7. Hearst supported Faithful Mary's work and even cast her in a Hollywood production, *Two-Gun Man from Harlem*. However, she returned to the Peace Mission movement in 1938 after a car accident possibly caused by her drinking (Watts, 159).

108. Weisbrot, *Father Divine*, 210; Watts, *God, Harlem U.S.A.*, 160–63; Mabee, *Promised Land*, 201–2, 209–10. Divinites sold the last Promised Land property, Kingston Mansion, in 1985 (Mabee, 217).

109. Braden, *"These Also Believe,"* 21; Mabee, *Promised Land*, 184–90. Mabee notes that fifty-six Divinites were conscientious objectors during the war (189).

110. Weisbrot, *Father Divine*, 202–12; Watts, *God, Harlem U.S.A.*, 165, 171.

111. Satter, "Marcus Garvey, Father Divine," 591; Weisenfeld, *New World A-Coming*, 188.

112. Watts, *God, Harlem U.S.A.*, 172.

113. Weisbrot, *Father Divine*, 213–15; Watts, *God, Harlem U.S.A.*, 167–69.

114. Jim Jones, the founder of the People's Temple, an interracial congregation, spent time at the Philadelphia Peace Mission intent on learning what kept Divinites in the fold. He also unsuccessfully tried to convince Peace Mission members to join his temple in 1971, bringing hundreds of his followers to Woodmont. Two decades later, in 1978, Jones oversaw the massacre of 918 followers at his compound in Guyana. See Weisbrot, *Father Divine*,

218–19; and Watts, *God, Harlem U.S.A.*, 174. The remaining members of the Father Divine movement continue to reside at the Woodmont estate.

115. Belstrom, *Rediscovering God*, 288.

116. Quoted in Weisbrot, *Father Divine*, 221. The telegram was reprinted in *New Day*, March 17, 1965, 1.

117. Harris, *Father Divine*, 188.

CHAPTER FOUR

1. Quoted in Quinton H. Dixie and Peter Eisenstadt, *Visions of a Better World: Howard Thurman's Pilgrimage to India and the Origins of African American Nonviolence* (Boston: Beacon Press, 2011), 171.

2. Rosa King Zimmerman, "Oral History Interview with Marjorie Penney Paschkis," July 20, 1976, p. 1, folder 158, box 5, series 1, Fellowship House Papers, Urban Archives, Temple University, Philadelphia, Pennsylvania (hereafter cited as Fellowship House Papers).

3. Howard Thurman, *Footprints of a Dream: The Story of the Church for the Fellowship of All Peoples* (New York: Harper & Brothers, 1959), 20; italics in the original.

4. Works on Thurman include Dixie and Eisenstadt, *Visions of a Better World*; Albert J. Raboteau, *American Prophets: Seven Religious Radicals and Their Struggle for Social and Political Justice* (Princeton, NJ: Princeton University Press, 2016), 95–118; Alton B. Pollard III, *Mysticism and Social Change: The Social Witness of Howard Thurman* (New York: Peter Lang, 1992); Amanda Brown, "Organized Religion for American Moderns: Howard Thurman's Fellowship Church and the Twentieth Century's Christian Left" (PhD diss., Lehigh University, 2007); Walter E. Fluker, *They Looked for a City: A Comparative Analysis of the Ideal of Community in the Thought of Howard Thurman and Martin Luther King, Jr.* (New York: University Press of America, 1989); Sarah Azaransky, *This Worldwide Struggle: Religion and the International Roots of the Civil Rights Movement* (New York: Oxford University Press, 2017), esp. 16–39; and Sarah Azaransky, "Resisting Jim Crow Colonialism: Black Christianity and the International Roots of the Civil Rights Movement," in *The Religious Left in Modern America: Doorkeepers of a Radical Faith*, ed. Leilah Danielson, Marian Mollin, and Doug Rossinow (New York: Palgrave Macmillan, 2018), 125–44.

5. Howard Thurman, *The Papers of Howard Thurman*, vol. 2, ed. Walter Early Fluker et al. (Columbia: University of South Carolina Press, 2012), xxiii.

6. "Relaxation and Race Conflict," reprinted in *Pacifism in the Modern World*, ed. Devere Allen (Garden City, NJ: Doubleday, 1929), 67–78, in Howard Thurman, *The Papers of Howard Thurman*, vol. 1, Walter Earl Fluker et al. (Columbia: University of South Carolina Press, 2009), 147. In *Breaking White Supremacy: Martin Luther King Jr. and the Black Social Gospel* (New Haven, CT: Yale University Press, 2018), Gary Dorrien notes that with this publication Thurman was "breaking into company that no black religious intellectual had experienced" (137). See also Dixie and Eisenstadt, *Visions of a Better World*, 60–63, who argue that the essay "is the beginning of a distinctively African American understanding of the potential for Christian nonviolence to address the African American condition, and its message would reverberate in the decades ahead" (63).

7. "To the American Negro: A Message from Mahatma Gandhi," *Crisis* 36, no. 7 (July 1929): 225.

8. Dorrien, *Breaking White Supremacy*, esp. 122–24, 161–71. On Thurman's mysticism, see Pollard, *Mysticism and Social Change*; and Brown, "Organized Religion for American Moderns," 64–85.

9. Dixie and Eisenstadt, *Visions of a Better World*, 49–53; Pollard, *Mysticism and Social Change*, 20–22; Brown, "Organized Religion for American Moderns," 64–79. Although Jones was willing to tutor Thurman, he never expressed any opinions on race. However, Leigh Eric Schmidt points out that "Jones tirelessly insisted on the practical social implications of a revived mysticism, which he himself lived out in his dedication to the Fellowship of Reconciliation." Schmidt, "The Making of Modern 'Mysticism,'" *Journal of the American Academy of Religion* 71, no. 2 (June 2003): 293.

10. Thurman, *The Papers of Howard Thurman*, 1:283.

11. Mahadev Desai, "Gandhi, with Our Negro Guests," *Harijan* 4 (March 14, 1936): 336, 337, reprinted in Thurman, *The Papers of Howard Thurman*, 1:332–37.

12. Bayard Rustin, *Down the Line: The Collected Writings of Bayard Rustin* (Chicago: Quadrangle Books, 1971), 103.

13. Thurman, *Footprints of a Dream*, 24.

14. Howard Thurman to John Nevin Sayre, May 26, 1936, reprinted in *The Papers of Howard Thurman*, 2:10.

15. Howard Thurman, *The Luminous Darkness* (New York: Harper and Row, 1965), 13.

16. Dixie and Eisenstadt, *Visions of a Better World*, 115, 165.

17. Marjorie Penney to Howard Thurman, October 22, 1942, reprinted in *The Papers of Howard Thurman*, 2:319.

18. Thurman, *The Papers of Howard Thurman*, 2:264.

19. Peter Dana, "Dr. Thurman Speaks on Indian Question," *Pittsburgh Courier*, August 29, 1942, 1.

20. Alfred Fisk to Howard Thurman, October 15, 1943, reprinted in *The Papers of Howard Thurman*, vol. 3, ed. Walter Earl Fluker et al. (Columbia: University of South Carolina Press, 2015), 2–3. On African Americans in San Francisco, see Albert S. Broussard, *Black San Francisco: The Struggle for Racial Equality in the West, 1900–1954* (Lawrence: University Press of Kansas, 1993).

21. Thurman, *The Papers of Howard Thurman*, 3:xxv–xxvi.

22. Alfred Fisk to Howard Thurman, November 6, 1943, reprinted in *The Papers of Howard Thurman*, 3:10.

23. Muriel Lester, *Training* (Nashville: Abingdon-Colesbury Press, 1940), reprinted in Muriel Lester, *An Ambassador of Reconciliation: A Muriel Lester Reader*, ed. Richard Deats (Philadelphia: New Society Publishers, 1991), 93; Thurman, *The Papers of Howard Thurman*, 2:1, 54.

24. Seth Koven, *The Match Girl and the Heiress* (Princeton, NJ: Princeton University Press, 2014), 20. Other works on Lester include Jill Wallis, *Muriel Lester: Mother of World Peace* (Middlesex, UK: Hisarlik Press, 1993); and Vera Brittain, *The Rebel Passion: A Short History of Some Pioneer Peacemakers* (London: Allen and Unwin, 1964).

25. Thurman, *Footprints of a Dream*, 24.

26. Dixie and Eisenstadt, *Visions of a Better World*, 166.

27. Angela D. Dillard, *Faith in the City: Preaching Radical Social Change in Detroit* (Ann Arbor: University of Michigan Press, 2007), 245, 247.

28. Albert B. Cleage Jr., "Fellowship Church: Adventure in Interracial Understanding," *NOW*, October 1944, reprinted in Thurman, *The Papers of Howard Thurman*, 3:93; Thurman, *Footprints of a Dream*, 33. On CORE's San Francisco campaigns, see Daniel Crowe, *Prophets of Rage: The Black Freedom Struggle in San Francisco, 1945–1969* (New York: Garland Press, 2000), 119–22.

29. Thurman, *Footprints of a Dream*, 32. Roosevelt continued to support the church for decades following its founding.

30. Howard Thurman, "The Fellowship Church of All Peoples," *Common Ground* 5 (Spring 1945): 29–31, reprinted in *The Papers of Howard Thurman*, 3:125.

31. "Looking Back, 1948–49," p. 1, folder 6, box 55, Howard Thurman Collection, Howard Gottlieb Archival Research Center, Boston University, Boston, Massachusetts (hereafter cited as Howard Thurman Collection); "Dear Friends of the Fellowship," Summer 1955, p. 1, folder 11, box 55, Howard Thurman Collection. Thurman was eager to move into a more integrated neighborhood, arguing that "the institution takes on the social pattern in which the people whom it serves are involved." Howard Thurman, "Outgrowing the Barriers," *The Growing Edge*, Summer 1950, p. 1, folder 13, box 57, Howard Thurman Collection.

32. Thurman, *Footprints of a Dream*, 46–51.

33. Thurman, 57; Dixie and Eisenstadt, *Visions of a Better World*, 172; Pollard, *Mysticism and Social Change*, 79; Brown, "Organized Religion for American Moderns," 213.

34. "Dear Friends of the Fellowship," Summer 1955, p. 2; Thurman, *The Papers of Howard Thurman*, 3:xli. Patricia Appelbaum, in *Kingdom to Commune: Protestant Pacifist Culture between World War I and the Vietnam Era* (Chapel Hill: University of North Carolina Press, 2009), argues that meditation was central to Protestant pacifist culture (127).

35. Thurman, *The Papers of Howard Thurman*, 2:xxxiii–xxxiv; "Background on Fellowship Church," August 6, 1954, p. 1, folder 11, box 55, Howard Thurman Collection; "The Fellowship Church of All Peoples," pamphlet, 1945, p. 2, folder 1, box 59, Howard Thurman Collection.

36. Pollard, *Mysticism and Social Change*, 22; Brown, "Organized Religion for American Moderns," 190–99; "Looking Back, 1948–49," 1; "The Fellowship Church of All Peoples," flyer, n.d., p. 1, folder 20, box 55, Howard Thurman Collection.

37. "The Church for the Fellowship of All Peoples," flyer, n.d., p. 1, folder 2, box 55, Howard Thurman Collection.

38. Alfred Fisk, Howard Thurman, Ayako Murota, and Anna Anderson to the National Association of the Church for the Fellowship of All Peoples, c. 1944, folder 6, box 55, Howard Thurman Collection.

39. Lester, *An Ambassador of Reconciliation*, 103. On Lester advising Thurman in advance of his trip, see Azaransky, *This Worldwide Struggle*, 93.

40. "Church for the Fellowship of All People," c. 1944, folder 20, box 55, Howard Thurman Collection.

41. W. E. B. Du Bois, "The Winds of Time," *Chicago Defender*, June 8, 1946; Thurman, *The Papers of Howard Thurman*, 3:128; Howard Thurman, *With Head and Heart: The Autobiography of Howard Thurman* (New York: Houghton Mifflin Harcourt, 1979), 144.

42. "Fellowship Church," *Time* 52, no. 4 (July 26, 1948): 42, 275–78. See also "Trumpet Ready in the West," *Christian Century*, September 12, 1951, 1041; and Brown, "Organized Religion for American Moderns," 213.

43. "The Community Bulletin," May 28, 1944, folder 6, box 55, Howard Thurman Collection; "Pledge Brotherhood," February 1952, p. 2, folder 7, box 55, Howard Thurman Collection; "Make Your Preaching Practice—Pledge Brotherhood This Year," pamphlet, folder 7, box 55, Howard Thurman Collection.

44. Thurman, *With Head and Heart*, 145; Thurman, *The Papers of Howard Thurman*, 3:xxix, xxxi; Brown, "Organized Religion for American Moderns," 225.

45. Thurman, *The Luminous Darkness*, 2.

46. Thurman, *With Head and Heart*, 154, 157.

47. Homer A. Jack, "The Emergence of the Interracial Church," *Social Action* 13, no. 1 (January 1947): 31–38.

48. Dan B. Genung to Howard Thurman, February 29, 1944, reprinted in *The Papers of Howard Thurman*, 3:37. During the 1940s, the Los Angeles church was a center of pacifism and civil rights activism. Bayard Rustin, James Farmer, and W. E. B. Du Bois all visited during this time. Thurman, *The Papers of Howard Thurman*, 3:37. See also Dan B. Genung, *A Street Called Love: The Story of All Peoples Christian Church and Center, Los Angeles* (Pasadena: Hope Publishing House, 2000).

49. Jack, "The Emergence of the Interracial Church," 37.

50. Lerone Bennett, "Howard Thurman: 20th Century Holy Man," *Ebony*, February 1978, 68–85. Gary Dorrien, in *Breaking White Supremacy*, suggests that Thurman was not suited to be a movement leader. "He was not a movement person. He was temperamentally reserved and a loner, he disliked politics and political strategizing, and his spirituality had a decidedly inward pull" (162).

51. Howard Thurman to Prentice Thomas, May 23, 1938, reprinted in *The Papers of Howard Thurman*, 2:154–55. See also James Farmer to Howard Thurman, December 15, 1944, reprinted in *The Papers of Howard Thurman*, 3:100–101; Dixie and Eisenstadt, *Visions of a Better World*, 159; and Howard Thurman to John Nevin Sayre, December 15, 1939, reprinted in *The Papers of Howard Thurman*, 2:239–40. The editors of Thurman's papers, Fluker et al., note: "It was Thurman who originally introduced Farmer to the study of Gandhi and encouraged the young scholar's analysis of the historical relationship between religion and racism" (2:239). Farmer earned his Bachelor of Divinity degree from Howard in 1941 and went on to co-found CORE. In *Visions of a Better World*, historians Quinton Dixie and Peter Eisenstadt argue, "Thurman introduced Farmer to the works and thought of Gandhi, and under his influence Farmer embraced pacifism and became a conscientious objector" (160). Sarah Azaransky, in *This Worldwide Struggle*, writes that Thurman was "one of Farmer's favorite teachers." She points out that Farmer's years at Howard corresponded with the period right after Thurman's return from India (96).

52. See, for example, Pauli Murray to Howard Thurman, May 5, 1949, reprinted in *The*

Papers of Howard Thurman, 3:320–21. On Farmer's and Murray's relationships with Thurman, see also Dixie and Eisenstadt, *Visions of a Better World*, 160–61. For descriptions of the campaign, see Pauli Murray, *Song in a Weary Throat: An American Pilgrimage* (New York: Harper and Row, 1987), 200–209, 222–31; "Howard Students Picket Jim Crow Restaurant," *Chicago Defender*, April 24, 1943, 5; Marian Mollin, *Radical Pacifism in Modern America: Egalitarianism and Protest* (Philadelphia: University of Pennsylvania Press, 2006), 24–26; Flora Bryant Brown, "NAACP Sponsored Sit-Ins by Howard University Students in Washington, DC, 1943–44," *Journal of Negro History* 85, no. 4 (Autumn 2000): 274–86; Lizabeth Cohen, *A Consumers' Republic: The Politics of Mass Consumption in Postwar America* (New York: Vintage, 2003), 98–99; and Glenda Elizabeth Gilmore, *Defying Dixie: The Radical Roots of Civil Rights, 1919–1950* (New York: Norton, 2008), 384–93.

53. Pauli Murray, *Pauli Murray: The Autobiography of a Black Activist, Feminist, Lawyer, Priest, and Poet* (Knoxville: University of Tennessee Press, 1987), 226, 228.

54. Bernice Fisher to Howard Thurman, January 20, 1943, reprinted in *The Papers of Howard Thurman*, 2:323–24; Howard Thurman to George Houser, July 17, 1945, reprinted in *The Papers of Howard Thurman*, 3:133. See also Howard Thurman to George Houser, October 14, 1946, reprinted in *The Papers of Howard Thurman*, 3:204; and Raboteau, *American Prophets*, 109.

55. Matthew Hedstrom, *The Rise of Liberal Religion: Book Culture and American Spirituality in the Twentieth Century* (New York: Oxford University Press, 2012), 218; Azaransky, *This Worldwide Struggle*, 16. See also Dixie and Eisenstadt, *Visions of a Better World*, 183–90.

56. Thurman, *Footprints of a Dream*, 21.

57. Howard Thurman, *Jesus and the Disinherited* (New York: Abingdon Press, 1949), 17, 15, 108.

58. Dixie and Eisenstadt, *Visions of a Better World*, 190–91; Dennis Dickerson, "African American Religious Intellectuals and the Theological Foundations of the Civil Rights Movement," *Church History* 74, no. 2 (June 2005): 231–33. Examples of public addresses using Thurman include Martin Luther King Jr., "A Religion of Doing," July 4, 1954, and "Overcoming an Inferiority Complex," July 14, 1957, reprinted in *The Papers of Martin Luther King, Jr.*, 6:170–74, 303–16.

59. Dixie and Eisenstadt, *Visions of a Better World*, 192; David Hardiman, *Gandhi in His Time and Ours: The Global Legacy of His Ideas* (New York: Columbia University Press, 2004), 258; Azaransky, *This Worldwide Struggle*, 49, 112; Thomas F. Jackson, *From Civil Rights to Human Rights: Martin Luther King, Jr., and the Struggle for Economic Justice* (Philadelphia: University of Pennsylvania Press, 2007), 24.

60. Brown, "Organized Religion for American Moderns," 90. King considered taking over the pastorate of the Fellowship Church before accepting his position in Montgomery. Dorrien, *Breaking White Supremacy*, 171. Howard Thurman to Martin Luther King Jr., March 14, 1956, reprinted in *The Papers of Martin Luther King, Jr.*, vol. 3, ed. Clayborne Carson (Oakland: University of California Press, 1997), 175; King Jr. to Thurman, March 16, 1956, reprinted in *The Papers of Martin Luther King, Jr.*, 3:177.

61. Thurman, *Footprints of a Dream*, 126.

62. Howard Thurman, in *The Growing Edge*, January 1949, p. 3, folder 2, box 57, Howard Thurman Collection.

63. "The Church of All Peoples," 1946, p. 2, folder 37, box 59, Howard Thurman Collection.

64. Zimmerman, "Oral History Interview," 3.

65. E. Phyllis Grossman, "Marjorie Penney and Her House of Fellowship," August 9, 1981, p. 3, folder 145: "History, Fellowship House, Beginnings," box 5, series 1, Fellowship House Papers; "The Young Peoples Interracial Fellowship," c. 1937, p. 1, folder 29: "Committees, Advisory Committee/Council, 1948–53," box 2, series 1, Fellowship House Papers; Stanley Keith Arnold, *Building the Beloved Community: Philadelphia's Interracial Civil Rights Organizations and Race Relations, 1930–1970* (Jackson: University Press of Mississippi, 2014), 19–25.

66. Zimmerman, "Oral History Interview," 3.

67. Zimmerman, 2.

68. Grossman, "Marjorie Penney and Her House of Fellowship," 3–6; "Report on Survey of Fellowship Houses," May 1955, p. 1, folder 2: "Board of Directors, Agenda, Minutes, etc., 1947–67," box 1, series 1, Fellowship House Papers; Marjorie Penney to Friends, June 11, 1940, folder 75: "Committees, Steering Committee, 1941–45," box 1, series 1, Fellowship House Papers. On the founding of the Young People's Interracial Fellowship, see Matthew J. Countryman, *Up South: Civil Rights and Black Power in Philadelphia* (Philadelphia: University of Pennsylvania Press, 2006), 17–18.

69. "Report on Survey of Fellowship Houses," May 1955, 5–6.

70. Martin Luther King Jr., *Stride toward Freedom: The Montgomery Story* (New York: Harper and Row, 1958), 78. This story is told in most works about King and Gandhi. See, for example, Sudarshan Kapur, *Raising Up a Prophet: The African-American Encounter with Gandhi* (Boston: Beacon Press, 1992), 146–47; Hardiman, *Gandhi in His Time and Ours*, 258; and Patrick Parr, *The Seminarian: Martin Luther King Jr. Comes of Age* (Chicago: Lawrence Hill Books, 2018), 98.

71. Zimmerman, "Oral History Interview," 37.

72. "History of Fellowship," document, 1946, p. 3, folder 12: "Basic Training," box 19, series 4, Fellowship House Papers.

73. "Guide to the Fellowship House," n.d., p. 1, Fellowship House, Philadelphia Folder, CDGA Collective Box: Federation of American Scientists through Fellowship Press, Inc., Swarthmore Peace Archives, Swathmore College, Swathmore, Pennsylvania (hereafter cited as CDGA Collective Box).

74. A 1949 report stated, "No one who went to Father Divine's 42nd Street Heaven will ever be quite the same again, and no one forgot it for very long during the remainder of the week." See "Report on Houseparty 1949," p. 2, folder 2: "Board of Directors, Agenda, Minutes, etc., 1947–67," box 1, series 1, Fellowship House Papers.

75. "What Is Fellowship House," pamphlet, c. 1950, folder 3: "Board of Directors, Agenda, Minutes, etc., 1950," box 1, series 1, Fellowship House Papers.

76. Countryman, *Up South*, 26.

77. Fellowship House Report, 1942, p. 1, folder 10: "Board of Directors, Correspondence, 1941–44," box 1, series 1, Fellowship House Papers.

78. Karen Johnson, *One in Christ: Chicago Catholics and the Quest for Interracial Justice* (New York: Oxford University Press, 2018), 78–93; Julie Leininger Pycior, "Bearing Witness: Catherine de Hueck Doherty and the 'Gospel of Dorothy Day,'" *U.S. Catholic Historian* 26, no. 1 (Winter 2008): 43–66; Nicholas Rademacher, "'Allow me to disappear . . . in the fetid

slums': Catherine de Hueck, Catholic Action, and the Growing End of Catholic Radicalism," *U.S. Catholic Historian* 32, no. 3 (Summer 2014): 71–100; Lorene Hanley Duquinn, *They Called Her the Baroness* (New York: Alba House, 1995); Catherine Doherty, *Fragments of My Life* (Notre Dame, IN: Ave Maria Press, 1979), esp. 145–56.

79. Thomas Merton, *The Seven Storey Mountain* (New York: Harcourt, Brace, 1948), 340.

80. "Handbook 1948–49," p. 2, folder 9: "Board of Directors, By-Laws, 1948–49, 1953, 1967," box 1, series 1, Fellowship House Papers. See also "Directors Report, October 19, 1950," p. 1, folder 3: "Board of Directors, Agenda, Minutes, etc., 1950," box 1, series 1, Fellowship House Papers; "Fellowship House Newsletter," February 1, 1943, p. 2, folder 29: "Committees, Advisory Committee/Council, 1948–53," box 2, series 1, Fellowship House Papers.

81. Fellowship House Report, 1942, 1; "Fellowship House Newsletter," July and August 1946, p. 2, folder 20: "Detroit Newsletter, Riots 1943," box 12, series 3, Fellowship House Papers.

82. "Extinguish Hatred," pamphlet, 1950, p. 2, folder: "Units for Unity, 1944–47, 1950," box 26, series 4, Fellowship House Papers; "History of Fellowship," 1946, 2; "Guide to the Fellowship House," 1; "History of Fellowship," 1946, 1; "Fellowship House, A Laboratory in Racial and Religious Understanding," leaflet, September 30, 1948, p. 1, Fellowship House, Philadelphia Folder, CDGA Collective Box; Arnold, *Building the Beloved Community*, 36–37.

83. Fellowship House Report, 1942, 1; "A Summary of Fellowship's Projects since May, 1931," n.d., p. 1, folder 75: "Committees, Steering Committee, 1941–45," box 2, series 1, Fellowship House Papers; "You Can Help Build 'Singing City,'" flyer, 1949, Fellowship House, Philadelphia Folder, CDGA Collective Box; Elaine Brown, "Singing City," n.d., p. 2, folder 371: "Singing City, 1950, 1953–54," box 26, series 4, Fellowship House Papers; "Singing City Director's Report," January 20, 1954, folder 371: "Singing City, 1950, 1953–54," series 4, box 26, Fellowship House Papers; "Pilgrim's Progress," pamphlet, n.d., p. 1, folder 42: "Church Pilgrimage, 1945–47," box 19, series 4, Fellowship House Papers.

84. Marjorie Penney, "Director's Report," March 23, 1950, p. 1, folder 1: "Board of Directors Agenda, 1942–70," box 1, series 1, Fellowship House Papers; "Speakers' Bureau," document, 1943, p. 1, folder 373: "Speakers 1940–44," box 26, series 4, Fellowship House Papers; "Handbook 1948–49," 2; "Directors Report, October 19, 1950," 1.

85. "A Summary of Fellowship's Projects since May, 1931," 2; "Minutes of the Steering Committee Meeting," October 22, 1935, folder 72: "Committees, Steering Committee Minutes, 1932–41," box 2, series 1, Fellowship House Papers; "A Summary of Fellowship's Projects since May, 1931," 3.

86. Document on Mass Arrests, November 1940, folder 4: "Cooperative Council, 1936–50," box 12, series 3, Fellowship House Papers.

87. Victoria W. Wolcott, *Race, Riots, and Roller Coasters: The Struggle over Segregated Recreation in America* (Philadelphia: University of Pennsylvania Press, 2012), 111–12; Jacques E. Wilmore to John Parker, June 18, 1954, folder 404: "Test Cases, Integration in Recreation, 1953–55," box 26, series 4, Fellowship House Papers.

88. "Suggestions for Testing Bowling Alleys," n.d.; Jacques Wilmore to Mile Manly, January 4, 1954; Minutes, February 10, 1954, Committee on Integration of Recreation; "Intergroup Tensions in Recreation Facilities," March 7, 1955; Mary Plunkett to Committee on

Integration of Recreation, memo, n.d.; and "Don't Support Jim Crow," leaflet, n.d.: all in folder 404: "Test Cases, Integration in Recreation, 1953–55," box 26, series 4, Fellowship House Papers; "Gung-Ho," newsletter, n.d., p. 2, folder 143: "Out of Town Fellowship, from 1950–51," box 79, series 7, Fellowship House Papers.

89. Dorothy M. Bristol, "Anti-Lynching Campaign," 1937, folder 4: "Cooperative Council, 1936–50," box 12, series 3, Fellowship House Papers; "The Young Peoples Interracial Fellowship," c. 1937, 1; "A Summary of Fellowship's Projects since May, 1931," 1.

90. Penney, "Director's Report," March 23, 1950, 1; "Facts and Figures about Fellowship, 1948–49," p. 2, folder 29: "Advisory Committee/Council, 1948–53," box 2, series 1, Fellowship House Papers; "Fellowship House Newsletter," July and August 1946, 2; "History of Fellowship," 1946, 2.

91. "A Summary of Fellowship's Projects since May, 1931," 2; National Sharecroppers Week Poster, n.d., folder 4: "Cooperative Council, 1936–50," box 12, series 3, Fellowship House Papers; Marjorie Penney to Alice Rex, August 20, 1937, folder 29: "Committees, Advisory Committee/Council, 1948–53, box 2, series 1, Fellowship House Papers.

92. Thomas J. Sugrue, *Sweet Land of Liberty: The Forgotten Struggle for Civil Rights in the North* (New York: Random House, 2008), 83. Sugrue notes that there were more than 1,100 "intergroup relations agencies" formed by 1949 (83). Countryman, *Up South*, 28–29.

93. Gene Zubovich, "For Human Rights Abroad, against Jim Crow at Home: The Political Mobilization of American Ecumenical Protestants in the World War II Era," *Journal of American History*, September 2018, 267–90.

94. Grossman, "Marjorie Penney and Her House of Fellowship"; Arnold, *Building the Beloved Community*, 26. Sinatra became more conservative in his final decades, changing his party affiliation to Republican in 1970.

95. Newsletter, May 1942, folder 10: "Pendle Hill, 1942–43," box 12, series 3, Fellowship House Papers.

96. "The Young Peoples Interracial Fellowship," c. 1937, 1; "Statement about Religious Fellowship," January 19, 1947, folder 361: "Religious Fellowship, 1947," box 25, series 4, Fellowship House Papers.

97. Zimmerman, "Oral History Interview," 8; Marjorie Penney to Edythe Smart, September 28, 1945, folder 361: "Religious Fellowship, 1947," box 25, series 4, Fellowship House Papers.

98. "Prayer Pilgrimage," program, May 17, 1957, folder 327: "Prayer Pilgrimage (Wash, DC)," 1957, box 25, series 4, Fellowship House Papers; "Community Units," document, 1947, p. 1, folder 140: "Neighborhood Fellowships," box 79, series 7, Fellowship House Papers.

99. "The Religious Fellowship of Fellowship House," pamphlet, n.d., p. 3, Fellowship House, Philadelphia Folder, CDGA Collective Box.

100. "Minutes of Board of Director's Meeting, Fellowship House," February 26, 1948, folder 18: "Board of Directors, Minutes, 1942–48," box 1, series 1, Fellowship House Papers.

101. "The Story of Fellowship House Farm," n.d., p. 2, folder 144: "Fellowship History," box 5, series 1, Fellowship House Papers; "Invest Your Summer at Fellowship House Farm," pamphlet, 1953, p. 1, Fellowship House, Philadelphia Folder, CDGA Collective Box.

102. Pamphlet, Fellowship Farm, n.d., p. 3, Fellowship House, Philadelphia Folder, CDGA Collective Box.

103. Pamphlet, Fellowship Farm, 1956, folder 358: "Recruitment, General, 1956," box 25, series 4, Fellowship House Papers; "Fellowship Facts," 1957, p. 1, folder 140: "Fellowship Facts," box 21, series 4, Fellowship House Papers; Zimmerman, "Oral History Interview," 30.

104. "Report from Committee on Rule of Federation of Fellowship Houses," 1950, p. 1, folder 1: "Board of Directors Agenda, 1942–70," box 1, series 1, Fellowship House Papers.

105. "Rule of Federation of Fellowship Houses," 1950, p. 1, folder 1: "Board of Directors Agenda, 1942–70," box 1, series 1, Fellowship House Papers.

106. "Report on Survey of Fellowship Houses," May 1955, 1, 10–12, 27; "We Are Not Alone," 1950, p. 1, folder 3: "Board of Directors, Agenda, Minutes, 1950," box 1, series 1, Fellowship House Papers; "Fellowship House Meeting of Directors," May 19, 1955, p. 3, folder 4: "Board of Directors, Agenda, minutes, Etc., 1955–58," box 1, series 1, Fellowship House Papers; Mitzi R. Jacoby to LeRoy Graf, May 4, 1955, p. 1, folder 126: "Knoxville, 1955," box 79, series 7, Fellowship House Papers.

107. "Bulletin of the Federation of Fellowship Houses," February 1951, p. 3, folder 131: "Federation of Fellowship Houses 1950s," box 79, series 7, Fellowship House Papers; Washington Fellowship House, brochure, 1949, p. 2, folder 5: "Washington D.C. 1949," box 78, series 7, Fellowship House Papers; Jerry Watts, Pauli Murray, and Robert Swenson to "Friends," April 8, 1944, p. 1, folder 144: "Prospective Fellowships up to 1949," box 80, series 7, Fellowship House Papers.

108. Murray, *Pauli Murray*, 228; Marjorie Penney to Mordecai Johnson, March 27, 1945, p. 1, folder 45: "Church Service, 1944–45," box 19, series 4, Fellowship House Papers. Penney wrote to Johnson in 1945, "You have come to us more often than any other friend who preaches for Fellowship Church, and you are still the most popular of all our guest ministers."

109. Marjorie Penney to George Houser, October 12, 1945, folder 361: "Religious Fellowship, 1947," box 25, series 4, Fellowship House Papers; George Houser to Marjorie Penney, October 5, 1945, folder 46: "Church Service, 1946–47," box 19, series 4, Fellowship House Papers; George Houser to Edmund Brooks, July 24, 1942, and Brooks to Houser, July 28, 1942, folder 15: "Other Fellowships, 1942," box 78, series 7, Fellowship House Papers.

110. "Inter-Racial Church-Visitation Project," 1947, p. 2, folder 46: "Church Service, 1946–47," box 19, series 4, Fellowship House Papers.

111. "Nonviolence, A Practical Guide," 1957, folder 372: "Sit-Ins 1960," box 26, series 4, Fellowship House Papers; Zimmerman, "Oral History Interview," 43; Countryman, *Up South*, 99.

112. "Report on the South," 1960, p. 3, folder 2: "Board of Directors, Agenda, Minutes, etc., 1947–67," box 1, series 1, Fellowship House Papers; Countryman, *Up South*, 209.

113. Faith S. Hosaert et al., eds., *Hands on the Freedom Plow: Personal Accounts by Women in SNCC* (Chicago: University of Illinois Press, 2010), 173. See also Courtney Pace, *Freedom Faith: The Womanist Vision of Prathia Hall* (Athens: University of Georgia Press, 2019).

114. Countryman, *Up South*, 209; "Prathia Hall," SNCC Digital Gateway, https:// snccdigital.org/people/prathia-hall/ (accessed July 5, 2019); Hosaert et al., *Hands on the Freedom Plow*, 174, 180. Pace points out that Hall's oratory skills were learned at the Fellowship House. Pace, *Freedom Faith*, 15.

115. Raymond Arsenault, *Freedom Riders: 1961 and the Struggle for Racial Justice* (New York: Oxford University Press, 2006), 39–40; Sean Chabot, *Transnational Roots of the Civil Rights Movement: African American Explorations of the Gandhian Repertoire* (New York: Lexington Books, 2012), 147–48.

116. John Lewis, *Walking with the Wind: A Memoir of the Movement* (New York: Simon and Schuster, 1998), 136.

117. Arsenault, *Freedom Riders*, 107–9.

118. Zimmerman, "Oral History Interview," 39.

119. For King's itinerary, see Martin Luther King Jr., *The Papers of Martin Luther King, Jr.*, vol. 7, ed. Clayborne Carson (Oakland: University of California Press, 2014), 60–61.

120. Zimmerman, "Oral History Interview," 39–40; Countryman, *Up South*, 175–76.

121. Howard Thurman, "The Historical Perspective," in "The Church for the Fellowship of All Peoples Bulletin," p. 7, folder 46, box 55, Howard Thurman Collection.

CHAPTER FIVE

1. Bayard Rustin, "The Negro and Non-Violence," *Fellowship* 8, no. 10 (October 1942): 167.

2. Krishnalal Shridharani, *War without Violence: A Study of Gandhi's Method and Its Accomplishments* (New York: Harcourt, Brace, 1939), 12.

3. James Farmer, *Lay Bare the Heart: An Autobiography of the Civil Rights Movement* (New York: Arbor House, 1985), 75, 358; James Farmer, *Freedom—When?* (New York: Random House, 1965), 54. In their seminal study, *CORE: A Study in the Civil Rights Movement* (Chicago: University of Illinois Press, 1975), August Meier and Elliott Rudwick downplay the significance of Farmer's memorandum in the founding of CORE. In *Pacifism in the Twentieth Century* (Toronto: University of Toronto Press, 1999), Peter Brock and Nigel Young note that "by the end of the 1940s CORE had expanded in membership and support far beyond FOR circles" (231).

4. Shridharani, *War without Violence*, 321. Paul R. Dekar, in *Creating the Beloved Community: A Journey with the Fellowship of Reconciliation* (Telford, PA: Cascadia, 2005), calls Shridharani's book the "semiofficial manual of CORE and FOR" (98). The early members of CORE also consulted Richard B. Gregg, *The Power of Nonviolence* (New York: Schocken, 1934). However, James Farmer, Bayard Rustin, George Houser, and James Peck all cite Shridharani's book more frequently. In *Civil Disobedience: An American Tragedy* (New Haven, CT: Yale University Press, 2013), Lewis Perry notes that CORE activist Homer Jack "informed me that *this* was the book, rather than Gregg's, that he and other founders of the Congress of Racial Equality (CORE) studied systematically in the early 1940s as they worked out a nonviolent strategy for confronting segregation" (185). On Gregg's influence, see Joseph Kip Kosek, "Richard Gregg, Mohandas Gandhi, and the Strategy of Nonviolence," *Journal of American History*, March 2005, 1318–48. Muste responded to Farmer's call for brotherhood mobilization in a letter: "The religious pacifist movement, like the early church, may find eventually that it has no alternative save that of weathering the storm in the form of small, compact fellowships, which manage to keep alive and which begin to rebuilt society from the bottom on a cooperative basis." A. J. Muste to James Farmer, January 3, 1942, folder:

"General Correspondence, 1940–47," box 1, section 2, series A-3, Fellowship of Reconciliation Papers, Swarthmore Peace Archives, Swarthmore, Pennsylvania (hereafter cited as Fellowship of Reconciliation Papers).

5. August Meier and Elliott Rudwick, "How CORE Began," *Social Science Quarterly* 49, no. 4 (March 1969): 789–99; "James Farmer: On the Beginnings and the End of the Congress of Racial Equality, 50 Years Later, an Interview by Robin Washington," *Fellowship* (April/May 1992): 6–8, 15–18. Other founding members of CORE included Bernice Fisher, Homer Jack, and James R. Robinson.

6. Leilah Danielson, *American Gandhi: A. J. Muste and the History of Radicalism in the Twentieth Century* (Philadelphia: University of Pennsylvania Press, 2014), 220–22; Heather A. Warren, *Theologians of a New World Order: Reinhold Niebuhr and the Christian Realists, 1920–1948* (New York: Oxford University Press, 1997), 12–15; David P. Cline, *From Reconciliation to Revolution: The Student Interracial Ministry, Liberal Christianity, and the Civil Rights Movement* (Chapel Hill: University of North Carolina Press, 2016).

7. Wini Breines, *The Great Refusal: Community and Organization in the New Left, 1962–1968* (New York: Praeger, 1982), 6.

8. Shridharani, *War without Violence*, 266. In *Transnational Roots of the Civil Rights Movement: African American Explorations of the Gandhian Repertoire* (New York: Lexington Books, 2012), sociologist Sean Chabot traces how American radicals translated the "Gandhian repertoire" beginning in the 1930s. See also Chabot, "The Gandhian Repertoire as Transformative Invention," *International Journal of Hindu Studies* 18, no. 3 (2014): 327–67.

9. Larry Gara and Lenna Mae Gara, *A Few Small Candles: War Resisters of World War II Tell Their Stories* (Kent, OH: Kent State University Press, 1999), 31.

10. For descriptions of Ahimsa, see Charles Chatfield, *For Peace and Justice: Pacifism in America* (Knoxville: University of Tennessee Press, 1971), 216–17; Patricia Appelbaum, *Kingdom to Commune: Protestant Pacifist Culture between World War I and the Vietnam Era* (Chapel Hill: University of North Carolina Press, 2009), 140, 149–51, 156–57; Sean Scalmer, *Gandhi in the West: The Mahatma and the Rise of Radical Protest* (Cambridge: Cambridge University Press, 2011), 126–27; Dekar, *Creating the Beloved Community*, 100–103; and Nico Slate, *Colored Cosmopolitanism: The Shared Struggle for Freedom in the United States and India* (Cambridge, MA: Harvard University Press, 2012), 210. On Antioch College, see Robert L. Straker, *The Unseen Harvest: Horace Mann and Antioch College* (Yellow Springs, OH: Antioch College, 1955). The college opened in 1850 as one of the first coeducational and nonsectarian schools on the grounds of a former Owenite utopian community.

11. Gara and Gara, *A Few Small Candles*, 59–60; Ahimsa Farm Leaflet, 1940, p. 1, folder: "Ahimsa Farm," box 1, Ahimsa Farm Papers, Swarthmore Peace Archives, Swarthmore, Pennsylvania (hereafter cited as Ahimsa Farm Papers).

12. Statement, July 8, 1940, p. 1, folder: "Ahimsa Farm," box 1, Ahimsa Farm Papers; Appelbaum, *Kingdom to Commune*, 131; Francesca Polletta, *Freedom Is an Endless Meeting: Democracy in American Social Movements* (Chicago: University of Chicago Press, 2002), esp. 27–29, 37–54. Polletta notes that "pacifists' well-known commitment to making 'the means reflect the ends' has been cited as inspiration for the utopian character of 1960s movements generally and, in particular, their commitment to participatory democracy" (27).

13. "Typical Week-End Program, Ahimsa Farm, Aurora, Ohio," n.d., p. 1, and "Aggressive Pacifism," August 1940, p. 1, folder: "Ahimsa Farm," box 1, Ahimsa Farm Papers.

14. "By-Laws of Ahimsa Farm," 1940, p. 1, folder: "Ahimsa Farm," box 1, Ahimsa Farm Papers.

15. Victoria W. Wolcott, *Race, Riots, and Roller Coasters: The Struggle over Segregated Recreation in America* (Philadelphia: University of Pennsylvania Press, 2012), 55; Art Dole, "Pattern in Black and White," c. 1941, CORE Papers (Sanford, NC: Microfilming Corporation of America, 1980), p. 70, microfilm, frame 422, reel 14, series 3; Rusty Brown, "Red-Led Group Tries to Stir Race Riot at Swimming Pool," undated clipping, p. 70, microfilm, frame 468, reel 14, series 3, CORE Papers; George Houser, *Erasing the Color Line* (New York: Fellowship Publications, 1945), 29–32; Thomas J. Sugrue, *Sweet Land of Liberty: The Forgotten Struggle for Civil Rights in the North* (New York: Random House, 2008), 156; Gara and Gara, *A Few Small Candles*, 1, 59–60; Todd M. Michney, *Surrogate Suburbs: Black Upward Mobility and Neighborhood Change in Cleveland, 1900–1980* (Chapel Hill: University of North Carolina Press, 2017), 163–64.

16. "A Project in Satyagraha," Summer 1941, p. 4, folder: "Direct Action Projects: Food for Europe Marches, Garfield Park Swimming Pool," box 1, Ahimsa Farm Papers.

17. Chatfield, *For Peace and Justice*, 217.

18. Brent Edwards, "Black Globality: The International Shape of Black Intellectual Culture" (PhD diss., Columbia University, 1998).

19. Works on the relationship of India to African Americans include Gerald Horne, *The End of Empires: African Americans and India* (Philadelphia: Temple University Press, 2008); Scalmer, *Gandhi in the West*, esp. 107–36; Sudarshan Kapur, *Raising Up a Prophet: The African-American Encounter with Gandhi* (Boston: Beacon Press, 1992); David Hardiman, *Gandhi in His Time and Ours: The Global Legacy of His Ideas* (New York: Columbia University Press, 2004), 255–77; and Slate, *Colored Cosmopolitanism*. See also John Munro, *The Anticolonial Front: The African American Freedom Struggle and Global Decolonization, 1945–1960* (New York: Cambridge University Press, 2017). Munro argues that "anticommunism did not eviscerate anticolonialism" (4).

20. "Peace Trek Ends in a Parade Here," *New York Times*, January 2, 1941, 5; Paul R. Dekar, "The Harlem Ashram 1940–1947: Gandhian Satyagraha in the United States," http://www.peacehost.net/HarlemAshram/dekar.htm (accessed July 10, 2016); Dekar, *Creating the Beloved Community*, 101; "'Hunger' Pilgrims Will Arrive Today," *New York Times*, January 1, 1941, 25.

21. "Long Range Program for Ahimsa," n.d., p. 1, folder: "Ahimsa Farm," box 1, Ahimsa Farm Papers.

22. "Ahimsa," *Antiochian* 5, no. 1 (October 4, 1940), in folder: "Periodical Articles," box 1, Ahimsa Farm Papers.

23. Quoted in Quinton H. Dixie and Peter Eisenstadt, *Visions of a Better World: Howard Thurman's Pilgrimage to India and the Origins of African American Nonviolence* (Boston: Beacon Press, 2011), 112.

24. "The Harlem Ashram," pamphlet, n.d., folder: "Harlem Ashram," box 13, section 2, series A-3, Fellowship of Reconciliation Papers, Swarthmore Peace Archives, Swarthmore, Pennsylvania (hereafter cited as Fellowship of Reconciliation Papers).

25. Joseph Kip Kosek, *Acts of Conscience: Christian Nonviolence and Modern American Democracy* (New York: Columbia University Press, 2009), 1. See also Appelbaum, *Kingdom to Commune*.

26. J. Holmes Smith, "Our New York Ashram," *Fellowship* 7, no. 1 (January 1941): 2.

27. J. Holmes Smith to Fellowship Friend, October 4, 1941, folder: "Harlem Ashram," box 13, section 2, series A-3, Fellowship of Reconciliation Papers.

28. J. Holmes Smith, "Ministers and the Revolution," n.d., folder: "General Correspondence, 1940-47, Smith, J. Holmes," box 4, section 1, Fellowship of Reconciliation Papers.

29. Shridharani, *War without Violence*, xxxvi. The Harlem Ashram is mentioned briefly in works on radical pacifism and civil rights. Representative works include Scalmer, *Gandhi in the West*, 125-26; Lawrence S. Wittner, *Rebels against War: The American Peace Movement, 1941-60* (New York: Columbia University Press, 1969), 63-64; Scott H. Bennett, *Radical Pacifism: The War Resisters League and Gandhian Nonviolence in America, 1915-1963* (Syracuse, NY: Syracuse University Press, 2003), 94-95; Glenda Elizabeth Gilmore, *Defying Dixie: The Radical Roots of Civil Rights, 1919-1950* (New York: Norton, 2008), 327-28, 386; Appelbaum, *Kingdom to Commune*, 150-51; Slate, *Colored Cosmopolitanism*, 208-10; Dekar, *Creating the Beloved Community*, 97-100; and Horne, *The End of Empires*, 139-42.

30. "The Harlem Ashram," 2.

31. J. Holmes Smith, "Non-Violent Direct Action," *Fellowship* 7, no. 12 (December 1941): 207.

32. Aldon D. Morris, *The Origins of the Civil Rights Movement: Black Communities Organizing for Change* (New York: Free Press, 1984), 139, 140.

33. J. Holmes Smith to Fellowship Friend, folder: "Harlem Ashram," box 13, section 2, series A-3, Fellowship of Reconciliation Papers; John M. Swomley Jr., "Youth News and Plans," *Fellowship* 7, no. 4 (April 1941): 63. Patricia Appelbaum notes that this training course marked a paradigm shift away from mainline Protestantism as the main source of pacifism to teachings in nonviolent action. Appelbaum, *Kingdom to Commune*, 67.

34. Harlem Ashram to the Members of the Board of Directors YMCA of the City of New York, folder: "Harlem Ashram," box 13, section 2, series A-3, Fellowship of Reconciliation Papers.

35. James L. Farmer Jr., "The Race Logic of Pacifism," *Fellowship* 8, no. 2 (February 1942): 25.

36. Kapur, *Raising Up a Prophet*, 115; Kosek, *Acts of Conscience*, 183; John D'Emilio, *Lost Prophet: The Life and Times of Bayard Rustin* (New York: Free Press, 2003), 61; Paula F. Pfeffer, *A. Philip Randolph, Pioneer of the Civil Rights Movement* (Baton Rouge: Louisiana State University Press, 1990), 54-55; David Welky, *Marching across the Color Line: A. Philip Randolph and Civil Rights in the World War II Era* (New York: Oxford University Press, 2013), 123-31; Cornelius L. Bynum, *A. Philip Randolph and the Struggle for Civil Rights* (Urbana: University of Illinois Press, 2010); "Randolph to Adopt Gandhi Technique," *Chicago Defender*, January 9, 1943, 4; E. Pauline Myers to Local Units of the MOWM, July 20, 1943, folder: "March on Washington Movement Conferences," A. Philip Randolph Papers, Library of Congress, Washington, DC (hereafter cited as A. Philip Randolph Papers). Following the meeting, the Harlem Ashram held a series of discussions led by Rustin and oth-

ers to explore the implications of the shift. "Non-Violent Methods for Racial Justice Aired at Public Meetings," *New York Amsterdam News*, September 4, 1943, 4.

37. Charles Wesley Burton to A. Philip Randolph, April 21, 1943, folder: "March on Washington Movement, A–C, 1943," box 26, A. Philip Randolph Papers.

38. "Memo on the Pilgrimage to the Lincoln Memorial," n.d., folder: "Harlem Ashram," box 13, section 2, series A-3, Fellowship of Reconciliation Papers; Simeon Booker, "The Force Behind the Pilgrimage," *Afro-American*, September 12, 1942, 8; "Interracial Group Marches to Washington," *Fellowship* 8, no. 2 (November 1942): 1.

39. Historian Joseph Kip Kosek notes in his analysis of Richard Gregg, author of *Power of Non-Violence*: "Gregg came to believe that in Gandhi nonviolence had become more than an inner conviction; it was now a performance, part of a public moral dialogue intended to elicit sympathy from both opponents and disinterested observers." Kosek, "Richard Gregg, Mohandas Gandhi, and the Strategy of Nonviolence," 1325.

40. David Scott Cooney, "A Consistent Witness of Conscience: Methodist Nonviolent Activists, 1940–1970" (PhD diss., University of Denver, May 2000), 206–8.

41. "Memo on the Pilgrimage to the Lincoln Memorial." The cities and towns that the marchers stopped at were Newark, NJ; New Brunswick, NJ; Princeton, NJ; Trenton, NJ; Philadelphia, PA; Chester, PA; Wilmington, DE; Elkton, MD; Havre de Grace, MD; Abingdon, MD; Baltimore, MD; Laurel, MD; and Washington, DC.

42. Booker, "The Force Behind the Pilgrimage," 8; Simeon Booker, "F.D. Snubs N.Y. to D.C. Pilgrimage," *Afro-American*, September 19, 1942, 27; "Interracial Group Marches to Washington," 1.

43. "Foot Pilgrimage to Washington to Visit Balto.," *Afro-American*, June 6, 1942, 9; "Pilgrimage Will Begin August 26," *Afro-American*, August 8, 1942, 13; "March on Capital," *Pittsburgh Courier*, September 5, 1941, 20; Booker, "F.D. Snubs N.Y. to D.C. Pilgrimage," 27.

44. Jay Holmes Smith, "The Gandhi of Puerto Rico," *Fellowship* 10, no. 11 (November 1944): 186–87. Smith's estimation of Campos was not shared by other pacifists, including Muste, who were more skeptical of his commitment to nonviolence and the level of popular support he had in Puerto Rico.

45. J. Holmes Smith to Fellowship Friend, October 4, 1941, folder: "Harlem Ashram," box 13, section 2, series A-3, Fellowship of Reconciliation Papers; Harlem Ashram to A. J. Muste, November 18, 1944, folder: "General Correspondence, 1940–47, Smith, J. Holmes," box 13, section 2, series A-3, Fellowship of Reconciliation Papers. Ashram member Ruth Reynolds moved to Puerto Rico after the community broke up to support the nationalist cause. In 1950 she was arrested for sedition and spent two years in prison. See "Dona Ruth Reynolds," http://www.peacehost.net/WhiteStar/Voices/eng-ruthreynolds.html (accessed June 20, 2016).

46. Smith and Templin fasted for eight days after their arrest in Washington. "Two Missionaries Held for Picketing Embassy," *New York Times*, February 24, 1943, 9; William K. Hefner, "Free India Committee," November 1960, folder: "Ahimsa Farm," box 1, Ahimsa Farm Papers. See also Slate, *Colored Cosmopolitanism*, 218.

47. J. Holmes Smith to Fellowship Friend, October 4, 1941; "The Work of the Harlem Ashram," c. 1946; Maude Pickett to "Dear Friend," March 12, 1943; and "Our Play Street," n.d.:

all in folder: "Harlem Ashram," box 13, section 2, series A-3, Fellowship of Reconciliation Papers; Cooney, "A Consistent Witness of Conscience," 158–59.

48. "The Work of the Harlem Ashram," c. 1946, p. 3, folder: "Harlem Ashram," box 13, section 2, series A-3, Fellowship of Reconciliation Papers.

49. "The Work of the Harlem Ashram," 3; "Follower of Gandhi Tells Why He Refuses to Fight," *Afro-American*, February 12, 1944, 10. For a discussion of Rustin's experiences in prison, see D'Emilio, *Lost Prophet*, 93–120. For reminiscences from former COs, see Gara and Gara, *A Few Small Candles*. While in prison, many COs used nonviolent direct action to protest racial segregation, tactics they had learned at the Harlem Ashram and Fellowship Houses.

50. Rachel Waltner Goossen, in *Women against the Good War: Conscientious Objection and Gender on the American Homefront, 1941–1947* (Chapel Hill: University of North Carolina Press, 1997), estimates that "approximately two thousand women, and perhaps half as many children, lived in and near Civilian Public Service camps" (2).

51. Meier and Rudwick, *CORE*, 14; John M. Swomley, *Confronting Systems of Violence: Memoirs of a Peace Activist* (New York: Fellowship Publications, 1998), 15; Slate, *Colored Cosmopolitanism*, 209–10; Rosalind Rosenberg, *Jane Crow: The Life of Pauli Murray* (New York: Oxford University Press, 2017), 100–101; Gilmore, *Defying Dixie*, 327–28; Perry, *Civil Disobedience*, 204; Patricia Bell-Scott, *The Firebrand and the First Lady: Portrait of a Friendship* (New York: Knopf, 2016), 117; William P. Jones, *The March on Washington: Jobs, Freedom, and the Forgotten History of Civil Rights* (New York: Norton, 2013), 54. Jones notes that by 1942, Murray "wondered if Gandhi's tactics of mass protest and civil disobedience might be more effective than the 'legalistic' approach that she associated with the NAACP" (54).

52. Dekar, "The Harlem Ashram 1940–1947."

53. Quoted in "Some Suggested Disciplines for Earnest Pacifists," p. 3, folder: "Harlem Ashram," box 13, section 2, series A-3, Fellowship of Reconciliation Papers.

54. "Some Suggested Disciplines for Earnest Pacifists," 1.

55. "A Memorandum Concerning a New York Ashram," n.d., p. 2, folder: "Harlem Ashram," box 13, section 2, series A-3, Fellowship of Reconciliation Papers.

56. "Dona Ruth Reynolds"; Farmer, *Lay Bare the Heart*, 150.

57. Kosek, *Acts of Conscience*, 30.

58. Farmer, *Lay Bare the Heart*, 150.

59. Quoted in Slate, *Colored Cosmopolitanism*, 210. See also Gilmore, *Defying Dixie*, 328; and Rosenberg, *Jane Crow*, 100.

60. On the connection between folk dancing and radical politics, see Daniel Walkowitz, *City Folk: English Country Dance and the Politics of the Folk in Modern America* (New York: New York University Press, 2010). See also Erica M. Nielson, *Folk Dancing* (New York: Greenwood, 2011).

61. A. J. Muste to E. Stanley Jones, July 3, 1942, folder: "Gen. Corresp., 1940–47, Smith, J. Holmes," box 4, section 1, Fellowship of Reconciliation Papers. Muste states in this letter, "There is some feeling that, without intending it, Jay wants followers and disciples, not co-workers."

62. "A Proposal Regarding the Future of the Ashram," n.d., p. 1, folder: "Harlem Ashram," box 13, section 2, series A-3, Fellowship of Reconciliation Papers.

63. John M. Swomley Jr., "Youth News and Plans," *Fellowship* 7, no. 2 (February 1941): 31. See also Douglas Van Steere, *A Manual on the Need, the Organization, and the Discipline of Cells for Peace* (New York: Fellowship of Reconciliation, 1947); and Appelbaum, *Kingdom to Commune*, 38–39.

64. On the Almanac House, see Emily Brennan, "Pete Seeger's New York Roots," *New York Times*, June 16, 2015; and Agnes Sis Cunningham and Gordon Friesen, *Red Dust and Broadsides: A Joint Autobiography* (Amherst: University of Massachusetts Press, 1999), 209–11, 339. Examples of antiwar songs at the eve of WWII include "C is for Conscription," "Plow Under," "Ballad of October 16," and "Billy Boy."

65. Marian Mollin, *Radical Pacifism in Modern America: Egalitarianism and Protest* (Philadelphia: University of Pennsylvania Press, 2006), 119–120; Interviews for *No Easy Victories: African Liberation and American Activists*, edited by William Minter, Gail Hovey, and Charles Cobb Jr. (Trenton, NJ: African World Press, 2007), http://www.noeasyvictories .org/interviews/int01_sutherland.php (accessed October 5, 2018); David Dellinger, *From Yale to Jail: The Life Story of a Moral Dissenter* (New York: Pantheon, 1993), 61–65; Appelbaum, *Kingdom to Commune*, 151–52.

66. Dellinger, *Yale to Jail*, 106, 107.

67. Bennett, *Radical Pacifism*, 127–29; Andrew E. Hunt, *David Dellinger: The Life and Times of a Nonviolent Revolutionary* (New York: New York University Press, 2006), 71–72; Appelbaum, *Kingdom to Commune*, 151; Leilah Danielson, "'It Is a Day of Judgement': The Peacemakers, Religion, and Radicalism in Cold War America," *Religion and American Culture: A Journal of Interpretation* 18, no. 2 (Summer 2008): 222; Danielson, *American Gandhi*, 222; Dellinger, *Yale to Jail*, 66–68, 106–7; "Newark Colony Gets a Farm," *Catholic Worker* 10, no. 2 (January 1943): 8.

68. Andrew Cornell, *Unruly Equality: U.S. Anarchism in the 20th Century* (Oakland: University of California Press, 2016), 172.

69. Bennett, *Radical Pacifism*, 161–67; Mollin, *Radical Pacifism*, 57; Danielson, "'It Is a Day of Judgement,'" 233; Hunt, *David Dellinger*, 91; Dellinger, *Yale to Jail*, 145–52; "Five on Hunger Strike over War in Korea," *New York Times*, July 7, 1950, 3; Timothy Miller, *The Quest for Utopia in Twentieth-Century America* (Syracuse, NY: Syracuse University Press, 1998), 170; Cornell, *Unruly Equality*, 213–27.

70. Danielson, "'It Is a Day of Judgement,'" 229; Hunt, *David Dellinger*, 93; Cornell, *Unruly Equality*, 176; Vincent J. Intondi, *African Americans against the Bomb: Nuclear Weapons, Colonialism, and the Black Freedom Movement* (Stanford, CA: Stanford University Press, 2015), 20–22; Judith A. Blackburn and Robert M. Coughlin, *Building the Beloved Community: Maurice McCrackin's Life for Peace and Civil Rights* (London: Trafford, 2006), 74; Jo Ann Ooiman Robinson, *Abraham Went Out: A Biography of A. J. Muste* (Philadelphia: Temple University Press, 1981), 94–95; Maurice Isserman, *If I Had a Hammer . . . The Death of the Old Left and the Birth of the New Left* (New York: Basic Books, 1987), 137; D'Emilio, *Lost Prophet*, 128–29. See also David L. Chappell, *A Stone of Hope: Prophetic Religion and the Death of Jim Crow* (Chapel Hill: University of North Carolina Press, 2004), esp. 44–

66; Wittner, *Rebels against War*, 156–60; and James Tracy, *Direct Action: Radical Pacifism from the Union Eight to the Chicago Seven* (Chicago: University of Chicago Press, 1996), 60–67.

71. Peacemakers, 1952, folder: "Marion Material (1952–1989)," box 6, Marion Bromley and Ernest Bromley Papers, Swarthmore Peace Archives, Swarthmore, Pennsylvania (hereafter cited as Bromley Papers).

72. Wolcott, *Race, Riots, and Roller Coasters*, 96–110.

73. Miller, *The Quest for Utopia*, 167. For a description of Skyview, see also Alfred Hassler, "Commuters' Community," *Fellowship* 19, no. 4 (April 1953): 5–11, 17–18; Kosek, *Acts of Conscience*, 210; Dan McKanan, *Prophetic Encounters: Religion and the American Radical Tradition* (Boston: Beacon Press, 2011), 185–86. McKanan notes that George Houser's wife, Jean Houser, served as president of the local PTA (185). A larger-scale interracial development was financed by FOR member Morris Milgram in Concord Park Homes near Philadelphia. See Alfred Hassler, "They Build Brotherhood," *Fellowship* 22, no. 2 (February 1956): 11–16; and Morris Milgram, *Good Neighborhood: The Challenge of Open Housing* (New York: W. W. Norton, 1977).

74. Selma Platt to Bayard Rustin, June 25, 1948, folder: "General Corresp., Feb. 1948–Dec. 1949," box 1, Bayard Rustin Papers, Library of Congress, Washington, DC (hereafter cited as Rustin Papers). See also Bayard Rustin, *I Must Resist: Bayard Rustin's Life in Letters*, ed. Michael G. Long (San Francisco: City Lights Books, 2012), 119.

75. Danielson, *American Gandhi*, 256–60; Mollin, *Radical Pacifism*, 62–64; Bennett, *Radical Pacifism*, 166, 208; Hunt, *David Dellinger*, 95–97. In 1961 the Peacemakers, Catholic Worker, and War Resisters League also sponsored a fast at CIA headquarters in support of Cuba. See "A Two Week Fast to Appeal to the American Conscience," p. 1, clipping from the Nonviolent Committee for Cuban Independence, folder: "Committee for Nonviolent Action," box 2, series B, Horace Champney Papers, Swarthmore Peace Archives, Swarthmore, Pennsylvania (hereafter cited as Champney Papers).

76. Appelbaum, *Kingdom to Commune*, 143. Appelbaum includes the Saline Valley Farm, Cello Community, Macedonia Cooperative Farm, Brookwood Labor College, Koinonia, Pendle Hill, Highlander Folk School, and the School for Living in this category. Some cooperative farms excluded African Americans, including Fairhope in Alabama. On Fairhope, see Paul M. Gaston, *Coming of Age in Utopia: The Odyssey of an Idea* (Montgomery, AL: NewSouth Books, 2010).

77. Tracy Elaine K'Meyer, *Interracialism and Christian Community in the Postwar South: The Story of Koinonia Farm* (Charlottesville: University Press of Virginia, 1997); Ansley L. Quiros, *God with Us: Lived Theology and the Freedom Struggle in Americus, Georgia, 1942–1976* (Chapel Hill: University of North Carolina Press, 2018), 15–40; Appelbaum, *Kingdom to Commune*, 151.

78. K'Meyer, *Interracialism and Christian Community*, 58.

79. "The Koinonia Story," 1957, folder: "Friends of Koinonia," box 7, Bromley Papers.

80. Quiros, *God with Us*, 96–98.

81. Alice Lynd and Staughton Lynd, *Stepping Stones: Memoir of a Life Together* (New York: Lexington Books, 2009), 45–54. On Macedonia, see also W. Edward Orser, *Searching*

for a Viable Alternative: The Macedonia Cooperative Community, 1937–58 (New York: Burt Franklin, 1981); Isserman, *If I Had a Hammer*, 135; Wittner, *Rebels against the War*, 159; John Egerton, *Speak Now against the Day: The Generation before the Civil Rights Movement in the South* (Chapel Hill: University of North Carolina Press, 1995), 127; and Miller, *The Quest for Utopia*, xviii, 158–60. On Staughton Lynd, see Vaneesa Cook, *Spiritual Socialists: Religion and the American Left* (Philadelphia: University of Pennsylvania Press, 2019), 170–82, 185–89.

82. Laurence Veysey, *The Communal Experience: Anarchist and Mystical Counter-Cultures in America* (New York: Harper and Row, 1973), 39; Cornell, *Unruly Equality*, 135–36; Cook, *Spiritual Socialists*, 58, 77–78, 91; Nancy L. Roberts, *Dorothy Day and the Catholic Workers* (Albany: SUNY Press, 1984), 11–20; James Terence Fisher, *The Catholic Counterculture in America, 1933–1962* (Chapel Hill: University of North Carolina Press, 1989), 41–53.

83. Polletta, *Freedom Is an Endless Meeting*, 38. There were intentional communities founded in the mid-twentieth century that isolated themselves from the broader society. Proponents of communes founded the Fellowship of Intentional Communities in 1937 in Ann Arbor, Michigan, and published *Cooperative Living* magazine from 1949–56. See Veysey, *The Communal Experience*, 38–40; McKanan, *Prophetic Encounters*, 185–86; and Wendell Barlow Kramer, "Criteria for the Intentional Community: A Study of the Factors Affecting Success and Failure in the Planned, Purposeful, Cooperative Community" (PhD diss., New York University, 1955).

84. "Proceedings of the National Conference of Peacemakers Olivet Institute, Chicago, April 1–3, 1949," folder: "Peacemaker Conferences/Committee Mtgs.," box 7, Bromley Papers. They also recommended that cells introduce cooperative economics and be founded in both urban and rural settings.

85. A. Philip Randolph, "March on Washington Movement Presents Program for the Negro," in *What the Negro Wants*, ed. Rayford W. Logan (Chapel Hill: University of North Carolina Press, 1944), 149. Randolph's anti-communist stance led to a major split in the National Negro Congress (NNC) in 1940, although local chapters of the NNC continued to carry out important organizing work. See Erik S. Gellman, *Death Blow to Jim Crow: The National Negro Congress and the Rise of Militant Civil Rights* (Chapel Hill: University of North Carolina Press, 2012); and Clarence Lang, "Freedom Train Derailed: The National Negro Labor Council and the Nadir of Black Radicalism," in *Anticommunism and the African American Freedom Movement: "Another Side of the Story,"* ed. Robbie Lieberman and Clarence Lang (New York: Palgrave Macmillan, 2009), 161–88. Eric Arnesen analyzes Randolph's life to argue that Black anti-communism has been misunderstood and that the Communist Party was, in fact, a destructive force by the early 1940s. Eric Arnesen, "A. Philip Randolph, Black Anticommunism, and the Race Question," in *Rethinking U.S. Labor History: Essays on the Working-Class Experience, 1756–2009*, ed. Donna T. Haverty-Stacke and Daniel J. Walkowitz (New York: Continuum, 2010), 137–67. See also his essay, Eric Arnesen, "Reconsidering the 'Long Civil Rights Movement,'" *Historically Speaking* 10, no. 2 (April 2009): 31–34. Despite their opposition to the Communist Party, Randolph and activists in CORE and FOR defended communists' civil liberties and were highly critical of the Red scare.

86. Nikhil Pal Singh, *Black Is a Country: Race and the Unfinished Struggle for Democracy* (Cambridge, MA: Harvard University Press, 2004), 111.

87. W. E. B. Du Bois, "As the Crow Flies," *New York Amsterdam News*, March 13, 1943, 10. In *The Nashville Way: Racial Etiquette and the Struggle for Social Justice in a Southern City* (Athens: University of Georgia Press, 2012), Benjamin Houston argues that "the etiquette associated with the strategy; the style of picketing, of direct action, of putting bodies directly on the line, was not to the NAACP's taste" (132). See also Manfred Berg, *"The Ticket to Freedom": The NAACP and the Struggle for Black Political Integration* (Gainesville: University Press of Florida, 2005), 172–79; and Gilbert Jonas, *Freedom's Sword: The NAACP and the Struggle against Racism in America, 1909–1969* (New York: Routledge, 2005), 104–7. Berg notes that the NAACP did not openly support nonviolence until its 1960 convention (175). In *Bayard Rustin: Troubles I've Seen* (New York: HarperCollins, 1997), Jervis Anderson states that neither Walter White "nor the traditionally nonconfrontational NAACP thought highly of the effort in direct action, however nonviolent its leaders were" (114). Local chapters of the NAACP, in contrast to the national office, sometimes cooperated with radical pacifists.

88. Thurgood Marshall, "Negroes Cautioned on Resistance Idea," *New York Times*, November 23, 1946, 14.

89. Lee Finkle, "The Conservative Aims of Militant Rhetoric: Black Protest during World War II," *Journal of American History* 60, no. 3 (December 1973): 709; A. Philip Randolph, "Randolph Blasts Courier as 'Bitter Voice of Defeatism,'" *Chicago Defender*, June 12, 1943, 13; Sean Chabot, "Transnational Diffusion and the African-American Reinvention of the Gandhian Repertoire," *Mobilization* 5, no. 2 (Fall 2000): 206; Slate, *Colored Cosmopolitanism*, 214. In *Transnational Roots of the Civil Rights Movement*, Sean Chabot points out that the Black press "generally believed that the NAACP's traditional protest methods remained more realistic and practical" (86).

90. Gunnar Myrdal, *An American Dilemma: The Negro Problem and Modern Democracy* (New York: Harper and Brothers, 1944), xvii.

91. Bayard Rustin to A. J. Muste, September 12, 1942, in Rustin, *I Must Resist*, 5; Rustin, "The Negro and Non-Violence," 166.

92. Randolph, "Randolph Blasts Courier as 'Bitter Voice of Defeatism,'" 13.

93. John Swomley, "F.O.R.'s Early Efforts for Racial Equality," *Fellowship*, July/August 1990, 7–9; Swomley, *Confronting Systems of Violence*, 20; Tracy, *Direct Action*, 54; D'Emilio, *Lost Prophet*, 142–44; Charles DeBenedetti, *The Peace Reform in American History* (Bloomington: Indiana University Press, 1980), 140–41. For an overview of these institutes, see Victoria W. Wolcott, "Radical Nonviolence, Interracial Utopias and the Congress of Racial Equality in the Early Civil Rights Movement," *Journal of Civil and Human Rights* 4, no. 2 (Fall/Winter 2018): 31–61.

94. Bayard Rustin suggested the works of Franz Boas, Margaret Mead, and Ruth Benedict. See Bayard Rustin, *Interracial Primer* (New York: Fellowship of Reconciliation, 1943), 7. Sunday morning was given to interracial worship, and the institutes closed with a speech on Gandhi, usually given by Muste, and often a song from the extraordinarily talented Bayard Rustin. Evenings were taken up with folk dancing and games. "Memorandum on Proposed Institutes of Non-Violent Action as Applied to Race Relationships in the United States,"

February 4, 1943, folder: "FOR, New York: Race Relations Work, 1942–48," box 6, section 3, series C, Fellowship of Reconciliation Papers.

95. Houser, *Erasing the Color Line*, 11; "Suggestions for Organizing a Race Relations Institute," n.d., folder: "Fellowship articles on race, 1942–66," box 19, section 3, series E, Fellowship of Reconciliation Papers.

96. Swomley, "F.O.R.'s Early Efforts for Racial Equality," 7; Clarence Holmes to George Houser, August 24, 1945, microfilm, frame 126, reel 6, series 2, CORE Papers; "Memorandum on Proposed Institutes of Non-Violent Action as Applied to Race Relationships in the United States," February 4, 1943. CORE and FOR did not ignore economic rights in their work. Most workshops and institutes addressed racial discrimination in hiring, and the groups continued to push for a permanent FEPC.

97. "Report to the FOR National Council about the Racial-Industrial Work," May 30, 1947, p. 2, folder: "Institutes, Workshops, Etc., 1944–59," box 19, section 3, series E, Fellowship of Reconciliation Papers. Typical was a 1945 Cleveland race institute held by George Houser that brought in three hundred participants. See A. J. Muste to Bayard Rustin, January 23, 1945, folder: "General Correspondence, Jan.–Dec. 1945," box 1, Rustin Papers.

98. Bayard Rustin to A. J. Muste, September 12, 1942, in Rustin, *I Must Resist*, 5.

99. "What Are Interracial Institutes and Workshops?" n.d., folder: "Fellowship articles on race, 1942–66," box 19, section 3, series E, Fellowship of Reconciliation Papers; "Windy City Sophisticates," *Chicago Bee*, August 12, 1945, clipping, microfilm, frame 131, reel 8, series 3, CORE Papers. Among other tactics, activists polled shoppers asking, "Would you be willing to be served by a Negro salesclerk?" They used the results (usually about 60 percent said yes) to bring publicity to the issue. For a history of department stores and segregation, see Traci Parker, *Department Stores and the Black Freedom Movement: Workers, Consumers, and Civil Rights from the 1930s to the 1980s* (Chapel Hill: University of North Carolina Press, 2019). On housing campaigns, see, for example, "Congress of Racial Equality Announces Summer Interracial Action Project," April 19, 1945, press release, microfilm, frame 76, reel 8, series 3, CORE Papers.

100. "Detroit Institute on Race Relations and Non-Violent Solutions," April 1943, folder: "Fellowship articles on race, 1942–66," box 19, section 3, series E, Fellowship of Reconciliation Papers. For descriptions of a variety of projects, see Bayard Rustin, "Institutes on Race and Nonviolence," 1943, folder: "Fellowship of Reconciliation, Misc., 1944–45, n.d.," box 45, Bayard Rustin Papers.

101. "Plan for Race Relations Institutes," n.d., folder: "Fellowship articles on race, 1942–66," box 19, section 3, series E, Fellowship of Reconciliation Papers; "Report to the FOR National Council about the Racial-Industrial Work," May 30, 1947, 1. The cities included West Chester, PA; Fort Wayne, IN; Pittsburgh, PA; Cincinnati, OH; Cleveland, OH; and St. Louis, MO.

102. "Pamphlet for 1946 Campaign," microfilm, frame 301, reel 8, series 3, CORE Papers.

103. "What Are Interracial Institutes and Workshops?" 3. Rustin was known for carrying out spontaneous sit-ins. In 1947, when he was refused a room at the Hamline Hotel in St. Paul, Minnesota, he sat in the lobby for hours. When local activists joined him, the management relented. "Passive Resistance Sit Down Cracks St. Paul Hotel Bias," *Chicago*

Defender, February 1, 1947, 4. When Rustin was traveling via train to Knoxville, Tennessee, he sat in the "white" dining car for six hours without being served. "Defies Dixie Diner Jim Crow Six Hours," *Chicago Defender*, October 4, 1947, 1.

104. "Report to the FOR National Council about the Racial-Industrial Work," May 30, 1947, 2.

105. On the Journey of Reconciliation, see James Peck, *Freedom Ride* (New York: Simon and Schuster, 1962), 10–16; Robinson, *Abraham Went Out*, 113–14; D'Emilio, *Lost Prophet*, 135–40; Raymond Arsenault, "'You Don't Have to Ride Jim Crow': CORE and the 1947 Journey of Reconciliation," in *Before Brown: Civil Rights and White Backlash in the Modern South*, ed. Glenn Feldman (Tuscaloosa: University of Alabama Press, 2004); Derek Charles Catsam, *Freedom's Main Line: The Journey of Reconciliation and the Freedom Rides* (Lexington: University Press of Kentucky, 2009), 13–46; and Marian Mollin, "The Limits of Egalitarianism: Radical Pacifism, Civil Rights, and the Journey of Reconciliation," *Radical History Review* 88 (2004): 112–13.

106. Bayard Rustin, "Civil Disobedience, Jim Crow, and the Armed Forces," April 11, 1948, "Speech Accepting the Thomas Jefferson Award by the Council Against Intolerance in America," in Bayard Rustin, *Down the Line: The Collected Writings of Bayard Rustin* (Chicago: Quadrangle Books, 1971), 50, 51.

107. "Report of the CORE Conference and Convention, June 15th to 19th, 1949," p. 3, microfilm, frame 65, reel 2, series 1, CORE Papers.

108. "Fourth Annual Convention," 1946, microfilm, frame 133, reel 9, series 3, CORE Papers; "What Is the Vanguard League," pamphlet, microfilm, frame 210, reel 9, series 3, CORE Papers; Sugrue, *Sweet Land of Liberty*, 150. The Vanguard League merged with CORE in 1950 (Letter from Barbee William to George Houser, June 8, 1948, microfilm, frame 160, reel 9, series 3, CORE Papers). "Committee for Racial Democracy in the Nation's Capital," February 15, 1947, microfilm, frame 211, reel 9, series 3, CORE Papers; "Report of George Houser's Trip to the West Coast, March 11th to April 15th, 1946," microfilm, frame 220, reel 9, series 3, CORE Papers.

109. Houser, *Erasing the Color Line*; Rustin, *Interracial Primer*; James Peck, *Cracking the Color Line: Non-Violent Direct Action Methods of Eliminating Racial Discrimination* (New York: CORE, 1960); "Workshop Report on an Interracial Primer for Negroes," n.d., folder: "Workshop: Race and Non-Violence, San Francisco," box 19, section 3, series E, Fellowship of Reconciliation Papers; George Houser, "CORE Convention, June, 1949," microfilm, frame 127, reel 9, series 3, CORE Papers; "Minutes of National Convention, June 10–14, 1953," p. 3, microfilm, frame 302, reel 10, series 3, CORE Papers; Wallace F. Nelson, "The Second Year of Field Work: A Report to the 1953 CORE Conference and Convention," pp. 2–3, microfilm, frame 299, reel 10, series 3, CORE Papers.

110. "CORE Conference Report," June 13, 14, 15, 1947, p. 2, microfilm, frame 264, reel 9, series 3, CORE Papers.

111. Press release on fourth annual convention, May 27, 1946, microfilm, frame 290, reel 9, series 3, CORE Papers.

112. George Houser, "CORE: A Brief History," 1949, p. 9, folder: "CORE, 1942–61," box 19, section 3, series E, Fellowship of Reconciliation Papers.

113. "Volunteer for Interracial Action," 1946, p. 1, folder: "CORE, 1942–61," box 19, section 3, series E, Fellowship of Reconciliation Papers.

114. Astor Kirk to Friend, September 11, 1943, folder: "Fellowship of Reconciliation, Miscellaneous, 1944–45, n.d.," box 45, Bayard Rustin Papers.

115. "Interracial workshops, July 1948, Washington DC and Southern California," folder: "Institutes, Workshops, etc., 1944–59," box 19, section 3, series E, Fellowship of Reconciliation Papers. See also Kosek, *Acts of Conscience*, 103. The FOR was officially a co-sponsor of the Washington workshops, but the leaders were all active in CORE.

116. Pauli Murray, *Song in a Weary Throat: An American Pilgrimage* (New York: Harper and Row, 1987), 200. On segregation in Washington, DC, see Myrdal, *An American Dilemma*, 632; Constance McLaughlin Green, *The Secret City: A History of Race Relations in the Nation's Capital* (Princeton, NJ: Princeton University Press, 1967); and National Committee on Segregation in the Nation's Capital, *Segregation in Washington: A Report of the National Committee on Segregation in the Nation's Capital* (Chicago, 1948).

117. For descriptions of the campaign, see Murray, *Song in a Weary Throat*, 200–209, 222–31; "Howard Students Picket Jim Crow Restaurant," *Chicago Defender*, April 24, 1943, 5; Mollin, *Radical Pacifism*, 24–26; Flora Bryant Brown, "NAACP Sponsored Sit-Ins by Howard University Students in Washington, DC, 1943–44," *Journal of Negro History* 85, no. 4 (Autumn 2000): 274–86; Lizabeth Cohen, *Consumers' Republic: The Politics of Mass Consumption in Postwar America* (New York: Vintage, 2003), 98–99; Rosenberg, *Jane Crow*, 124–27, 133–36; Bell-Scott, *The Firebrand and the First Lady*, 113–18, 128–31; and Gilmore, *Defying Dixie*, 384–93.

118. "The following places were visited by Margaret Draper and Leroy Fennell on Saturday, July 26, 1947 between 12:30 and 2:15 PM," and "Account of visit to Southern Café by Paul Jacobs and Bayard Rustin," 1947, folder: "Interracial Workshop, Washington, D.C.," box 19, section 3, series E, Fellowship of Reconciliation Papers; "Interracial Workshop Progress Report," pp. 1–2, 5, folder: "Interracial Workshop, Washington, D.C.," box 19, section 3, series E, Fellowship of Reconciliation Papers; "Negroes Can Ride Non-Jim Crow into the South," May 27, 1948, press release, microfilm, frame 65, reel 8, series 3, CORE Papers.

119. Radio Transcript from WWDC, July 27, 1947, folder: "Interracial Workshop, Washington, D.C.," box 19, section 3, series E, Fellowship of Reconciliation Papers.

120. Interracial Workshop Bulletin, July 15, 1949, pp. 4, 13, folder: "Institutes, Workshops, etc., 1944–59," box 19, section 3, series E, Fellowship of Reconciliation Papers.

121. Polletta, *Freedom Is an Endless Meeting*. Farmer noted that as a result of the workshops, "literally thousands of interracial organizations which came into being to fight the good fight became themselves temporary models of integrated living." Farmer, *Freedom—When?*, 115.

122. George Houser, "Project: Brotherhood," *Fellowship* 16, no. 2 (February 1950): 13–16. For analysis of the Anacostia pool riot, see Wolcott, *Race, Riots, and Roller Coasters*, 81–85; and Jeff Wiltse, *Contested Waters: A Social History of Swimming Pools in America* (Chapel Hill: University of North Carolina Press, 2007), 184–85.

123. Houser, "Project: Brotherhood," 16–18; "Summer Interracial Workshop," July 1954, folder: "Institutes, Workshops, etc., 1944–59," box 19, section 3, series E, Fellowship of Rec-

onciliation Papers. The participants came from fifteen states; many of them were students in undergraduate and graduate schools.

124. Wilson Head, *A Life on the Edge: Experiences in "Black and White" in North America* (Toronto: University of Toronto Press 1995), 222.

125. Juanita Nelson, "Interesting Phases of Sis Robinson's Life," *The Peacemaker* 13, no. 3 (February 20, 1960): 6.

126. Wolcott, *Race, Riots, and Roller Coasters*, 109-10; Meier and Rudwick, *CORE*, 52-53; Summer Interracial Workshop, "Brotherhood Bulletin," July 31, 1952, folder: "CORE Projects: Interracial Workshops, 1947-54," box 1, Congress of Racial Equality Papers, Swarthmore Peace Archives, Swarthmore, Pennsylvania (hereafter cited as Congress of Racial Equality Papers); "Rosedale—2 Years Later!" "Brotherhood Bulletin," July 20, 1954," folder: "CORE Newsletters, 1947-54," box 2, Congress of Racial Equality Papers.

127. Summer Interracial Workshop, "Brotherhood Bulletin," July 31, 1952.

128. "1952 CORE Convention," p. 2, microfilm, frame 191, reel 10, series 3, CORE Papers; George Houser, "CORE: A Brief History," 1949, p. 10, folder: "CORE, 1942-61," box 19, section 3, series E, Fellowship of Reconciliation Papers.

129. Swomley, *Confronting Systems of Violence*, 20. For memories of the institutes, see also Dekar, *Creating the Beloved Community*, 103.

130. Houser, *Erasing the Color Line*, 63.

131. Houser, 62.

132. Scalmer, *Gandhi in the West*, 178-90; Kosek, "Richard Gregg, Mohandas Gandhi, and the Strategy of Nonviolence," 1343; Kosek, *Acts of Conscience*, 193, 212, 229; Slate, *Colored Cosmopolitanism*, 220-28. Because of his arrests for homosexuality, and the ensuing concerns about his "respectability," Rustin soon returned to New York, leaving Smiley to work with King. The Fellowship of Reconciliation also published a comic book detailing the events at Montgomery.

133. In 1957 alone, for example, Rustin traveled to "Alabama, Georgia, Florida and Louisiana," where "he [had] consulted with leaders engaged in bus protests; in Mississippi and South Carolina, with those faced with economic boycotts and reprisals; in Tennessee and North Carolina, with groups seeking integration in Public Schools." Bayard Rustin, "Nonviolence in the South," 1957, pamphlet, p. 1, folder: "War Resisters League, 1943, 1951-64," box 33, Bayard Rustin Papers.

134. Scalmer, *Gandhi in the West*, 182; Houston, *The Nashville Way*, 85, 120; Dennis Dickerson, "African American Religious Intellectuals and the Theological Foundations of the Civil Rights Movement," *Church History* 74, no. 2 (June 2005): 233-35; Peter Ackerman and Jack DuVall, *A Force More Powerful: A Century of Nonviolent Conflict* (New York: St. Martin's Press, 2000), 306-10; Wesley C. Hogan, *Many Minds, One Heart: SNCC's Dream for a New America* (Chapel Hill: University of North Carolina Press, 2007), 13-31. Hogan notes that Glenn E. Smiley and James Lawson acted as a "reconciliation team," traveling throughout the South and running nonviolent workshops (15). This activism paralleled the work of Houser and Rustin in the North during the 1940s.

135. Inge Powell Bell, *CORE and the Strategy of Nonviolence* (New York: Random House, 1968), 41.

136. Eric Arnesen, for example, points out that "activism came in fits and starts." "Reconsidering the 'Long Civil Rights Movement,'" 34. For similar critiques, see Sundiata Keita Cha-Jua and Clarence Lang, "The 'Long Movement' as Vampire: Temporal and Spatial Fallacies in Recent Black Freedom Studies," *Journal of African American History* 92, no. 2 (2007): 265–88; Arnesen, "A. Philip Randolph, Black Anticommunism, and the Race Question"; David L. Chappell, "The Lost Decade of Civil Rights," *Historically Speaking* 10, no. 2 (April 2009): 37–41. Kevin Boyle makes the opposite criticism of long movement scholarship, arguing that it exaggerates the *differences* between the character of struggle in the 1940s and the 1960s. See Kevin Boyle, "Labour, the Left, and the Long Civil Rights Movement," *Social History* 30, no. 3 (August 2005): 366–72.

AFTERWORD

1. Quoted in Courtney Pace, *Freedom Faith: The Womanist Vision of Prathia Hall* (Athens: University of Georgia Press, 2019), 19.

2. "Across the Editor's Desk," *Student Voice* 1, no. 1 (June 1960): 5.

3. Pace, *Freedom Faith*, 18. On the Raleigh conference, see Barbara Ransby, *Ella Baker and the Black Freedom Movement: A Radical Democratic Vision* (Chapel Hill: University of North Carolina Press, 2003), 239–47; Clayborne Carson, *In Struggle: SNCC and the Black Awakening of the 1960s* (Cambridge, MA: Harvard University Press, 1981); Wesley C. Hogan, *Many Minds, One Heart: SNCC's Dreams for a New America* (Chapel Hill: University of North Carolina Press, 2007); and David J. Garrow, *Bearing the Cross: Martin Luther King, Jr., and the Southern Christian Leadership Conference* (New York: Quill, 1999).

4. James Lawson, "Statement of Purpose," *Student Voice* 1, no. 1 (June 1960): 1; Claude Sitton, "Negro Criticizes N.A.A.C.P. Tactics," *New York Times*, April 17, 1960, 32.

5. James M. Lawson Jr., "Eve of Nonviolent Revolution," *Southern Patriot*, November 1961, 132.

6. Editorial, *Liberation*, April 1960, 3.

7. David Riesman, *Individualism Reconsidered* (New York: Free Press, 1954), 67. In *Visions of Progress: The Left-Liberal Tradition in America* (Philadelphia: University of Pennsylvania Press, 2008), Doug Rossinow notes that "Riesman called for a revival of the kind of small-scale collectivist experiment first derided as 'utopian' by Karl Marx" (210).

8. Richard Flacks and Nelson Lichtenstein, eds., *The Port Huron Statement: Sources and Legacies of the New Left's Founding Manifesto* (Philadelphia: University of Pennsylvania Press, 2015), 241.

9. Van Gosse, *Rethinking the New Left: An Interpretive History* (New York: Palgrave Macmillan, 2005); Marc Stears, *Demanding Democracy: American Radicals in Search of a New Politics* (Princeton, NJ: Princeton University Press, 2010); Michael Kazin, *American Dreamers: How the Left Changed a Nation* (New York: Vintage, 2011); Wini Breines, *The Great Refusal: Community and Organization in the New Left, 1962–1968* (New York: Praeger, 1982).

10. Helen Nearing and Scott Nearing, *Living the Good Life: How to Live Sanely and Simply in a Troubled World* (New York: Schocken Books, 1954). Two decades later they published a second book, *Continuing the Good Life: Half a Century of Homesteading* (New York: Schocken

Books, 1979). On homesteading and its relationship to the pacifist movement, see Patricia Appelbaum, *Kingdom to Commune: Protestant Pacifist Culture between World War I and the Vietnam Era* (Chapel Hill: University of North Carolina Press, 2009), 144–62; and Dona Brown, *Back to the Land: The Enduring Dream of Self-Sufficiency in Modern America* (Madison: University of Wisconsin Press, 2011), 197–201. See also Scott Nearing, *The Making of a Radical: A Political Autobiography* (New York: Harper and Row, 1972).

11. Leilah Danielson, *American Gandhi: A. J. Muste and the History of Radicalism in the Twentieth Century* (Philadelphia: University of Pennsylvania Press, 2014), 90.

12. On Gregg, see Joseph Kip Kosek, *Acts of Conscience: Christian Nonviolence and Modern American Democracy* (New York: Columbia University Press, 2009), 224. On the Nearing's influence on the political counterculture, see Peter Richardson, *No Simple Highway: A Cultural History of the Grateful Dead* (New York: St. Martin's Griffin, 2014), 119–22.

13. Historian Steven Conn points out, "Almost no African Americans joined communes, and many who studied them made this observation." Conn, *Americans against the City: Anti-Urbanism in the Twentieth Century* (New York: Oxford University Press, 2014), 268.

14. "Father Divine's Righteous Government Platform," pamphlet, n.d., box 3, folder 4, Father Divine Papers, Schomburg Center for Research in Black Culture, New York, New York; "Black Panther Party Platform and Program," in *Modern Black Nationalism: From Marcus Garvey to Louis Farrakhan*, ed. William L. Van Deburg (New York: New York University Press, 1997), 249–51.

15. Joshua Clark Davis, *From Head Shops to Whole Foods: The Rise and Fall of Activist Entrepreneurs* (New York: Columbia University Press, 2017), 22.

16. Maulana Karenga, "The Seven Principles," in *Modern Black Nationalism*, ed. Van Deburg, 282; Scot Brown, *Fighting for US: Maulana Karenga, The US Organization, and Black Cultural Nationalism* (New York: New York University Press, 2003), 14–15.

17. Mark Dery coined the term "Afrofuturism" in his chapter "Black to the Future: Interviews with Samuel R. Delany, Greg Tate, and Tricia Rose," in *Flame Wars: The Discourse of Cyberculture*, ed. Mark Dery (Durham, NC: Duke University Press, 1994), 179–222. Works on Afrofuturism include Alondra Nelson, ed., *Afrofuturism: A Special Issue of Social Text* (June 2002); Alex Zamalin, *Black Utopia: The History of an Idea from Black Nationalism to Afrofuturism* (New York: Columbia University Press, 2019); Wilson J. Moses, *Afrotopia: The Roots of African American Popular History* (New York: Cambridge University Press, 1998); Richard Iton, *In Search of the Black Fantastic: Politics and Popular Culture in the Post–Civil Rights Era* (New York: Oxford University Press, 2010); Walter Greason and Julian Chambliss, eds., *Cities Imagined: The African Diaspora in Media and History* (New York: Kendall Hunt, 2015); Jayna Brown, *Black Utopias: Speculative Life and the Music of Other Worlds* (Durham, NC: Duke University Press, 2021).

18. In "'We Can't Grow Food on All This Concrete': The Land Question, Agrarianism, and Black Nationalist Thought in the Late 1960s and 1970s," *Journal of American History* 103, no. 4 (March 2017): 956–80, historian Russell Rickford defines "agrarian nationalism" as "veneration of the countryside, and especially the rural American South, as the crucial realm of Black nationality" (958). On the Federation of Southern Cooperatives, see Monica M. White, *Freedom Farmers: Agricultural Resistance and the Black Freedom Movement*

(Chapel Hill: University of North Carolina Press, 2018), 97–116; and Jessica Gordon Nembhard, *Collective Courage: A History of African American Cooperative Economic Thought and Practice* (University Park: Pennsylvania State University Press, 2014), 193–212. In 1985 the federation merged with the Emergency Land Fund to become the Federation of Southern Cooperatives/Land Assistance Fund (FSC/LAF) (Nembhard, 193). FSC/LAF still operates across seven southern states, providing education and financial support to Black farmers, landowners, and cooperatives.

19. "The Anti-Depression Program of the Republic of New Africa," in *Modern Black Nationalism*, ed. Van Deburg, 200. On the RNA, see Edward Onaci, *Free the Land: The Republic of New Afrika and the Pursuit of a Black Nation-State* (Chapel Hill: University of North Carolina Press, 2020). For a discussion of contemporary Black towns, some dating back to the nineteenth century, see Karla Slocum, *Black Towns, Black Futures: The Enduring Allure of a Black Place in the American West* (Chapel Hill: University of North Carolina Press, 2019). The role of decolonization in the Black Power movement is explored in Brenda Gayle Plummer, *In Search of Power: African Americans in the Era of Decolonization, 1956–1974* (New York: Cambridge University Press, 2013).

20. Onaci, *Free the Land*, 79–112; Kali Akuno and Ajamu Nangwaya, *Jackson Rising: The Struggle for Economic Democracy and Black Self-Determination in Jackson, Mississippi* (Ottawa: Daraja Press, 2017), xii. They changed the spelling of Africa to the Swahili spelling, Afrika.

21. "Cooperation Jackson," https://cooperationjackson.org/ (accessed October 10, 2019); Akuno and Nangwaya, *Jackson Rising*. In "Transforming Capitalism through Real Utopias," *American Sociological Review* 78, no. 1 (2013), Erik Olin Wright points to participatory budgeting and worker-owned cooperatives as prime examples of "real utopias" (9–10).

22. Floyd B. McKissick, *Soul City North Carolina* (Soul City, NC: The Company, 1974), 2; Floyd McKissick, *Three-Fifths of a Man* (New York: Macmillan, 1969), 15.

23. Christopher Strain, "Soul City, North Carolina: Black Power, Utopia, and the African American Dream," *Journal of African American History* 89, no. 1 (Winter 2004): 7–74.

24. Nembhard, *Collective Courage*, 219–20.

25. MOVE is not an acronym; rather founder John Africa chose it to reflect the unity of all living things that move. Works on MOVE include John Anderson and Hilary Hevenor, *Burning Down the House: MOVE and the Tragedy of Philadelphia* (New York: Norton, 1987); Robin Wagner-Pacifici, *Discourse and Destruction: The City of Philadelphia vs. MOVE* (Chicago: University of Chicago Press, 1984); and Richard Kent Evans, *Move: An American Religion* (New York: Oxford University Press, 2020). The organization still exists and promotes the values it first propagated in the 1970s. MOVE also supports the bombing survivors and those MOVE members still imprisoned. "On a Move: Website of the Move Organization," http://onamove.com/ (accessed May 1, 2020).

26. On gender and Black Nationalism, see Tracye Matthews, "No One Ever Asks What a Man's Role in the Revolution Is: Gender and the Politics of the Black Panther Party," in *Black Panther Party Reconsidered*, ed. Charles Jones (Baltimore: Black Classic Press, 1998), 267–304; Robyn Spencer, *The Revolution Has Come: Black Power, Gender, and the Black Panther Party in Oakland* (Durham, NC: Duke University Press, 2016); Keisha N. Blain, *Set the*

World on Fire: Black Nationalist Women and the Global Struggle for Freedom (Philadelphia: University of Pennsylvania Press, 2018); and Ula Taylor, *Promise of Patriarchy: Women and the Nation of Islam* (Chapel Hill: University of North Carolina Press, 2017).

27. Chris Dixon, *Another Politics: Talking Across Today's Transformative Movements* (Berkeley: University of California Press, 2014), 2, 6.

28. Kim Parker, Juliana Menasce Horowitz, and Monica Anderson, "Amid Protests, Majorities Across Racial and Ethnic Groups Express Support for the Black Lives Matter Movement," Pew Research Center, June 12, 2020, https://www.pewsocialtrends.org/2020/06/12/amid-protests-majorities-across-racial-and-ethnic-groups-express-support-for-the-black-lives-matter-movement/ (accessed December 1, 2020). This white support declined in the fall of 2020 but still remained substantial. Deja Thomas and Juliana Menasce Horowitz, "Support for Black Lives Matter Has Decreased since June but Remains Strong among Black Americans," Pew Research Center, September 16, 2020, https://www.pewresearch.org/fact-tank/2020/09/16/support-for-black-lives-matter-has-decreased-since-june-but-remains-strong-among-black-americans/ (accessed December 1, 2020).

29. On the novelty of white participation in the 2020 protests, see Thomas J. Sugrue, "2020 Is Not 1968: To Understand Today's Protests, You Must Look Further Back," *National Geographic*, June 11, 2020, https://www.nationalgeographic.com/history/2020/06/2020-not-1968/ (accessed November 15, 2020); Dana R. Fisher, "The Diversity of the Recent Black Lives Matter Protests Is a Good Sign for Racial Equality," Brookings, July 8, 2020, https://www.brookings.edu/blog/how-we-rise/2020/07/08/the-diversity-of-the-recent-black-lives-matter-protests-is-a-good-sign-for-racial-equity/ (accessed November 15, 2020); Douglas McAdam, "We've Never Seen Protests Like These Before," *Jacobin*, June 20, 2020, https://jacobinmag.com/2020/06/george-floyd-protests-black-lives-matter-riots-demonstrations (accessed November 15, 2020).

30. Wright, "Transforming Capitalism through Real Utopias." Wright directed the "Real Utopias Project" from 1992 until his death in 2019. See also Erik Olin Wright, *Envisioning Real Utopias* (New York: Verso, 2010).

31. Tom Moylan, *Becoming Utopian: The Culture and Politics of Radical Transformation* (New York: Bloomsbury, 2020); Rutger Bregman, *Utopia for Realists: How We Can Build the Ideal World* (New York: Little, Brown, 2017).

32. David Graeber, "The New Anarchists," *New Left Review* 13 (January–February 2002): 12. See also his reflections on the Occupy movement and prefigurative politics in *The Democracy Project: A History, a Crisis, a Movement* (New York: Random House, 2013). On the alter-globalization movement, see Marianne Maeckelbergh, *The Will of the Many: How the Alterglobalisation Movement Is Changing the Face of Democracy* (London: Pluto Press, 2009); and Maeckelbergh, "Doing Is Believing: Prefiguration as Strategic Practice in the Alterglobalization Movement," *Social Movement Studies* 10, no. 1 (2011): 1–20. On contemporary prefigurative movements, see Luke Yates, "Rethinking Prefiguration: Alternatives, Micropolitics and Goals in Social Movements," *Social Movement Studies* 14, no. 1 (2015): 1–21.

33. Angela Y. Davis and Dylan Rodriguez, "The Challenge of Prison Abolition: A Conversation," *Social Justice* 27, no. 3 (Fall 2000): 212–18; Keeanga-Yamahtta Taylor, *From #Blacklivesmatter to Black Liberation* (Chicago: Haymarket Books, 2016).

34. "New Brookwood Labor College," https://newbrookwood.org/mission (accessed July 15, 2020). Reflecting on the original Brookwood, they state: "Brookwood saw the labor movement as an instrument for workers to achieve higher wages and better working conditions with the ultimate goal of a new social order free from exploitation and a good life for all" (https://newbrookwood.org/history).

35. "Highlander Research and Education Center," https://highlandercenter.org/ (accessed December 1, 2020).

36. "The Freedom Georgia Initiative," https://thefreedomgeorgiainitiative.com/ (accessed September 6, 2020).

37. In *Spiritual Socialists: Religion and the American Left* (Philadelphia: University of Pennsylvania Press, 2019), Vaneesa Cook also lists the "Amos Project in Cincinnati; the Interfaith Coalition for Worker Justice in Madison, Wisconsin; and PICO (People Improving Communities Through Organizing)" (211). On the Poor People's Campaigns, see William J. Barber II with Jonathan Wilson-Hartgrove, *The Third Reconstruction: How a Moral Movement Is Overcoming the Politics of Division and Fear* (Boston: Beacon Press, 2016). On the contemporary religious Left, see Leilah Danielson, Marian Mollin, and Doug Rossinow, eds., *The Religious Left in Modern America: Doorkeepers of a Radical Faith* (New York: Palgrave Macmillan, 2018); and Jack Jenkins, *American Prophets: The Religious Roots of Progressive Politics and the Ongoing Fight for the Soul of the Country* (New York: HarperCollins, 2020).

38. "The Catholic Worker Movement," https://www.catholicworker.org/ (accessed December 1, 2020).

39. Martin Luther King Jr., "The Birth of a New Age," August 11, 1956, in *The Papers of Martin Luther King, Jr.*, vol. 3, ed. Clayborne Carson (Oakland: University of California Press, 1997), 340, 344. In *God and Human Dignity: The Personalism, Theology, and Ethics of Martin Luther King, Jr.* (Notre Dame, IN: University of Notre Dame Press, 2006), Rufus Burrow Jr. argues that the 1956 Buffalo speech may be the first time King invoked the term "beloved community."

40. On Cooperation Buffalo, see Cooperation Buffalo, https://www.cooperationbuffalo.org/ (accessed April 20, 2020). For PUSH, see PUSH Buffalo: People United for Sustainable Housing, https://www.pushbuffalo.org/ (accessed April 20, 2020). On the West Side Bazaar, see West Side Bazaar: Bringing the World to Buffalo, https://www.westsidebazaar.com/ (accessed April 20, 2020). For the Fruit Belt Community Land Trust, see Steve Dubb, "Buffalo Decides to Set Aside Land for Nonprofit Community Land Trust," 2018, University at Buffalo, Center for Urban Studies, http://centerforurbanstudies.ap.buffalo.edu/news-items/buffalo-vows-to-set-aside-land-for-nonprofit-community-land-trust/ (accessed April 20, 2020).

41. Yi-Ling Liu, "Dream State: The Radical Imagination of the Hong Kong Protest Movement," *Harper's* 340, no. 2040 (May 2020): 42.

42. Howard Thurman, *The Search for Common Ground: An Inquiry into the Basis of Man's Experience of Community* (Richmond, IN: Friends United Press, 1971), 44.

Index